CONCEPTS AND CONTEXTS OF VATTEL'S POLITICAL AND LEGAL THOUGHT

Swiss-born Emer de Vattel (1714–1767) was one of the last eminent thinkers of natural law. He shaped the later part of early-modern natural jurisprudence. At the time, the subject had become a fashionable academic sub-discipline in both jurisprudence and philosophy. Vattel's considerable impact on statesmen, political thinkers, diplomats, and lawyers during his lifetime and after rested primarily on the fact that his *The Law of Nations* (1758) transformed natural law into the basis of a more comprehensive and practicable theory of interstate relations. His ideas served to promote reform programmes whose comprehensive natures spanned the domains of economic reform, constitutionalism, international diplomacy, and foreign trade policy. Vattel's conception centred round the principle that defined all sovereign states as nations composed of societies of free men and profoundly influenced legal and political debates in the eighteenth and nineteenth centuries.

Peter Schröder is Professor of the History of Political Thought at University College London. He was visiting Professor at universities in Seoul, Rome, and Paris and has held numerous senior research fellowships. Recent publications include *Trust in Early Modern International Political Thought, 1598–1713* (2017), and a German translation of R. Filmer's *Patriarcha* (2019).

Concepts and Contexts of Vattel's Political and Legal Thought

Edited by
PETER SCHRÖDER
University College London

CAMBRIDGE
UNIVERSITY PRESS

CAMBRIDGE
UNIVERSITY PRESS

University Printing House, Cambridge CB2 8BS, United Kingdom

One Liberty Plaza, 20th Floor, New York, NY 10006, USA

477 Williamstown Road, Port Melbourne, VIC 3207, Australia

314–321, 3rd Floor, Plot 3, Splendor Forum, Jasola District Centre, New Delhi – 110025, India

79 Anson Road, #06–04/06, Singapore 079906

Cambridge University Press is part of the University of Cambridge.

It furthers the University's mission by disseminating knowledge in the pursuit of education, learning, and research at the highest international levels of excellence.

www.cambridge.org
Information on this title: www.cambridge.org/9781108489447
DOI: 10.1017/9781108784009

First published 2021

A catalogue record for this publication is available from the British Library.

Library of Congress Cataloging-in-Publication Data
NAMES: Schröder, Peter, 1965– editor.
TITLE: Concepts and contexts of Vattel's political and legal thought / edited by Peter Schröder, University College London.
DESCRIPTION: Cambridge, United Kingdom ; New York, NY : Cambridge University Press, 2021. | Includes index.
IDENTIFIERS: LCCN 2021006947 (print) | LCCN 2021006948 (ebook) | ISBN 9781108489447 (hardback) | ISBN 9781108746533 (paperback) | ISBN 9781108784009 (epub)
SUBJECTS: LCSH: Vattel, Emer de, 1714-1767–influence. | International law–Early works to 1800.
CLASSIFICATION: LCC KZ2414 .C66 2021 (print) | LCC KZ2414 (ebook) | DDC 341-dc23
LC record available at https://lccn.loc.gov/2021006947
LC ebook record available at https://lccn.loc.gov/2021006948

ISBN 978-1-108-48944-7 Hardback

Contents

Contributors

Marco Barducci (Honorary Fellow at Durham University's Institute of Medieval and Early Modern Studies) is an intellectual historian specialising in the exchange and reception of political and religious ideas between Britain and Continental Europe in the early modern period. He taught at the University of Florence, he has held fellowships at, among others, Durham University, the Institute for Advanced Study (Princeton) and the Centro Studi sul Pensiero Politico (Turin). His recent books are *Hugo Grotius and the Century of Revolution, 1613–1718* (Oxford University Press, 2017), and *Order and Conflict. Anthony Ascham and English Political Thought, 1648–1650* (Manchester University Press, 2015).

Camilla Boisen is a historian of political thought and Lecturer in the Writing Program at New York University, Abu Dhabi. Her main area of research is the intellectual history of empire and political theory in relation to the development of ideas of rights and trusteeship and their influence on contemporary problems such as postcolonial restitution. She is the author of numerous articles in journals such as *The History of European Ideas*, *Settler Colonial Studies* and *Journal of International Political Theory*.

Nathaniel Boyd (post-doc Research Fellow at University of York) is a member of the *European Society for the History of Political Thought* and received his PhD in politics and history from Brunel University London. Specialising in the early modern and modern European history of political thought and conceptual history, he has publications in these fields, most recently in *History of Political Thought* and *Hobbes Studies*. Currently, he is working on a monograph on Hegel's early political theory and its relationship to the German constitutional tradition.

Theodore Christov is Associate Professor of History and International Affairs at George Washington University in Washington DC. He received his PhD in Political Theory at UCLA and was previously a visiting assistant professor of political theory at Northwestern University. His research interests lie in early modern intellectual history and modern political and international thought, with a focus on political theories of empire and imperialism, the history of international law and theories of international relations. He is the author of *Before Anarchy: Hobbes and His Critics in Modern International Thought* (Cambridge University Press, 2015). His current book project is on a critical history of self-determination.

Richard Devetak is Associate Professor of International Relations in the School of Political Science and International Studies at the University of Queensland. His research focuses on the history of international thought, history of the states-system and critical theories of international relations. His publications include articles in *History of European Ideas*, *International Affairs*, *International Theory* and *Review of International Studies* and a recent book on *Critical International Theory: An Intellectual History* (Oxford University Press, 2018).

Elisabetta Fiocchi Malaspina is Assistant Professor of Legal History at the Law Faculty of the University of Zurich. Her main research fields include history of international law, circulation and diffusion of natural law and law of nations theories between the eighteenth and nineteenth centuries, history of water law and history of land ownership and registration (nineteenth and twentieth centuries). She is the author of *L'eterno ritorno del Droit des gens di Emer de Vattel (secc. XVIII–XIX). L'impatto sulla cultura giuridica in prospettiva globale* (Max Planck Institute for European Legal History, 2017).

Ben Holland is an Associate Professor in the School of Politics and International Relations at the University of Nottingham. His research is concerned with the intellectual history of the European state, its sovereignty and the connections between political and theological discourse. A fellow of the Royal Historical Society and a graduate of the University of Cambridge and the London School of Economics and Political Science, he is the author of *The Moral Person of the State: Pufendorf, Sovereignty and Composite Polities* (Cambridge University Press, 2017) and *Self and City in the Thought of Saint Augustine* (Palgrave Macmillan, 2020).

Francesca Iurlaro holds a PhD in Law from the European University Institute in Florence (2018). She was also a research fellow of the University of Milan and global postdoctoral fellow at NYU School of Law (USA). She graduated in the history of philosophy (University of Macerata, 2014) and has an LLM in Comparative, European and International Laws (European University Institute, 2015). She is currently Alexander von Humboldt Postdoctoral Fellow at the Max Planck Institute for comparative Public Law and International Law (Heidelberg). Her book *The Invention of Custom. Natural Law and the Law of Nations, 1550–1750* is forthcoming with Oxford University Press.

Pablo Kalmanovitz is Research Professor and Head of the International Studies Division at CIDE (Centro de Investigación y Docencia Económicas) in Mexico City. He has held permanent or visiting positions at the Universidad de los Andes in Bogotá, the European University Institute, Yale University, McGill University and the University of Ulster. His research focuses on historical and theoretical aspects of the international regulation of armed force, on which he has published numerous articles and book chapters. His book *The Laws of War in International Thought* was published by Oxford University Press in 2020.

Ere Nokkala is a University Researcher at the University of Helsinki. He has published widely on aspects of cameralism and early modern political thought. Nokkala is the author of *From Natural Law to Political Economy: J. H. G. von Justi on State, Commerce and International Order* (LIT Verlag, 2019). He is the co-editor of *Cameralism and the Enlightenment: Happiness, Governance and Reform in Transnational Perspective* (Routledge, 2020). Nokkala is codirector of the *International Research Network on Cameralism across the World of Enlightenment*. He has held fellowships at the Swedish Collegium for Advanced Study, The Göttingen Institute for Advanced Study and Herzog August Bibliothek.

Peter Schröder is Professor of the History of Political Thought at University College London. He has published widely in this field. Recent publications include a monograph on *Trust in Early Modern International Political Thought, 1598–1713* (Ideas in Context 116) (Cambridge University Press, 2017), as well as two edited volumes: German translation and edition of T. Hobbes, *Behemoth or the Long Parliament* (Meiner Verlag, 2015) and German translation and edition of R. Filmer, *Patriarcha* (Meiner Verlag,

2019). He has been a visiting professor at universities in Paris, Rome and Seoul and held numerous senior research visiting fellowships.

Gabriella Silvestrini is Associate Professor in the History of Political Thought at the University of Eastern Piedmont (Vercelli, Italy). She has published widely in this field and is author of *Diritto naturale e volontà generale. Il contrattualismo repubblicano di Jean-Jacques Rousseau* (Turin, 2010). Her main research areas include the natural law tradition, theories of war and peace and early modern republicanism; she is working on an intellectual history of the power to punish.

Mark Somos holds the Deutsche Forschungsgemeinschaft's Heisenberg position at the Max Planck Institute for Comparative Public Law and International Law. He studied history, political science and law at Cambridge, Harvard, Sussex and Leiden. He is the author of *Secularisation and the Leiden Circle* (Brill, 2011), *American States of Nature: The Origins of Independence, 1761–1775* (Oxford, 2019) and over 40 scholarly papers; co-author, with Dániel Margócsy and Stephen Joffe, of *The Fabrica of Andreas Vesalius* (Brill, 2018); and edited *Trust and Happiness in the History of European Political Thought* (Brill, 2017) with László Kontler. He is co-editor-in-chief of *Grotiana* and the *History of European Political and Constitutional Thought* series.

Koen Stapelbroek is an Academy of Finland senior research fellow at the University of Helsinki, associate professor of the History of Political Theory at Erasmus University Rotterdam and director of the Helsinki Centre for Intellectual History. He has published numerous articles and edited volumes on eighteenth-century political thought, intellectual history and the institutional development of trade.

Antonio Trampus is Full Professor of Early Modern History at Ca' Foscari University Venice. His work on the Masonic culture, on the emergence of the political concept of happiness and on the political thought of Gaetano Filangieri and Benjamin Constant focuses on the impact of the Enlightenment's legacy in the Mediterranean area, in Europe and the Americas. He is working on a comparative study of the European reception and practical use of Vattel's conceptualisations of the constitutional state. His most recent book is *La Naissance du langage politique moderne* (Classiques Garnier, 2017).

Nadir Weber is an Ambizione Fellow of the Swiss National Science Foundation at the Historical Institute of the University of Bern. His main research interests lie in diplomatic history, the history of political thought and the history of human–animal relations. He is the author of a monograph on Neuchâtel and the foreign relations of eighteenth-century Prussia (Böhlau, 2015), co-editor of a volume on the history of political protection and international intervention (Böhlau, 2016) and co-editor of a volume on diplomats and political cultures in early modern Switzerland (Schwabe, 2018).

Acknowledgements

This volume is the result of a process of collaborative work during a time of crisis and strain. The authors of the individual chapters were extremely generous with their time and input on the whole of the volume. I would not have been able to edit such a work without their indefatigable dedication and my thanks go to all of them. My friends David Saunders and Ian Hunter were always there when I asked for their advice and criticism. Such a dedicated group of people made the editing process a pleasure and an intellectually stimulating enterprise. I can only hope that this transpires in the result of this volume. I would also like to acknowledge the tremendous help from Ana-Maria Radu for putting the index together.

Concepts and Contexts of Vattel's Political and Legal Thought

An Introduction

PETER SCHRÖDER

INTRODUCTION

The study of natural law and the law of nations in the early-modern period has expanded remarkably during the last decades. This has partly been inspired by contemporary concerns, in particular by the interest in the genealogy of human rights and the foundations of international law. However, natural law in this period has also been studied in its own historical right, with a view to understanding its intellectual sources and cultural and political uses. Early modern natural law emerged in a variety of forms at the volatile interface of theology, moral philosophy, political thought and jurisprudence. These 'different models of natural law' have been described 'as conflicting ways of configuring access to ethical and political norms in the service of rival cultural–political programmes'.[1] Within the language and concepts of natural law doctrines, then, quite divergent approaches were pursued to regulate and protect human society. Some operated at the level of the domestic state, with a view to rationalising and legitimating its political and juridical authority. Others operated beyond the borders of the territorial state, with a view to regulating interstate relations via the laws of war and peace.

The Swiss-born Emer de Vattel (25 April 1714–28 December 1767) is one of the last eminent proponents of the natural law tradition. In reworking and integrating aspects of the natural law doctrines of Hugo Grotius (1583–1645), Thomas Hobbes (1588–1679), Samuel Pufendorf (1632–1694) and Christian Wolff (1679–1754), Vattel developed his own model of the law of nature and nations. Grotius's views in many ways dominated the early modern debate on

[1] I. Hunter, 'The invention of human nature: The intention and reception of Pufendorf's *entia moralia* doctrine', *History of European Ideas* 45 (2019), 950.

the law of nations well into the eighteenth century.[2] Hobbes's influence was also felt throughout Europe, but rather in an infamous way; he was a bête noir and gave endless cause for polemics.[3] In his natural law work, Pufendorf responded to both Grotius and Hobbes, while Grotius's natural law flowed into Wolff's, such that through them Grotius continued to influence natural law thought into the eighteenth century. Only with Vattel was Grotius's influence on the law of nature and nations eclipsed by other writers and concerns.

Vattel's considerable impact on statesmen, political thinkers, diplomats, and lawyers in the eighteenth and nineteenth centuries rested primarily on the fact that in his *Le Droit des Gens* (*The Law of Nations*, 1758) he transformed natural law into the basis of a more comprehensive and practicable theory of interstate relations, as is indicated by the full title of his treatise: *The Law of Nations, Or, Principles of the Law of Nature, Applied to the Conduct and Affairs of Nations and Sovereigns*. This title sets out clearly the agenda Vattel intended to work through. The doctrines of the law of nature and their application to the relations between sovereign states are the two aspects which were highlighted by Vattel from the outset. I will discuss these two aspects in the next two sections of the Introduction, before providing an overview of the rationale and structure of the present volume in the following sections.

VATTEL AND THE NATURAL LAW TRADITION

The reach of natural law was limited within human society because it lacked the force of public authority to compel compliance. In this argumentative

[2] See C. Thomasius, 'On the history of natural law until Grotius', in I. Hunter, T. Ahnert and F. Grunert (eds.), *Essays on Church, State and Politics* (Indianapolis, 2007), 44. This essay was the foreword by Thomasius to the first German translation of Grotius's *De jure belli ac pacis*. Adam Friedrich Glafey made a very similar point. A. F. Glafey, *Vollständige Geschichte des Rechts der Vernunfft, worinnen in dieser Wissenschaft ans Licht getretenen Schriften nach ihrem Inhalt und wahren Werth beurtheilet* (Leipzig, 1739), 111. See also the discussion by F. Grunert, 'The reception of Hugo Grotius's De jure belli ac pacis in the early German Enlightenment', in T. Hochstrasser and P. Schröder (eds.), *Early Modern Natural Law Theories: Contexts and Strategies in the Early Enlightenment* (Dordrecht, 2003), 89–105 and J. B. Schneewind, *The Invention of Autonomy. A History of Modern Moral Philosophy* (Cambridge, 1998), 66–70. R. Tuck, *The Rights of War and Peace: Political Thought and the International Order from Grotius to Kant*, (Oxford, 2001), 195 saw in 'Vattel's '*Le Droit de Gens* . . . a more or less faithful version of the Grotian argument'.

[3] See, F. Palladini, *Samuel Pufendorf Disciple of Hobbes*, translated by D. Saunders (Leiden, 2020) and J. Parkin, *Taming the Leviathan. The Reception of the Political and Religious Ideas of Thomas Hobbes in England 1640–1700* (Cambridge, 2007). On Hobbes's and Pufendorf's influence on Vattel see Chapter 2 by Ben Holland; and T. Christov, *Before Anarchy. Hobbes and His Critics in Modern International Thought* (Cambridge, 2015), 241–253.

context, Vattel reformulated the dualism between perfect and imperfect laws and rights, and between internal and external right.[4] In doing so, he used the limitations of the earlier approaches of Hobbes and Pufendorf to clarify his own approach:

> Hobbes was . . . the first who gave a distinct though imperfect idea of the law of nations. He divides the *law of nature* into that of *man*, and that of *states*: and the latter is, according to him, what we usually call the law of nations. . . . This author has well observed, that the law of nations is the law of nature applied to states or nations.[5] But we shall see in the course of this work, that he was mistaken in the idea that the law of nature does not suffer any necessary change in that application . . . Pufendorf declares he unreservedly subscribes to this opinion espoused by Hobbes. He has not therefore separately treated of the law of nations but has every-where blended it with the law of nature properly so called. (*LN*, preface 8)

The law of nature is applicable to states but, for Vattel, for this to happen it was necessary to distinguish between the conduct of states and that of individual men, because there 'are many cases . . . in which the law of nature does not decide between state and state in the same manner as it would between man and man' (*LN*, prelim. 6). Nor had Grotius made such a distinction and, as we will see later, Vattel was rather critical of him in this regard.

Despite his use of Hobbes and Pufendorf, Vattel reserved his main praise for Wolff.

> It is better to acknowledge here, once and for all, the obligations I am under that great master [i.e. Wolff]. Although my work be very different from his . . ., I confess that I should never have had the courage to launch into so extensive a field, if the celebrated philosopher of Halle had not preceded my steps, and held forth a torch to guide me on my way. (*LN*, preface 12)

Wolff is of such importance to Vattel's project because, unlike Hobbes and Pufendorf who had left the law of nations as a subordinate part of natural law, Wolff had realised that it was necessary to develop an independent basis for the law of nations, including an account of how to *apply* the law of nature to the law of nations (cf. *LN*, preface 10). All this is indicative for the composition

4 For this reason, states were constituted, to establish 'a public authority, adding a positive obligation to natural obligation, through the means of punishment'. E. Vattel, 'Dissertation on this question: "Can natural law bring society to perfection without the assistance of political laws?"', translated by T. Hochstrasser, in *The Law of Nations*, ed. B. Kapossy and R. Whatmore (Indianapolis, 2008), 779.

5 Vattel refers to the last paragraph of chapter 30 of Hobbes's *Leviathan*. T. Hobbes, *Leviathan*, ed. R. Tuck (Cambridge, 1992), 244.

of Vattel's own work. He would develop these findings into one of the most influential writings on the law of nations. In doing so, he not only developed a post-Grotian law of nations, but also provided a new model for the organisation of interstate relations.

This change was helped by the fact that during the early modern period significant peace treaties had ended major European wars. In particular, the Peace of Westphalia of 1648 became the main reference point, and subsequent peace treaties such as the Peace of Nijmegen 1678 or the Peace of Utrecht 1714 explicitly referred to it. Many authors provided collections and analysis of the numerous peace treaties.[6] Vattel built this evolving corpus of treaty law into his theory of interstate relations. In doing so, he adopted a pragmatic and historical viewpoint, declaring that a 'treaty of peace can be no more than a compromise. Were the rules of strict and rigid justice to be observed in it, so that each party should precisely receive every thing to which he has a just title, it would be impossible ever to make a peace' (*LN*, IV-II-18). Here, Vattel was taking note of the fact that European diplomacy and praxis of interstate relations had developed into customs (tacit consent) and positive international law in the form of treaty agreements (express consent) between sovereign states.[7] 'Vattel seeks to provide a conciliation of principles of natural law and state practice'.[8] His incorporation of treaty practice and diplomatic conventions puts his account of the law of nations on a very different footing in comparison to Wolff and his abstract reasoning.

Vattel's use of Wolff's *The Law of Nations* in his own work of this title, does, however, shed interesting light on Vattel's key concepts and the way he constructed his own law of nations.[9] In terms of the development of his

6 Next to the above-mentioned peace treaties see, for example, C. Freschot, *The Compleat History of the Peace of Utrecht as also that of Gertruydenberg: Containing All the Acts, Memorials, Representations, Complaints, Demands, Letters, Speeches, Treaties and other Authentick Pieces relating to the Negotiations there* (London, 1715), 2 vols; and Abbé de Mably, *Le Droit public de l'Europe. Fondé sur les Traitez conclus jusqu'en l'année 1740* (Amsterdam, 1748). Invaluable for modern research is the data base at the *Leibniz-Institut für Europäische Geschichte*, Mainz: www.ieg-friedensvertraege.de/

7 R. Lesaffer, 'Peace treaties and the formation of international law' in B. Fassbender and A. Peters (eds.), *The Oxford Handbook of the History of International Law* (Oxford, 2012), 71–94.

8 F. Iurlaro, 'Vattel's doctrine of customary law of nations between sovereign interests and the principles of natural law', in S. Zurbuchen (ed.), *The Law of Nations and Natural Law 1625–1800* (Leiden, 2019), 289.

9 In his correspondence with Formey (1711–1797), one of the founding members of the Academy in Berlin and son of French Huguenot immigrants to Brandenburg–Prussia, Vattel repeatedly indicated that he was engaged with Wolff's *Law of Nations*. See A. Bandelier (ed.), *Emer de Vattel à Jean Henri Samuel Formey: correspondances autour du Droit des gens* (Paris, 2012), 34, 67. Formey also had great interest in Wolff's work. He eventually provided a French translation

innovative conception of the law of nations, Vattel's criticisms of Wolff turn out to be no less interesting than his borrowings from him.[10] At the heart of their differences lies a profoundly different understanding of interstate relations, which boils down to a fundamentally different conception of the sovereign state.[11] Each nation and each society of men united politically is, according to natural law, free and sovereign. Hobbes, Pufendorf, Wolff and Vattel all agree that because of this sovereign independence states find themselves in a state of nature. All four also insist on the legal equality of sovereign states, irrespective of their de facto political, military or economic power. Here both Wolff and Vattel use the same analogy of the giant and dwarf as being morally equal human beings, despite their difference in size, to underscore the equality of all states, regardless of their power or size. But that is as far as Vattel is prepared to follow Wolff.[12]

Vattel's conception rested on the principle that defined all sovereign states as nations composed of societies of free men. Nations, or states, are sovereign political bodies, each with their own interests. Here, Vattel employed the fiction of the state being a moral person with its own intentions and will, able to fulfil obligations and observe rights. This intellectual fiction stemmed from Hobbes and Pufendorf, who had used it to argue for the independent sovereign state.[13] Wolff too used this idea, but he crucially pushed this fiction in a

of Wolff's *Jus naturae* (*Law of Nature*). See also, with interesting archival material, F. Ieva, '"A poor imitation of Grotius and Pufendorf" biographical uncertainties and the laborious genesis of Vattel's *droit des gens*', in K. Stapelbroek and A. Trampus (eds.), *The Legacy of Vattel's Droit des gens* (Cham, 2019), 68–75.

10 An overview of Wolff's *Law of Nations* is provided by T. Kleinlein, 'Christian Wolff: System as an episode?', in S. Kadelbach, T. Kleinlein and D. Roth-Isigkeit (eds.), *System, Order, and International Law: The Early History of International Legal Thought from Machiavelli to Hegel* (Oxford, 2017), 216–239. Next to Chapter 3 by Ere Nokkala on Vattel and Wolff, see P. Kalmanovitz, 'Sovereignty, pluralism, and regular war: Wolff and Vattel's enlightenment critique of just war', *Political Theory* 46 (2018), 218–241, where the emphasis of the discussion is on the convergence between Wolff's and Vattel's thought.

11 See F. G. Whelan, 'Vattel's doctrine of the state', *History of Political Thought* 9 (1988), 88f; and S. Beaulac, 'Emer de Vattel and the externalization of sovereignty', *Journal of the History of International Law/Revue d'histoire du droit international* 5 (2003), 247f, 266f.

12 C. Wolff, *The Law of Nations Treated by the Scientific Method*, ed. T. Ahnert (Indianapolis, 2017), §16, and for Vattel (*LN*, prelim. 75). See also the discussion by P. Haggenmacher, 'L'État souverain comme sujet du droit international, de Vitoria à Vattel', *Droits* 15–16 (1992–1993), 11–20.

13 This argument is made in T. Hobbes, *Leviathan*, 121; and further developed by Pufendorf in, for instance, S. Pufendorf, *Two Books of the Elements of Universal Jurisprudence*, ed. T. Behme (Indianapolis, 2009), (I-XIII-24) 225; S. Pufendorf, *Of the Law of Nature and Nations*, translated and ed. B. Kennet (London, 1717), (VII-V-13) 678; and S. Pufendorf, *On the Duty of Man and Citizen*, ed. J. Tully (Cambridge, 1991), (II-6-10) 137. Wolff claimed that 'all moral persons and, too, the supreme state itself in the law of nature and nations have something fictitious in them'.

very different direction which culminated in his equally fictitious idea of a global state or *civitas maxima*.[14] While both Wolff and Vattel referred to the state as a moral person, their understandings of interstate relations differed profoundly. In Wolff, the idea of the state as a global moral person is employed to curtail the independence deriving from the idea of sovereign territorial states. Whereas Hobbes, Pufendorf and – as we shall see – Vattel also used the fiction of the state as a moral person to legitimise state sovereignty, Wolff pushed the potential of legitimising political power and structures by these fictitious ideas to their universalist extreme.[15] He argued that, because individual states were moral persons, they could be regarded as subordinating themselves to the global state or *civitas maxima*, in relation to which individual states 'are understood to have bound themselves to the whole'.[16] This assumed contractual obligation resulted in a right vested in the *civitas maxima* 'of coercing the individual nations, if they are unwilling to perform their obligations'.[17]

The whole purpose of setting out this idea of a supreme state has to be seen as part of Wolff's attempt to confer 'some sovereignty over individual nations'.[18] This was in turn necessary in order to establish 'the voluntary [and enforceable] law of nations, which is derived from the concept of the supreme state [*civitas maxima*]'.[19] As is often stressed, but perhaps not

Wolff, *The Law of Nations*, §21. See also the discussion in B. Holland, *The Moral Person of the State: Pufendorf, Sovereignty and Composite Polities* (Cambridge, 2017), esp. 109–130; Q. Skinner, 'A genealogy of the modern state', *Proceedings of the British Academy* 162 (2008), 349–352; and I. Hunter, 'Vattel's *Law of Nations*: Diplomatic casuistry for the protestant nation', *Grotiana* 31 (2010), 123–126.

14 Wolff, *The Law of Nations*, §9: 'all nations are understood to have come together into a state, whose separate nations are separate members or individual states'.

15 Francis Cheneval emphasized the importance of Wolff's fictitious approach for legitimising his concept of an enforceable law of nations. Rather than being dismissive about this concept (like Vattel), he urged his readers to take this approach seriously, not least because it informed Kant's understanding of the social contract and his approach to interstate relations in his *Perpetual Peace*. F. Cheneval, 'Der präsumtiv vernünftige Konsens der Menschen und Völker – Christian Wolffs Theorie der civitas maxima', *Archiv für Rechts- und Sozialphilosophie/Archives for Philosophy of Law and Social Philosophy* 85 (1999), 563–580; and F. Cheneval, 'Auseinandersetzungen um die civitas maxima in der Nachfolge Christian Wolffs', *Studia Leibnitiana* 33 (2001), 125–144. Given Vattel's profound disagreement with Wolff's approach, and given Kant's intellectual debt to Wolff, this in turn explains Kant's dismissive attitude towards Vattel.

16 Wolff, *The Law of Nations*, §13.

17 Ibid.

18 Ibid., §15.

19 Cf. Ibid., §22. On the problems of how to translate *civitas maxima* into English see the discussion in N. G. Onuf, 'Civitas Maxima: Wolff, Vattel and the fate of republicanism', *The American Journal of International Law* 88 (1994), 287–292.

sufficiently explained, at the heart of Vattel's famous refutation of Wolff's concept of the *civitas maxima* lies his very different understanding of state sovereignty, which was rather inspired by, or at least resembled, that of Hobbes and Pufendorf.[20] This is why we read in Vattel,

> I differ entirely from Monsieur Wolf [sic] in the manner of establishing the foundations of that species of law of nations which we call *voluntary*. Monsieur Wolf deduces it from the idea of a great republic (*civitas maximae*) instituted by nature herself, and of which all nations of the world are members. According to him, the voluntary law of nations is, as it were, the civil law of that great republic. (*LN*, preface 14)

This is a fair account of Wolff's argument and Vattel makes absolutely clear why he disagrees profoundly:

> This idea does not satisfy me; nor do I think the fiction of such a republic either admissible in itself, or capable of affording sufficiently solid grounds on which to build the rules of the universal law of nations which shall necessarily claim the obedient acquiescence of sovereign states. I acknowledge no other natural society between nations than that which nature has established between mankind in general. It is essential to every civil society that each member has resigned a part of his right to the body of the society, and that there exists in it an authority capable of commanding all the members, of giving them laws, and of compelling those who should refuse to obey. *Nothing of this kind can be conceived or supposed to subsist between nations. Each sovereign state claims and actually possesses an absolute independence on all the others*. They are all, according to Monsieur Wolf himself, to be considered as so many individuals who live together in the state of nature, and who acknowledge no other laws but those of nature, or of her Great Author. (*LN*, preface 14; emphasis added)

It would be difficult to be more outspoken. Although it is easy to see why Vattel disagreed with Wolff, the obvious question should be raised: why did the former nevertheless hail the latter as his most illuminating guide? The answer appears equally simple: Wolff only argued for the *civitas maxima* and its role to safeguard and enforce the voluntary law of nations in the prolegomena (that is to say only in the first 26 of the 1068 paragraphs) of his *Law of Nations*. The remaining part was presented in the traditional structure, discussing in nine different chapters in great detail inter alia the duties of nations to themselves and others, treaties, methods of settling disputes, *ius ad bellum*

[20] See R. Koselleck, *Critique and Crisis. Enlightenment and the Pathogenesis of Modern Society* (Cambridge, MA, 1988), 45.

and *ius in bello*, peace treaties and the law of embassies. This enabled Vattel to dismiss the idea of the *civitas maxima* without losing the wealth of legal and theoretical arguments about the law of nations he readily found in Wolff's treaties. Effectively Vattel could change the foundations of the law of nations, bringing the individual sovereign states centre stage, and still use the bulk of Wolff's *Law of Nations* rather faithfully.

THE SOVEREIGN STATE AND WAR IN DUE FORM

Within the natural law tradition, Vattel positioned the sovereign state centre stage and this in turn informed how he deployed the ideas of his predecessors in this tradition. Interstate relations had to be organised on the assumption that 'no state has the smallest right to interfere in the government of another. Of all rights that can belong to a nation, sovereignty is, doubtless, the most precious, and that which other nations ought the most scrupulously to respect' (*LN*, II-IV-54). Vattel excluded the possibility that sovereign states could exit the conundrum of the state of nature. Each state remained judge in its own case (cf. *LN*, prelim. 16) and the law of nature, applied as the *necessary law of nations* to sovereign states, could only be binding internally (*LN*, prelim. 17 and III-XII-189).[21] War as a means to pursue the interests of a sovereign state remained a realistic possibility, and the right to wage war was actually an essential aspect of state sovereignty. A main aim of Vattel's *Law of Nations* was to show how war itself could be regulated and restricted in order to at least mitigate its devastating consequences. Each state was expected to think first about its own self-interest, before any further expectations of mutual help could be reasonably demanded. Natural law was only binding on the conscience of the sovereign: 'A nation . . . is mistress of her own actions . . . so long as she is only *internally* [i.e. by the law of nature] bound, and does not lie under any *external* and *prefect* obligation' (*LN*, prelim. 20) which it might have made by contract or treaty with another nation. The absolute freedom and independence of sovereign states determined interstate relations.

Nevertheless, relations between states should be regulated by rules and laws. But, contrary to the Thomist natural law tradition to which Grotius and Wolff were indebted, Vattel insisted that these rules and laws provided only a general framework within which the competing interests of states should be balanced and regulated. In this context his insistence on the importance of state neutrality, including commercial neutrality, provided additional aspects of

[21] In this section of the preliminaries Vattel reproduced almost verbatim the conundrum of Hobbes's state of nature.

how the competing interests of states could be balanced. Although the conduct of sovereign states should be guided by the evolving voluntary law of nations and natural law, Vattel did not regard the law of nations as enforceable in the manner of domestic law. As in Hobbes's and Pufendorf's conceptions, the very notion of a sovereign state excluded such an idea. Nor should the precepts of the law of nature mean that 'the good become the dupes and prey of the wicked' (*LN*, II-I-16). Contrary to Wolff's claim that the *civitas maxima* informs and regulates interstate relations, Vattel maintained that there cannot be a general set of rules or laws, which would always apply in the same way to all potential conflicts. An alternative stabilising mechanism was required, such that: 'In the absence of a *civitas maxima*, it was the commercial interest of these states that supported the continuation of an international order beyond the limitations of the balance of power'.[22] Vattel was wary of Grotius's or Wolff's appeal to higher truths and values, and sought for viable alternatives, having seen how such claims had fuelled the confessional wars in Europe. Consequently, he criticised Grotius:

> It is strange to hear the learned and judicious Grotius assert, that a sovereign may justly take up arms to chastise nations which are guilty of enormous transgressions of the law of nature. ... What led him into this error, was his attributing to every independent man, and of course to every sovereign, an odd kind of right to punish faults which involve an enormous violation of the laws of nature, though they do not affect either his rights or his safety. But we have shewn ... that men derive the right of punishment solely from their right to provide for their own safety; and consequently they cannot claim it except against those by whom they have been injured. Could it escape Grotius, that ... his opinion opens a door to all the ravages of enthusiasm and fanaticism, and furnishes ambition with numberless pretexts? (*LN*, II-i-7)[23]

[22] I. Nakhimovsky, 'Vattel's theory of the international order: Commerce and the balance of power in the *Law of Nations*', *History of European Ideas* 33 (2007), 170.

[23] Vattel has been interpreted as a (critical) commentator of Grotius, but on this and other important issues related to the concept of sovereignty he was taking up Pufendorf's and to a lesser extent Wolff's position. Cf. Pufendorf, *The Law of Nature and Nations*, VIII-x-7, 1298: 'the evils inflicted by right of war have properly no relation to punishments, since they neither proceed from a superior as such, nor have as their direct object the reform of the guilty party or others, but the defense and assertion of my safety, my property, and my rights. To secure such ends it is permissible to use whatever means I think will best prevail'. See, also, Pufendorf, *The Law of Nature and Nations*, VIII-III-4, 1163. It has to be noted, though, that Wolff was less outspoken than Pufendorf in refuting Grotius's claim of punishment by one belligerent state of another. Wolff, *The Law of Nations*, §636–637. See also Ian Hunter's account of Vattel's different, state-based 'conception of justice'. I. Hunter, 'Kant and Vattel in context: Cosmopolitan philosophy and diplomatic casuistry', *History of European Ideas* 39 (2013), 492.

Rather than appealing to abstract higher values such as universal justice or a *civitas maxima*, Vattel insisted that no state could claim exclusive access to such values. Instead, he found that 'each nation in fact maintains that she has justice on her side in every dispute that happens to arise: and it does not belong to either of the parties interested, or to other nations, to pronounce a judgement on the contested question' (*LN*, prelim. 21). In the absence of a binding norm of international justice, Vattel's aim was to explore ways to mitigate the consequences of this conundrum in which sovereign states necessarily found themselves. What is needed, therefore, is, firstly, to establish rules, customs and laws of nations that should inform more effectively the conduct of self-interested sovereign states and, secondly, 'to apply the rules to particular cases' (*LN*, III-III-50).

In this view, all nations have the right to self-defence. War is, therefore, one among the legitimate options sovereign states have at their disposal to pursue their interests and rights towards others by force. However, Vattel qualified war. It was something more specific than just the eruption of violence. Only a public war, i.e. a war 'which takes place between nations or sovereigns' (LN III-I-2) qualifies as a regular war. All other conflicts are private and not regulated by the law of nations. In order to balance the various interests and resulting conflicts, decisions will have to be made on each specific case and claim. It is significant that in his *Law of Nations*, Vattel explicitly postpones discussion 'of the justice of war' (*LN*, III-I-5) in the third book, which deals with war. Instead, he indicates 'the various objects for which a nation takes up arms, – objects which may furnish lawful reasons, or unjust pretences, but which are at least susceptible of a colour of right' (*LN*, III-I-5). Vattel's insistence on judging individual cases, rather than relying on the universal theory of international justice of Wolff's *civitas maxima*, provided the basis for developing the strategic and argumentative aim of book III, *On War*. That is to say, to establish regulations which will bridle ensuing war between nations.[24] This approach echoes significant aspects of Gentili's doctrine of the *just enemy*.[25] Vattel insisted that 'regular war [i.e. war between sovereign states] is to be accounted just on both sides' (*LN*, III-XII-190).

[24] Cf. (*LN*, III-I-3). See also, C. Schmitt, *The Nomos of the Earth in International Law of the Jus Publicum Europeum*, translated by G. L. Ulmen (New York, 2003), 152ff; and R. Lesaffer, 'A schoolmaster abolishing home-work? Vattel on peacemaking and peace treaties', in V. Chetail and P. Haggenmacher (eds.), *Vattel's International Law from a XXIst Century Perspective/Le Droit International de Vattel vu du XXIe Siècle* (Leiden, 2011), 361.

[25] Cf. A. Gentili, *The Three Books on the Law of War*, ed. J. C. Rolfe (Oxford, 1933), I–IV, 25: 'For the word *hostis*, "enemy", while it implies equality, like the word "war" ... is sometimes extended to those who are not equal, namely to pirates, proscribed persons and rebels;

Furthermore, Vattel maintained that war was not capable of resolving controversies about justice. He saw clearly that the just war doctrine not only aimed – in vain as far as Vattel was concerned – at articulating normative constraints on the right to go to war (jus ad bellum), but that at the same time it could also be (mis-)used for legitimising going to war. Claims to justice are a vain and dangerous exercise in the case of war and cannot be decided among sovereign states. Vattel's insistence on legal equality and non-discrimination of belligerent states forestalled the abuse of a moral high ground or the claim of a moral superiority during war by any of the warring states. Setting aside the notion of a just war, states would have to accept their opponent as an equally just enemy. This in turn allowed Vattel to obviate the embarrassing consequence of just war doctrine, that the just would also be the victorious: 'It is an error, no less absurd than pernicious, to say that war is to decide controversies between those who acknowledge no superior judge – as is the case with nations. Victory usually favours the cause of strength and prudence rather than that of right and justice' (*LN*, III-III-38).

Replacing the claim to universal justice on which the just war doctrine was based, was the pre-condition for Vattel to circumscribe the conduct of European wars. The result of this move was a more 'humane' conduct of war between the sovereign European states.[26] It also meant adopting a morally non-discriminatory stance towards the enemy. Again the praxis of early modern treaty-making endorsed Vattel's claim, because 'not [in] a single peace treaty [in the early modern period] was judgement rendered on the justice of the war, nor did a single treaty contain an attribution of guilt to one of the belligerents'.[27] Seen in this perspective, Vattel's discussions of justice and the concept of a just war in book III of the *Law of Nations* fit within the history of European treaty-making.[28]

Vattel wrote in the context of European conflict. He had seen the expansionist drive of the Prussian King Frederick II during the Silesian Wars (1740–1742 and 1744–1745) against Austria and the interests of his employer,

nevertheless it cannot confer the rights due to enemies, properly so called, and the privileges of *regular warfare*' [emphasis added].

26 'The humanity with which most nations in Europe carry on their wars at present, cannot be too much commended' (*LN*, III-VIII-140).

27 R. Lesaffer, 'Peace Treaties and the Formation of International Law', 89.

28 See the controversial discussion in I. Hunter, 'Vattel's *Law of Nations*'; E. Jouannet, *Emer de Vattel et l'émergence doctrinale du droit international classique* (Paris, 1993); G. Silvestrini, 'Justice, war and inequality. The unjust aggressor and the enemy of the human race in Vattel's theory of the law of nations', *Grotiana* 31 (2010), 44–68; S. Zurbuchen, 'Vattel's *Law of Nations* and just war theory', *History of European Ideas* 35 (2009), 408–417; and Kalmanovitz, 'Sovereignty, pluralism, and regular war'.

the Prince Elector of Saxony. These conflicts culminated in the Seven Years' War (1756–1763), a full scale European war which soon became the first global conflict.[29] It has been observed that the 'Prussian king was aware that all of his efforts took place within the context of world politics, and that his struggle was part of the global conflict between Great Britain and France'.[30] Vattel saw the conflict between France and Britain in America during the Seven Years' War as a key threat to European peace and equilibrium. Indeed, he scolded the negotiators during the peace undertakings at Utrecht.

> Since the least encroachment on the territory of another is an act of injustice, – in order to avoid the commission of any such act, and to prevent every subject of discord, every occasion of quarrel, the limits of territories ought to be marked out with clearness and precision. *If those who drew up the treaty of Utrecht had bestowed on so important a subject all the attention it deserved, we should not see France and England in arms, in order to decide by a bloody war what are to be the boundaries of their possessions in America.* But the makers of treaties often designedly leave in them some obscurity, some uncertainty, in order to reserve for their nation a pretext for a rupture: – an unworthy artifice in a transaction wherein good faith alone ought to preside! (*LN*, II-VII-92; emphasis added)

Vattel was even less interested in colonial questions or justifications for European expansion and actually severely criticised European conquest in America.[31] However, there is a polemical tendency among some modern scholars to reproach Vattel and other early modern European thinkers for not having provided a more balanced and sensitive approach to global injustices. Such arguments often culminate in the – at best anachronistic – accusation that Vattel and others justified European hegemony and expansion.[32]

[29] See J. Luh, 'Frederick the Great and the first "World" war', in M. H. Danley and P. J. Speelman (eds.), *The Seven Years' War: Global Views* (Leiden, 2012), 1–21. For a general account see T. Pocock, *Battle for Empire. The Very First World War 1756–63* (London, 1998) and F. A. J. Szabo, *The Seven Years War in Europe 1756–1763* (Harlow, 2008).

[30] Luh, 'Frederick the Great and the first "World" war', 21.

[31] *LN*, II-I-28: 'Those ambitious Europeans who attacked the American nations, and subjected them to their greedy dominion, in order, as they pretended to civilise them, and cause them to be instructed in the true religion, – those usurpers, I say, grounded themselves on a pretext equally unjust and ridiculous'. See E. Tourme-Jouannet, 'Des Origines coloniales du droit international: à propos du droit des gens modern au 18ème siècle', in P.-M. Dupuy and V. Chetail (eds.), *The Roots of International Law/Les fondements du droit international* (Leiden, 2014), 655–661.

[32] See, for instance, B. Bowden, 'The colonial origins of international law: European expansion and the classical standard of civilisation', *Journal of the History of International Law* 7 (2005), 13f; and G. Gozzi, *Rights and Civilisations. A History and Philosophy of International Law*, translated by F. Valente (Cambridge, 2019), 70: 'There clearly emerges here [in Vattel's *Law of*

Vattel distinguished between civilised and barbarous nations. Among the civilised nations he counted European and non-European nations (notably China or the South-American Empires) alike (cf. *LN*, I-VII-80f.).[33] Such a distinction was not motivated by an idea of European superiority, but rather by the concern that during the Seven Years' War 'civilised' European states were sliding back into barbarism. Among the historical examples of this backsliding that Vattel gave in his *Law of Nations*, the most striking example refers to France – surely the most civilised nation in the world in the perception of eighteenth century Europe – which became the 'scourge of mankind' when during the reign of Louis XIV it 'ravaged and burnt the Palatinate' (*LN*, III-IX-167). Extreme and wanton violence during war makes any such aggressor, even if it is the most civilised state, 'an enemy to mankind' (*LN*, III-IX-168).

The *Law of Nations* quickly became central to the academic discussion and institutionalisation of the subject, exercising a remarkable influence throughout Europe and the new world. In fact, Vattel's ideas served to promote reform programmes whose comprehensive natures spanned the domains of economic reform, constitutionalism and international diplomacy and foreign trade policy. Not surprisingly, his work has led to different, in some cases almost mutually exclusive interpretations. So far I have outlined my own stance on Vattel. However, the present collection of essays seeks to embrace the range of these diverse views, rather than to reduce the richness of his work into one ostensibly coherent interpretation. The following essays, therefore, aim to shed light on various aspects of Vattel's work, by providing access to a diverse array of modern scholarly interpretations.

Vattel used the natural law tradition to frame a pragmatic and treaty-oriented model of the law of nations, centred on the sovereign state and a morally non-discriminatory conception of the enemy and of war. But what

Nations] the conceit of the European peoples' superiority over the "savages" of the primeval world'. W. Rech, *Enemies of Mankind – Vattel's Theory of Collective Security* (Leiden, 2013), 118, argued that Vattel's doctrine denied 'non-Europeans . . . the opportunity to play according to their own rules'.

33 Next to Chapter 7 by Pablo Kalmanovitz, see, G. Cavallar, 'Vitoria, Grotius, Pufendorf, Wolff and Vattel. Accomplices of European colonialism and exploitation or true cosmopolitans?', *Journal of the History of International Law* 10 (2008), 181–209; A. Anghie, 'Vattel and colonialism: Some preliminary observations', in V. Chetail and P. Haggenmacher (eds.), *Vattel's International Law from a XXIst Century Perspective/Le Droit International de Vattel vu du XXIe Siècle* (Leiden, 2011), 237–253; S. Zurbuchen, 'Das Verhältnis Europas zu den Staaten der Alten und der Neuen Welt. Die Idee einer *société générale du genre humain* in Emer von Vattels Völkerrecht', in O. Asbach (ed.), *Europa und die Moderne im langen 18. Jahrhundert* (Hannover, 2014), 181–185; and P. Piirimäe, 'Men, monsters and the history of mankind in Vattel's *Law of Nations*', in S. Zurbuchen (ed.), *The Law of Nations and Natural Law 1625–1800* (Leiden, 2019), 159–185.

were the specific contexts that governed his elaboration of this legal and political model in *The Law of Nations*? This collection of essays seeks to address this question from three distinct angles and is accordingly divided into three parts: (I) contexts, (II) concepts and (III) receptions. Whereas Part I puts the emphasis on different aspects of the historical contexts and the influence of other thinkers in order to illuminate the way Vattel developed his legal and political concepts, Part II focusses on key concepts of Vattel's thought. The far-reaching legacy of Vattel's *Law of Nations* is examined in Part III.

PART I: HISTORICAL AND INTELLECTUAL CONTEXTS

Vattel's life and work are closely related to the context of eighteenth-century Switzerland, 'a country of which liberty is the soul, the treasure, and the fundamental law', as he prominently stated at the very end of the preface to his *Law of Nations* (*LN*, preface 20). In Chapter 1, Nadir Weber offers an original interpretation that situates Vattel's political thought within the complicated Swiss context, which also helps to explain from this particular angle the apparent tension of some of his key positions.

Vattel was born in the Principality of Neuchâtel, an allied territory of the Swiss Cantons, but which was de jure also under the hereditary – though rather distant – sovereignty of the Prussian monarchy.[34] He studied in Basel and Geneva and, after having failed to secure a post in Prussian service, served as a Saxon diplomat in Bern, the major centre for mercenary service and state financing, from 1747 to 1759. This put him in the uncomfortable position of having to pursue diplomatic undertakings against the interests of his sovereign king, Frederick II, in the employment of one of Prussia's enemies. Although Vattel officially represented Saxon-Polish interests in Bern, in the 1750s, he was also directly involved in Swiss politics. Soon after the publication of his *Law of Nations* he was employed at the Saxon court in Dresden, and later in Warsaw, Frederic August II also being elective king of Poland. He remained in diplomatic services for Saxony until his death in 1767.

[34] For Vattel's views on hereditary states and the necessary consent of the people, see *LN* I-v-58f. The direct line of the ruling family in Neuchâtel died out in 1707. Several European contenders, backed respectively by the French and English monarchies, competed for the right of succession. Eventually, Frederick I of Prussia was adopted as the new sovereign by the estates in Neuchâtel. This outcome was ultimately confirmed by the Peace of Utrecht. For a detailed account of the Prussian succession, see N. Weber, *Lokale Interessen und grosse Strategie. Das Fürstentum Neuchâtel und die politischen Beziehungen der Könige von Preussen (1707–1806)* (Cologne, 2015), 65–84.

Vattel wrote articles for the *Mercure Suisse* and *Journal Helvétique*, corresponded with Swiss savants and magistrates and frequented literary circles in Neuchâtel and Bern. Weber shows the extent to which he participated in discussions of public law, political economy and administration taking place in the Confederacy. The idea of the relative self-sufficiency of the state in contrast to individuals in the state of nature was based on his proposals for economic reform and improvement of agriculture. His insistence on the cultivation of agriculture was foremost motivated by his republican leanings.[35] He advocated republican frugality and criticised corrupting luxury.[36]

The *Law of Nations* was published in the turbulent context of the Seven Years' War. Although Vattel's legacy was arguably derived mostly from the reception of the later posthumous edition, in Chapter 5 Koen Stapelbroek proposes that his position towards contemporary French, Prussian and British politics can be reconstructed from the *Law of Nations* and other sources of the time.[37] Although this was a war with truly global implications, Vattel's interest focused firmly on the challenges for the European state system. In this regard, he viewed the wars undertaken by the Prussian King Frederick II as no less threatening to the system than the extra-European antagonism between France and Britain.

While contexts of Swiss republicanism and the Seven Years War are the focus of Chapters 1 and 5 by Weber and Stapelbroek, respectively, other contributors are concerned to elucidate Vattel's intellectual context and the writers on whom he drew. As Ben Holland and Ere Nokkala show in Chapters 2 and 3, respectively, an intricate network of references to leading natural law thinkers can be traced in Vattel's various writings. In Chapter 3, Nokkala considers the important role that Christian Wolff played for Vattel, observing that as early as the 1740s Vattel was already defending the rationalist philosophy of Wolff. In his *Défense du système leibnitzien* (1741), a response to

35 E. Vattel, 'Dialogue between the prince of **** and his confidant, on certain essential elements of public administration', translated by K. Goodwin, in *The Law of Nations*, ed. B. Kapossy and R. Whatmore (Indianapolis, 2008), 789f. A very similar point is made by Vattel in his 'General considerations on political economy', translated by B. Kapossy and R. Whatmore, 'Emer de *Vattel's Mélanges de littérature, de morale et de politique*', *History of European Ideas* 34 (2008), 91. The criticism of Vattel by Anthony Anghie is thus misleading, because it ignores Vattel's republican motivation. Cf. A. Anghie, *Imperialism, Sovereignty and the Making of International Law* (Cambridge, 2004), 270.

36 See Vattel, 'Dialogue', 788.

37 In addition to Chapter 5 by Koen Stapelbroek, see, K. Stapelbroek, 'The foundations of Vattel's "system" of politics and the context of the seven years' war: Moral philosophy, luxury and the constitutional commercial state', in K. Stapelbroek and A. Trampus (eds.), *The Legacy of Vattel's* Droit des gens (Cham, 2019), 95–163.

critics of Leibnizian–Wolffian philosophy, Vattel argued that adherence to the premises of rationalist philosophy would not serve the cause of atheists. Holland's discussion focuses on why Vattel was to a certain extent oscillating between concepts found in Hobbes and Pufendorf on the one hand, and those he drew from Leibniz and Wolff on the other. In the *Law of Nations*. Vattel approved of Jean Barbeyrac (1674–1744), the French translator and commentator of Pufendorf, for teasing out differences between natural law and the law of nations (*LN*, preface 10). But, in the argument that had broken out over Leibniz's critique of Pufendorf's conception of natural law, Vattel took Leibniz's side against Barbeyrac's support for Pufendorf.[38] Vattel's last book, *Questions de droit naturel et observations sur le traité du droit de nature par le Baron de Wolf* (1764), was another critical assessment of Wolff's natural law doctrine. Nokkala's essay addresses the question: to what extent did the general philosophical framework of Vattel's thought remain true to Wolff? Or did his republican political convictions lead him away from the political theory of enlightened absolutism as advocated by Pufendorf and Wolff in political and international thought? Vattel's prominent statement in his *Law of Nations* that he mainly aimed at making Wolff more approachable was, Nokkala suggests, more than a mere rhetorical gesture.

In Chapter 4, Francesca Iurlaro studies an aspect of Vattel which has so far escaped scholarly interest. She draws attention to the fact that Vattel's *Law of Nations* provides historical examples of a general customary law of moderation, to be applied as a prudential principle in international affairs. Vattel does not resort to the standard examples of *pietas* and *clementia*, drawn from the classical humanism that was of such importance for Gentili, Grotius or Pufendorf. Rather, he drew his examples from a novel selection of historical sources and engaged in a discussion of more contemporary (mostly, French) historiography. In her case-study, Iurlaro scrutinizes Vattel's reliance on the French historian François Timoléon de Choisy (1644–1724). She argues that Vattel's selective reading of Choisy provides us with a valuable means to address the relationship between universal and regional customs. Whereas the former are applicable to humankind as a whole for the universality of the principles they enshrine, respect of the latter is restricted to culturally

38 E. Vattel, 'Essay on the foundation of natural law and on the first principle of the obligation men find themselves under to observe laws', translated by T. Hochstrasser, in *The Law of Nations*, ed. B. Kapossy and R. Whatmore (Indianapolis, 2008), 761–771. See J. Barbeyrac, 'The judgement of an anonymous writer on the original of this abridgement', in S. Pufendorf (ed.), *The Whole Duty of Man, According to the Law of Nature*, ed. I. Hunter and D. Saunders (Indianapolis, 2003), 267–305. Aspects of the complexity of these relationships are explored in Chapter 3 by Ere Nokkala and Chapter 2 by Ben Holland.

homogeneous environments (i.e. Europe) and, as such, they are more subject to contestation. In her contribution, Iurlaro asks what kind of ideas of universality of the law of nations Vattel was conveying when looking through the eyes of Choisy's histories of France? For her, Vattel's reading of Choisy sheds new light on the originality of his use of historical examples and exemplifies a new language of historical authenticity. Though Choisy's memoires were not cited in Vattel's works, Vattel specifically used the genre of memoir to address questions of war and politics. Iurlaro thus offers new insight into the relationship between the stylistic freshness of memoires as a genre and Vattel's more general doctrinal treatment of the law of nations.

PART II: CONCEPTS

The chapters in the second part of this volume trace key concepts of Vattel's political and juridical thought. Focusing on the internal organisation of the state, Antonio Trampus (Chapter 8) thus studies constitutionalism, while Gabriella Silvestrini (Chapter 9) explores the social contract. In shifting the focus to external relations between states, Camilla Boisen (Chapter 6) writes on the balance of power, and Pablo Kalmanovitz (Chapter 7) on civilisation and irregular war. This list of concepts is far from exhaustive. Thus, neutrality and sovereignty resonate in these chapters and are explored from different interpretative angles. From their specific perspectives, contributors ask to what extent Vattel's *Law of Nations* remained indebted to existing traditions of political thought or was coloured by the multi-layered contexts that the Swiss diplomat experienced in the employment of the Saxon Prince Elector.

In Chapter 9, Silvestrini explores an important but neglected topic in Vattel's political and international thought, namely his social contract theory. She shows that Vattel endorses a theory of the double contract, the act of association and the compact of government, which is however different from Pufendorf's doctrine. Whereas the latter considers the contract of government the source of political obligation, Vattel – following Wolff – thinks that political obligation already exists by virtue of the act of association, without excluding the possibility of a contract of government that reciprocally binds the prince and the people. She shows how Vattel's theory of the social contract functions in historical contexts (for example in his interpretation of the relationships between the prince of Prussia and the communities of Neuchâtel and Valangin) and in his rational deduction of the principles of public law. She also draws attention to the marriage contract and the exclusion of women from politics as an example of Vattel's conceptualisation of the contract. Finally, she points out that, despite similar language, Vattel's theory of the social contract and the inalienability of sovereignty is very different conceptually from the theory of the social contract that Rousseau elaborated in the same period.

Closely related to Silvestrini's analysis, Trampus's focus in Chapter 8 is on Vattel's contribution to constitutionalism, a key issue in the eighteenth and nineteenth centuries. Centred on the principle that defined all sovereign states as nations composed of societies of free men, in Vattel's conception, as Trampus shows, nations or states are independent political bodies, each with their own interests. The nation that becomes a state assumes the form of a moral person with its own intentions and will, able to fulfil obligations and observe rights. Trampus explores how Vattel's assertion that each nation is, according to natural law, free and sovereign – irrespective of what degree of power or political and economic autonomy it possesses – fed into discussions of constitutionalism, in particular for smaller states that found themselves in a situation of inequality because militarily weak or geographically small. As Trampus demonstrates, on the basis of Vattel's *Law of Nations* these smaller states were still able to make claims to sovereign independence and freedom, internally and externally.

The concept of independent sovereign states led Vattel to reformulate a range of political concepts – the social contract, constitutionalism, neutrality, the balance of power or the war in due form – that were most importantly applied to the European state system. They were also intended to make good the shortcomings of natural law in interstate relations. Sovereign states at war recognised the opponent as a just enemy, and sovereign states that stayed neutral maintained their trade. As shown by Camilla Boisen in Chapter 6, the balance of power envisaged by Vattel thus had multiple layers, providing a more realistic and more flexible approach to accommodate competing economic and political interests. In Vattel's view, the European state system had been successful in balancing trade and war, with Vattel commenting: 'that the commerce of neutral nations may subsist in as great a degree of freedom as is consistent with the laws of war, there are certain rules to be observed, on which Europe seems to be generally agreed' (*LN*, III-VII-111).[39] As Boisen demonstrates, Vattel's idea of the balance of power was largely descriptive. He

39 Next to Chapter 6 by Camilla Boisen, see Nakhimovsky, 'Vattel's theory of the international order', 162–166; R. Devetak, 'Law of nations as reason of state: Diplomacy and balance of power in Vattel's *Law of Nations*', *Parergon* 28 (2011), 105–128; and R. Devetak, '"The fear of universal monarchy": Balance of power as an ordering practice of liberty', *Proceedings of the British Academy* 190 (2013), 121–137.

viewed the balance of power as an important factor promoting a stable system of sovereign states as the basis for international peace.

> Europe forms a political system . . . closely connected by the interests of the nations inhabiting this part of the world. . . . The continual attention of sovereigns to every occurrence, the constant residence of ministers, and the perpetual negotiations, make of modern Europe a kind of republic, of which the members – each independent, but all linked together by the ties of common interest – unite for the maintenance of order and liberty. Hence arose that famous scheme of the political balance, or the equilibrium of power; by which is understood such a disposition of things, as that no one potentate be able absolutely to predominate, and prescribe laws to others. (*LN*, III-iii-47)

This citation summarises many of Vattel's key-concepts and indicates that his main concern focused on establishing a political system for the European context.

In Chapter 7, Pablo Kalmanovitz examines the extent to which standards of justice or norms of civilization informed Vattel's construction of the laws of war. Many scholars have argued that Vattel 'relegated' natural justice to the realm of morality or conscience and restricted the scope of legal obligations to the positivist rules of voluntary law, effectively replacing just war with formal war. Vattel, rather than just presenting an abstract system of rights and duties in war, embedded his argument in a specific Enlightenment account of history where sovereigns aspire towards an ever greater degree of civility. These European sovereigns are contrasted with 'enemies of mankind' who do not qualify as subjects of the voluntary law of nations. Kalmanovitz concentrates on this concept by studying Vattel's arguments about regular war, irregulars, and savages. He examines the extent to which standards of civilization were relevant or present in Vattel's construction of the laws of war. By analysing Vattel's treatment of non-Europeans, Kalmanovitz's chapter emphasizes the contrasts between Vattel and the more familiar nineteenth century constructions. Instead of using a crude distinction between Europeans and non-Europeans, Kalmanovitz's Vattel produced a set of nuanced distinctions to construct categories of irregularity and savagery which he applied to both Europeans and non-Europeans.

PART III: RECEPTIONS

The numerous editions and early translations produced throughout the eighteenth century enabled the broad dissemination of Vattel's *Law of Nations.*

The contributors to the third part of the present collection investigate the reception and impact of the *Law of Nations* with regard to different political realities and historical and legal contexts. They also discuss the attempts, mechanisms and strategies used to put Vattel's ideas into practice and establish a new international legal doctrines between the eighteenth and nineteenth centuries.[40] These contributors analyse how the *Law of Nations* was received, rejected or altered to meet the needs of political practice, to justify war – often explicitly against Vattel's intentions – and to direct diplomacy, the prudence of which was contingent on the interests of the different state actors involved. Case studies of Vattel's translators, editors and readers in the Greek and Italian contexts by Elisabetta Fiocchi Malaspina or the English and Scottish contexts by Marco Barducci show how readers and translators assimilated and transformed Vattel's vocabulary regarding obligations, rights and duties; societies, nations and state; ownership and possession; sovereignty and freedom. In Chapter 12, Fiocchi Malaspina is centrally concerned with analysing, on the one hand, how the decision to translate the *Law of Nations* served a political–constitutional purpose in the case of Greek independence between 1821 and 1832 and, on the other hand, examining how Vattel's treatise was used during the Italian Risorgimento. While, in Chapter 13, Barducci focuses on Vattel as a leading authority on matters concerning international law and as the continuator of the continental natural law tradition in England and Scotland. Vattel can thus be seen as a *trait-d'union* between this continental strand of thought and British legal and intellectual culture.

This transformative assimilation of Vattel's thought can equally be discerned in North America, where politicians and legislators were keen to seek arguments from Vattel for their struggle of independence. His concepts of sovereignty (*LN*, I-I-4) and constitutional reform (*LN*, I-III-32f) could be adopted as forceful arguments for the emancipation and self-government of the American colonists. The declaration of independence of 1776 echoes Vattel's convictions but was not, however, primarily aimed at the internal affairs of North America. Rather, this famous declaration was the deliberate attempt – using Vattelian language and concepts – to gain recognition as an independent nation within the European state system.[41] These are well researched and established aspects of Vattel's reception in North America.[42]

[40] See also, E. Fiocchi Malaspina, *L'eterno ritorno del Droit des gens di Emer de Vattel (secc. XVIII–XIX), L'impatto sulla cultura giuridica in prospettiva* (Frankfurt, 2017).

[41] E. H. Gould, *Among the Powers of the Earth. The American Revolution and the Making of a New World Empire* (Cambridge, MA, 2012).

[42] Next to Chapter 10 by Mark Somos, see B. Richardson, 'The use of Vattel in the American Law of Nations', *The American Journal of International Law* 106 (2012), 547–571; V. Chetail, 'Vattel

In Chapter 10, Mark Somos focusses on the period of 1761–1775, which predated the 'classical' reception of Vattel by the founding fathers. Drawing on newly unearthed source material, he is able to shed fresh light on the history of Vattel's reception in America. Somos shows that the founding fathers' use of Vattel was not limited to international law, but that he was first cited as an authority on domestic constitutional norms and procedures.

The history of different adaptations of Vattel's thought in these contexts is not a mere episode of a reception of foreign ideas. Rather, as is shown in Chapter 10 by Somos and Chapter 11 by Nathaniel Boyd, it is a history of the creative adaptation of materials in order to combine the new vocabulary of the law of nations with the particular political and constitutional foundations of the specific context in which Vattel was being appropriated. In this way these contributors offer a new way of viewing the historical fortunes of Vattel's juridical and political thought by underscoring how political contexts shape the formation of concepts, thereby determining the development or reception of a political theory.

As the two concluding contributions by Theodore Christov in Chapter 14 and Richard Devetak in Chapter 15 demonstrate, Vattel's influence and legacy reached well beyond the nineteenth century and are still felt today. The turn of the nineteenth century is widely seen in histories of international law as a watershed moment, when the naturalism of the eighteenth century paved the way for positivism in the nineteenth and twentieth centuries. Christov reassesses such a narrative by tracing the question of the scope of the law of nations through the reception and use of Vattel, particularly in the international law literature. According to Christov, the changing reception of Vattel's work from the first to the second half of the nineteenth century illustrates not only the increasing professionalisation of international lawyers, but also his authoritative status in respect of Europe's imperial expansion. He sees Vattel's most enduring effect on colonial jurisprudence in judicial thought concerning the relations between European and non-European people. Christov further suggests that the reception of Vattel in modern international law can also be perceived in the way the ambiguous status of the universality of the law of nations was exploited.

and the American dream: An inquiry into the reception of the *Law of Nations* in the United States', in P.-M. Dupuy and V. Chetail (eds.), *The Roots of International Law/Les fondements du droit international* (Leiden, 2014), 251–300; and W. Ossipow and D. Gerber, 'The reception of Vattel's *Law of Nations* in the American colonies: From James Otis and John Adams to the Declaration of Independence', *American Journal of Legal History* 57 (2017), 521–555.

In his critical revisionist approach, Devetak demonstrates how the discipline of international relations has conventionally approached Emer de Vattel by pigeon-holing him in one or other of the dominant theories. Some have identified Vattel as a realist for his defence of the sovereign state's unfettered liberty in a Hobbesian state of nature, others as a liberal or idealist for his appeal to universally valid natural laws. Still others have aligned him with a *via media* between the extremes of Hobbesian realism and Kantian idealism in which Vattel, like Grotius, upholds the existence of an international society of states. These different treatments, Devetak argues, are a function of the dominance in international relations of theoretical 'isms', abstract philosophies of history, and the correlative failure to contextualise Vattel's thinking. Devetak concludes that by projecting twentieth and twenty-first century theories onto Vattel, international relations has failed to grasp his nuanced thinking, resulting in simplistic or ambivalent accounts. Having shown the limitations of the dominant patterns of Vattel's reception in international relations, Devetak proposes an alternative stance: a contextual form of intellectual history that would enable a richer appreciation of Vattel's thinking than international relations theory generally recognises. In many ways, the essays in the present volume may be regarded as a contribution to this contextualised approach to Vattel's thought.

It should have become evident by now that 'Vattel appears to have articulated ... different framings of the character of international legal order'.[43] Vattel believed in the betterment and perfection of the human condition. Such idealism accounts not least for a certain ambiguity or tension of argument detected throughout the *Law of Nations*, fuelling competing interpretations – resonating in this volume – of how to understand his concepts.[44] However, Vattel was always clear about what was desirable and what was realistic and possible regarding interstate relations:

> How happy would mankind be, were these amiable precepts of nature every where observed! Nations would communicate to each other their products and their knowledge; a profound peace would prevail all over the earth, and enrich it with its invaluable fruits; industry, the sciences, and the arts, would

[43] B. Holland, 'The moral person of the state: Emer de Vattel and the foundations of international legal order', *History of European Ideas* 37 (2011), 438.

[44] An overview of competing interpretations can be found in I. Nakhimovsky, 'Carl Schmitt's Vattel and the *Law of Nations* between enlightenment and revolution', *Grotiana* 31 (2010), 141–164. See also G. Cavallar, 'The *Law of Nations* in the age of enlightenment: Moral and legal principles', *Jahrbuch für Recht und Ethik/Annual Review of Law and Ethics* 12 (2004), 222–225; and B. Kapossy, 'Rival histories of Emer de Vattel's *Law of Nations*', *Grotiana* 31 (2010), 12–14.

> be employed in promoting our happiness ... violent methods of deciding contests would be no more heard of: all differences would be terminated by moderation, justice and equity: the world would have the appearance of a large republic; men would live everywhere like brothers, and each individual be a citizen of the universe. (*LN*, II-1-16)

What Vattel described here, in words similar to those previously used by Hobbes,[45] are the agreeable effects to be found once sovereign states leave the bellicose state of nature and enter into the law of nations. He immediately emphasised, however, 'that this idea should be but a delightful dream' (*LN*, II-1-16). No matter how delightful such an idea might be, Vattel was resolute that dreaming about the universal brotherhood of mankind did not recommend itself as the instrument for regulating the potentially antagonistic interests of sovereign states.[46] Instead, he insisted, interstate political relations depended on political compromise (*LN*, IV-11-18).

FURTHER READING

Writings by Vattel

Vattel, E., *The Law of Nations*, ed. B. Kapossy and R. Whatmore (Indianapolis, 2008).

'Essay on the foundation of natural law and on the first principle of the obligation men find themselves under to observe laws', translated by T. Hochstrasser, in B. Kapossy and R. Whatmore (eds.), *The Law of Nations* (Indianapolis, 2008), 747–771.

'Dissertation on this question: "Can natural law bring society to perfection without the assistance of political laws?"', translated by T. Hochstrasser, in B. Kapossy and R. Whatmore (eds.), *The Law of Nations* (Indianapolis, 2008), 773–781.

'Dialogue between the Prince of **** and his confidant, on certain essential elements of public administration', translated by K. Goodwin, in B. Kapossy and R. Whatmore (eds.), *The Law of Nations* (Indianapolis, 2008), 783–796.

45 Hobbes, *Leviathan*, 89: 'In such condition [of the state of nature], there is no place for Industry; because the fruit thereof is uncertain: and consequently no Culture of the Earth; no Navigation, nor use of the commodities that may be imported by Sea; no commodious Building; no Instruments of moving, and removing such things as require much force; no Knowledge of the face of the Earth; no account of Time; no Arts; no Letters; no Society; and which is worst of all, continuall feare, and danger of violent death'. On the importance of Hobbes for Vattel see, P. Haggenmacher, 'Introduction. Le modèle de Vattel et la discipline de droit internationale', in V. Chetail and P. Haggenmacher (eds.), *Vattel's International Law from a XXIst Century Perspective/Le Droit International de Vattel vu du XXIe Siècle* (Leiden, 2011), 34–38.

46 This is not least the case, because 'melancholy experience shews that most nations aim only to strengthen and enrich themselves at the expense of others, – to domineer over them, and even, if an opportunity offers, to oppress and bring them under the yoke' (*LN*, II-1-16).

Défense du système leibnitzien contre les objections et les imputations de Mr de Crousaz, contenues dans l'Examen de l'Essai sur l'homme de Mr Pope … (Leyden, 1741).

Questions de droit naturel et observations sur le traité du droit de nature par le Baron de Wolf (Bern, 1762).

Kapossy, B. and Whatmore, R. (eds.), 'Emer de *Vattel's Mélanges de littérature, de morale et de politique*', *History of European Ideas* 34 (2008), 77–103.

Bandelier, A. (ed.), Emer de Vattel à Jean Henri Samuel Formey: correspondances autour du Droit des gens (Paris, 2012).

Selected Secondary Literature

Beaulac, S., 'Emer de Vattel and the externalization of sovereignty', Journal of the History of International Law/Revue d'histoire du droit international 5 (2003), 237–292.

Chetail, V., 'Vattel and the American dream: An inquiry into the reception of the *Law of Nations* in the United States' in P.-M. Dupuy and V. Chetail (eds.), The Roots of International Law/Les fondements du droit international (Leiden, 2014), 251–300.

Fenwick, C. G., 'The authority of Vattel', *The American Political Science Review* 7 (1913), 395–410.

'The authority of Vattel' *The American Political Science Review* 8 (1914), 375–392.

Holland, B., 'The moral person of the State: Emer de Vattel and the foundations of international legal order', *History of European Ideas* 37 (2011), 438–445.

Hunter, I., 'Vattel's *Law of Nations*: Diplomatic casuistry for the protestant nation', *Grotiana* 31 (2010), 108–140.

Kalmanovitz, P., 'Sovereignty, pluralism, and regular war: Wolff and Vattel's enlightenment critique of just war', *Political Theory* 46 (2018), 218–241.

Kapossy, B., 'Rival histories of Emer de Vattel's *Law of Nations*', *Grotiana* 31 (2010), 5–21.

Lesaffer, R., 'A schoolmaster abolishing home-work? Vattel on peacemaking and peace treaties', in V. Chetail and P. Haggenmacher (eds.), Vattel's International Law from a XXIst Century Perspective/Le Droit International de Vattel vu du XXIe Siècle (Leiden, 2011), 353–384.

Nakhimovsky, I., 'Vattel's theory of the international order: Commerce and the balance of power in the *Law of Nations*', *History of European Ideas* 33 (2007), 157–173.

Stapelbroek, K., 'The foundations of Vattel's "system" of politics and the context of the seven years' war: Moral philosophy, luxury and the constitutional commercial state', in K. Stapelbroek and A. Trampus (eds.), *The Legacy of Vattel's* Droit des gens(Cham, 2019), 95–163.

Whelan, F. G., 'Vattel's doctrine of the State', *History of Political Thought* 9 (1988), 59–80.

Zurbuchen, S., 'Emer de Vattel on the society of nations and the political system of Europe', in S. Kadelbach, T. Kleinlein and D. Roth-Isigkeit (eds.), *System, Order, and International Law. The Early History of International Legal Thought from Machiavelli to Hegel* (Oxford 2017), 263–282.

PART I

Historical and Intellectual Contexts

1

In Search of a Nation

Vattel, Neuchâtel, and the Swiss Confederacy

NADIR WEBER

In the preface of his *Law of Nations*, Emer de Vattel stated that 'I was born in a country of which liberty is the soul, the treasure, and the fundamental law; and my birth qualifies me to be the friend of all nations'. At first sight, it seems evident that this country is Switzerland. Vattel's statement perfectly dovetails with the eighteenth-century discourse that praised the country as a haven of peace and frugality and applauded the republican autonomy of the Swiss. In scholarly literature, Vattel is usually considered as a Swiss legal scholar. However, the question of which country Vattel considered as his native country is not trivial when we take a closer look – and it may offer us a key to a better understanding of important parts of his work.

This chapter will first show how the *Law of Nations* reflects the transnational experiences of an author who was born in the small principality of Neufchatel in Switzerland. Then we will see that, for his Swiss contemporaries, Vattel was not only an *homme de lettres* and theorist of international law. He was also a controversial actor on the political scene of his home country who used his legal concepts to challenge the rule of the prince of Neuchâtel, king Frederick II of Prussia. These long-neglected political involvements help to explain Vattel's fervent insistence on the principle of national sovereignty that probably constitutes the main innovation of his oeuvre in the context of eighteenth-century political and legal discourse.[1]

A CITIZEN OF ALL NATIONS?

The idea of a 'Westphalian system of states' has been heavily challenged by historians in the last two or three decades. This concept, introduced by the

[1] I am indebted to Béla Kapossy, Antonio Trampus and Simone Zurbuchen for critical readings of an earlier version of this chapter.

legal scholar Leo Gross in 1948, seems to have more to do with concerns about collective security, national independence and parity among nation states after the end of World War II than with the political realities in Europe after the peace of Westphalia.[2] While it is true that the concept of sovereignty became a key issue in seventeenth-century political discourse and diplomatic practice, one has to consider that the concept did not only denote a legal quality within an emerging, yet still unaccomplished state system, but also a social status within the society of princes.[3] Thus, the recognition of sovereignty was intrinsically tied to the *honores regii* that were granted in ceremonial interaction, while heterogeneous composite monarchies and largely autonomous small territories still made up a large part of the political scene in eighteenth-century Europe.[4]

Accordingly, when contemporaries of Emer de Vattel talked about their country or *patrie*, they still referred rather to their communal or regional affiliation than to a national identity.[5] In 1714, Vattel was born in Couvet, a village in the Val-de-Travers close to the French border, before the family moved to Saint-Aubin on the shores of Lake Neuchâtel.[6] As a son of the reformed pastor David Vattel, Emer was also a member of the citizenry of Neuchâtel, the most important municipal corporation in the principality of Neuchâtel and Valangin. As the name indicates, the territory with its population of about 30,000 inhabitants was ruled by a prince – the king of Prussia – but was seen as *principauté souveraine* independent from the other territories under the rule of the same monarch.[7] Vattel would spend most of his life in

[2] H. Duchhardt, '"Westphalian System". Zur Problematik einer Denkfigur', *Historische Zeitschrift* 269 (1999), 305–315; A. Osiander, "Sovereignty, international relations, and the Westphalian myth", *International Organization* 55 (2001), 251–287.

[3] S. Beaulac, *The Power of Language in the Making of International Law. The Word 'Sovereignty' in Bodin and Vattel and the Myth of Westphalia* (Leiden 2004); A. J. Krischer and H. von Thiessen, 'Diplomacy in a global early modernity: The ambiguity of sovereignty', *The International History Review* 41 (2019), 1100–1107.

[4] J. H. Elliott, 'A Europe of composite monarchies', *Past and Present* 137 (1992), 48–71; A. Krischer, 'Souveränität als sozialer Status. Zur Funktion des diplomatischen Zeremoniells in der Frühen Neuzeit', in R. Kauz, G. Rota and J. P. Niederkorn (eds.), *Diplomatisches Zeremoniell in Europa und dem Mittleren Osten in der Frühen Neuzeit* (Vienna, 2009), 1–32.

[5] R. von Friedeburg (ed.), *'Patria' und 'Patrioten' vor dem Patriotismus. Pflichten, Rechte, Glauben und die Rekonfigurierung europäischer Gemeinwesen im 17. Jahrhundert* (Wiesbaden, 2005).

[6] For details on Vattel's biography, see especially E. Béguelin, 'En souvenir de Vattel', *Recueil de travaux publié par la Faculté de droit de l'Université de Neuchâtel à la Société suisse des juristes* (Neuchâtel, 1929), 33–176.

[7] W. Stirbrny, *Die Könige von Preußen als Fürsten von Neuenburg-Neuchâtel (1707–1848). Geschichte einer Personalunion* (Berlin, 1998); N. Weber, *Lokale Interessen und große Strategie. Das Fürstentum Neuchâtel und die politischen Beziehungen der Könige von Preußen (1707–1806)* (Cologne, 2015).

this territory, often described as a sort of mini-Switzerland with beautiful mountains and lakes and a population that profited from extremely low taxes and extensive local privileges, according to contemporary observers.[8] When staying abroad, Vattel praised the fresh air in Neuchâtel and the simple manners of its inhabitants in his letters in a similar way. Neuchâtel always remained his primary *patrie*, and like many of his compatriots, he was eager to defend the autonomy of the extremely small yet sovereign principality.

Being Neuchâtelois did not preclude being Swiss. In his *Law of Nations*, Vattel repeatedly uses the formula 'Neufchatel in Switzerland' when discussing the case of Neuchâtel (cf., for instance, *LN*, I-I-9; I-XIX-225; II-VII-85). Yet defining Neuchâtel as a part of Switzerland already contained a political message, as it was a controversial issue in the eighteenth century to which national entity the principality actually belonged. Since the late middle ages, several local municipal corporations of Neuchâtel were allied to the four Swiss city-states of Bern, Lucerne, Fribourg and Solothurn.[9] However, Neuchâtel did not belong to the circle of thirteen cantons that had a vote at the Swiss diet, the main federal institution in early modern Switzerland.[10] After the Prussian succession in 1707, the Catholic cantons of Switzerland even refused to accept Neuchâtel as an ally of the Swiss Confederacy. Thus, when Vattel was born, Neuchâtel was only a formal ally of the canton of Bern, while it was also part of the composite Prussian monarchy. Furthermore, during the entire eighteenth century, the court of Versailles and several noble families remained deeply interested in the principality and were waiting for an opportunity to bring Neuchâtel back under French rule.[11]

Given this political situation, the elites governing the principality were divided into pro-Prussian and pro-French families.[12] Both sides might have

8 P. Henry, 'Libertés neuchâteloises et liberté suisse. Regards étrangers sur les institutions de la principauté de Neuchâtel au XVIIIe siècle', in Ph. Henry (ed.), *Des chartes de franchises à la nouvelle Constitution. Une histoire des institutions neuchâteloises* (Neuchâtel, 2002), 143–167.

9 L. Montandon, L.-E. Roulet, A. Schnegg and F. Faessler, *Neuchâtel et la Suisse* (Neuchâtel, 1969).

10 A. Würgler, *Die Tagsatzung der Eidgenossen. Politik, Kommunikation und Symbolik einer repräsentativen Institution im europäischen Kontext* (1470–1798) (Epfendorf, 2013); A. Würgler, '"The League of Discordant Members" or how the old Swiss Confederation operated and how it managed to survive for so long' , in A. Holenstein, Th. Maissen and M. Prak (eds.), *The Republican Alternative. The Netherlands and Switzerland Compared* (Amsterdam, 2008), 29–50.

11 J. Courvoisier, 'Essai sur les projets de cession de Neuchâtel à la France entre 1707 et 1789', *Schweizerische Zeitschrift für Geschichte* 9 (1959), 145–167.

12 N. Weber, 'Divide and rule? Rival factions and Prussian state management in eighteenth-century Neuchâtel', in M. Caesar (ed.), *Factional Struggles. Divided Elites in European Cities and Courts (1400–1750)* (Leiden, 2017), 176–195.

bonds of parentage and friendship with patricians in the Swiss cantons, where similar factional divides between pro-French and anti-French families existed within the ruling councils. Through the alliance with the family of Emer's mother, Marie de Montmollin, the Vattel family originally belonged to the patricians that profited from the Prussian reign.[13] Vattel's uncle, the powerful chancellor and diplomat Emer de Montmollin (from whom he had inherited his first name), had been a key actor in the Prussian succession. The ennoblement of Vattel's father by king Frederick William I in 1727 (which added *de* to the family name) stood in a line of favours granted to loyal subjects by the Prussian crown. Thus it seemed only natural that Emer de Vattel, after finishing his studies, first travelled to Berlin in order to obtain a post as a professor of philosophy in Neuchâtel or as a Prussian diplomat.[14] He took with him his first philosophical treatise, the *Défense du système leibnitien* (1741), in which he presented himself as a 'faithful subject' of the young philosopher-king Frederick II of Prussia.

Rather coincidentally, after having failed to obtain the favour of the king, Vattel then turned to Dresden where he had more luck. The elector of Saxony and king of Poland-Lithuania, Augustus III, granted him a post as a *conseiller d'ambassade* with a modest, but regular pension in 1747. Although his plan to negotiate the cession of Neuchâtel from the Prussian to the Saxon monarch proved to be unfeasible,[15] Vattel would stay in Saxon service until his death. Services for foreign monarchs were a widespread phenomenon in Neuchâtel and in the Confederacy; many Swiss served as soldiers, physicians, diplomats, educators or governesses at European courts.[16] Vattel's elder brother, Jean Frédéric de Vattel, had already entered the French military service and recruited soldiers for king Louis XV in the principality with Emer's support. Military service for foreign powers was formally allowed by the so-called *articles généraux* that the Prussian representative had to sign when the princi-

[13] On Vattel's family, see P. A. Borel, 'Branche anoblie de la famille Vattel communière de Peseux et bourgeoise de Neuchâtel', *Généalogie suisse: annuaire* (2006), 61–83.

[14] A. Bandelier, 'De Berlin à Neuchâtel. La genèse du Droit des gens d'Emer de Vattel', in M. Fontius and H. Holzhey (eds.), *Schweizer im Berlin des 18. Jahrhunderts* (Berlin, 1996), 45–56

[15] T. Toyoda, Theory and Politics of the Law of Nations. Political Bias in International Law Discourse of Seven German Court Councilors in the Seventeenth and Eighteenth Centuries (Leiden, 2011), 171–173. Toyoda has convincingly pointed out Vattel's Neuchâtel bias in his chapter on 'Vattel's doctrine of national sovereignty in the context of Saxony-Poland and Neuchâtel' (ibid., 161–190).

[16] A. Holenstein, *Mitten in Europa. Verflechtung und Abgrenzung in der Schweizer Geschichte* (Baden, 2014); D. Tosato-Rigo, S. Moret Petrini, *L'appel de l'est. Précepteurs et gouvernantes suisses à la Cour de Russie (1760–1820)* (Lausanne, 2017).

pality had passed to the king in 1707[17] – a fact that Vattel explicitly mentions in his *Law of Nations* (*LN*, I-I-9). While the foreign services of the Vattel brothers seemed not to cause any problems during the Franco–Prussian alliance, they had significant effects a decade later, as we will see.

In any case, for an eighteenth-century Neuchâtelois like Emer de Vattel, being Swiss, Prussian or French was rather a matter of individual choice than of a pre-determined national identity. Especially for the compatriots engaged in business affairs, this proved to be a very lucrative situation. Depending on their needs, they could profit from Prussian protection, Swiss neutrality and commercial privileges or French connections – or from all at the same time. For instance, the Neuchâtel-based merchant and banker Jacques-Louis de Pourtalès, who created one of the major enterprises of global capitalism in the late eighteenth century, was notorious for being a 'citizen of all nations' ('*citoyen de toutes les nations*'); he always assumed the role that was most profitable at a given point in time.[18] The same experience of a fluid nationality influenced Vattel's rather pragmatic, non-essentialist definition of national membership in his *Law of Nations*, where he sees no problem in 'choos[ing] another country, that is, to become a member of another society' and simply defines country as 'the state of which a man is an actual member' (*LN*, I-XI-122). Consequently, when a friend asked him to inform him about the current affairs in his country, Vattel replied with the question of whether he should talk about his 'native country [i.e. Neuchâtel] or the one that I serve at the moment [Saxony]?'[19]

However, Vattel was also fully aware that the ambiguous status of Neuchâtel, combined with its geographical situation, could have disastrous consequences. In times of Franco–Prussian antagonism, the inclusion within the Swiss system of neutrality and military defence was a *condition d'être* for the Neuchâtelois. As a formally recognised ally of the Swiss, the principality would not only be protected against French military aggression, but also against any aims of the Prussian court to intensify its rule over the territory. For this reason, local elites of all factions constantly aimed to strengthen their

17 On this topic, see A. Bachmann, *Die preussische Sukzession in Neuchâtel. Ein ständisches Verfahren um die Landesherrschaft im Spannungsfeld zwischen Recht und Utilitarismus (1694–1715)* (Zürich, 1993).

18 Statement by Augustino Augostini to the French Directory, January 1799, A. Du Pasquier, 'Un mémoire sur la réunion de Neuchâtel à la République française', *Musée neuchâtelois* 48 (1911), 155–184, 211–229, at 169.

19 E. de Vattel to J. H. S. Formey, Neuchâtel, 25 March 1753: E. Vattel, Emer de Vattel à Jean Henri Samuel Formey. Correspondances autour du Droit des gens, ed. André Bandelier (Paris, 2012), 143. [*Correspondances*].

ties to the Swiss cantons not only through political, but also through literary and historiographical means. One of the first and most prominent defenders of this becoming-Swiss strategy had been Vattel's uncle Emer de Montmollin who had written long statements on this issue when participating in the peace negotiations at Utrecht in 1712–1713.[20] Later, the same statements were reused and combined with information from a forged late medieval chronicle by partisans of Helvetism (a literary intellectual trend in eighteenth-century western Switzerland) in order to corroborate Neuchâtel's supposedly ancient membership in the Swiss nation.[21] Vattel himself used his influence to support Neuchâtel's integration into the Helvetic body. Even in his last letter as a Saxon envoy to the Republic of Bern, he did not miss the opportunity to tell the Bernese that being 'tenderly attached to my country [i.e. Neuchâtel], I know that your powerful republic is its most firm column'.[22]

Finally, by claiming to be Swiss and not Saxon, Prussian or French, Vattel also underlined his personal neutrality – and credibility – as an author of international law. In the midst of the Seven Years' War, it was not only the Swiss liberty, but also the Swiss neutrality that 'qualified' him 'to be a friend of all nations' (*LN*, preface). His Swiss nationality thus also served the author's editorial strategy and his self-positioning within the European republic of letters.[23]

VATTEL AND THE SWISS *RÉPUBLIQUE DES LETTRES*

The question of what it actually meant to be Swiss was not only discussed in border territories such as Neuchâtel, but also in the core regions of the Confederacy. While for diplomats, travellers, merchants, cartographers or historians, 'Switzerland' was a well-established entity in the eighteenth-century, their different visions were rarely fully congruent, whether they lived in the cantons or came from abroad.[24] Different kinds of

[20] L. Montandon, 'Emer de Montmollin et l'indigénat helvétique', *Musée neuchâtelois* (1955), 16–21.

[21] A. Besson, *Le Moyen Âge mythique des neuchâtelois. Réécrire l'histoire pour devenir suisse. Sur les traces d'un faussaire du XVIIIe siècle* (Neuchâtel, 2014).

[22] E. de Vattel to the Council of Bern [Warsaw, 8 May 1762], *Correspondances*, 201.

[23] Consequently, some contemporaries considered Vattel as a Swiss author and even as a citizen of the Republic of Bern. Cf. A. Alimento, 'The French reception of Vattel's *Droit des gens*: Politics and publishing strategies', in K. Stapelbroek and A. Trampus (eds.), *The Legacy of Vattel's Droit des gens* (Cham, 2019), 135–163, at 137–138.

[24] A. Würgler, 'Which Switzerland? Contrasting conceptions of the early modern Swiss confederation in European minds and maps', in Beat Kümin (ed.), *Political Space in Pre-industrial Europe* (Farnham, 2009), 197–213.

frictions – confessional, political and economic – complicated the communication between the cantons and prevented any plans of building up central structures. Even the Swiss diet remained a congress of envoys rather than an institution of national decision-making. After the civil war between the Catholic and the Protestant cantons in 1712 and the following separate alliance of the Catholic cantons with the French king, the political fragmentation even seemed to increase. However, the elites of the small states knew that they could only maintain their commercial privileges and their independence with regard to the expanding monarchical neighbours if they stayed together. Far from being an integrated modern nation state, the cohesion of the Helvetic body remained a permanent issue of political negotiations and learned debates throughout the century.[25]

Thanks to the expanding printing industry, the intermediary position between the German, French and Italian language regions and the general economic prosperity in the Protestant city states, western and northern Switzerland became major hubs of the European Enlightenment that also inspired Swiss reform discourse. Internationally known figures such as Albrecht von Haller, Jean-Jacques Rousseau and Isaak Iselin participated in the debates about the need of political and social reform in Switzerland.[26] In the emergence of a Swiss public sphere, Neuchâtel played a special role. It was in Neuchâtel that the professor of philosophy and mathematics Louis Bourguet founded the *Mercure suisse*, the first transregional literary periodical in Switzerland, in 1732. Thanks to its immediate success, the journal soon split into a political periodical, later called *Nouvelliste suisse*, and a literary journal, the *Journal helvétique*.[27] For young Emer de Vattel, who was a student of Bourguet, this journal offered the perfect opportunity to enter the public stage of the *république des lettres*.

In April 1737, a letter by 'Aaron Monceca' to 'Jacob Brito' appeared in the *Mercure suisse* – probably the first publication written by Vattel. Using the fictional figure of a Jewish traveller residing in Paris, the anonymous author presented a positive view of Switzerland and the Reformation, countering some (supposed) insults against the Swiss by 'Jacob Brito' that had been published in the *Lettres juives* by the Marquis d'Argens.[28] By publishing this

[25] A. Holenstein, C. Jaquier, T. Léchot and D. Schläppi (eds.), *Politische, gelehrte und imaginierte Schweiz. Kohäsion und Disparität im Corpus helveticum des 18. Jahrhundert* (Geneva, 2019).

[26] See B. Kapossy, *Iselin contra Rousseau. Sociable Patriotism and the History of Mankind* (Basel, 2006)

[27] S. Huguenin and T. Léchot (eds.), *Lectures du Journal helvétique, 1732–1782* (Geneva, 2016).

[28] Béguelin, 'En souvenir de Vattel', 81–83.

text, Vattel – who soon unveiled the secret of his name – entered a long-standing debate on the national honour of the Swiss.[29] While Vattel, as a 'good cosmopolitan', later distanced himself from too fervent reactions against d'Argens and other authors (*Poliergie*, 314), he still praised the military virtues of the ancient confederates and contradicted authors who had criticised the venality of the country's mercenaries and politicians in his *Law of Nations* (*LN*, I-XI-124 and IV-VI-79, note against Abram de Wicquefort). Furthermore, the disproportionate frequency of examples taken from Swiss history in the same work seems to have a more substantial reason than the easy and direct access to the relevant books. By repeatedly quoting from late medieval Swiss chronicles and more recent works of Swiss historiography such as Alexander Ludwig von Wattenwyl's *Histoire de la Confédération helvétique* (1754), and by evoking heroic national legends such as Arnold von Winkelried's martyrdom in the battle of Sempach (1386), the author himself performed his 'Swissness' in a work that was intended to serve humanity.

Other poems, literary essays and learned treatises that Vattel published in the *Mercure suisse* and the *Journal helvétique* were less directly concerned with the subject of the Swiss nation. Nevertheless, through his defence of Wolff's rationalism against the religious criticism of the Lausanne academy professors Jacob Bessonet and Jean-Pierre de Crousaz and other interventions, Vattel contributed to the rise of a public sphere of philosophical debates in Switzerland.[30] Local debates also shaped Vattel's choice of topics and arguments. His literary activities for Swiss periodicals facilitated contact with other learned men and women (including the famous Bernese *salonnière* Julie Bondeli), printers and magistrates in the Confederacy, a fact that would prove to be useful during his later diplomatic activities. Even before publishing his *Défense du système leibnitien* and establishing himself in Germany, Vattel had already become a known figure in Swiss literary circles. Later, he would republish most of these earlier texts in his collections *Les loisirs philosophiques* (1747), *Poliergie* (1757) and *Mélanges de littérature* (1760). It is also noteworthy that Vattel's *Law of Nations* (1758) and the *Questions du droit naturel* (1762)

[29] On the concepts of Swiss national honour, see Thomas Lau, *'Stiefbrüder'. Nation und Konfession in der Schweiz und in Europa (1656–1712)* (Cologne, 2008).

[30] Already in 1737, Vattel published an article in the *Mercure Suisse* countering the arguments that 'professor B' (the theologian Bessonet) had formulated against Wolff; see Béguelin, 'En souvenir de Vattel', 83–84, and on the Swiss debates on Wolff's philosophy, S. Zurbuchen, 'Die Schweizerische Debatte über die Leibniz-Wolffsche Philosophie und ihre Bedeutung für Emer von Vattels philosophischen Werdegang', in P. Coleman, A. Hofmann and S. Zurbuchen (eds.), *Reconceptualizing Nature, Science, and Aesthetics. Contribution à une nouvelle approche des Lumières helvétiques* (Geneva, 1998), 91–113.

were first printed in Neuchâtel and Bern. Thus, in the eyes of his contemporaries, Emer de Vattel was and remained a full member of the Swiss *république des lettres*.

VATTEL AND THE SWISS REPUBLICS

In the eighteenth century, being Swiss and writing on political theory usually entailed being a republican in one way or another. The core of the Swiss Confederacy was composed of thirteen independent cantons of different sizes and confessions, though all under non-monarchical rule. For this reason, the members of the ruling elites were usually eager to present the advantages of collective decision-making in a Europe dominated by monarchies, while their opponents pleaded for a broader participation of the people in government.[31] Authors from abroad also participated in this discourse and discussed the advantages and disadvantages of republican rule by analysing the constitutions of the cantons in state descriptions, travel accounts and works of political theory. On the one hand, the Swiss were praised for their frugality and collective liberty, and especially Bern became a sort of model state for a wisely governed and prosperous aristocratic republic.[32] On the other hand, the differences between aristocratic, democratic and mixed republics and the advantages and disadvantages of these forms of government made for controversial discussion by contemporary observers.

These debates on different forms of republican constitutions in Switzerland echoed inner conflicts between governing elites and the broader population in various Swiss cantons. In eighteenth-century Switzerland, democracy was not only a theoretical or historical concept derived from antiquity, but, according to contemporary observers, an asserted political reality in the rural cantons where the *Landsgemeinden* – assemblies of all adult male citizens – elected the magistrates and took important decisions by majority vote. In practice, social elites governed through large networks of patronage, yet they still had to respect the established forms of decision-making and – if they did not – were repeatedly removed from power during popular unrests led by malcontents

[31] T. Maissen, *Die Geburt der Republic. Staatsverständnis und Repräsentation in der frühneuzeitlichen Eidgenossenschaft* (Göttingen, 2006); Holenstein, Maissen and Prak (eds.), *The Republican Alternative*.

[32] B. Kapossy, 'Neo-Roman republicanism and commercial society. The example of eighteenth-century Berne', in M. van Gelderen and Q. Skinner (eds.), *Republicanism. A Shared European Heritage, vol. II: The Values of Republicanism in Early Modern Europe* (Cambridge, 2002), 227–247.

who invoked the principle of popular sovereignty.[33] In the cantons dominated by a city, the rural population remained almost completely excluded from the government (an exception was Zug). However, the question of whether sovereignty lay in the city's commune as a whole, or in the guilds, or only in councils that were renewed by co-optation, resulted in feelings running high and provoked repeated unrest and debate that found their way into printed European media.[34]

Emer de Vattel was fully aware of these tensions within the Swiss republics. Basel, where he began his studies in theology and philosophy in 1728, had been a scene of popular unrests some decades before, and Geneva, where he continued his studies between 1733 and 1736, remained a hotspot of inner conflicts and republican theorizing throughout the eighteenth century.[35] It was in Geneva where Vattel supposedly listened to the lectures of Jean-Jacques Burlamaqui who was involved in the *troubles* of the 1730s. Burlamaqui argued for a mixed form of government, that is, an elective aristocracy moderated by democracy, where the sovereign power is divided between the assembled people and the councils.[36] Shortly after Vattel had assumed his role as a diplomatic representative of the elector of Saxony in Bern (even though he stayed in Neuchâtel most of the time), the capital of the largest and most powerful city state in Switzerland also became the scene of unrests. On 3 July 1749, about seventy citizens planning to overturn the Bernese government were arrested. Only two weeks later, three leaders of the 'complot' were executed – an event that was debated in newspapers all over Europe.[37] Vattel, who may have known one of these leaders personally, was far from

[33] F. Brändle, *Demokratie und Charisma. Fünf Landsgemeindekonflikte im 18. Jahrhundert* (Zürich, 2005). A similar case was Grisons, an allied territory of the Swiss: R. C. Head, *Early Modern Democracy in Grisons. Social Order and Political Language in a Swiss Mountain Canton, 1470–1620* (Cambridge, 1995).

[34] A. Würgler, *Unruhen und Öffentlichkeit. Städtische und ländliche Protestbewegungen im 18. Jahrhundert* (Tübingen, 1995); N. Weber, 'Eine vollkommene Aristokratie? Debatten um die Regierungsform der Republik Bern im 18. Jahrhundert', *Berner Zeitschrift für Geschichte* 75 (2013), 3–38.

[35] H. Rosenblatt, *Rousseau and Geneva. From the First Discourse to the Social Contract, 1749–1762* (Cambridge, 1997); R. Whatmore, *Against War and Empire. Geneva, Britain, and France in the Eighteenth Century* (New Haven, 2012).

[36] On Burlamaqui, Barbeyrac and the 'École romande du droit des gens', see the contributions in S. Zurbuchen (ed.), *The Law of Nations and Natural Law 1625–1800* (Leiden, 2019), 229–326. On Bourlamarqui's theory of a mixed government, see also A. Riklin, *Machtteilung. Geschichte der Mischverfarrung* (Darmstadt, 2006), 257–267.

[37] A. Würgler, 'Conspiracy and denunciation: A local affair and its European publics (Bern, 1749)', in J. van Horn Melton (ed.), *Cultures of Communication from Reformation to Enlightenment. Constructing Publics in the Early Modern German Lands* (Aldershot, 2002), 119–131.

sympathetic with the insurgents. In a letter to his close friend Jean Henri Samuel Formey in Berlin, he condemned their 'awful purpose' to murder the top magistrates.[38] Later, while defending the right of a nation to change its sovereign, he distanced himself from all '*rebels* ... who unjustly take up arms against the ruler of the society' (*LN*, III-XVIII-288).

In 1753, Vattel even defended the aristocratic government of Bern in public. In his *Pensées*, the French protestant writer Laurent Angliviel de La Beaumelle had severely attacked Bern's aristocracy as an aberration of the originally democratic republic, denouncing the 'tyranny' of the Bernese bailiffs in the Pays de Vaud.[39] In a letter published in Formey's *Nouvelle bibliothèque germanique*, Vattel countered that Bern had a legal aristocratic system and described the republic as 'the steadiest boulevard of Switzerland'.[40] The intervention testifies to the author's will to find a moderate position in the debate on different forms of government; in his *Law of Nations*, he simply stated that a nation could either be ruled democratically, or aristocratically or monarchically without indicating a preference among them (*LN*, I-I-3). At the same time, his famous expression that 'a dwarf is as much a man as a giant; a small republic is no less a sovereign state than the most powerful kingdom' (*LN*, prelim. 18) was certainly in line with the consistent aim of the Swiss republics to be accepted as full members of the European state system.[41]

The Bernese magistrates were very content with Vattel's public defence of their republic, as he told his friend Formey in a letter.[42] This goodwill surely also facilitated the later reception of Vattel's work. While his Genevan counterpart Jean-Jacques Rousseau became a persona non grata in Switzerland because he had associated Bern with a 'hereditary aristocracy' that he considered to be the 'worst of all governments' in his Social Contract and propagated ideas that were generally seen as too democratic (even though he favoured the idea of an 'elective aristocracy'),[43] Vattel's works remained

38 E. Vattel to J. H. S. Formey, Neuchâtel, 10 October 1749, *Correspondances*, 106–107.

39 L. A. La Baumelle, *Mes pensées* (Copenhagen, 1751), ch. CCIV, 351–354. On the affair, see also A. Bandelier, *Des Suisses dans la République des lettres. Un réseau savant au temps de Frédéric le Grand* (Geneva, 2007), 148–156.

40 Anonymous [E. de Vattel], 'Seconde Lettre à l'Auteur du Journal', *Nouvelle bibliothèque germanique* 12 (1753), 99–102.

41 T. Maissen, 'Inventing the sovereign republic. Imperial structures, French challenges, Dutch models, and the early modern Swiss confederation', in Holenstein, Maissen and Prak (eds.), *The Republican Alternative*, 125–150.

42 E. de Vattel to J. H. S. Formey, Neuchâtel, 24 January 1753, *Correspondances*, 138.

43 Cf. J.-J. Rousseau, 'Of the social contract' (1762), in *The Social Contract and Other Later Political Writings*, 2nd ed., translated by and ed. V. Gourevitch (Cambridge, 2018), 39–155, 95 (ch. III–V). On Rousseau's reception in the Swiss context, see S. Zurbuchen, 'Reacting to

acceptable in the aristocratic city states. For instance, as a student, the Bernese patrician and future councillor Johann Anton von Tillier copied whole chapters of Vattel's *Law of Nations*.[44] This becomes even more notable when considering that Vattel was convinced that his political theory was based on the same ideas as Rousseau's – that is, most probably, the principle of popular sovereignty. In a letter to his friend Abram de Pury in Neuchâtel, who personally knew Rousseau, he even suspected the citizen of Geneva to be guilty of a sort of plagiarism or at least concealment: 'At the end of his Emile, he [Rousseau] harshly criticizes all those who have written about public law; he says that he will be the first who gives its true principles, and these principles are the same that I have already established in my work.[45]

However, Vattel's relation to the Swiss republics and especially to the Republic of Bern was not without tensions. When the armies of Brandenburg–Prussia attacked Saxony in autumn 1756, Vattel soon realized that this would leave him in a problematic position. As a theorist, he defended the rather contradictory Swiss practice to remain neutral and supply war powers with large numbers of mercenaries (*LN*, III-VII-110).[46] As a Saxon diplomat, he was nevertheless obliged to protest sharply against the Prussian aggression and, more implicitly, the participation of Bernese regiments in Frederick's II service.[47] His personal situation became considerably more uncomfortable in Neuchâtel, where he still lived. Being in the service of the sovereign's enemy, he could not visit the Prussian governor anymore and thus came into conflict with loyal magistrates. While his different roles as the Prussian king's subject, the Saxon elector's envoy and a Swiss intellectual clashed, Vattel wished for a less ambiguous national identity: 'How happy is

Rousseau. Difficult relations between erudition and politics in the Swiss republics', in A. Holenstein, H. Steinke and M. Stuber (eds.), *Scholars in Action. The Practice of Knowledge and the Figure of the Savant in the 18th Century* (Leiden, 2013), 481–501.

44 A. Trampus, '"Good government" and the tradition of small states. The eighteenth- and nineteenth-century reception of the Droit des gens', in K. Stapelbroek and A. Trampus (eds.), *The Legacy of Vattel's Droit des gens* (Cham, 2019), 167–188, at 178–83. On Vattel's relationship with the Bernese learned reformers, see also the contribution by Radoslaw Szymanski in the same volume.

45 'À la fin de son Emile, il maltraitte le fort tous ceux qui ont écrit sur le Droit Public, il dit qu'il va le premier en donner les vrais Principes; & ces Principes sont les mêmes que j'ai établis dans mon Ouvrage'. Vattel to Abram de Pury, Warsaw, 24 November 1762, Archives de l'État de Neuchâtel, Archives de Pury, VI (6a). The hitherto unknown letters will soon be edited by the author.

46 On the neutrality debate in late eighteenth- and early nineteenth-century Switzerland, see P. Lehmann, *Die Umdeutung der Neutralität. Eine politische Ideengeschichte der Eidgenossenschaft vor und nach 1815* (Basel, 2020).

47 E. de Vattel to the Avoyer and Council of Bern, 28 February 1757, *Correspondances*, 181–184.

our Switzerland! And how happy I would be, if I was attached to Switzerland alone!'[48]

VATTEL, A POLITICAL FIREBRAND?

Vattel was not the only one in Neuchâtel to come into conflict with the Prussian ruler and his representatives after the outbreak of the seven years' war. As we have seen, mercenary services for the king of France had a long-standing tradition in the principality and were also guaranteed under Prussian rule. However, did this also imply that the Neuchâtelois could fight their own ruler on foreign battlefields? For this is exactly what happened in the famous battle of Rossbach on 5 November 1757. Several hundred Neuchâtelois participated as combatants of the Swiss regiments of France, among which also figured Vattel's brother, Jean Frédéric, who later even received an *ordre du mérite militaire* for his services. Surprised that several officers among the prisoners of war came from his own principality, king Frederick II of Prussia instructed his governor in Neuchâtel, George Keith, to remind his subjects of their duties towards their sovereign. While some citizenries re-affirmed their loyalty and even promised to exclude all mercenaries for France from their municipal corporations, the citizenry of the city of Neuchâtel defended the privilege to serve foreign powers and openly protested against this attack against their liberty.[49]

In this context, a remarkable 'statement establishing the rights of the subjects of the principality of Neuchâtel and Valangin regarding the service for foreign powers was discussed in Neuchâtel's city council.[50] The manuscript, of which copies were also sent to the French embassy in Solothurn and the Republic of Bern, argues that every nation should have its proper sovereign. When a prince like the king of Prussia possesses different territories, each should be treated as if it had a different ruler. Furthermore, according to the statement, the Neuchâtelois were not only subjects of the king of Prussia. They were also members of the Swiss nation. Because the alliance of the Swiss with France (dating back to 1516–1521) was much older than the obligations towards the present sovereign (dating back to 1707), the first obligations

48 E. Vattel to J. H. S. Formey, 17 February 1757, *Correspondances*, 180. ('Que notre Suisse est heureuse! Et que je serois heureux moi-même, si je ne tenois qu'à la Suisse!')

49 A. Schnegg, 'De la guerre à la paix 1756–1763', *Musée neuchâtelois* 17 (1980), 5–34.

50 Archives de la ville de Neuchâtel, Neuchâtel, P 105.02, [Frédéric Samuel Ostervald], *Mémoire où l'on établie le droit des sujets de la principauté de Neuchâtel & de Valengin relativement au service des puissances étrangères* [manuscript, May 1758]. For more details, see Weber, *Lokale Interessen*, 453–455.

preceded the others. Evoking the already-mentioned *articles généraux* (art. 3) which granted free mercenary services to the Neuchâtelois, the statement concluded: 'The Neuchâtelois are thus a free people in the matter under discussion, and having been acknowledged as Swiss, they had the right to take sides in the service of France during the present war as did their compatriots'.[51]

It is not by chance that the arguments of this manuscript perfectly dovetail with the statements in Vattel's *Law of Nations* that had been printed in Neuchâtel only some months before (cf. *LN*, I-I-9; II-XVII-309). The mayor Frédéric Samuel Ostervald, the leader of the rebellious citizens to whom the statement has been attributed, was a close friend of Vattel. It even seems very probable that Vattel himself composed the central points of the manuscript. In a letter, Vattel told the Saxon prime minister von Brühl that 'I did not shy away from illuminating and encouraging our magistrates on this issue, acting not only as a servant of the king [i.e. Augustus III of Poland] who is allied to France, but also as a good patriot'.[52] At the same time, the Prussian representatives in Neuchâtel, to whom these activities were known, discussed how they could get rid of Vattel. In a letter to the Prussian court, governor Keith described Vattel (whom he knew personally) as a 'dangerous quarreller' and 'the firebrand behind all the troubles we have had here as of late'.[53] In the meantime, Vattel continued his subversive activities, probably claiming that he was not only protected by the local privileges of the citizens of Neuchâtel but also by the law of nations that – according to himself – granted immunity to foreign ministers even when they were subjects of the state where they were employed (*LN*, VI-VIII-112). Two weeks later, Keith commented indignantly on Vattel: 'He believes that with the title of a minister of the king of Poland everything is permitted to him'.[54] Shortly afterwards, the Prussian court addressed two letters to the local authorities in Neuchâtel to obtain Vattel's banishment from the principality, but without success.

[51] *Mémoire*, p. 4. ('Les Neuchatelois etant donc un Peuple libre dans l'objet dont il s'agit et reconnûs comme Suisses, ils ont été en droit de prendre parti au service de France pendant la presente guerre à l'imitation de leurs compatriotes'.)

[52] E. de Vattel to Count Heinrich von Brühl, Neuchâtel, 24 July 1758, Sächsisches Hauptstaatsarchiv Dresden, 10026 Geheimes Cabinett, Loc. 2778/7, fol. 182v ('je me suis pas épargné à éclaircir & encourager là-dessus nos Magistrats, agissant en cela, non seulement comme serviteur du Roi, Allié de la France, mais encore comme bon Patriote.'). I am indebted to Béla Kapossy for providing a copy of this letter.

[53] G. Keith to king Frederick II of Prussia, Neuchâtel, 1 July 1758, Geheimes Staatsarchiv Preussischer Kulturbesitz Berlin-Dahlem, I. HA, Rep. 64/IV/II/I, Convol. 1758–1762, fol. 425 ('c'est un brouillon dangereux'; 'le boutefeu de toutes les brouilleries depuis peu ici').

[54] G. Keith to king Frederick II of Prussia, Neuchâtel, 13 July 1758, ibid., fol. 435 ('Il croit que sous le titre de Ministre du Roy de Pologne tout lui est permis.')

In the following years, the Prussian king's authority in Neuchâtel decreased more and more. In a time when even the capital Berlin was occupied by foreign powers, it was impossible for King Frederick II to reply to the distant subjects' demands with any force. The inhabitants of Neuchâtel continued to serve the armies of the king of France, and in 1760, the rebellious subjects established a sort of counter-institution to the sovereign's council: the assembly of the *corps et communautés de l'État* (bodies and communities of the state) that claimed to represent the principality's will as an 'assembly of the nation'.[55] At the end of the Seven Years' War, the balance of powers between ruler and subjects turned in favour of the ruler. Yet three years later, in 1766, Prussian attempts to extract more resources from the principality by reforming the tax regime again provoked popular resistance. The great 'troubles of Neuchâtel', discussed in printed media all over Europe, soon became an issue in the cabinets of Potsdam and Versailles and in the Swiss councils. While some Neuchâtelois hoped for French protection in order to get rid of their sovereign and turn into a republic, the crisis was finally resolved by a military intervention of the four allied Swiss cantons. It was only a mixture of Prussian pragmatism, local disagreements and Swiss disinterest in having a new canton with equal rights and privileges that secured Neuchâtel's ambiguous status for another three decades.

During these troubles, Emer de Vattel himself did not act openly in favour of the opposition. Having become a European celebrity after the publication of the *Law of Nations*, he had left his country of birth to join the Saxon court in 1760. He only returned to Switzerland for some weeks in 1766, and once again in autumn 1767 – but for reasons of health rather than for political support. Having hoped to regain forces by breathing the 'salubrious air of Switzerland', Vattel eventually died in Neuchâtel on 28 December 1767.[56] During his absence, however, Vattel had stayed in contact with leading figures of the opposition such as Abram de Pury who later pleaded for a transformation of the principality into a sovereign Swiss republic.[57] The popular resistance in Neuchâtel also seems to have been inspired by the reading of the *Law of Nations*. As we have seen, Vattel condemns unlawful rebellions, yet simultaneously he acknowledges the right of a nation to resist their sovereign or even change the government, as long as the resistance is led by a representative institution of the nation (*LN*, I-III-32). By revitalizing the *corps*

[55] See Weber, *Lokale Interessen*, 487–489; Stirbrny, *Die Könige von Preußen*, 149–152.

[56] E. de Vattel to J. H. S. Formey, Dresden, 14 July 1767, *Correspondances*, 223.

[57] J. Jeanjaquet, 'Un projet d'émancipation de Neuchâtel en 1768', *Musée neuchâtelois* (1902), 202–210.

et communautes de l'État and redefining this corporative institution as an 'assembly of the nation', the local opponents of Frederick the Great based their resistance on the same principles their compatriot had defined in his major work published in the same place some months before. Vattel's ambiguous if not positive attitude towards foreign protection and intervention may have served as an additional argument for the opposition to negotiate secretly with the French crown and the Swiss cantons during the troubles.[58]

The reception of Vattel's work in Switzerland and beyond is not the primary concern of this chapter. Nevertheless, it is noteworthy that, despite enthusiastic reactions by contemporary Swiss authors such as Isaak Iselin who praised the *Law of Nations* as a moment of glory in the history of mankind,[59] Vattel was also harshly criticized by some learned compatriots. Thirty years after its publication, the Neuchâtelois patrician and Prussian diplomat in Turin Jean-Pierre de Chambrier d'Oleyres attacked Vattel for precisely those passages of the *Law of Nations* that could be read as a legitimization of the Neuchâtelois opposition against their distant Prussian sovereign – and, more globally, of rebellions against 'foreign rule' in general. In two statements presented to the Berlin Academy of Sciences in 1789 and 1790 – at a time when the Revolution in France was already under way – Chambrier d'Oleyres criticized Vattel's positions concerning the right of subjects to revolt, the service of mercenaries for foreign powers and the status of local municipal corporations in international affairs as well as his view of Swiss neutrality. Printed in Berlin in 1793 and again in Italy in 1795, the *Essai sur le droit des gens* by Chambrier d'Oleyres testifies that Vattel could still be seen as a dangerous political 'firebrand' years after his death.[60]

CONCLUSION

In the middle of the eighteenth century, there was no international state system in the strict sense of the word. Large composite monarchies such as

[58] See Weber, *Lokale Interessen*, 501–533, and on Vattel's attitude towards intervention: L. Cello, 'The legitimacy of international interventions in Vattel's *The Law of Nations*', *Global Intellectual History* 2 (2017), 105–123.

[59] See I. Iselin, *Geschichte der Menschheit* (1764), ed. S. Henny (Basel, 2018), 336.

[60] J.-P. de Chambrier d'Oleyres, *Essai sur le droit des gens* (Parma, 1795). On Chambrier d'Oleyres' critique and its late eighteenth-century contexts, see also Isaac Nakhimovsky, 'Carl Schmitt's Vattel and the "Law of Nations" between enlightenment and revolution', *Grotiana* 31 (2010) (Special Issue *Rival Histories of Emer de Vattel's 'Law of Nations'*, ed. by Béla Kapossy), 141–164, and A. Trampus, *Emer de Vattel and the Politics of Good Government. Constitutionalism, Small States and the International System* (Cham, 2020).

the state conglomerate of the kings of Prussia, mid-sized heterogeneous confederacies such as the Helvetic body and petty yet quasi-autonomous territories such as the principality of Neuchâtel all remained players on Europe's political scene. Only around 1800, between the outbreak of the French Revolution and the new order settled at the Congress of Vienna, the *Theatrum Europaeum* became something similar to a system of nation states.[61] By imposing the principle of national sovereignty instead of the patrimonialism of the hereditary monarchies or the corporatism of early modern republics as a basis of power relations (without however giving up the idea of a 'society of the human race'), Emer de Vattel's *Law of Nations* largely shaped the discursive transition that would merge into the paradigm of classical international law in the nineteenth and early twentieth centuries.[62] At the same time, Vattel's work remains deeply embedded in the practices of foreign relations of his time, arguing casuistically rather than from a systematic perspective of public natural law in many details. In this view, it was legal for a municipal city to receive foreign ministers in order to negotiate treatises (*LN*, IV-v-60) or for subjects to enter mercenary services to fight against their own sovereign when this was granted in ancient privileges. Thus, Vattel's work is Janus-faced, mirroring established practices of foreign relations in a society of orders and simultaneously pointing to a future order based on sovereign and legally equal nation states.

This chapter has shown that many of the paradoxes in Vattel's work become more comprehensible when we read it within its Neuchâtelois and Swiss context. With his positive attitude towards the republican form of government and his insistence on the equality between dwarf and giant states, he argued in line with his Swiss contemporaries. Discussing a bulk of questions that especially concerned the situation of his home country Neuchâtel, he intervened in local debates concerning the rights of the subjects in relation to their Prussian sovereign. At the same time, the contextual reading reveals that Vattel's idea of distinct national societies was rather a wishful anticipation

[61] See e.g. M. Belissa and G. Ferragu (eds.), *Acteurs diplomatiques et ordre international. Fin XVIIIe siècle–XIXe siècle* (Paris, 2007); Weber, *Lokale Interessen*, 541–588, and the literature discussed above, notes 2 and 3.

[62] For nuanced analyses of the innovative aspects in Vattel's work, see esp. E. Jouannet, *Emer de Vattel et l'émergence doctrinale du droit international classique* (Paris, 1998); Y. Sandoz (ed.), *Réflexions sur l'impact, le rayonnement, et l'actualité de 'Le droit des gens, ou, Principes de la loi naturelle appliqués à la conduite et aux affaires des nations et des souverains' d'Emer de Vattel à l'occasion du 250ème anniversaire de sa parution* (Brussels, 2010); V. Chétail and P. Haggenmacher (eds.), Vattel's International Law in a XXIst Century Perspective (Leiden, 2011); and E. Fiocchi Malaspina, *L'eterno ritorno del Droit des gens di Emer de Vattel (secc. XVIII–XIX). L'impatto sulla cultura giuridica in prospettiva globale* (Frankfurt, 2017).

than a description of what he could observe during his lifetime. Born in a small principality that was neither fully Swiss nor Prussian nor French, Vattel shared his compatriots' experience that you could indeed be a 'friend of all nations' – though you could never be certain to which larger entity your country would belong after the next political crisis. Lost in a network of conflicting interests and exposed to a state system that became more and more dynamic, being 'Swiss and Swiss alone' became an attractive alternative to reduce complexity and uncertainty. While this remained something of a literary dream in the eighteenth century, Neuchâtel would become a full member of the new Swiss Confederation in 1814–1815. However, as is known, the nineteenth-century nation state generated its own problems and aporias.

FURTHER READING

Writings by Vattel

Vattel, E. *Défense du système leibnitien contre les objections et les imputations de Mr de Crousaz* (Leiden, 1741).

Poliegrie, ou mélange de littérature et de poësies (Amsterdam, 1757).

The Law of Nations, ed. B. Kapossy and R. Whatmore (Indianapolis, 2008).

Emer de Vattel à Jean Henri Samuel Formey. Correspondances autour du Droit des gens, ed. André Bandelier (Paris, 2012).

Selected Secondary Literature

Holenstein, A., Maissen, Th. and Prak, M. (eds.) *The Republican Alternative. The Netherlands and Switzerland Compared* (Amsterdam, 2008).

Kapossy, B., *Iselin contra Rousseau. Sociable Patriotism and the History of Mankind* (Basel, 2006).

Kapossy, B. (ed.) 'Rival histories of Emer de Vattel's "Law of Nations"', *Grotiana* 31:1 (2010) (Special Issue).

Toyoda, T. *Theory and Politics of the Law of Nations. Political Bias in International Law Discourse of Seven German Court Councilors in the Seventeenth and Eighteenth Centuries* (Leiden, 2011)

Zurbuchen, S. 'Emer de Vattel on the society of nations and the political system of Europe', in S. Kadelbach, Th. Kleinlein and D. Roth-Isigkeit System (eds.), *Order, and International Law: The Early History of International Legal Thought from Machiavelli to Hegel* (Oxford, 2017), 263–282.

Zurbuchen, S. (ed.) *The Law of Nations and Natural Law 1625–1800* (Leiden, 2019).

2

Sovereignty Contested

Vattel's Use of Leibniz, Hobbes, and Pufendorf

BEN HOLLAND

The modern state is the institution to which human beings have entrusted the coercive power they deem necessary and legitimate to regulate the lives that they lead together in a bounded community. The name for the legitimate coercive power of the modern state is sovereignty. The state is sovereign internally because it possesses the effective *monopoly* on this legitimate coercive power within its own clearly demarcated territory; it gives force to the law that it makes. It is also sovereign internally because it is the only *author* of the laws that have jurisdiction within its territory. The state is sovereign externally because its monopoly of power within its boundaries excludes its domination by or dependence upon any other state. It is also sovereign externally because its sole authority over itself means that it brooks no interference from other states affecting its constitution or government, and nor does it accept the writ of other states. It is, in short, subject to no other power or authority and must chart its own course as a *free actor* on the world stage. Finally, the modern state is externally sovereign because it is the only entity in a position reciprocally to *recognise* others as its sovereign equals. There is no higher authority from which a modern state may draw its claim to assume for itself the powers of the earth.

These are conventional definitions and distinctions. Emer de Vattel's principal contribution to the political theory of the state and its sovereignty, it has been argued, was to focus squarely on the character and implications of the external sovereignty of the state, which too often had only been implicit in theories focussing overwhelmingly on internal sovereignty. Vattel's *Law of Nations* is a book about the diplomatic and commercial consequences, both practically and normatively, of the independence of sovereign states in their dealings with each other. 'The law of nations is the law of sovereigns: free and independent states are moral persons, whose rights and obligations we are to establish in this treatise' (*LN*, I-I-12). Vattel was keen to insist that external sovereignty means that a state must be free from interference by outside powers in its internal affairs. 'No state', he maintains, 'has the smallest right to interfere in the government of another' (*LN*, II-IV-54). Moreover, external sovereignty indicates that no state be dependent on any other to the extent that its liberty is curtailed. 'Every nation', he writes, 'that governs itself, under what form soever, without dependence on any foreign power, is a *sovereign state*' (*LN*, I-I-4). Vattel's is a book written on the basis of a change of perspective: It has less regard than some earlier treaties on sovereignty of its vertical dimensions within the state than of its lateral implications, as a plurality of sovereign states must coexist together in an international system. According to Stéphane Beaulac, Vattel thus did nothing less than 'externalise' the concept of sovereignty, transposing it 'from the internal plane to the international plane'.[1]

Yet these conventional definitions and distinctions begin to chafe when we put them under pressure. With respect to internal sovereignty, the definition in the previous paragraph concerns the state's power and authority over potential objects of control within its borders. Theorists focusing on the internal sovereignty of a state, however, are as likely to want to see it as turning on the relationship between constituent and constituted powers, between the power and authority of the political community and its members and the power and authority of those who must discharge sovereign responsibilities. With respect to external sovereignty, we are bound to say that the state's internal constitution as a juridical object will impact on the kind of freedom that it can exercise and the nature of the relationships that it can establish. The 'absoluteness' of its liberty is not only compromised by the empirical limits to its exterior power but also in virtue of the state's existence as a particular kind of legal and moral entity.

The *Law of Nations* is not merely a book about external sovereignty as independence. Vattel writes about sovereignty in its multifarious manifestations. I have given thought to various ways of providing an account of Vattel on sovereignty in this chapter. I considered writing a conceptual and textual analysis under the fourfold headings of power, authority, liberty and recognition, as per the definitions and distinctions given at the outset; but in view both of their interweaving and what they leave out, I soon put that idea aside. I also contemplated a systematic and philosophical threefold, whether an Aristotelian one on *efficient* (constitutional relations of sovereignty), *formal* (the state's sovereignty over itself) and *final* (international) dimensions of state sovereignty, or an Hegelian one, on the sovereign state *in itself* (on the essence

[1] S. Beaulac, *Power of Language in the Making of International Law: The Word 'Sovereignty' in Bodin and Vattel and the Myth of Westphalia* (Leiden, 2004), 133.

of relations of sovereignty inside the state), *for itself* (the 'comprehension' of those relations when the state is at home with itself) and *in-and-for* itself (when the state finds itself in the other). As tempting as each of these manners of presentation was, they seemed to me to be unhistorical: anachronistic in the first case and proleptic in the second. In the end, I have proceeded analogically, and therefore in accordance with the twofold relationship of source and target domains. This is how Vattel himself proceeded, so it has that to recommend it.

The analogy is between the person and the state. The first great theorist of the modern sovereign state, Thomas Hobbes, in a rare digression on its external dimension, wrote that each state has 'an absolute Libertie, to doe what it shall judge' conduces to its own benefit.[2] And as Isaiah Berlin argued in a celebrated (if gendered) elucidation of liberty, 'conceptions of freedom directly derive from views of what constitutes a self, a person, a man'.[3] It is thus no coincidence that Hobbes understood the modern state as analogous to the person, in a move which Vattel recognises as decisive in establishing the modern field of international law, and which he will continue (*LN*, preface). In this chapter, I draw out some implications of Vattel's description of sovereign states as *moral persons*.

In the first section, I trace the outlines of the state-personality tradition from Hobbes through Samuel Pufendorf, with whom the moral person locution originates, to Vattel. In the second, I argue that we can learn more about the kind of freedom that Vattel considers to be characteristic of states as moral persons from the writings of one of his chief influences, namely G. W. Leibniz. Leibniz had an entirely different account of what it means to be a free agent than, for instance, Hobbes and Pufendorf. Real freedom, according to Leibniz, requires the achievement of self-consciousness in thinking and enabling the mind's ability to attend to the world – both of which capacities are heightened through the publicity of ourselves to others and acting together with them. In the third section, I show how these contexts bear on Vattel's sense that the internal and external sovereignty of states are amplified by their association with one another in accordance with rules that they have mutually established. This chapter therefore seeks to provide an account of what is perhaps the master concept in Vattel's political lexicon, but it does so in terms of his navigation between some rival traditions of conceiving of free human agency and community.

[2] T. Hobbes, *Leviathan*, vol. 2: *The English and Latin Texts (i)*, ed. N. Malcolm (Oxford, 2012), chap. 21, 332.

[3] I. Berlin, 'Two concepts of liberty', in *Liberty* (Oxford, 2002), 181.

THE SOVEREIGN STATE AS MORAL PERSON

It is to Hobbes that we owe the modern concept of the sovereign state. His framework was a theatrical one. The word 'person', he wrote in chapter 16 of *Leviathan* (1651), was originally a dramaturgical term, naming the mask donned by an *actor*, the purpose of which was to help him to project his voice (hence the etymology: *per* and *sona*, 'through' and 'sound') but also to make clear to the *audience* an important intention of the *author* of the play, namely to signify the *character* that the actor had assumed. Soon enough, Hobbes argued, the concept of person had been stretched to refer to anyone who represented another, including some inanimate thing, not only onstage but even in a court of law, by speaking for them. As he only got around to clarifying in chapter 42, it was further extended to apply to the representee, by being spoken for. Developing the political implications of his account of personhood in chapter 17, Hobbes argued that when the 'multitude' – his name for the agglomerate of individuals and family heads living together on some territory but without a common power to keep them from harming each other – speaks together, with one voice, to confer their own capacities and claims of self-defence on some nominated individual or group, then we can point to the new presence of three kinds of person. First, each person of the multitude has authorised the power of that individual or group on whom they have bestowed their powers and rights of self-preservation, so that each person of the multitude is individually an *author* of something. Second, the individual or group which has been so authorised to act for the collective protection of the covenanters has taken up a role and thus become an *actor*: the sovereign. The name of the third person, that of the *character* played, is, said Hobbes, the state. The appellation that is given to the *performance* is sovereignty. Each particular author of the state, then, has given up his powers of self-defence, including his right to judge what is a threat to him, to the person of the state. Yet the state only ever speaks directly once, when all together unanimously and univocally say 'Him!' or 'Them!'; thereafter, the state only speaks and acts through its representative, because that is the deal to which the covenanters have explicitly signed up. Everything that the authorised individual or group says and does thereafter counts as authorised by each individual and, more to the point, as the words and deeds of the state itself, for the sovereign is but an actor, playing the part of the state, however terrifying and world-changing that performance may be.[4]

[4] The best systematic account of Hobbes' person-theory of the state is now S. Fleming, 'The two faces of personhood: Hobbes, corporate agency and the personality of the state', *European Journal of Political Theory* 20.1 (2021), 5–26.

Hobbes' state is the abstract or fictional person in whose name sovereignty is exercised by its authorised representative. This is a conception of the state and sovereignty taken up almost entirely by Vattel. Hobbes had now done most of the hard work of thinking about the internal sovereignty of the state, for his concerns were principally about civil war, and he arrived at his person-theory precisely because he regarded the hegemonic metaphor of political society as a 'body politic' as further contributing to political strife by inviting the question as to whether its life source – its sovereignty – lay with the (monarchical) head or the body (of the people).[5] It is necessary, though, to acknowledge a further influence on Vattel's picture of the state: Pufendorf's theory of the state as a moral person. In *The Law of Nature and Nations* (1672), Pufendorf maintained that Hobbes' elaborate theatrical metaphor devalued human personhood, which was, according to Pufendorf, properly about rational freedom. Rational freedom entailed that action was the consequence of the mental faculties of the understanding and the will, each making its proper contribution to that deed. In the case of the understanding this was to uphold the action's rationality, and in the case of the will, this meant safeguarding the freedom of the choice of that act.[6] Human exploits, after all, leave behind them 'moral effects', and any conceptualisation of personhood as fundamentally involving a guessing game about the attribution of words and deeds, as turning on the relationships between authors, actors and characters, left little distinction in place between ethics and aesthetics, valuing human endeavours 'only according to the Dexterity and Artifice of the Performance'.[7] Like Hobbes, however, Pufendorf went on to declare that the state was also a person, but because the state was constituted in such a way that it emulated the human person who governed himself (*sic*) according to the twofold work of understanding and will. In a decently constituted state, Pufendorf held, these capacities would be represented by a council of advisors and a sovereign prince, respectively. Pufendorf sought to guard against a malevolent or capricious sovereign will by arguing that the exercise of will in the human person was circumscribed by certain conditions, such as the cognisance of there being some reason to act at all, which were the province of the understanding, and that the same conditions applied for the application of sovereign will in

5 Q. Skinner, 'Hobbes and the concept of the state', in *From Humanism to Hobbes: Studies in Rhetoric and Politics* (Cambridge, 2018).

6 I have written about Pufendorf's faculty psychology at greater length in B. Holland, *The Moral Person of the State: Pufendorf, Sovereignty and Composite Polities* (Cambridge, 2017), esp. 78–80.

7 S. Pufendorf, *The Law of Nature and Nations*, ed. J. Barbeyrac and B. Kennet, 5th ed. (London, 1749), I.I.15.

the state. A king simply could not will something if his counsellors did not deem it reasonable.[8]

Vattel's understanding of the state and its sovereignty sits very clearly in the person-theory tradition coming down from Hobbes through Pufendorf. His definition of the state is as follows:

> A political society is a moral person inasmuch as it has an understanding and a will of which it makes use for the conduct of its affairs, and is capable of obligations and rights. When therefore a people confer the sovereignty on any one person, they invest him with their understanding and will, and make over to him their obligations and rights, so far as relates to the administration of the state, and to the exercise of the public authority. (*LN*, I-iv-40)

We can take note of Vattel's adoption of Pufendorf's terminology in relation to the state, namely its categorisation as a moral person. Vattel, moreover, seems to have a conception of a people as pre-existing their incorporation into the state, and this is powerfully *not* Hobbesian, for Hobbes repudiated entirely the notion that individuals and families living together before the state had any kind of corporate identity, or that sovereignty was something that could antedate the state. Pufendorf, on the other hand, had been prepared to grant that individuals and families might inhabit a 'society' before they were united as one under the abstraction of the state.[9] And yet then Vattel makes a move which looks much more absolutist than anything advanced by Pufendorf, which is to argue that the granting of sovereignty to a single person involves the renunciation of 'understanding *and* will'.

Pufendorf defined the state as 'a Compound Moral Person, whose Will, united and tied together by those Covenants, is deemed the Will of all'.[10] He scrupulously left the capacities of understanding belonging to the contractors out of this process involving the forfeiture of faculties. His state has an understanding of its own, represented by a council, but the understandings of the parties to the social contract are not relinquished to that individual whom Vattel calls the 'conductor of the state', the sovereign. For Vattel, however, state-making involves simultaneously the bestowal upon the

8 Holland, *Moral Person*, 80–93. See also Ian Hunter, 'The invention of human nature: The intention and reception of Pufendorf's *entia moralia* doctrine', *History of European Ideas* 45 (2019), 933–952.

9 T. J. Hochstrasser, *Natural Law Theories in the Early Enlightenment* (Cambridge, 2000), 87–92; I. Hont, 'The language of sociability and commerce: Samuel Pufendorf and the theoretical foundations of the "four-stages" theory', in *Jealousy of Trade: International Competition and the Nation-State in Historical Perspective* (Cambridge, MA, 2005).

10 Pufendorf, *Law of Nature*, VII.ii.13.

sovereign not only of our executive capacities of choosing and deciding but also of our cognitive capacities of judging and reasoning. Vattel's sovereign does not simply play the part of the state on the world stage, as its representative; he, the 'depositary of empire', absorbs it almost without residuum (*LN*, I-IV-42). The 'moral person resides in those who are invested with the public authority', Vattel argues later (*LN*, I-XI-117). One might be forgiven for thinking that Pufendorf's constitutionalist controls on sovereign will have vanished in Vattel's moral person of the state.[11]

REASON, WILL AND FREEDOM IN THE LEIBNIZIAN TRADITION

Understanding and will are evidently critical to Vattel's theory of the state and its sovereignty. His moral person of the state comes into being as a sovereign entity precisely when individual faculties of understanding and will are alienated by its prospective subjects to a single 'director' (*LN*, I-XXI-259). The terminology is principally from Pufendorf but, in a twist, Vattel's theory appears to take a much more absolutist turn.

However, all is not as it may seem. This is because Vattel's thinking about the state and its sovereignty was at least as significantly influenced by Leibniz as by Pufendorf.[12] Vattel's first publication was in fact a *Defence of the Leibnizian System* (1741), for 'everyone now talks about the Leibnizian philosophy, and yet few people have a proper idea of it' (*DSL*, Pref. [unnumbered]). Most of the book consists of long quotations from Leibniz's *Theodicy* (1710), in which that universal genius had argued that our world is the best possible world – and in fact Vattel's argument is even more optimistic than Leibniz's, such as Vattel's insistence that 'ALL IS GOOD in relation to God' (*DSL*, 49). (Leibniz himself had concluded that the bad that necessarily existed in the best possible world would still be bad in God's eyes.) Vattel, though, endorsed comprehensively Leibniz's account of freedom and the relationship of understanding and will in securing it (*DSL*, 248–250). Leibniz's thought is complex and architectonic, and a compressed account of any aspect of it will inevitably be crude and incomplete. Simply put, though, Leibniz posited an argument about freedom which arrogated the will as a power to choose between reasons for acting to the faculty of understanding,

[11] See also Chapter 8 by Antonio Trampus.

[12] By and large, Vattel sided with Leibniz over Pufendorf wherever the two disagreed, such as on the proper definition of law. See *FNL*, 766. I do not deal with the (admittedly even greater) impact on Vattel's thought of Christian Wolff, who inspired many of Vattel's ideas in his own right as well as indirectly mediating many of Leibniz's concepts and theories, in this chapter. For Wolff's influence on Vattel, see Chapter 3 by Ere Nokkala.

reconceiving will as a zeal or resolution on the part of the agent to be increasingly self-conscious in the process of action. As I shall try to spell out towards the end of this chapter, I think that grasping Vattel's Leibnizian ontology takes us a long way towards apprehending why his theory of internal sovereignty is not as absolutist as initially supposed; that is to say, it is not prepared to give up constitutional protections of citizens for the sake of a strong sovereign will. It also undergirds Vattel's emphasis on the external dimension of sovereign agents interacting with each other.[13]

Leibniz argued against a tradition – one of the adherents of which was Pufendorf – of conceiving of freedom as 'indifference' to causes, secured by a free will which can act or not act in the presence of all antecedent conditions.[14] The three ingredients of his alternative conception of freedom were 'intelligence, which involves a clear knowledge of the object of deliberation'; 'spontaneity, whereby we determine' ourselves; and 'contingency, that is, in the exclusion of logical or metaphysical necessity'.[15] The third of these components is easiest to deal with quickly. The exclusion of metaphysical necessity means that God chose freely from all the possible worlds the world in which this particular action took place and that His choosing was not caused by something outside of Himself, which of course it never is. The exclusion of logical necessity entails a distinction, within the possible world that God has chosen to actualise, between the essences of things that even God cannot alter (that a circle is round, for example) and the essences of things which could very well have been otherwise (God could have created a world in which Julius Caesar did not cross the Rubicon, Leibniz held, because the opposite of 'Caesar crossed the Rubicon' involves no contradiction).[16]

Leibniz's condition of spontaneity is even more contentious as an aspect of freedom. He meant by it that every free substance is the causal source of all of its own non-initial states. This ends up being a trivial condition of freedom, because every single human action is spontaneous according to Leibniz. 'Our spontaneity', he wrote, 'admits of no exception at all, and external things have

[13] L. Glanville, 'Responsibility to perfect: Vattel's conception of duties beyond borders', *International Studies Quarterly* 61 (2017), 385–395, covers some other Leibnizian influences on Vattel's international theory.

[14] See Holland, *Moral Person*, 32–37; and B. Holland, *Self and City in the Thought of Saint Augustine* (New York, 2019), 52–57.

[15] G. W. Leibniz, *Theodicy: Essays on the Goodness of God, the Freedom of Man and the Origin of Evil*, ed. A. Farrer and E. M. Huggard (London, 1952), 303.

[16] Leibniz, *Theodicy*, 242, on the essence of circles; G. W. Leibniz, 'Discourse on metaphysics', in R. S. Woolhouse and R. Francks (eds.), *Philosophical Texts* (Oxford, 1998), 65, on Caesar crossing the Rubicon.

no physical influence on us at all'.[17] To know the full concept of 'Julius Caesar' is not only to know that the predicate 'crossed the Rubicon' is included in that concept, but it is also to know, in virtue of the fact that all attributes are relational and conjunctive, that the Rubicon would cease to be the northern border of Italy seven years after his crossing it, and that all of Italy's borders would be closed on 9 March 2020. 'If we consider carefully the interconnectedness of all things, we can say that in the soul of [Caesar] there are for all time remnants of everything that will happen to him – and even traces of everything that happens in the universe, although it is only God who can recognise them all'.[18] Every living substance is 'a perpetual living mirror of the universe', and

> just as the same town when seen from different sides will seem quite different, and is as it were multiplied *perspectivally*, the same thing happens here: because of the infinite multitude of simple substances it is as if there were as many different universes; but they are all perspectives on the same one, according to the different *point of view* of each.[19]

What this finally comes down to is that each substance, as a microcosm of all Creation, is the cause of its own successive states, which are representations of the complete physical universe. 'For it is plain that every simple substance embraces the whole universe in its confused perceptions or sensations, and that the succession of these perceptions is regulated by the particular nature of this substance, but in a manner which always expresses all the nature in the universe'.[20] If a man sneaks up behind a dog while it is eating from its bowl and whacks it with a stick, still the 'principle of change' from pleasure to pain 'is in the dog', for the dog 'acts upon itself, in so far as it is disposed and influenced by this representation' of the universe which includes the blow, and produces its own subsequent state, advancing it to the next representation of the entire universe.[21] In this respect are its actions spontaneous.

Intelligence, then, must be the most decisive capacity in securing human freedom, and indeed Leibniz described it as 'the soul of freedom'.[22] Such intelligence, however, does not assure for the agent the kind of indifference to causes that had been the mainstay of older accounts of free will. Every action taken by a human being, he argued, has a cause, and intelligence is purely the

[17] Leibniz, *Theodicy*, 304.
[18] Leibniz, 'Discourse', 60.
[19] G. W. Leibniz, 'Monadology', in *Philosophical Texts*, §§ 56–57, 275.
[20] Leibniz, *Theodicy*, 365.
[21] Ibid., 428.
[22] Ibid., 303.

capacity to be cognisant of such causes so that they become reasons. The agent who acts freely, in Leibniz's eyes, is one who acts self-consciously with respect to her motives. Leibniz simply had no conception of will as a facility of moving oneself to action on the basis of a power to choose freely between different reasons for action. Understanding 'in the mind of a wise being, and motives in any mind whatsoever, do that which answers to the effect produced by weights in a balance', and choice always 'follows the strongest inclination'.[23] The ends of action are first in respect of intention; and 'the representation of the end in the soul is the efficient cause of the representation of the means in the same', so that the cognitive perception of the best means to an end determines the choice itself.[24] Will as a capacity to choose is completely subsumed by understanding, and that is entirely determined, or so it seems, by a causal chain over which the human being has no control.

Leibniz's will, however, has two sides: it is a faculty of choice wholly subservient to understanding, but it is also a conscious force, 'effort or endeavour' on the part of the human being to attend to the world. Leibniz more often called this aspect of the will 'volition'.[25] Although ideas in the mind are formed 'in accordance with our nature and that of things', so as to be beyond our control, the process of thinking is driven in part also by a *desire* over which free agents can exercise some direction.[26] 'This one thing we recognise to be within the power of the will: to command attention and exertion'.[27] What we know and remember can be consequent on how we direct our attention and how hard we try. And volition in the present may positively affect volition in the future:

> Although our choice *ex datis*, with respect to all internal and external circumstances taken together, is always determined, and although, for the present, we cannot alter our will, it is true, nevertheless, that we have great power with respect to our future volitions, by choosing to be attentive to certain objects and by accustoming ourselves to certain ways of thinking. In

[23] G. W. Leibniz, 'Leibniz's fifth paper to Samuel Clarke', in L. E. Loemker (ed.), *Philosophical Papers and Letters*, 2nd ed. (Dordrecht, 1969), 696; G. W. Leibniz, 'Letter to Coste, on human freedom', in R. Ariew and D. Garber (eds.), *Philosophical Essays* (Indianapolis, 1989), 194.

[24] G. W. Leibniz, 'Animadversions concerning certain assertions of the *True Medical Theory*', in F. Duchesneau and J. E. H. Smith (eds.), *The Leibniz-Stahl Controversy* (New Haven, 2016), 23.

[25] G. W. Leibniz, *New Essays on Human Understanding*, ed. P. Remnant and J. Bennett (Cambridge, 1996), 172.

[26] Leibniz, *Theodicy*, 364.

[27] G. W. Leibniz, 'Critical thoughts on the general part of the principles of Descartes', in *Papers and Letters*, 384–385.

this way we accustom ourselves to resist [certain] impressions better and have our reason behave better, so that we can contribute to making ourselves will what we should.[28]

Or as he put it in the *New Essays*, although 'we cannot will what we want to, just as we cannot judge what we want to, we can nevertheless act ahead of time in such a way that we shall eventually judge or will what we would like to be able to judge or will today'.[29] In this way the mind might 'work from afar' to cultivate a growing control over itself.[30]

One of the ways in which a person may 'prepare the mind in advance', according to Leibniz, is 'by training [it] to follow a definite series and method when thinking, so that later the required attitude offers itself spontaneously'.[31] He argued that human beings think for the most part with words. We can use words 'philosophically', as mnemonic devices, to draw inferences, to verify propositions and to heighten the powers of the imagination. There is also, though, the 'civil use of words', when we use them to communicate our thoughts to others and in the 'practice of civil life'.[32] The philosophical use of words can fall victim to error, particularly when 'ideas are very composite', while the civil use of words can lead to incivility because words are often oblique or multifarious, 'as are those of most moral words', which 'have seldom, in the minds of two different men, the same precise signification', and also because the imaginative connotations of words can excite sensibilities that cloud common understanding.[33] Leibniz's solution to these problems, on which he worked for much of his life, was his universal characteristic.[34] This was to be a method for providing rules for the substitution of thoughts by characters and for the combination of characters, so that one could express formally the composition of any concept on the basis of a set of primitive concepts, such 'that there will be no equivocations nor ambiguities, and everything which can be said intelligibly will be said properly'.[35] The universal characteristic would also supply rules for the transition from expression to expression in a 'chain of definitions' and according to a calculus for expressing

28 Leibniz, 'Letter to Coste', 195.
29 Leibniz, *New Essays*, 182.
30 Leibniz, *Theodicy*, 158.
31 Leibniz, 'Critical thoughts', 388.
32 Leibniz, *New Essays*, 334–335.
33 Leibniz, *New Essays*, 335.
34 M. R. Antognazza, *Leibniz: An Intellectual Biography* (Cambridge, 2009), 92–100.
35 G. W. Leibniz, 'Préface à la science générale', in Louis Couturat (ed.), *Opuscules et fragments inédits de Leibniz*, (Paris, 1903), 156–157 ('D'autant qu'il n'y aura point d'equivocations ny amphibolies; et que tout ce qu'on y dira intelligiblement, sera dit à propos'.)

the relations of identity and inclusion between concepts.[36] Thus, 'a certain alphabet of human thoughts can be worked out' and 'through the combination of the letters of this alphabet and through the analysis of words produced from them, all things can be discovered and judged'.[37] According to Leibniz, using the universal characteristic in order to produce metaphysical or moral reasoning would solve the problems associated with the philosophical and civil uses of words, because 'symbolic or blind thinking', when our thoughts are replaced by formal elements, would ensure that sensibilities do not intrude into our thinking, that private mental contents are exceeded by public material marks, and moreover that minds are afforded 'an Ariadne's thread' to lead them, 'without agitation, without litigation, without fear of error'.[38]

Most importantly, though, in respect of our concern with Leibniz's account of freedom, he intended that the universal characteristic would improve people's self-consciousness about their thinking and ease their effort to attend to the world. Since, he maintained, 'the analysis of concepts thus corresponds exactly to the analysis of a character, we need merely to see the characters in order to have adequate notions brought to our mind freely and without effort'.[39] The universal characteristic would grease the wheels of volition and thereby improve the quality of human freedom, as the reasons that determined action would increasingly be rational ones of which individuals would have a gradually clearer awareness. Furthermore, the initial effort involved in concentrating the mind to 'follow a definite method and series in thinking' would give rise to new habits of effortless reasonableness.

Leibniz considered that a free mind was a mind trained to abide by certain public rules. The public dimension is important in other ways.[40] The right reasons for acting, he argued, are likeliest to emerge when they are publicly aired, tested and refined, while the habit of rational action is most likely to be propagated in society. Publicity is important to 'enlighten the understanding', for claims to truth discovered in the application of 'the methods of judging and inventing which is that true logic that is the source of all objects of knowledge' must be subject to rigorous examination and then inventoried.[41]

[36] G. W. Leibniz, 'Letter to Herman Conring', in *Papers and Letters*, 187.

[37] G. W. Leibniz, 'Preface to a universal characteristic', in *Philosophical Essays*, 6–7.

[38] G. W. Leibniz, 'De logica nova condenda', in F. Schupp (ed.), *Die Grundlagen des logischen Kalküls* (Hamburg, 2000), 14 ('sine agitatione mentis, sine litibus, sine formidine errandi, non minus secure procedamus, ac is, qui in labyrintho filum habet Ariadnaeum').

[39] G. W. Leibniz, 'Letter to Walter von Tschirnhaus', in *Papers and Letters*, 193.

[40] See especially M. Losonsky, *Enlightenment and Action from Descartes to Kant* (New York, 2001), 180–184.

[41] G. W. Leibniz, 'Memoir for enlightened persons of good intention', in Patrick Riley (ed.), *Political Writings*, 2nd ed. (Cambridge, 1988), 106.

In addition, people must be fortified 'in the exercise of virtues, that is, in the habit of acting according to reason', and nothing works better to confound the 'want of attention or application' that so often afflicts even those with 'enough mental energy to see what [they] ought to do' than finding others 'with whom one dares to be open' and with whom one can work together for the 'general good'.[42]

> For when each person thinks by himself, it happens that different people do the same thing, which is so much time wasted . . . a thousand things can be done by two or three or by several who understand each other, which will never be done, or never be well done, if they work without communicating.[43]

Freedom, or our sovereignty over our own deeds, is only enhanced, Leibniz maintained, through joint application of our desires and efforts to understand together with others the problems thrown up in the course of lives lived in common places and times, and a shared commitment to work towards practical solutions.

A UNIVERSAL CHARACTERISTIC FOR INTERNATIONAL SOCIETY

Leibniz did not write a great deal about state sovereignty, but, when he did, he was always keen that it should have no absolutist connotations. His account of choice as always following the stipulations of reason he illustrated metaphorically in a manner that we may suppose was as much intended to revise received understandings of sovereignty as an executive capacity defined by will – a will that could not be beholden to reason if it were to count as the will of a sovereign agent – as it was designed to illuminate his argument about human freedom.

> One will have it that the will is alone active and supreme, and one is wont to imagine it to be like a queen seated on her throne, whose minister of state is the understanding, while the passions are her courtiers or favourite ladies, who by their influence often prevail over the counsel of her ministers. One will have it that the understanding speaks only at this queen's order . . . But it is a personification or mythology somewhat ill-conceived. If the will is to judge, or take cognizance of the reasons and inclinations which the understanding or the senses offer it, it will need another understanding in itself.[44]

42 Ibid., 104–105.
43 Ibid., 109.
44 Leibniz, *Theodicy*, 421.

And Leibniz was moreover at pains to insist that federations and alliances involved no abrogation of sovereignty, because in his view they worked to increase a sovereign's control over his decisions by strengthening his comprehension of them and by buttressing his volition.[45]

Reading Vattel's *Law of Nations* in light of its author's avowed adherence to Leibniz's theory of freedom helps us to understand the discussions of the internal and external sovereignty of the state presented in that work. On the former, I earlier characterised Vattel's insistence that soon-to-be subjects renounce their faculties of understanding and will to their imminent sovereign in the social compact as having the appearance of a considerably more absolutist model of sovereignty than in Pufendorf, with whom the notion of the state as a moral person originated. We are now in a position to reconsider that preliminary depiction. For if will, as a power of choice, is always determined by causes, and if such causes attain the status of reasons at the point at which they are cognised by intelligence, then it simply makes no sense, even on the basis of a 'facultative' conception of state personality, to say that sovereign willpower can be compartmentalised and segregated from the state's understanding. Will, thus conceived, is part and parcel of understanding. Vattel writes of the '*sufficient reason* for an act of the will' and uses that locution 'to express whatever has produced that act – whatever has determined the will on a particular occasion; whether the will has been determined by a single reason, or by many concurrent reasons' (*LN*, II-xvii-289). Will is simply never indifferent to its causes; and if an agent be self-conscious of her own causes through reason's reflection on itself as a cause, then her freedom has been secured. To hold back reason at the conception of the state would be to make any kind of sovereign willing impossible.

Second, external sovereignty. Vattel's book is an attempt to establish some principles and rules the end of which ought to satisfy three general requirements of the freedom of states: to heighten their self-consciousness in acting; to lessen the struggle to attend to the world; and together to produce moral reasoning about the world. Vattel's problems resemble Leibniz's inasmuch as natural languages are seen to stand in the way of developing virtuous habits – and virtuous statecraft. 'If the ideas of men were always distinct and perfectly determinate', he wrote, and 'if, for the expression of those ideas, they had none but proper words, no terms but such as were clear, precise, and susceptible only of one sense – there would never be any difficulty in discovering their meaning in the words by which they intended to express it' (*LN*, II-xvii-262).

[45] G. W. Leibniz, 'Caesarinus Fürstenerius', in *Political Writings*, 117–120.

But, of course, words are not like this; and the problem is compounded in international politics, where 'men designedly throw obscurity and ambiguity into their treaties' and where 'it is impossible to foresee and point out all the particular cases that may arise', where 'conjunctures vary, and produce new kinds of cases, that cannot be brought within the terms of the treaty or the law, except by inferences drawn from the general views of the contracting parties' (*LN*, II-XVII-262). The *Law of Nations* is a kind of universal characteristic for an international society of sovereign states, an endeavour 'to establish rules founded on reason, and authorised by the law of nature, capable of diffusing light over what is obscure, of determining what is uncertain' (*LN*, II-XVII-262). For 'virtue is, even for sovereigns and political bodies, the most certain road to prosperity and happiness' (*LN*, II-I-1), and states will need to legislate for themselves certain common directions in order that they can work together to better their mutual condition. They stand in need of their own Ariadne's thread to lead them ever more surely in their mutual intercourse.

To be sovereign is to be free. The power of state sovereigns to be conscious of their causes, to attend productively to the world – and to do both of these things with growing facility – turns, Vattel maintains, on their speaking and understanding the same language. Vattel thus lays down some 'fixed rules calculated to determine' the interpretation of international legal agreements, which, because they 'are founded on right reason', are 'approved and prescribed by the law of nature', and so 'every sovereign is obliged to admit and to follow them' (*LN*, II-XVII-268). These rules do not contradict but in fact enable sovereignty. Vattel spends a good deal of chapter XVII of Book II, 'Of the Interpretation of Treaties', setting out such rules of mutual understanding. He deals, for instance, with the handling of figurative expressions (such as to '*hatch a plot* or to *carry fire and sword into a country*') and equivocal expressions (when words 'signify two or more different things' and where phrases may be 'susceptible of more than one sense') (*LN*, II-XVII-278–279). His rules sound a lot like common sense, and so they should: they all follow, he thinks, from the right use of right reason; but he identifies historical sovereign offenders of each rule, so he considers that the lessons continue to need to be spelled out. We ought, Vattel says, 'to affix such meaning to the expressions, as is most suitable to the subject or matter in question'; and on this basis Quintus Fabius Labeo is condemned for his interpretation of his treaty with Antiochus III, 'for a sovereign who stipulates that the half of his fleet or of his vessels shall be restored to him, undoubtedly means that the other party shall restore to him vessels which he can make use of, and not the half of each vessel, sawed in two' (*LN*, II-XVII-280; emphasis suppressed). And yet 'if any one of those expressions which are susceptible of different significations occurs more than once in the same piece, we cannot make it a rule to take it everywhere in the same signification' (*LN*, II-XVII-281; emphasis suppressed). Each expression must be interpreted on a case-by-case basis, and everything 'which leads to an absurdity ought to be rejected', and especially such interpretations as would lead to moral absurdity (*LN*, II-XVII-282).

Vattel leans quite heavily in developing his own principles of common interpretation on older ones, such as rule sixty-five from canon law, that 'in equal crimes or cases the position of the possessor is stronger': that is, when property (or territory, for sovereigns) is disputed and there is no other legal presumption in favour of either side, then the contested property ought to be retained by its current possessor, so long as he has it in good faith (*LN*, II-XVII-305).[46] With only a little adjustment, Vattel reaches his fourth rule for dealing with 'a collision or opposition between two laws, two promises, or two treaties, when [such] a case occurs' (*LN*, II-XVII-311), which is that 'if there be a collision between two treaties made with different powers, the more ancient claims the preference' (*LN*, II-XVII-315). Rule sixty-five had long been a tenet of casuistry, or case-based reasoning in law and ethics, and Vattel's rules very much have the character of a rubric for proceeding to conclusion in 'cases of doubt' (*LN*, II-IX-128; II-XII-190), where what is called for is 'extensive interpretation' (*LN*, II-XVII-290).[47] Conductors of states who together habituate themselves to observing rules such as these in their exchanges will thereby accustom themselves to making rational decisions, seeing the logic of the causes of their declarations of will, and with compounding ease. The payoffs of rule-based association will further incentivise cooperation.

Vattel's ruminations on conscience bear more responsibility than any other aspect of his work for the fairly well-consolidated view in the secondary literature that he endorsed a 'radical state-libertarianism'.[48] Vattel wrote about the 'necessary law of nations', which was 'the internal, and consciential, law' to do what needed to be done for the good of the state (*LN*, preface). If it were possible for one sovereign to compel another in virtue of some contracted obligation, the latter 'would no longer enjoy the freedom of determination respecting the conduct he is to pursue in order to obey the dictates of his own conscience' (*LN*, prelim. 17). 'As a consequence of that liberty and independence' entailed by sovereignty, he holds, 'it exclusively belongs to

46 Holland, *Moral Person*, 53–56.

47 See I. Hunter, 'Vattel's *Law of Nations*: Diplomatic casuistry for the protestant nation', *Grotiana* 31 (2010), 108–140; and L. Cello, 'The legitimacy of international interventions in Vattel's *The Law of Nations*', *Global Intellectual History* 2 (2017), 105–123, at 109–111.

48 A. Linklater, *Men and Citizens in the Theory of International Relations*, 2nd ed. (Basingstoke, 1990), 87.

each nation to form her own judgment of what her conscience prescribes to her – of what she can and cannot do – of what it is proper or improper for her to do' (*LN*, prelim. 16) and that may mean having to break promises. Or most succinctly: 'Let us leave the strictness of the necessary law of nations to the conscience of sovereigns' (*LN*, III-XII-189). Again, however, we must correct our first assumptions about Vattel's intentions. 'Conscience' did not in mid-eighteenth-century Europe carry quite the same privatised imputation that it does now, when we tend to speak of 'personal' conscience based on individual value systems. The etymology of *conscientia* points to 'knowing something (in company) with someone else', a joint knowledge of it.[49] Vattel takes it that association helps to produce self-consciousness about one's motives for acting and to improve the quality of moral action. Association does both of these things by sustaining certain rules about thinking to which associates habituate themselves and which help to invigorate volition. Conscience for Vattel was of course internal, but it had a public facet as well. It is not for nothing that even a fairly recent account of conscience defines it 'a sort of educated emotional habit'.[50] Pufendorf thought that a person acquired conscience 'from the general manner of life in his society, or from habit'.[51] And commenting on the eighteenth-century grasp of the voice of conscience inspired in large part by Pufendorf,[52] D. D. Raphael writes that it was pictured as reflecting 'what I imagine that I, with all my knowledge of the situation, would feel if I were a spectator instead of an agent', that it was understood as being 'a social product, a mirror of social feeling'.[53] The metaphor of the mirror is significant: Vattel subscribes to the Leibnizian ontology according to which all things are interconnected through their mutual mirroring of each other as reflections of the universe. When he writes of states as beings whose status as moral entities requires that they cannot be compelled by each other to observe agreements, he is referring explicitly to bilateral conventions. Obligations of conscience take precedence because conscience, as something perceived interiorly but shared intersubjectively, and as revealing the underlying reasons of things, enmeshes states in a more thoroughgoing set of moral relations with each other than one-to-one agreements. Appealing to conscience is not, as it

49 T. C. Potts, *Conscience in Medieval Philosophy* (Cambridge, 1980), 2

50 P. D. Ouspensky, *Conscience: The Search for Truth* (London, 1979), 54.

51 S. Pufendorf, *On the Duty of Man and Citizen according to Natural Law*, ed. J. Tully and M. Silverthorne (Cambridge, 1991), I.1.5.

52 H. Haara, *Pufendorf's Theory of Sociability: Passions, Habits and Social Order* (Cham, 2018), 35–41.

53 D. D. Raphael, *The Impartial Spectator: Adam Smith's Moral Philosophy* (Oxford, 2007), 35–36.

may first seem, Vattel's way of investing states with an inviolate right of independence, but rather speaks to the interdependence of states and the dependence of their liberty on their productive association. As Pablo Kalmanovitz has argued in relation to Vattel's stipulations about the principles and practices of war, 'valid public reasons must control or discipline persuasive reasons' and 'multilateralism operates as a filter against spurious claims'.[54] Jennifer Pitts, on the other hand, contrasts the 'Vattelian model of sovereignty', with 'self-determination not as sovereignty, but in terms of nondomination and relational autonomy'.[55] Relational autonomy, however, seems to me to be a good description of precisely what Vattel himself means by sovereignty.

CONCLUSION

Vattel's work is rooted in a number of traditions, not always natural bedfellows, so he tends to write about both freedom and sovereignty in liberal terms, where non-interference is constitutive, and in republican terms, where independence is central. He draws, as we have seen, some of his thinking on freedom and sovereignty from Hobbes, the great proto-liberal; but some of his reflection on the same topics also rests, as we have observed, on Hobbes's critic, Pufendorf. The Leibnizian tradition is strongest in its influence on Vattel, however. According to that, self-government, whether of the individual or the sovereign state, is about overcoming the irresolution of the will in order to enter into relationships which both enlighten and discipline reason through the careful mutual manipulation of some symbol system: this is a theory of a kind of positive liberty, in Berlin's sense, as opposed to two different pictures of negative liberty. It seems to me that Vattel anticipates the likes of Tocqueville's associative liberalism or even Cass R. Sunstein's account of freedom as navigability.[56] It is a theory of sovereignty that is so much more than what is usually thought to be.

54 P. Kalmanovitz, 'Sovereignty, pluralism, and regular war: Wolff and Vattel's Enlightenment critique of just war', *Political Theory* 46 (2018), 218–241, at 231–232. See also W. Rech, *Enemies of Mankind: Vattel's Theory of Collective Security* (Leiden, 2013), 54.

55 J. Pitts, 'Intervention and sovereign equality: Legacies of Vattel', in S. Recchia and J. M. Welsh (eds), *Just and Unjust Military Intervention: European Thinkers from Vitoria to Mill* (Cambridge, 2013), 132–153, at 151–153.

56 C. R. Sunstein, *On Freedom* (Princeton, 2019).

FURTHER READING

Writings by Vattel

Vattel, E., *Défense du système leibnitien contra les objections et les imputations de M. de Crousaz* (Leiden, 1741). [*DSL*]

'Essay on the foundation of natural law and on the first principle of the obligation men find themselves under to observe laws', in *The Law of Nations*, ed. B. Kapossy and R. Whatmore (Indianapolis, 2008). [*FNL*]

Selected Secondary Literature

Beaulac, S., Power of Language in the Making of International Law: The Word 'Sovereignty' in Bodin and Vattel and the Myth of Westphalia (Leiden, 2004), chap. 7.

Holland, B., The Moral Person of the State: Pufendorf, Sovereignty and Composite Polities (Cambridge, 2017), chap. 3.

Hunter, I., 'Vattel's *Law of Nations*: Diplomatic casuistry for the protestant nation', *Grotiana* 31 (2010), 108–140.

3

The Development of the Law of Nations

Wolff and Vattel

ERE NOKKALA

INTRODUCTION

The debate over Emer de Vattel's originality as a thinker has a long history. He himself gave impetus to the question in the preface of his main work, the *Law of Nations*,[1] by emphasising that the book owed a serious debt to Christian Wolff (1679–1754). Wolff was the leading German philosopher of the generation, preceding Immanuel Kant. He was the main advocate of Prussian school philosophy, also known as Wolffianism or alternatively as Leibnizian–Wolffian philosophy. The irony is that when one then picks up almost any standard account on Wolff, one soon learns that scholars have spent decades debating Wolff's originality. Until relatively recently, Wolff was considered a mere follower and populariser of Gottfried Wilhelm Leibniz's (1646–1716) philosophy.[2] Simultaneously, adding a touch of further irony, Wolff, 'Leibniz's popularizer', has been accused of being pedantic and boring. During the past three decades, Wolff has been increasingly recognised as an independent thinker with considerable originality, especially in the field of political thought, including his work on the law of nations.[3] The aim of this

[1] E. de Vattel, *The Law of Nations, or, Principles of the Law of Nature, Applied to the Conduct and Affairs of Nations and Sovereigns, with Three Early Essays on the Origin and Nature of Natural Law and on Luxury*, ed. B. Kapossy and R. Whatmore (Indianapolis, 2008).

[2] M. Stewart, *The Courtier and the Heretic: Leibniz, Spinoza and the Fate of God in the Modern World* (New Haven, 2005), 308.

[3] N. G. Onuf, 'Civitas Maxima: Wolff, Vattel and the fate of republicanism', *American Journal of International Law* 88 (1994), 280–303; F. Cheneval, 'Auseinandersetzungen um die civitas maxima in der Nachfolge Christian Wolffs', *Studia Leibnitiana* 33.2 (2001), 125–144; On the relationship between Leibniz and Wolff see L. Strickland and J. Weckend, 'Making waves: Leibniz's legacy and impact', in J. Weckend and L. Strickland (eds.), *Leibniz's Legacy and Impact* (New York, 2019), 1–19. According to Strickland and Weckend, 'Wolff borrowed numerous definitions, principles, and doctrines from Leibniz, often without acknowledging his debt, such that Wolff's philosophy draws from and depends upon Leibniz's philosophy as

chapter is to revisit Vattel's relationship to Wolff in a balanced manner, with attention given to the similarities and differences between these two major advocates of natural law and the law of nations in the eighteenth century.

By the time of the publication of the *Law of Nations* in 1758, Vattel had engaged himself with Wolff's work for a good ten years. His original plan had been to translate Wolff's German and Latin pieces into the language of the diplomats, French, and to act as a kind of mediator between the German and French intellectual cultures. What started as a translation and compilation project grew to be a significant, independent and, in fact, an original work by Vattel.[4] The preface to the *Law of Nations* is a good starting point when assessing the affinities between Wolff and Vattel. While Vattel wrote, he held Wolff's work on the law of nations as precious and wanted to make it known to the wider intellectual world. What Vattel found problematic was Wolff's manner of presentation, finding his work dry and incomplete. However, according to Vattel, Wolff's general principles and definitions were approvable and worthy of serious attention. Although Vattel was clearly influenced by Wolff's work, he made sure to state that differences between his and Wolff's work were obvious to everyone who bothered to make a comparison (*LN*, preface 13).

I will show in this chapter that Vattel followed Wolff's act of transforming the law of nations into an independent discipline. In order to accomplish this, Vattel drew on Wolff's ideas of states as moral persons and as the main subjects in the international arena, but he distanced himself from Wolff in two ways. First, Vattel did not approve of Wolff's mathematical method, which Wolff himself considered his main contribution to philosophy. Second, he disagreed with Wolff on how the so-called voluntary law of nations that bound sovereigns in their actual relationships should be understood. Wolff wanted to deduce the law from the idea of the greatest republic (*civitas maxima*), whereas Vattel wanted to replace it with voluntary law derived from natural law. Vattel's voluntary law of nations consisted of a body of rules connected

much as it diverges from it', at page 7; see also J. Ecole, 'Des rapports de Wolff avec Leibniz dans le domaine de la métaphysique', in A Heinekamp (ed.), *Beiträge zur Wirkungs- und Rezeptionsgeschichte von Gottfried Wilhelm Leibniz* (Stuttgart, 1986), 88–96.

4 F. Ieva, '"A poor imitation of Grotius and Pufendorf" biographical uncertainties and the laborious genesis of Vattel's *Droit des gens*', in K. Stapelbroek and A. Trampus (eds.), *The Legacy of Vattel's* Droit des gens (Cham, 2019), 53–76, 76.

with the European state practice,[5] leading to Vattel's rejection of Wolff's idea of 'the state of all states'.[6]

VATTEL'S CRITIQUE OF WOLFF'S METHOD

Independent of his high praise of Wolff, Vattel first and foremost wanted to distance himself from Wolff's method, which he believed made Wolff's work inaccessible. Wolff's notoriety as a pedantic and dry writer was – and still is – bound with his mathematical way of proceeding deductively from axioms. No less a figure than the Prussian king Frederick II, known as Frederick the Great, wrote to Wolff and asked him to present truths in a shorter manner and with fewer proofs. According to Frederick II, this would be pleasant to the intellect of the reader.[7] Although even Wolff's contemporaries at times ridiculed his pedantic presentation, it is worth noting that he was the most influential German philosopher of his lifetime and had followers in the whole of Europe, from Sweden to Italy.[8] Wolff's philosophical system is best described by his method that had many descriptions, including mathematical, geometrical, demonstrative, philosophic and scientific. Wolff and his students preferred to call their favoured method mathematical.[9] As a trained mathematician, Wolff wanted to make the chain of proofs the same way in psychology, ethics, politics and the law of nations as he did in mathematics, by deriving truths deductively.[10] His method was the leading paradigm in German-speaking Europe until the second half of the 1770s.[11] Beginning in the 1750s, his work was increasingly challenged and criticised – including in the work of Vattel – which explains Hegel's exaggerated comment

[5] P. Piirimäe, 'Men, monsters and the history of mankind in Vattel's *Law of Nations*', in S. Zurbuchen (ed.), *The Law of Nations and Natural Law 1625–1800* (Leiden, 2019), 159–85, 161.

[6] Vattel pointed out further differences in *LN*, preface 13–16. Vattel's conception of political order and defence of freedom and independence of states made him reluctant to approve of Wolff's praise of patrimonial kingdoms. Furthermore, unlike Wolff, Vattel did not approve of the use of poisonous weapons in war. This was a difference in their understanding of *jus in bello* (*LN*, III-VIII-§156).

[7] H.-M. Bachmann, *Die naturrechtliche Staatslehre Christian Wolffs* (Berlin, 1977), 57.

[8] Ibid., 14, 50.

[9] B. Stollberg-Rilinger, *Der Staat als Maschine Zur politischen Metaphorik des absoluten Fürstenstaats* (Berlin, 1986), 89.

[10] T. Ahnert, 'Introduction', in C. Wolff, *The Law of Nations Treated According to the Scientific Method*, ed. T. Ahnert, translated by J. H. Drake, translation revised by T. Ahnert (Indianapolis, 2017), xxi.

[11] Stollberg-Rilinger, *Der Staat als Maschine*, 95.

regarding Wolff having outlived his fame and seeing empty auditoriums during his final years before his death in 1754.[12]

As noted, Wolff's aim was to present all human knowledge in a mathematical method. His methodological starting point was that no principle was to be used unless it was fully proven. New principles could not be approved unless they were deduced from proven principles. Wolff strived for precision in his usage of concepts. If new concepts were to be introduced, they would need to be defined duly. In addition, previously accepted definitions of philosophical terms could not be changed.[13] In short, axioms, definitions and distinctions formed the core of Wolffianism. Wolff sought to build a unified system of sciences in which the last conclusion related to the original axiom. By following the rules of philosophy and using a deductive method, philosophers should be able to arrive at timeless truths of reason. In this manner, philosophy could provide us with truths as equally reliable as those of mathematics. In other words, Wolff universalised the claims of reason.

The content of Wolff's philosophy was defined by Leibnizian–Wolffian perfectionist metaphysics. Perfectibility was about the interconnectedness of the manifold (*Zusammenstimmung des Mannigfaltigen*). Perfectibility meant that complicated entities worked in harmony towards a common purpose. According to Leibniz and Wolff, the world that we live in is the best of possible worlds because all its parts work together to honour God, who is forever perfect. Wolff argued that the task of philosophy was to prove what the capacities of the soul can accomplish; this is to say, to show what is possible as human beings. Only after proving this could practical philosophy begin. Wolff began his inquiry into the soul by pointing out that we know from our experience that the soul has two capacities: the capacity of knowing and the capacity of willing.[14] Wolff defined the soul as a non-bodily substance that gives us a representation of the world. The representations given by the soul can differ; some are clearer than others.[15] The more precise our representations, the closer to perfection they are. Perceiving the world in a precise

[12] G. W. F. Hegel, *Vorlesungen über die Geschichte der Philosophie, als Vorschule zur Encyklopaedie, mit einigen Ausführungen und Anmerkungen zur Erlaeuterung, Verteidigung oder Berichtigung, für den akademischen Gebrauch*, ed. G. J. P. J. Bolland (Leiden, 1908), 940; T. Kleinlein, 'Christian Wolff: System as an episode?', in S. Kadelbach, T. Kleinlein, and D. Roth-Isigkeit (eds.), *System, Order, and International Law: The Early History of International Legal Thought from Machiavelli to Hegel* (Oxford, 2017), 216–239, 218.

[13] Stollberg-Rilinger, *Der Staat als Maschine*, 89.

[14] C. Wolff, *Der vernünfftigen Gedancken von Gott, der Welt und der Seele des Menschen, auch allen Dingen überhaupt* (Frankfurt, 1740 [1720]), §404, §873.

[15] Ibid., §745–746.

manner makes ourselves more perfect. Wolff explained that our recognition of perfection gives us pleasure, which connects to our wilful choice of perfection, this is to favour moral goodness.[16] In this way, feeling pleasure was only a manifestation of perfection. The pleasure that we felt was relative to the degree of perfection derived from our perceptions. What made our state more perfect was morally good.[17] When our actions were founded in such a manner that their aim was common (perfection and happiness), the path of a human being was perfect.[18]

For Wolff, practical philosophy was a science that guided the capacity of will to choose the good and shun the bad. In this way, psychological action defined morality in Wolff's philosophy.[19] From psychology, Wolff proceeded to ethics and from there to politics. The overarching concepts that combined all of these fields to build a system of philosophy were the intertwined concepts of happiness and perfection.[20] When our intellect developed and we could distinguish elements of the world with more precision, we would act as we want. In this way, our profound inclination to seek perfection, or good, forms our will. In short, according to Wolff, to implement human nature is to perfect. This was the same as to implement good, which again related to a lasting state of happiness.[21] In that way, knowledge about morality was dependent on metaphysical and 'psychological' knowledge. It was possible for human beings to become happy if they possessed certain moral truths.[22]

Wolff's teleological vision of human destiny, as individuals and as a collective, was perfectibility. He treated the collective in the service of perfectibility in terms of ascending associations. They included marriage (*Ehestand*), family (*väterliche Gesellschaft*), master society (*herrschaftliche Gesellschaft*) and state (*Staat*), and together they culminated in the greatest republic (*civitas maxima*), which was a collective formed by all states. All these collectives were based on social contracts that aimed for the perfectibility of the collective and of all its members. There was an undeniable paternalist trait in Wolff's

[16] Ibid., §404–405; J. Brückner, *Staatswissenschaften, Kameralismus und Naturrecht: Ein Beitrag zur Geschichte der politischen Wissenschaft in Deutschland des späten 17. und frühen 18. Jahrhunderts* (München, 1977), 216.

[17] Wolff, *Der vernünfftigen Gedancken von Gott*, §422.

[18] Ibid., §152.

[19] J. B. Schneewind, *The Invention of Autonomy: A History of Modern Moral Philosophy* (Cambridge, 1998), 435.

[20] Ibid., 436.

[21] Brückner, *Staatswissenschaften*, 216–217.

[22] M. Wundt, *Die deutsche Schulphilosophie im Zeitalter der Aufklärung* (Hildesheim, 1964 [1945]), 174–175; Schneewind, *The Invention of Autonomy*, 433.

contractual theory, since those who governed the collective were to be the judges of the perfectibility and happiness of the collective.[23]

The key concepts of Wolff's natural law and the law of nations that derived from it were human perfection and happiness. Drawing heavily on scholastic predecessors, Wolff claimed that the principles of natural law (i.e. the duties and rights of men) could be derived from the correct definition of human nature, namely that man ultimately seeks the realisation of his natural abilities and attainment of happiness.[24] As Jerome Schneewind has argued, 'in his metaphysics he [Wolff] refers back to his logic to explain the order of his argument, in the ethics back to the metaphysics for his principles, and so on through the series of expositions, as he reminds us each time he expounds the later stages. The whole constitutes a modern protestant scholastic system'.[25] Wolff's law of nations was part of this system. Vattel's original plan was to detach the law of nations from the scholastic detail of Wolffian metaphysics in order to make it accessible.[26] But at the end, as he himself recognised, Vattel ended up writing a completely new work.[27] This new work, however, did make significant use of the language of Wolff's philosophy.

Vattel subscribed to Leibnizian–Wolffian metaphysics, but he took a position of decisive distance from Wolff's method. He also found it problematic that Wolff's

> law of nations is dependent on all those of the same author on philosophy and the law of nature. In order to read and understand it, it is necessary to have previously studied sixteen or seventeen quarto volumes which precede it. Besides, it is written in the manner and even in the formal method of geometrical works. . . . The method followed by Monsieur Wolf has had the effect of rendering his work dry, and in many respects incomplete. The different subjects are scattered through it in a manner that is extremely fatiguing to the attention . . . (*LN*, preface 12)

Unlike Wolff, whose main audience were scholars, Vattel wrote to European sovereigns, ministers and diplomats with the aim of making a lasting impact on European political practice.[28] In a way, Vattel was responding to the wish

23 K. Haakonssen, 'Christian Wolff (1679–1754)', in B. Fassbender and A. Peters (eds.), *The Oxford Handbook of the History of International Law* (Oxford, 2012), 1106–1109. On Vattel's conception of social contract see Chapter 9, by Gabriella Silvestrini.

24 I. Hunter, *Rival Enlightenments: Civil and Metaphysical Philosophy in Early Modern Germany* (Cambridge, 2001), 12.

25 Schneewind, *The Invention of Autonomy*, 433.

26 Kleinlein, 'Christian Wolff', 237.

27 Ieva, 'A poor imitation', 76.

28 S. Zurbuchen, 'Emer de Vattel on the society of nations and the political system of Europe', in S. Kadelbach, T. Kleinlein and D. Roth-Isigkeit (eds.), *System, Order, and International Law:*

that Frederick II had expressed to Wolff – to be more readable and concise. Vattel's preferred presentation was clear, crisp and fluent, which made him abandon what Wolff considered his own greatest achievement, his method.[29] What Vattel took from Wolff were the general principles and definitions. Above all, Vattel implemented in his own work Wolff's concept of the nation as a moral person and secondly Wolff's conception of perfection, the idea that we owe duties and rights of perfection to ourselves, others and God. These were key Wolffian principles in Vattel's political and international political thought, including the field of law of nations.

THE DEVELOPMENT OF THE LAW OF NATIONS INTO AN INDEPENDENT DISCIPLINE: MORALITY OF THE STATE

Despite his severe criticism of Wolff, Vattel considered Wolff the greatest of his predecessors in the field of the law of nations.[30] Vattel appreciated Wolff's attempt to transform the law of nations into an independent discipline. Whereas Wolff's predecessors treated the law of nations mainly in footnotes and side comments, Wolff dedicated a whole book to the topic, *Jus gentium methodo scientifica pertractatum*, in 1749.[31] It was a follow-up to his eight-volume work on the law of nature, *Jus Naturae methodo scientifica pertractatum*, published between 1740 and 1748. Wolff's law of nature and law of nations were later compiled as *Institutiones Juris Naturae et Gentium*, which was prepared mainly for teaching purposes, and it was translated into German in 1754 under the title *Grundsätze des Natur- und Völkerrechts*.[32] Vattel was interested in taking the autonomisation of the law of nations even further by detaching it from Wolff's other works and giving it a new form in his *Law of Nations*. To accomplish this, Vattel built on Wolff's account of nations as moral persons.[33] For Wolff and Vattel, nations understood as moral persons were the main subjects of the law of nations.

The Early History of International Legal Thought from Machiavelli to Hegel (Oxford, 2017), 263–282; Piirimäe, 'Men, monsters', 160.

[29] Kleinlein, 'Christian Wolff', 220-221; Ieva, 'A poor imitation', 54.

[30] B. Holland, *The Moral Person of the State: Pufendorf, Sovereignty and Composite Polities* (Cambridge, 2017), 123.

[31] C. Wolff, *Jus Gentium Methodo Scientifica Pertractatum*, ed. O. Nippold, translated by J. H. Drake and F. J. Hemelt (Oxford, 1934 [1749]).

[32] C. Wolff, *Grundsätze des Natur- und Völkerrechts, worinn alle Verbindlichkeiten und alle Rechte aus der Natur des Menschen in einem beständigen Zusammenhange hergeleitet werden* (Halle, 1754).

[33] B. Holland, 'The moral person of the state: Emer de Vattel and the foundations of international legal order', *History of European Ideas* 37 (2011), 438–445.

Wolff's ideas concerning the law of nations that Vattel drew on had a prehistory.[34] The modern concept of the law of nations (*Völkerrecht, law of nations, droit des gens, jus gentium*), which considers free and independent states as the main legal subjects, originates in the political thought of Thomas Hobbes and Samuel Pufendorf. As Peter Haggenmacher has argued, Grotius and Suárez were the first scholars to redefine *jus gentium* – in Grotius' case, famously in conjunction *ius naturae et gentium* – as a properly international law. However, for these earlier thinkers, *jus gentium* bound individuals as opposed to states.[35] Some scholars have equally pointed to Alberico Gentili (1552–1608) as the father of the law of nations. However, Gentili regarded it as a form of private law that consisted of common rules used by different nations, which also applied to relations between states.[36] The modern understanding of the law of nations rests on two distinctions outlined in the political thinking of Pufendorf and Hobbes. They were the first theorists to make a clear distinction between universal rational natural law and the positive law based on the will of the legislator. This dualism paved the way for the modern understanding of the law of nations, since it left no room for the older concept of *jus gentium*, understood as a law shared by all peoples. Even more significant, in terms of the contribution of Pufendorf and Hobbes, was the introduction of the idea of the state as a person.[37] According to Hobbes, the state is a fictional person (a person who only exists when represented) represented by an artificial person (one who acts in the name of another), who may or may not also be a natural person (an assembly of men can represent the state and therefore is an artificial person but not a natural person). For Pufendorf, the state was a moral entity in the form of a moral person imposed by men on themselves.[38] While both thinkers allowed for a theoretical distinction between the authority of the state and the person of the sovereign, this was

[34] On Vattel's relationship to Leibniz, Hobbes and Pufendorf, see Chapter 2, by Ben Holland.

[35] P. Haggenmacher, 'Hugo Grotius (1583–1645)', in B. Fassbender and A. Peters (eds.), *The Oxford Handbook of International Law* (Oxford, 2012), 1098–1111.

[36] M. Scattola, 'Alberico Gentili (1552–1608)', in B. Fassbender and A. Peters (eds.), *The Oxford Handbook of International Law* (Oxford, 2012), 1092–1097. On Gentili's role in law of nations see B. Kingsbury and B. Straumann (eds.), *The Roman Foundations of the Law of Nations: Alberico Gentili and the Justice of Empire* (Oxford, 2010).

[37] J. Schröder, 'Die Entstehung des modernen Völkerrechtsbegriffs im Naturrecht des frühen Neuzeit', *Jahrbuch für Recht und Ethik* 8 (2000), 47–71.

[38] Holland, *The Moral Person of the State*, 65–103. On the differences between Hobbes's and Pufendorf's conceptions of law of nature and law of nations, see Kari Saastamoinen, 'Pufendorf on the law of sociality and the law of nations', in S. Zurbuchen (ed.), *The Law of Nations and Natural Law 1625–1800* (Leiden, 2019), 107–131, 119–120, 123–124; On Hobbes, see Quentin Skinner. 'Hobbes on persons, authors and representatives', in P. Springborg (ed.), *The Cambridge Companion to Hobbes's Leviathan* (Cambridge, 2007), 157–180.

not a clear feature of their writings, where one was often identified with the other.[39] With Wolff and Vattel, this changed.

The work of Hobbes and Pufendorf laid the groundwork for the establishment of state's legal personality as it became understood by Wolff and Vattel and the subsequent eighteenth-century thinkers in the field of the law of nations. Vattel alone is often credited with first formulating what we now know as 'classic international law', the law of nations as the law of independent and free states. The mentioned key move by Wolff foreshadowed what Vattel was to clearly distinguish as the body of the state, i.e. the body politic to whom the authority originally belonged, from the person or the persons who exercised this authority. In this way, nations or states as 'bodies politic' became the proper subjects of the law of nations. In *Jus Gentium Methodo Scientifica Pertractatum* (1749), Wolff had argued that 'By the Law of Nations we understand the science of that law which nations or peoples use in their relations with each other and the obligations corresponding thereto'. Since Wolff regarded nations as individual free persons living in the state of nature, 'nations also must be regarded in relation to each other as individual free persons living in the state of nature'. Wolff concluded that 'Since nations are regarded as individual persons living in a state of nature, moreover, as men in a state of nature use nothing except natural law, nations also originally used none other than natural law; therefore, the law of nations is originally nothing except the law of nature applied to nations.' Wolff distinguished between several parts of the law of nations, and the part that was based on the law of nature, which was immutable, he called the necessary law of nations.[40] Similar to individual men living in the state of nature, nations or states were governed by the law of nature. In other words, entire nations in their actions were subject to natural law. The starting point was that all nations were free and no nation was entitled to restrain another from enjoying its freedom. However, according to Wolff, the states owed the duty of perfection to themselves and to other states. While self-preservation always came prior to aiding other nations in their endeavour to perfect themselves, the latter was nonetheless, for Wolff, a duty that had to be respected.[41]

Already in his German *Politik* (1721), Wolff had made use of the analogy between an individual in relation to a state and a state in relation to other states. He argued that every state was, in its relation to other states, a person.[42]

39 Schröder, 'Die Entstehung', 67 ff.

40 Wolff, *Jus Gentium*, §1–4.

41 Wolff, *Grundsätze*, §1088–1089.

42 C. Wolff, *Vernünftige Gedanken von dem Gesellschaftlichen Leben der Menschen und Insonderheit dem Gemeinen Wesen* (Halle, 1721), §220.

Once the state itself was understood as a person, it could be perceived as an actor in the international sphere in a way similar to that in which the individual was positioned in the 'domestic sphere'.[43] Wolff deduced from this that states as moral persons had natural obligations that could be generated from general principles. These principles were deduced from the nature of the state, from the nature it had as a moral person.[44] In sum, the concept of the person of the state, as a moral person, offered Wolff a way of conceptualising international relations in terms of rights and duties. He believed that states owed the same rights and duties towards one another as did individuals in the state of nature. For Wolff, the most important of these duties was the duty of perfection, and this was the most important general principle Vattel picked up from Wolff. Drawing heavily on Wolff, Vattel argued that the law of nations was the law of nature applied to the moral persons of nations (*LN*, preface 12). Vattel argued that 'The first general law that we discover in the very object of the society of nations, is that each individual nation is bound to contribute every thing in her power to the happiness and perfection of all the others' (*LN*, prelim. 13; 73). Emphasising the duties of nations as moral persons, Vattel argued that,

> Since the object of the natural society established between all mankind is that they should lend each other mutual assistance in order to attain perfection themselves and to render their condition as perfect as possible – and since nations, considered as so many free persons living together in a state of nature, are bound to cultivate human society with each other, – the object of the great society established by nature between all nations is also the interchange of mutual assistance for their own improvement and that of their condition. (LN, prelim. 12; 73)

Wolff and Vattel were by no means unique in extending natural law to the implied law of nations. In fact, many eighteenth-century natural law theorists advocated the idea that natural law was at least to some extent applicable to the law of nations. Already Hobbes had famously made this point in *Leviathan* when he stated that 'Concerning the Offices of one Sovereign to another, which are comprehended in that Law, which is commonly called the Law of Nations, I need not to say any thing in this place; because the Law of Nations, and the Law of Nature, is the same thing.'[45] However, very few thinkers were ready to admit that states and humans were identical, preferring to highlight

43 H. Suganami, *The Domestic Analogy and World Order Proposals* (Cambridge, 1989), 13.

44 T. J. Hochstrasser, *Natural Law Theories in the Early Enlightenment* (Cambridge, 2000), 177–178.

45 T. Hobbes, *Leviathan*, ed. R. Tuck, rev. ed. (Cambridge, 1996 [1651]), 244.

certain differences in their nature. According to Vattel, the states were moral persons, but they conducted themselves in a different manner from individuals. He praised Jean Barbeyrac (1674–1744), the French natural lawyer and famous translator and commentator of Pufendorf, for going beyond Hobbes in realising that although the principles behind natural law and the law of nations were very similar, there were differences in application.[46] For Wolff and Vattel, the field that dealt with the differences in application was called voluntary law of nations. According to Wolff, the voluntary law of nations could be deduced from the idea of *civitas maxima*. Vattel again rejected the idea of *civitas maxima* as fictitious and at odds with state sovereignty,[47] and he emphasised that the voluntary law of nations could be deduced only from the natural liberty of nations (*LN*, preface 16).

THE VOLUNTARY LAW OF NATIONS: FROM *CIVITAS MAXIMA* TO THE NATURAL LIBERTY OF NATIONS

The originality of Vattel's intervention in relation to Wolff becomes clear if we analyse the conception of the voluntary law of nations elaborated by Wolff. Wolff divided the field of the law of nations into the necessary law of nations and the voluntary law of nations. For Wolff, the concept of *civitas maxima* was central to the latter. Vattel subscribed to Wolff's necessary law of nations, which was applied law of nature. However, Vattel attacked Wolff's idea of the *civitas maxima* and consequently his notion of a voluntary law of nations. Vattel accused Wolff of making a confusing equation between civil law within a nation and voluntary law between nations, this is to say, with the voluntary law of nations.

Concerning the analogy between men in the state of nature and states as moral persons living in the state of nature, the question arose as to whether states should not also set a sovereign above themselves, either to escape the insecurity of the state of nature or in order to reciprocally pursue greater perfection and happiness. If the states were assumed to be like humans in the state of nature, why did they not then become citizens of the greatest republic. Why did they not form a universal state, for example, in the form of a republic or of a monarchy? Wolff gave a decisive answer to these questions. For Wolff the greatest republic already existed:

46 Hochstrasser, *Natural Law Theories*, 177–178.

47 B. Kapossy and R. Whatmore, 'Introduction', in *The Law of Nations*, ed. B. Kapossy and R. Whatmore (Indianapolis, 2008), xv. It is worth pointing out that Wolff would have not denied that *civitas maxima* was fictitious.

> All nations are understood to have come together into a state, whose separate members are separate nations, or individual states. For nature herself has established society among all nations and compels them to preserve it, for the purpose of promoting the common good by their combined powers. Therefore since a society of men united for the purpose of common good by their combined powers, is a state, nature herself has combined nations into a state.[48]

According to Wolff, the states formed together the greatest republic (*civitas maxima*). Whereas a necessary law of nations was natural law applied on states, a voluntary law of nations was supposed to reflect the presumed consensus of the nations united in *civitas maxima*.[49] Wolff's distinction between necessary and voluntary law of nations recalls Grotius' distinction between a law of nations that follows directly from natural law and the voluntary law of nations, which was positive law. Wolff and Vattel have consequently been counted among Grotius' most prominent eighteenth-century followers.[50] Grotius understood the notion of a voluntary law of nations as customary, unwritten law applicable to the whole society of mankind. According to Grotius, the voluntary law of nations was based on the tacit convention of the majority of peoples.[51]

Despite the affinities between Grotius and Wolff, Wolff's greatest republic was not inspired in the first place by Grotius. Rather, his *civitas maxima* issued from the unitary worldview, Wolff took from Leibniz's metaphysical holism, which owed a large debt to stoic cosmopolitanism.[52] For Leibniz, the world was a single community, the 'City of God'. Not unlike his mentor Leibniz, Wolff thought that the core of the natural world was a whole. The problems of this whole, of the community of nations, had already been resolved. It was the task of the philosopher to make the underlying harmony visible and unobjectionable through deductive reasoning.[53] Martti Koskenniemi has argued that it 'was sheer scholastic nostalgia that made Christian Wolff, in his late excursus

48 Wolff, *Jus Gentium*, §9; R. Tuck, *The Rights of War and Peace: Political Thought and the International Order from Grotius to Kant* (Oxford, 1999), 188.

49 G. Silvestrini. 'Justice, war and inequality: The unjust aggressor and the enemy of human race in Vattel's Theory of the law of nations', *Grotiana* 31 (2010), 44–68, 51.

50 P. P. Remec, *The Position of the Individual in International Law according to Grotius and Vattel* (The Hague, 1960), 69; J. Manz, *Emer de Vattel: Versuch einer Würdigung; unter besonderer Berücksichtigung seiner Auffassung von der individuellen Freiheit und der souveränen Gleichheit* (Zürich, 1971), 34.

51 S. Zurbuchen, 'Vattel's law of nations and just war theory', *History of European Ideas* 35 (2009), 409.

52 P. S. Onuf, *Federal Union, Modern World: The Law of Nations in an Age of Revolutions, 1776–1814* (Madison, 1993), 13.

53 M. Koskenniemi, '"International community" from Dante to Vattel', in V. Chetail and P. Haggenmacher (eds.), *Vattel's International Law in a XXIst Century Perspective – Le droit international de Vattel vu du XXIe siècle* (Leiden, 2011), 51–75, at 67–70.

into the law of nations in 1749, speak of all nations joined together in a *civitas maxima* as a functional equivalent to civil society.'[54] Indeed, in his notion of *civitas maxima* Wolff presented the civil law of the world.[55] For Wolff, *civitas maxima* was the tool that helped to deduce the unobjectionable voluntary law of nations, laws that could be considered as the political laws of this universal state. Wolff's *civitas maxima* had the same purpose for states as the state had for its citizens: to facilitate the pursuit of happiness and the perfection of the states and their members. With united powers the states would seek to make themselves and each other more perfect. An underlying assumption of Wolff's international thought was that there is a common interest of everyone. As Francis Cheneval has argued, *civitas maxima* was a methodological innovation, which has a long history of misunderstanding it in the terms of tacit factual consensus whereby the innovative idea of presumed normative consensus (normative fiction of reason) was lost. To avoid this misunderstanding and the inadequate critique that followed from the misunderstanding, Wolff's *civitas maxima* should be reduced neither to a natural nor a metaphysical reality.[56]

Wolff followed the 'domestic analogy' further and argued innovatively that states were citizens, citizens of the greatest republic.[57] Wolff's analogy raises a further question about will formation in the greatest republic. Whose will was it that all nations were presumed to want to accept? Nicholas Onuf has argued that Wolff's *civitas maxima* was a republic – not in the eighteenth-century sense of a generic term for any state but as a commonwealth governed by the citizens.[58] The republic of states would then be governed by the states that were members of the republic of states. It is true that Wolff stated that the laws of *civitas maxima* must correspond with the assumed wills of the states. In addition, he argued that *civitas maxima* was a democracy of free and equal nations: 'The supreme state is a kind of democratic government.'[59] However, it is a very particular democracy:

> Nevertheless, since in a democratic state it is necessary that individuals assemble in a definite place and declare their will as to what ought to be done, since moreover all the nations scattered throughout the whole world

[54] M. Koskenniemi, 'The advantage of treaties: International law in the enlightenment', *Edinburgh Law Review* 13 (2009), 52.

[55] Kapossy and Whatmore, 'Introduction', xv.

[56] Cheneval, 'Auseinandersetzungen', 125.

[57] Wolff, *Grundsätze*, §1090.

[58] Onuf, 'Civitas Maxima', 287–292, 296.

[59] Wolff, *Jus Gentium*, §19.

> cannot assemble together, as is self-evident, that must be taken to be the will of all nations which they are bound to agree upon, if following the leadership of nature they use right reason. Hence it is plain, because it has to be admitted, that what has been approved by the more civilized nations is the law of nations.[60]

Wolff considered the 'more civilized nations' the ones that possessed 'perfect intellect' as the decision-makers of the will of all nations, this is to say of the civil law of the greatest republic (i.e. the voluntary law of nations). The civilised nations could therefore expect that less cultivated nations would oblige themselves to the voluntary law of nations.[61] According to Wolff, non-civilised nations should accept the civilised states' law of nations as the starting point of their relations. Not unlike the civil law of a state, Wolff considered the civil law of the *civitas maxima* obligating. This was because 'if a state is established, individuals bind themselves to the whole, because they wish to promote the common good'. From this, Wolff concluded that 'In the supreme state the nations as a whole have a right to coerce the individual nations, if they should be unwilling to perform their obligations'.[62] We move from Wolff's view of all nations as equal and free to the view that disobliging nations can be rightfully coerced. Hereby, Wolff's voluntary law of nations was in a Hobbesian and Pufendorfian sense a law in the proper sense of the word: law implied obligation, which in turn presupposed the existence of a subject and of a superior.[63] For Wolff, states remain in a state of nature and nevertheless he argues for the existence of enforceable law between states. He does this to overcome Hobbes's and Pufendorf's argument. This was precisely what fictitious *civitas maxima* is meant to legitimise in Wolff's law of nations. In this sense Wolff is decisively anti-Hobbesian and anti-Pufendorfian, which does not come as a surprise considering that he was an essentially Leibnizian thinker.

For Vattel, independence and freedom of states could not be jeopardised in the name of *civitas maxima*. According to him, the alterations between the law of nature and law of nations could be deduced from the natural liberty of

60 Ibid., §20.

61 I. Nakhimovsky, 'Vattel's theory of the international order: Commerce and the balance of power in the law of nations', *History of European Ideas* 33 (2007), 161, fn 13; Liliana Obregón Tarazona, 'The civilized and the uncivilized', in B. Fassbender and A. Peters (eds.), *The Oxford Handbook of the History of International Law* (Oxford, 2012), 917–939; For Vattel's rejection of this division, see Simone Zurbuchen, 'Vattel's "Law of Nations" and the principle of non-intervention', *Grotiana* 31 (2010), 69–84, 83.

62 Wolff, *Jus Gentium*, §11–13.

63 S. Zurbuchen, 'Vattel's "Law of Nations"', 409.

nations, similar to what Wolff had done in his treatise on natural law with respect to individuals (*LN*, preface 16). He prioritised the sovereignty of states and argued that independence was necessary for states to properly discharge the duties they owe to themselves and their citizens and to govern themselves in the manner that best suited their circumstances. For Vattel, it was enough that nations conformed 'to what is required of them by the natural and general society established between all mankind' (*LN*, preface 15). States required full independence and freedom for their self-perfection. Vattel did think that there was unity among nations, but it did not go further than the 'general society of mankind'. He directly refuted Wolff's idea that the voluntary law of nations is, as it were, the civil law of the great republic:

> This idea does not satisfy me; nor do I think the fiction of such a republic either admissible in itself, or capable of affording sufficiently solid grounds on which to build the rules of the universal law of nations which shall necessarily claim the obedient acquiescence of sovereign states. I acknowledge no other natural society between nations than that which nature has established between mankind in general. It is essential to every civil society (civitati) that each member has resigned apart of his right to the body of the society, and that there exists in it an authority capable of commanding all the members, of giving them laws, and of compelling those who should refuse to obey. Nothing of this kind can be conceived or supposed to subsist between nations. Each sovereign state claims and actually possesses an absolute independence on all the others. They are all, according to Monsieur Wolf himself, to be considered as so many individuals who live together in the state of nature, and who acknowledge no other laws but those of nature, or of her Great Author. (LN, preface 14)

It is worth noting that, as political theorists Vattel and Wolff differed significantly from each other, and this is reflected in their work on the law of nations. Vattel was a quintessentially republican thinker. Wolff's political thought, on the other hand, was profoundly conservative and paternalistic. With justification, he can be regarded as an advocate of the political theory of enlightened absolutism. As Frank Grunert has demonstrated, Wolff's political absolutism followed inevitably from his theoretical absolutism. Wolff's theoretical absolutism morphed into political absolutism once the philosopher was called upon to give the right insight dependent on the truth of the *bonum commune*.[64] As Knud Haakonssen has argued, for Wolff, those who govern

[64] F. Grunert, 'Absolutism(s): Necessary ambivalences in the political theory of Christian Wolff', *Tijdschrift voor Rechtsgeschiedenis* 73 (2005), 141–152, 146.

were judges of the perfectibility of the collective.[65] The theoretical and political absolutisms of Wolff's international thought becomes apparent once he states that the *civitas maxima* can be thought of as having a ruler:

> Since in the supreme state that is to be considered as the will of all nations, to which they ought to agree, if following the leadership of nature they use right reason, and since the superior in the state is he to whom belongs the right over the actions of the individuals
>
> ... he can be considered the ruler of the supreme state who, following the leadership of nature, defines by right use of reason what nations ought to consider as law among themselves ...[66]

Wolff emphasised that the ruler of the greatest republic was a fiction. Such a ruler was the hypothetical leader who could define by the right use of reason the law of nations that all nations should follow. Wolff's *civitas maxima* itself can be interpreted as an invention of reason. Indeed, Richard Tuck's remark that Wolff's treatise itself is the *civitas maxima* and that Wolff himself was the rector is convincing.[67] Since there was no mechanism for law in the greatest republic, it was the task of scholars, also Wolff's task, to formulate the rules of the voluntary law. In other words, the greatest republic and its rector were a very useful tool for Wolff in terms of deducing the voluntary law of nations.[68] In this way, the voluntary law of nations could form a coherent system whose principles were derived from the aim of the greatest republic – the happiness of the *civitas maxima*. Vattel's republican convictions and his insistence on the sovereignty and independence of states made it impossible for him to support Wolff's intellectualist idea of the state of the states.

CIVILISED NATIONS AND THE ENEMIES OF MANKIND

There has been much scholarly debate on whether Vattel, like Wolff, advocated a dichotomy between civilised and barbarous nations and whether this was a significant feature of his thought. Walter Rech has argued that Vattel advocated a hegemony of the civilised European nations.[69] Emmanuelle Tourme-Jouannet has questioned this view and pointed out that Vattel's law of nations was not intended and formulated in order to provide a backbone to

[65] Haakonssen, 'Christian Wolff', 1107.
[66] Wolff, *Jus Gentium*, §22.
[67] Tuck, *The Rights*, 188–189.
[68] Onuf, 'Civitas Maxima', 295.
[69] W. Rech, *Enemies of Mankind: Vattel's Theory of Collective Security* (Leiden, 2013), 11.

the endeavour of colonial conquest.[70] Similarly, Ian Hunter has emphasised that Vattel was not a spokesman for colonial aims. Rather, his focus was intra-European and he aimed in the first place to draw the voluntary law of nations from the European state practice.[71] As Pablo Kalmanovitz shows in Chapter 7, Vattel did deploy nuanced distinctions to categorise savagery in Europe and elsewhere, but the issue was less about deploying a dichotomy between European and non-European. Rather Vattel tried to open up for a more diverse understanding of Europe.

It has been suggested that Wolff's contention about the superiority of the more civilised nations is in accordance with the claims of recent secondary literature that has regarded natural law theorists as Eurocentric and as theorists who justified colonialism.[72] For example, Grotius has been accused of having had double standards, 'a dualistic or concentric conception of international society'.[73] According to Martin Wight, Grotius' society was a society established between civilised nations, which restricts the universality of Grotius' argument.[74] Richard Tuck has seen the role of Wolff differently. Tuck stressed that Pufendorf and Wolff should be seen as anomalous among the natural law thinkers in their relation to non-European nations. According to Tuck, Pufendorf and Wolff (both German) were against international punishment. Wolff's discussion of the question of conquering land from native peoples revealed a critical approach to Grotius' law of nations. Indeed, Wolff argued that families which 'have no settled abode but wander through uncultivated wilds' will have what he termed a 'mixed community holding' in the land.[75] I argue that in Wolff's case the appearance is deceptive. After all, his conviction was that the voluntary law of nations consisted of what had been approved

70 E. Tourme-Jouannet, 'Des Origines colonials du droit international: à propos du droit des gens modern au 18ème siècle', in P.-M. Dupuy and V. Chetail (eds.), *The Roots of International Law/ Les fondements du droit international (Liber Amicorum Peter Haggenmacher)* (Leiden, 2014), 649–671; in particular 655–661.

71 I. Hunter, 'Global justice and regional metaphysics: On the critical history of the law of nature and nations', in S. Dorsett and I. Hunter (eds.), *Law and Politics in British Colonial Thought* (Basingstoke, 2010), 11–29, at 19. For a convincing discussion of Rech's and Hunter's positions, see Piirimäe, 'Men, monsters', 161–162.

72 From the extensive literature see the historical chapters in S. J. Anaya, *Indigenous Peoples in International Law* (Oxford, 2004); and A. Anghie, *Imperialism, Sovereignty and the Making of International Law* (Cambridge, 2005). For a rejection of this position see E. Tourme-Jouannet, 'Des Origines colonials', 655–661.

73 M. Wight, *System of States* (Leicester, 1977), 128.

74 For this point see T. Christov, 'Liberal internationalism revisited: Grotius, Vattel, and the international order of states', *The European Legacy* 10 (2005), 565.

75 Tuck, *The Rights*, 188–189.

by the more civilised nations. Wolff understood a cultured or civilised nation to consist of the following:

> a cultural nation which cultivates intellectual virtues, consequently desires to perfect the intellect, and therefore develops the mind by training. And that is a civilized nation which has civilized usages or usages which conform to the standard of reason and politeness.[76]

Wolff defined barbarous nations as nations that neglected the perfecting of intellect and cared little for intellectual virtues. Wolff argued that barbarous nations do not train their minds and only follow natural inclinations and aversions, on which most uncivilised usages depend.[77] Still, Wolff's intellectualism often led him to formulate conceptions of an international order that appear Eurocentric. Europeans could be regarded as representatives of civilised nations, whose reason barbarous and uncivilised nations were to follow. Moreover, while he speaks of the Chinese as being prominent among the 'more civilized nations', he also noted that the Chinese had not made true advances in metaphysics or physics, not to speak of mathematics, where they have not acquired the fame of Europeans.[78] Nevertheless, for Wolff the decisive criteria was whether the nation was civilised according to Wolff's own standards, already mentioned in this section. It was not a question of the nation being European or non-European. Any state which strove to perfect itself qualified as civilised.

Vattel rejected a crude distinction between civilised and barbarian nations. He did not use such a distinction to justify European intervention in non-European states. For Vattel, the decisive criteria was sovereignty. According to him, states as sovereigns were free and equal, and therefore the law of nations was to be applied to all states in a reciprocal way.[79] However, there were exceptions. As argued by Pärtel Piirimäe, Vattel introduced the concepts of the enemy of mankind and monster as notions that could be applied in the international context. Monsters and enemies of mankind were not to be considered subjects of voluntary law, and the natural equality between nations ceased to exist between enemies of mankind and the civilised nations. Rights and duties deduced from the voluntary law of nations did not hold anymore.[80] An example of an enemy of a mankind was a state that attacked another

76 Wolff, *Jus Gentium*, §53.

77 Ibid., §52.

78 Ibid., §54. This said, passages in Wolff's writing also criticize the capture of lands from the natives and reflect a negative view of punitive wars.

79 Zurbuchen, 'Vattel's "Law of Nations"', 83.

80 Piirimäe, 'Men, monsters', 163–164; Zurbuchen, 'Emer de Vattel', 279.

without a formal declaration of war.[81] Vattel's distinction between monsters, enemies of mankind and civilised nations could be successfully applied to European as well as non-European nations. In this sense Vattel's thought was not Eurocentric, although there is no denying that he was concerned mainly with European state practice. According to Vattel, all states ought to perfect themselves and destroy barbarism through a process of civilising. Vattel considered a nation that realised the duty of self-perfection – an obligation imposed by the nature of mankind – as a civilised nation. According to this minimalist notion of civilised Vattel could regard, for instance, Russia as an example of a nation that had recently become civilised. Vattel recognised also that there was a danger that tyrants could rise among civilised European peoples.[82] Once again, the question was not about being European or non-European.

CONCLUSION

Vattel wrote his *Law of Nations* for diplomats, ministers and European sovereigns. To secure their attention, he adopted a style of presentation that differed significantly from Wolff's. The success of Vattel's treatise was beyond his expectations. Vattel's departure from Wolff's method should not lead us to consider him as an anti-Wolffian thinker. The famous statement in the preface of the *Law of Nations* regarding his primary aim of making Wolff more approachable is to be taken seriously and not as a mere rhetorical framing of his book. The general philosophical framework of Vattel's thought remained true to Wolff. Vattel's law of nations relies on Wolff's principles and distinctions, most prominently on Wolff's conception of nations as moral persons. Vattel's political convictions led him away from the political theory of enlightened absolutism as advocated by Wolff's political and international thought. Wolff's notion of *civitas maxima* was incompatible with Vattel's understanding of independent, free and equal sovereign states. In sum, Vattel rejected what Wolff considered his main contribution to philosophy, namely his method. Equally, Vattel dismissed Wolff's idea of *civitas maxima*, which scholars have considered Wolff's most original achievement. Still, Vattel managed to write a most original work, which owed a great debt to Wolff. Vattel detached himself from the Wolffian context, while still writing a Wolffian text. Vattel was much

81 Zurbuchen, 'Vattel's "Law of Nations"', 83.
82 Piirimäe, 'Men, monsters', 163, 167, 176–177, 182.

more influential outside of Germany in his own time than Wolff. His *Law of Nations* proved to be critical to the development of law of nations in the new states of North America. This could have been a point of transfer of the text from one context to another, by making the context of Wolff's philosophical writings obsolete for understanding the text.

FURTHER READING

Writings by Vattel

Vattel, E., *Defense du système leibnitien* (Leiden, 1741).

The Law of Nations, ed. B. Kapossy and R. Whatmore (Indianapolis, v2008).

Questions de droit naturel, et observations sur le traité du droit de nature par le Baron de Wolf (Bern, 1762).

Selected Secondary Literature

Haakonssen, K., 'Christian Wolff (1679–1754)', in B. Fassbender and A. Peters (eds.), *The Oxford Handbook of the History of International Law* (Oxford, 2012), 1106–1109.

Holland, B., *The Moral Person of the State: Pufendorf, Sovereignty and Composite Polities* (Cambridge, 2017).

Ieva, F., '"A poor imitation of Grotius and Pufendorf" biographical uncertainties and the laborious genesis of Vattel's *droit des gens*', in K. Stapelbroek and A. Trampus (eds.), *The Legacy of Vattel's* Droit des gens (Cham, 2019), 53–76.

Jouannet, E., 'Emer de Vattel (1714–1767)', in B. Fassbender and A. Peters (eds.), *The Oxford Handbook of the History of International Law* (Oxford, 2012), 1118–1121.

Kleinlein, T., 'Christian Wolff: System as an episode?', in S. Kadelbach, T. Kleinlein and D. Roth-Isigkeit (eds.), *System, Order, and International Law: The Early History of International Legal Thought from Machiavelli to Hegel* (Oxford, 2017), 216–239.

Onuf, N. G., 'Civitas Maxima: Wolff, Vattel and the fate of republicanism', *American Journal of International Law* 88 (1994), 280–303.

Piirimäe, P., 'Men, monsters and the history of mankind in Vattel's *Law of Nations*', in S. Zurbuchen (ed.), *The Law of Nations and Natural Law 1625–1800* (Leiden, 2019), 159–185.

Zurbuchen, S., 'Emer de Vattel on the society of nations and the political system of Europe', in S. Kadelbach, T. Kleinlein and D. Roth-Isigkeit (eds.), *System, Order, and International Law: The Early History of International Legal Thought from Machiavelli to Hegel* (Oxford, 2017), 263–282.

4

Vattel and the Abbé de Choisy

French Historiography, Piety, and Law of Nations

FRANCESCA IURLARO

VATTEL'S *DROIT DES GENS*: A NEW HISTORIOGRAPHICAL GENRE FOR THE LAW OF NATIONS

In his *Law of Nations*, Emer de Vattel not only recurs to common examples of *pietas* and *clementia* drawn from Roman history, but also refers to more contemporary historical events to frame his vision of the international legal order. Literary exemplarity was a fundamental value for authors like Alberico Gentili and Hugo Grotius, who used classical history as a powerful rhetorical arsenal of arguments to construct customary rules of the law of nations. Such rules were often legal idealisations of the values, myths and virtues of the classical past. Against this traditional framework, Vattel seems no longer under the ideological spell of classical history. Instead, he claims that, in the study of the law of nations, modern historiography should be preferred over ancient literary history. Vattel not only claims that Grotius already gave us plenty of information about the past and that it is time to move on to more contemporary and urgent questions; but also warns that indulgence in antiquarian arguments produces a mere 'parade of erudition' that alienates readers (*LN*, preface 19–20).[1]

Thus, Vattel's innovative methodological stance is motivated not only by the stylistic urge to make his work more palatable to his audience, but also by the need to find a new method for what he refers to as the 'arbitrary law of nations', the positive law based on the will of nations, rather than on natural

[1] On innovative forms of history writing and their relation with the method of the law of nations, see the recent P. Piirimäe, 'Official historiography and the state in early modern Europe', *Storia della storiografia* 71.1 (2017), 47.

law principles.[2] Customs and treaties play a fundamental role in Vattel's positive law of nations.[3] Vattel relies on different historical sources to construct genealogies of power and to find alternative ways to mediate between natural law principles and the factuality of European *droit public*. While acknowledging that sovereign equality rests upon natural law, Vattel suggests that the realm of customary practices is a realm of distinction, where the various degrees and modes of expression of sovereign power are at full display. Ceremonials, customs and rites do not only serve the construction of a shared European political discourse, but also provide sovereigns with a useful strategic means to demolish the authority of their adversaries, or demand equal standing with them in the international arena.

From a doctrinal point of view, Vattel envisages the existence of 'universal customs' that are directly derived from the 'natural law of nations' and that are more cogent and universally applicable than 'particular ones'. Whereas the first are applicable to humankind as a whole, for the universality of the principles they enshrine, respect of the latter is restricted to culturally homogeneous environments (i.e. Europe) and, as such, is subject to contestation. 'Particular customs' are, thus, geographically or temporally limited and capable of being surpassed by better, more perfect new regulations – Vattel calls such customs 'indifferent' as far as their normative content is concerned (*LN*, prelim. 26).[4] Although they are not based on principles of natural law, their usage is well established 'between those of a certain continent, as of Europe, for example, or between those who have a more frequent intercourse with each other' (*LN*, prelim. 26). Vattel observes:

> ... with regard to things of institution and custom, that, when a practice is so established, as to impart, according to the usages and manners of the age, a real value and a settled signification to things which are in their own nature indifferent, the natural and necessary law of nations requires that we should pay deference to such institution, and act, with respect to such things in the

2 On Vattel's doctrine of the law of nations, see P. P. Remec, *The Position of the Individual in International Law according to Grotius and Vattel* (The Hague, 1960); E. Jouannet, *Emer de Vattel et l'émergence doctrinal du droit international classique* (Paris, 1998); P. Haggenmacher, 'Introduction: Le modèle de Vattel et la discipline du droit international', in Vincent Chetail and Peter Haggenmacher (eds.), *Vattel's International Law from a XXIst Century Perspective / Le Droit International de Vattel vu du XXIe Siècle* (Leiden, 2011), 1–48; S. Zurbuchen, 'Emer de Vattel on the Society of Nations and the Political System of Europe', in S. Kadelbach, T. Kleinlein and D. Roth-Isigkeit (eds), *System, Order and International Law: the Early History of International Thought from Machiavelli to Hegel* (Oxford, 2017), 263–382.

3 I have treated the matter in F. Iurlaro, 'Vattel's doctrine of the customary law of nations between sovereign interests and the principles of natural law', in S. Zurbuchen (ed.), *The Law of Nations and Natural Law 1625–1850* (Leiden, 2019), 278–303.

4 This does not mean, however, that they can violate natural law.

> same manner *as if* they really possessed all that value which the opinion of mankind has annexed to them. (*LN*, IV-VI-79; emphasis added)

History is essential in ascertaining the value and opinion that 'mankind has annexed' to a given custom. Examples from the past help the jurist tracing back a customary rule's first occurrence and unchallenged observance over time; or, conversely, they offer useful arguments to rule in favour of the potential desuetude of certain customary practices.

In this chapter, I will first argue that Vattel's reading of a specific French historian and memorialist – the French crossdresser and missionary *abbé* François-Timoléon de Choisy (1644–1724) – provides us with an interesting example of how Vattel treats the relationship between universal and particular customs. Reflecting on Vattel's historical method and citation practices is particularly revealing not only of the specific aspects of his doctrine of *jus gentium*, but also, more in general, of the politics behind the structure and the ideological orientation of his arguments. Second, and consequently, I will claim that Vattel's reading of Choisy might help us cast new light on the notion of piety, which has a fundamental importance in the Swiss jurist's theory of state. By piety, Vattel means 'a disposition of soul that leads us to direct all our actions towards the Deity, and to endeavor to please him in everything we do. To the practice of this virtue all mankind are indispensably obliged' (*LN*, I-XV-125). Piety should, however, be pursued with knowledge and awareness. Zealous fanaticism, on the contrary, should be avoided altogether (*LN*, I-XV-126). As I will show, the virtue of piety provides Vattel with a fundamental normative criterion to discern the quality of customs under the law of nations. In its healthy form, piety provides a rationale for universally applicable customs; in its devious, more fanatic manifestations, it leads to an unjust interference of religion in matters of state, as Vattel's polemical mention of the French missions in Canada points out (*LN*, IV-II-60). Customs based on the undue, surpassed and dangerous interference of the Church into state affairs should be abandoned.

French Historiography, Mémoires *and Propaganda: The Power of History*

François-Timoléon de Choisy is an extremely fascinating historical figure. Gambler, crossdresser, famous historian, memorialist, missionary and strenuous defender of Christianity,[5] he has deserved much attention by

[5] See A. Monod, *De Pascal à Chateaubriand: les défenseurs du christianisme de 1670 à 1802* (Paris, 1916); J. Y Vialleton, 'La nouvelle diffamatoire dans la France de l'âge classique: le cas

contemporary scholarship.[6] Born in Paris in 1644, Choisy was from his early years very well acquainted with Louis XIV's courtly environment. His mother, being part of the circle of Anne of Austria,[7] introduced him both to court and to the art of crossdressing, which Choisy practiced until the age of eighteen. His literary and sentimental escapades as a crossdresser are the subject of his famous *Aventures de l'Abbé de Choisy habillé en femme*, published posthumously.[8]

In 1684, after a grave illness, Choisy decides to change his dissolute lifestyle and joins the *Société des Missions Étrangères de Paris*, a recently founded institution whose mission was the conversion to Roman Catholicism of infidels in China and South-East Asia. Choisy leaves as a missionary to Siam (Thailand) accompanying the ambassador Alexandre de Chaumont (a former Huguenot converted to Catholicism), in the attempt to convert Siamese people.[9] He becomes a priest in 1686 and publishes his experiences as a missionary in his *Journal du Voyage du Siam* (1687, 1688). After his return to France, he devotes himself to the writing of history and published four works on the kings of France (including *La Vie de Saint Louis*, 1689, and the *Histoire de Charles cinquième*, 1689, both quoted by Vattel) and a monumental, 11-volumes *Histoire d'Église* (1703–1723). By relying on what has been defined as 'textual transvestitism',[10] dabbling between practices of

particulier de La Vie de Monsieur l'abbé de Choisy', *Cahiers d'études italiennes* 10 (2010) 159–180, at 164.

6 Van der Cruysse has devoted many studies to Choisy, to which I refer for further bibliographical references: D. van der Cruysse, *L'Abbé de Choisy: androgyne et mandarin* (Paris, 2000); D. van der Cruysse, *De branche en branche: études sur le XVIIe et XVIIIe siècles français* (Louvain, 2005).

7 As he will later recall in his *Mémoires* on the history of Louis XIV, which he based on his personal memories and his mother's experiences at court: François-Timoléon de Choisy, *Mémoires à servir pour l'histoire de Louis XIV* (Utrecht, 1727).

8 Published later on in the nineteenth century and translated into English as *The Transvestite Memoirs: the Abbé de Choisy*, ed. R. H. F. Scott (London, 2008).

9 Van der Cruysse describes how the whole missionary project is based on a misunderstanding from Bénigne Vachet, a missionary from the Missions Étrangères. Vachet misinterprets Phra Naraï's attempt at tightening his diplomatic relations with France, as a means to seek protection against the Dutch's buoyant interventionism in the region, with his desire to convert to Catholicism. This, according to Van der Cruysse, bears witness to France's fundamental cultural ignorance of South-East Asia. D. Van der Cruysse, 'L'abbé de Choisy, historien du Siam et de l'Asie du Sud-Est', *Aséanie* 1 (1998), 107–122, at 108–110.

10 P. Schott, 'Authenticity and textual transvestitism in the memoirs of the Abbé de Choisy', *French Studies* 49.1 (2014), 14–29; J. Harris, 'Transvestite traditions and narrative discontinuities: d'Eon and the abbé de Choisy', in S. Burrows, J. Conlin, R. Goulbourne and V. Mainz (eds.), *The Chevalier d'Eon and His Worlds: Gender, Espionage, and Politics in the Eighteenth Century* (London, 2010), 177–186.

autobiographical re-invention, implausibility and entertainment, Choisy mixes the genre of *mémoir* with historiography. He thus replaces the general view that history should be something objective and impartial, with the irreducibility of personal experiences as the ultimate means to entertain the reader and lead him to believe the narrator regardless of historical authenticity. Choisy died in 1724.

In the eighteenth-century, French historiography was undergoing a general process of renovation.[11] Choisy comfortably navigated the fluidity of genres that would lead to such 'schizophrenic' consequences in later eighteenth-century developments of French historiography.[12] On the one hand, official national historiography generally presented an effort 'to ground the narrative in properly authenticated documents',[13] and, thus, to build the French nation with the language of official solemnity.[14] However, *grand histoires* like those of Gabriel Daniel, historiographer of France in 1713, and François Eudes de Mézeray's,[15] gradually lost their appeal in the mid-eighteenth century.[16] Jacob-Nicolas Moreau, appointed royal historiographer by Louis XV, seems to ride this wind of change: in his *Mémoire sur les fonctions d'un historiographe de France*, he urges the crown to assert its dominion over history (*maîtrise sur l'histoire*), or else, other political actors would succeed in dominating the realm of the past and acquire full control of historical narratives.[17] To protect and ensure the monarchy with the monopoly of sources, Moreau suggested creating a *Cabinet des Chartes* (1762) of which he became director, but ultimately failed to accomplish his mission.[18] Moreau was also the editor of the *Observateur Hollandois*, a periodical propaganda magazine published

[11] On the eighteenth-century development of the historical discipline and on the role of memorialists, see C. Grell, *Pratiques et Concepts de l'Histoire en Europe XVIème-XVIIIème siècles* (Paris, 1990).

[12] M. Fumaroli, 'Introduction', in M. Fumaroli and C. Grell (eds.), *Historiographie de la France et mémoire du royaume au XVIIIe siècle* (Paris, 2006), 9–22, at 20.

[13] L. Gossman, 'History as (auto)biography: A revolution in historiography', in M. Donaldson-Evans, L. Frappier-Mazur and G. Prince (eds.), *Autobiography, Historiography, Rhetoric: A Festschrift in Honor of Frank Paul Bowman* (Amsterdam, 1994), 103–129, at 103.

[14] P. Nora, *Les lieux des mémoire*, vol. III (Paris, 1997); D. A. Bell, *The Cult of the Nation in France: Inventing Nationalism, 1680–1800* (Cambridge, MA, 2001).

[15] The first volume of his *Histoire de France* appeared in 1643 (see footnote 47).

[16] C. Grell, 'Au fil du siècle: histoire et mémoire du passé national dans la France des Lumières', in M. Fumaroli and C. Grell (eds.), *Historiographie de la France et mémoire du royaume au XVIIIe siècle* (Paris, 2006), 23–68, at 23.

[17] Grell, 'Au fil du siècle', 51; see also K. M. Baker, *Inventing the French Revolution: Essays on French Political Culture in the Eighteenth Century* (Cambridge, 1990), at 59–85.

[18] Moreau collects such archival materials with the purpose of centralising them to 'aider la legislation, épurer l'histoire, conserver les principes essentiels de la monarchie'. Grell, 'Au fil du siècle', 52–53.

from 1755 to raise support for French colonial expansion in North America during the Seven Years' War.[19]

Historical knowledge was a powerful way for kings to assert political dominance, but also, if well disseminated, a successful means of propaganda. To inform and engage with a wider public, it was necessary to master a new style of history writing and to go beyond the dryness of academic historiography, while maintaining a balance between presenting archival data and a writing according to a more popular literary taste. While the genre of war memoir was a well-established literary tradition already in the Renaissance,[20] *mémoires* were the new eighteenth-century literary fashion in France.[21] Although it is hard to provide a single definition of the genre, it has been argued that *mémoires* (especially in the plural, as opposed to the singular *mémoire*) were conceived of as 'memoranda', rather than as proper journal or autobiographic reports: the incredible amount of texts typically titled '*Mémoires pour servir à l'histoire de …*' are often notes on historical subjects, that might serve as a starting point for further, more systematic elaboration of the topic.[22] Nonetheless, this poses the question of the relationship between *mémoires* and history, authenticity and objectivity – an ambiguity first acknowledged and exploited by Choisy himself. If *mémoires* are rarely autobiographical but, rather, are more likely to offer a reinvention of past events, their imaginative power can very well be used to voice the author's own political and personal agenda.

19 K. Stapelbroek, 'The foundations of Vattel's system of politics and the context of the seven years' war: Moral philosophy, luxury, and the constitutional commercial state', in K. Stapelbroek and A. Trampus (eds.), *The Legacy of Vattel's* Droit des gens: *Contexts, Concepts, Reception, Translation and Diffusion* (Cham, 2019), 95–133, at 96. See also Chapter 5 by Koen Stapelbroek.

20 Y. N. Harari, *Renaissance Military Memoirs: War, History and Identity* (Woodbridge, 2004), at 187 ff; see also Y. N. Harari, 'Military memoirs: A historical overview of the genre from the middle ages to the late modern era', *War in History* 14.3 (2007), 289–309.

21 Pierre Girault de Coursac and Pierrette Girault de Coursac (eds.), *Histoire, Historiens et Mémorialistes* (Paris, 1997); M. Bertaud and F. X. Cuche (eds), *Le Genre des mémoires: essai de definition* (Paris, 1995); A. Niderst (ed.), *Les Français vus par eux-mêmes. Le siècle de Louis XIV, une anthologie des mémorialistes du siècle de Louis XIV* (Paris, 1997); A. de Maurepas and F. Bayard (eds.), Les Français vus par eux-mêmes. Le xviiie siècle, anthologie des mémorialistes du xviiie siècle (Paris, 1999); F. Briot, *Usage du monde, usage de soi. Enquête sur les mémorialistes d'Ancien Régime* (Paris, 1994); F. Charbonneau, *Les Silences de l'Histoire. Les mémoires français du XVII siècle* (Paris, 2016); N. Hepp (ed.), *La Cour au miroir des mémorialistes, 1530–1682* (Paris, 1991).

22 J. Mesnard, 'Conclusion: Les Mémoires comme genre', in M. Bertaud and F. X. Cuche (eds.), *Le Genre des mémoires: essai de definition* (Paris, 1995), 361–372, at 364; M. Fumaroli, 'Introduction', in M. Fumaroli and C. Grell (eds.), *Historiographie de la France et mémoire du royaume au XVIIIe siècle* (Paris, 2006), 9–22, at 16.

Whereas Choisy's *mémoires* are not quoted in Vattel's *Law of Nations*, various *mémoires* have been attributed to Vattel, although their paternity is extremely contested by scholars.[23] The story of such texts is deeply entangled not only with the story of the circulation of Vattel's editions,[24] but also with the particular historical context of the Seven Years' War and the conflict between Britain's commercial power and French hegemonic pretenses. In a recent contribution, while questioning Vattel's alleged anglophilia, Stapelbroek has argued that between the Peace of Utrecht and the Seven Years' War, France was perceived as a threat by Britain not because it was a bellicose nation, but because it was 'a formidable peaceful economic competitor'.[25] According to Moreau, engaged, as we know well, in the construction of French patriotism through the language of historical propaganda, 'the reason why Britain had managed to win the last wars was not a presumed constitutional supremacy, but the outcome of the Peace of Utrecht, which had created a false balance of power'.[26] It has been suggested that Moreau's journal *Observateur Hollandais* might have played an active role in publishing these *Mémoires*: in 1758, the *Observateur* announced the periodical publication of *Mémoires politiques concernant la guerre, ou principes de la loi naturelle appliques à la conduit et aux affaires des nations et des souverains, par Mr. de V.*, containing a reproduction Book III and IV of Vattel's *Law of Nations*.[27] While an analysis of these *mémoires* would fall beyond the scope of this contribution, it is worth noting that, in line with the historiographic tendencies I have outlined, they seek to achieve the purpose of systematically treating questions of war and politics while pleasing the reader with a more 'refreshing' style.[28] The editor argues in the *Avertissement* that Vattel's novelty precisely relies in this stylistic innovation, accompanied by Vattel's substantial reliance on modern history. For this reason, his work succeeds better than those of Vattel's predecessors

[23] C. Good, *Emer de Vattel (1714–1767): Naturrechtliche Ansätze einer Menschenrechtsidee und des humanitären Völkerrechts im Zeitalter der Aufklärung* (Baden-Baden, 2011); E. Fiocchi Malaspina, *L'eterno ritorno del* Droit des Gens *di Emer de Vattel, secc. XVIII-XIX* (Frankfurt, 2017), at 44–45; Stapelbroek, 'The foundations of Vattel's system', 122–123; Jouannet, *Emer de Vattel*, 430–431.

[24] Fiocchi Malaspina, *L'eterno ritorno*, 44–45.

[25] Stapelbroek, 'The foundation of Vattel's system', 100; see also, on Vattel's alleged "anglophilia", R. Whatmore, *Against War and Empire: Geneva, Britain and France in the Eighteenth Century* (New Haven, 2012), 103–118.

[26] Stapelbroek, 'The foundation of Vattel's system', 119–120.

[27] *Mémoires politiques concernant la guerre, ou principes de la loi naturelle appliques à la conduit et aux affaires des nations et des souverains, par* Mr. *de* V., a Francfort et Leipsig aux Depens de la Compagnie, 1758, at 2.

[28] *Avertissement*, in *Mémoires politiques*.

(Grotius) in providing a key to the interpretation of 'present events'.[29] While the inclusion of Vattelian books into such *mémoires* might have contributed to the further popularisation of his works, it is interesting to note, once again, that Vattel's original use of history was perceived as a successful means to address urgent contemporary questions.

VATTEL READING CHOISY: THE *LIFE OF ST. LOUIS* AND THE *HISTORY OF CHARLES V*

While references to contemporary politics are indeed abundant in the *Law of Nations*, Vattel also relies on two of Choisy's works dedicated to the Middle Age: the *Vie de Saint Louis*,[30] on the French canonised king, leader of the Seventh Crusade, Louis IX (1214–1270), and the *Histoire de Charles Cinquième*.[31] If Louis IX was remembered for his sanctity, the fame of King Charles V (1338–1380) was traditionally associated to his wisdom and to his military success in the Hundred Years' War. As it often happened with Choisy, both works perfectly represented his tendency to talk about himself, rather than about the Middle Ages.[32] From a more general perspective, however, it could be argued that the increasing eighteenth-century interest into medieval genealogies (a phenomenon referred to in the scholarship as *médiévisme*) responded, on the one hand, to the urge to celebrate France's glorious past; on the other, to contribute to the political aggrandisement of the present.[33] Against potential accusations of impartiality, however, Choisy defends himself by clarifying that he is not claiming for himself the role of royal historiographer ('on ne se méfie point de moi; je n'ai point abordé l'étendard d'Historien du Roi').[34].

In the *Vie de Saint Louis*, Choisy adds that he has no interest in writing a political history of Louis IX's kingdom, nor into crafting the latest hagiographic portrait of the canonised king. Rather, Choisy is interested in portraying his personal life, so as to let him emerge as the 'truly Christian hero' he

[29] *Mémoires politiques*, at 3.

[30] *Vie de Saint Louis, par Mr. l'Abbè de Choisy*, Paris, Chez Claude Barbin, 1689.

[31] *Histoire de Charles cinquième, Roi de France, Par Mr. l'Abbè de Choisy*, Paris, Chez Antoine Dezallier, 1689.

[32] D. Van der Cruysse, 'Choisy historien de Louis XIV, du Moyen Âge, de l'église et de lui-même', in *De branche en branche: études sur le XVIIe et XVIIIe siècles français* (Louvain, 2005), 195–213, at 206.

[33] Van der Cruysse, *L'Abbé de Choisy: Androgyne et Mandarin*, chapter XIV.

[34] Van der Cruysse, 'Choisy historien', 205.

was.[35] However, Choisy writes that he will not neglect his military deeds, provided they are well described – again, the eighteenth-century obsession for a pleasant literary style emerges. While celebrating Louis IX's piety and missionary zeal,[36] Choisy lavishes in the ritual praises of Louis XIV, to whom the dedicatory epistle is addressed. In his view, Louis XIV, by combining the glory of arms with his constant *bonheur*, has surpassed Saint Louis himself in the practice of the Christian virtues of justice and piety. A dedication in the same vein precedes Choisy's *Histoire de Charles cinquième*, published 11 months after the *Vie de Saint Louis*: the author explains that, although this great prince ('the wisest of all your predecessors') was being attacked from all sides, he nonetheless managed to vanquish all his enemies. 'We hope, Sir', Choisy wishes, 'that, after you have surpassed his virtue, you also exceed him in the good fortune of your victories'.[37]

In his *Law of Nations*, Vattel quotes an excerpt from Choisy's *Vie de Saint Louis* precisely as a paradigmatic example of such virtues, in the context of a discussion of the independence and inviolability of ambassadors. While being based on the 'natural and necessary principles of the law of nations', such inviolability is 'farther confirmed by the uniform practice and general consent of mankind' (*LN*, IV-VII-103). By quoting a number of instances of non-European nations respecting the inviolability of ambassadors (Chinese, Mexicans, North-American tribes and Arabs), Vattel seeks to prove the general acceptance of this customary rule by insisting on the cultural value that various and diverse nations have annexed to it (*LN*, IV-VII-103). However, Vattel points out that 'it would be quite unnecessary, in this place, to accumulate the various examples with which the history of the European nations presents us: the enumeration would be endless; and the established customs of Europe on this subject are sufficiently known' (*LN*, IV-VII-103). Against the proliferation of examples, Vattel only quotes one 'remarkable instance of the protection due to public ministers': Louis IX's treatment of the ambassador of Old Man of the Mountain, or the prince of Assassins, who spoke insolently to the French monarch:

[35] *Vie de Saint Louis*, 2.

[36] Van der Cruysse, 'Choisy historien', 203. This also celebratory intent reflects Choisy's interest in contemporary politics: 'car la guerre de la Ligue d'Augsburg, qui oppose la France à toute l'Europe, vient de commencer. Malgré la politique d'agression de Louis XIV, Choisy ne doute pas de ses intentions pacifiques'.

[37] 'Ce grand prince, le plus sage de vos prédécesseurs, se vit seul attaqué de tous côtés. ... Il vainquit tous ses ennemis et nous espérons, Sire, qu'après l'avoir surpassé dans la vertu, vous le surpasserez encore dans le Bonheur de ses victoires'. 'Epitre au Roi', in *Histoire de Charles cinquième*.

> ... The grand masters of the orders of the Temple and the Hospital informed that minister, that, 'were it not for the respect paid to the character with which he was invested, they would cause him to be thrown into the sea'. The King however dismissed him without suffering the slightest injury to be done him. Nevertheless, as the prince of the Assassins was on his own part guilty of grossly violating the most sacred rights of nations, it would have been reasonable to suppose that his ambassador had no claim to protection, except indeed on this single consideration, that, as the privilege of inviolability is founded on the necessity of keeping open a safe channel of communication, through which sovereigns may reciprocally make proposals to each other, and carry on negotiations both in peace and in war, the protection should therefore extend even to the envoys of those princes, who, guilty themselves of violating the law of nations, would otherwise have no title to our respect. (*LN*, IV-vii-103)

This example of Saint Louis' piety shows that it is better to leave an ambassador unpunished, even when caught in flagrant violation of the law of nations, than to violate his immunity: it is better to overlook such instances of violation, than to put at risk the necessity of nations to communicate with each other and to carry on negotiations.

This anecdote from *Saint Louis* portrays the King's sanctity consistent with Choisy's intent to describe him as a 'truly Christian hero'. The same event, briefly quoted by Vattel, is treated profusely by Choisy in book four of the *Vie*, which deals with Saint Louis' mission to Palestine (1250–1254).[38] The ambassador's 'act of insolence' consisted in the fact that he dared to ask the King whether he knew the Old Man of the Mountain; to which Louis replied, 'coldly', that he did.[39] 'Sir, continued the Ambassador, since you have heard of Monsigneur, how come you have not sent gifts to him?'[40] The ambassador suggests that this amicable gesture was a practice successfully observed by other sovereigns (the Emperor of Germany, the King of Hungary and the Sultan of Egypt). Sending gifts was their only chance at having their lives spared by the ferocious Old Man of the Mountain. Choisy continues the anecdote by writing that the French King listened to the envoy 'impassibly' and told him to come back in the evening for his response. When the ambassador comes back, the Grand Master of the Temple and that of the Hospital urged him to come back on the next day.[41] Choisy reports that

[38] Choisy, in turn, relies on Louis IX's biographer, Jean de Joinville (1224–1317).

[39] *Vie de Saint Louis*, Livre Quatrième, 2.

[40] Ibid.

[41] Ibid., 3.

the ambassador of the Assassins 'was not accustomed to these manners', but that he was even more shocked when the Grand Masters told him that his was not an acceptable way to address the King of France and that, as also quoted in Vattel's passage, if it was not for the respect due to his role, 'they would have thrown him into the sea'.[42] Choisy writes that the moral height shown by Louis in this situation (arguably, the outcome of a divine intervention) produced a very good effect, with the ambassador returning the day after bearing gifts from the Old from the Mountain. The latter 'was terrified by a Prince that had so little fear of himself'.[43] In turn, the French King was moved by the 'secret joy' of having forced a barbarian into humiliating himself. After this event, Louis became 'even more sweet and human, and even further he thought about correcting his flaws'.[44]

In the example from the *Vie de Saint Louis*, a far away, romanticised middle age (with a taste for orientalism)[45] is evoked by Vattel to conjure up ideals of piety that could help inspire observance of such a universal custom. Additionally, the medieval example shows that the customary rule concerning the inviolability of ambassadors dates back to the very early stages of European history. Choisy seems to be evoked by Vattel in the attempt both to construct a linear historical narrative and as a paradigmatic example of the inherent *pieté* of the law of embassy. However, Vattel, differently from Choisy, also uses this anecdote as proof of the fact that Arabs *do* respect that custom. As a matter of fact, Vattel much less profusely insists on the Assassins' inferiority than Choisy's text does.

Indeed, this example also shows that there are certain formalities attached to the respect of the law of embassy that can be exploited to assert political superiority. The Assassins do respect the law, as shown by the fact that they are sending one of their, however insolent, envoys before Louis IX: nonetheless, they are 'unaccustomed' to European ceremonials and, for Louis IX, this suffices to mark the diplomatic territory with the aura of his divine superiority. An interesting counter-example in this respect, among other sources quoted,[46]

[42] Ibid.

[43] Ibid.

[44] '. . . encore plus doux et plus humain, et songea encore davantage à se corriger de ses deffauts'. *Vie de saint Louis*, Livre Quatrième, 4.

[45] See E. Said, *Orientalism* (London, 1977), at 216, mentioning Vattel's lack of colonial awareness; D. Van der Cruysse and M. Smithies (eds.), *Siam and the West: 1500–1700* (Chiang Mai, 2002); D. F. Lach and E. J. van Kley (eds.), *Asia in the Making of Europe*, vol. 3 (Chicago, 1998), pp. 1185 ff. On the question of evangelisation, see J. van Eijnatten, 'Getting the message: Towards a cultural history of the sermon', in J. van Eijnatten (ed.), *Preaching, Sermon and Cultural Change in the Long Eighteenth Century* (Leiden, 2009), 343–388, at 368.

[46] Together with the omnipresent reference to Abraham de Wicquefort's *L'ambassadeur et ses fonctions* (1681), Vattel quotes authors of sixteenth century war memoirs to provide evidence of

is taken from Mézeray's *Histoire de France*.[47] The protagonist of the example in question is the already quoted French King Charles V. If the law of embassy is an unalienable right under the law of nations, diplomatic formalities and ceremonials can become as malleable as to dampen the opponent's desires of superiority:

> Some people would have us to look upon the precedency of the emperor as something more than the first place among equals: they would fain attribute to him a superiority over all kings, and in a word make him the temporal head of Christendom. And it in fact appears, that many emperors entertained ideas of such pretensions, – as if, by reviving the name of the Roman empire, they could also revive its rights. Other states have been on their guard against these pretensions. We may see in Mézeray the precautions taken by King Charles V when the emperor Charles IV. visited France, 'for fear,' says the historian, 'lest that prince, and his son the King of the Romans, should found any right of superiority on his courtesy. (*LN*, II-III-40)[48]

Such precautions are described, as mentioned by Vattel in his footnotes to this passage, by Mézeray. In his *Histoire de France*, in a section devoted to the explanation of medals portraying Charles V, Mézeray explains that Emperors were accustomed, in Germany, to make their entrance on white horses. Charles V, during Charles IV of Luxembourg's visit to Paris, to convey the message that he was not inferior to the Emperor, sent him two black ones, one for him and one for his son. The medal's inscription reads 'by order of their prince, the citizens gladly appear before Charles, emperor of the West' and confirms the subjects' devotion to the commands of the King, rather than to those of the Emperor.[49] However, whether these 'precautions' might be useful in taming imperial pretensions, they might also result in the unjust

the immunity of public ministers in different historical and geographic contexts. Such works include memoirs from Duc de Nevers, Martin du Bellay, Duc de Sully and Philip de Commines. The only more contemporary memoire quoted by Vattel is Antoine de Pas, *Mémoires de M. le Marquis de Feuquiere, Lieutenant General des Armées du Roi, Contenans ses Maximes sur la Guerre, et l'application des examples aux Maximes*, Nouvelle ed., Tome Premier (London, Chez Pierre Dunoyer, 1736).

47 F. E. de Mézeray, *Histoire de France depuis Faramond just'au Regne de Louis le Juste*, Tome Seconde (Paris, Chez Denys Thierry, Jean Guignard, et Claude Barbin, 1685).

48 Mézeray, *Histoire de France*, 502: 'crainte que ce Prince et son fils le Roi des Romains ne pussent foner quelque droit de supériorité sur sa courtoisie'.

49 The image on the medal at 501 portrays three men on two horses entering the city of Paris. On this specific event, see J. Fantysová-Mateková, 'The holy Roman emperor in the toils of the French protocol: The visit of Charles IV to France', *Imago Temporis. Medium Aevum* 6 (2012), 223–248.

humiliation of smaller republics.[50] As an instance of this, Vattel mentions that the usage of receiving an ambassador wearing a hat, for instance, is a sign of deference due to his *persona* as a representative of the sovereign. To make this point, Vattel mentions that, in 1663, ambassadors from Switzerland 'suffered the King of France, and the nobles of his court, to refuse them those honours which custom has rendered essential to the ambassadors of sovereigns, and particularly that of being covered before the King at their audience' (*LN*, IV-VI-78). Later on, Vattel reports that when Louis XV visited Alsace in 1755, the Swiss sent no ambassadors precisely because their 'just demand' had been rejected. According to Brandli, these concerns of Vattel correspond to the reality of French diplomatic practices in Geneva. While acknowledging that sovereign equality rests upon natural law, Vattel suggests that the realm of customary practices is a realm of distinction, where the various degrees and modes of expression of sovereign power are at full display. In other words, Vattel seeks to strike a balance between the formal legal equality of sovereigns and the 'historical validation' provided by 'ceremonial distinctions'. The mere fact that they exist as historical facts makes it impossible to ignore their real, shared value in the European diplomatic discourse.[51] Learning the technicalities of such discourse, by respecting and demanding honours accordingly, helps nations neutralise their differences through the language of reciprocity and the ritualised execution of gestures that showcase their formal equivalence.[52]

Vattel refers again to Charles V in his *Law of Nations*. Vattel quotes two examples from Choisy's *Histoire de Charles V*: the first, that a prince cannot alienate the property of the crown (*LN*, IV-II-11).[53] The second example, much more interesting to our purposes, concerns Vattel's condemnation of

[50] P. Brandli, *Le nain et le géant. La Républic de Genève et la France au XVIIIème siècle* (Rennes, 2019).

[51] 'Vattel concilie l'égalité juridique des nations avec la validation historique des usages de la distinction cérémonielle qui oblige à les considérer comme dotés d'une «valeur réelle», certes subordonnés aux impératifs du droit naturel des gens, mais que ce dernier ne peut toutefois pas ignorer'. Brandli, *Le nain et le géant*, 157.

[52] Brandli, *Le nain et le géant*, 162.

[53] The event recalled by Vattel here concerns succession to the throne of Naples. Jane I of Naples was excommunicated by the Roman Pope Urban for her support to the Avignon pope Clemens VII. Persecuted by one Pope, 'Jane implores the assistance of the other', and adopts the Duke of Anjou, brother of Charles V and a valid military combatant, to protect herself against the enemies. The official act of adoption was signed in 1380 and was later confirmed by Clemens VII: 'et voila le fondement du droit que les Princes de la second maison d'Anjou ont eu au Royaume de Naples, et que nos Rois y ont encore selon les Loix fondamentales de l'Etat, qui les empêchent d'y renoncer au prejudice de leurs Successeurs par aucun Traité, ni libre, ni forcé'. de Choisy, *Histoire de Charles cinquième*, 445–446.

Charles V's support to what we have referred to as a 'particular custom': that of swearing oaths upon the signing of treaties – a practice, according to Vattel, introduced by the Pope to assume the right to himself to eventually exempt parties from respect of the treaty. In order to argue that such custom should now be considered an abuse (*LN*, II-xv-223–225), Vattel claims that oaths add nothing to the nature of the obligations, which are valid per se; at the same time, he also uses Choisy's passage to assert that religious piety should never overstep the boundaries of the welfare and safety of the State:

> Who does not see, that these daring acts of the popes, which were formerly very frequent, were violations of the law of nations, and directly tended to destroy all the bands that could unite mankind, and to sap the foundations of their tranquillity, or to render the pope sole arbiter of their affairs? But who can restrain his indignation at seeing this strange abuse authorized by princes themselves? In the treaty concluded at Vincennes, between Charles V. King of France, and Robert Stuart King of Scotland, in 1371, it was agreed, that the pope should absolve the Scots from all the oaths they had taken in swearing to a truce with the English, and that he should promise never to absolve the French or Scots from the oaths they were about to make in swearing to the new treaty. The custom, generally received in former times, of swearing to the observance of treaties, had furnished the popes with a pretext for claiming the power of breaking them, by absolving the contracting parties from their oaths. But in the present day, even children know that an oath does not constitute the obligation to keep a promise or a treaty: it only gives an additional strength to that obligation, by calling God to bear witness. A man of sense, a man of honour, does not think himself less bound by his word alone, by his faith once pledged, than if he had added the sanction of an oath. Cicero would not have us to make much difference between a perjurer and a liar. 'The habit of lying (says that great man) paves the way to perjury'. (*LN*, II-xv-223–225)

The French–Scottish treaty is also mentioned by Choisy in his *Histoire*, although with a completely different tone. Choisy reports that when the deputy of the King of Scotland signed and swore on the treaty, 'the French King took this as a great manifestation of his loyalty'. However, Choisy makes clear, such fidelity had an historical precedent: during the Crusade, Saint Louis used four Scottish men as his own personal guards. The reliability of Scots 'had already been proven under eight French kings and Charles V himself was about to create a company of one hundred [Scottish] guards'.[54] Quite understandably from his position, Choisy not only does not question the

[54] de Choisy, *Histoire de Charles cinquième*, 257.

Pope's authority, but also grounds the political validity of oaths on the amicable relations between France and Scotland – and, again, on the rhetorical weight of his genealogical reference to Saint Louis.[55] Vattel suggests, instead, that guarantees are a better legal device to ensure that treaties are respected. Violating treaties already in itself amounts to a violation of the law of nations and all nations have an interest to respect the faith of treaties (*LN*, II-XV-222). By condemning the Pope's criticism towards the Treaty of Westphalia, Vattel attacks his failure to grasp that it was 'a treaty in which all Europe was interested' (*LN*, II-XV-223).[56] While the Pope clearly has his own agenda, Vattel shows no toleration for princes authorising this 'strange abuse' (*LN*, II-XV-224).

This criticism is also reflected in Vattel's concern towards missionary practices, as shown by other passages in the *Law of Nations*, especially those conducted by the French missionaries in North America (*LN*, I-XII-140). Instead, Vattel suggests that there should be better regulations overseeing the conduct of such missions. It is precisely the duty of sovereigns to take care that no disturbing element from religion disrupts the 'welfare and safety' of their society (*LN*, I-XII-139). Against the French missionary zeal in New France (Canada), Vattel argues that the missionaries were the principal cause of the ruin of the indigenous population of Huron. The 'wild reveries, seraphic devotions, and sublime speculations' of faith introduce various elements of disruption into society: first, they weaken populations and diminish their interest into 'business and honest labour' (*LN*, I-XII-140). Second, Vattel argues that a society of saints, where both sexes are devoted to the practice of chastity, would be against the 'designs of their creator', and would not 'survive the first generation' (*LN*, I-XII-140).[57]

CONCLUSION

In invoking Choisy's works on French medieval history, Vattel succeeds in tracing narratives of historical linearity, whenever he needs to show that a given custom deserves universal respect or, rather, in articulating narratives of disruption, by comparing an idealised past of abuses with the customs and aspirations of a more just and secularised present. However, when compared

[55] He also quotes Ms. 8354 of the *Bibliothéque Royale* as a source.

[56] Vattel refers here to the papal bull *Zelo Domus Dei* (1648).

[57] By using a similar argument, Vattel justifies the rape of the Sabine Women by the Romans as an act of just war, as a nation cannot preserve and perpetuate itself except for propagation (*LN*, II-IX-122). A 'nation of women, if it even existed, put itself, by its own fault, out of a condition to support itself without foreign assistance'.

to Choisy's religious *esprit*, and his pompous celebration of Saint Louis IX's sanctity, Vattel's reference to piety as the ultimate foundation of the law of nations amounts more to a void invocation to the good manners of civilisation than to an invitation to export faith. That is, indeed, where Vattel draws the line between custom and abuse. Interestingly, Vattel never quotes Choisy's *Journal to Siam*.

As it has been shown, medieval histories are perceived, by both Choisy and Vattel, as genealogies of power: ceremonials, customs and rites do not only serve the construction of political authority, but also provide sovereigns with a useful strategic means to demolish that of the adversaries – a practice that can backfire in the present, as showed by Vattel's example of Switzerland being denied respect of diplomatic rituals from France. For this reason, learning the specifics of diplomatic discourse, respecting and demanding honours accordingly, helps nations neutralise their mutual differences through the language of reciprocity and the ritualised execution of gestures that showcase their formal equivalence. This ties in with Vattel's urge to consider Europe's historical configuration as a 'fact' that, in the attempt to build a balance of power, should be part of the equation as much as political and commercial considerations. Indeed, the latter are nothing but social structures resulting from historical processes, which is imperative to reconstruct up until to their present developments. To a certain extent, however, Vattel's original historical method lacked the authoritativeness that was guaranteed, in Grotius, by ancient history. Such authoritativeness resided in that fact that classical history was sufficiently detached from the present to serve as a guide to manipulate it. Instead, by changing language of *jus gentium* from the *topoi* of ancient history to the vocabulary of contemporary history and politics, one could argue that Vattel unwillingly subjected himself and his works to political contestation and manipulation.[58]

To conclude with, Vattel's legal obsession with formalities goes hand in hand, from an argumentative point of view, with his appropriation of French literary and historiographic modes of expression. Further research on the literary quality of Vattel's writing style could provide more insights into his construction of a language of good manners, both literary and political. From Vattel's perspective, knowledge of the formalities of (French) diplomacy is as empowering as the mastery of a genuinely refreshing style of French writing.

[58] On Vattel's fear of the potential political manipulations of *LN*, see Chapter 5, by Koen Stapelbroek.

FURTHER READING

Chetail, V. and Haggenmacher, P. (eds.), Vattel's International Law from a XXIst Century Perspective / Le Droit International de Vattel vu du XXIe Siècle (Leiden, 2011).

Fumaroli M. and Grell, C. (eds.), *Historiographie de la France et mémoire du royaume au XVIIIe siècle* (Paris, 2006).

Jouannet, E., *Emer de Vattel et l'émergence doctrinal du droit international classique* (Paris, 1998).

Kalmanovitz, P., 'Sovereignty, pluralism, and regular war: Wolff and Vattel's Enlightenment critique of just war', *Political Theory* 45 (2017), 1–24.

Silvestrini, G., 'Justice, war and inequality. The unjust aggressor and the enemy of the human race in Vattel's theory of the law of nations', *Grotiana* 31 (2010), 44–68.

Toyoda, T., Theory and Politics of the Law of Nations: Political Bias in International Law Discourse of Seven German Court Councilors in the Seventeenth and Eighteenth Centuries (Leiden, 2011).

Van der Cruysse, D., L'Abbé de Choisy: androgyne et mandarin (Paris, 2000).

De branche en branche: études sur le XVIIe et XVIIIe siècles français (Louvain, 2005).

Zurbuchen, S., 'Vattel's Law of Nations and the principle of non-intervention', *Grotiana* 31 (2010), 69–84.

'Emer de Vattel on the society of nations and the political system of Europe', in S. Kadelbach, T. Kleinlein and D. Roth-Isigkeit (eds), *System, Order and International Law: The Early History of International Thought from Machiavelli to Hegel* (Oxford, 2017), 263–382.

5

Vattel and the Seven Years' War

KOEN STAPELBROEK

INTRODUCTION

Vattel's *Law of Nations* appeared in the midst of the Seven Years' War. Vattel's lasting fame was, however, not an instant effect of the initial reception of his main work as the *Law of Nations* spread throughout Europe on a much larger scale after its second enlarged edition was posthumously published in 1773. The context of the Seven Years' War is nonetheless important. To understand the *Law of Nations* and its enduring legacy and influence on international law, constitutionalism and political thought, its immediate reception as well as its proximity to the mechanisms of diplomacy, war and peace need to be taken into account. By assessing the *Law of Nations* in the context of the Seven Years' War and along with other sources of the time, Vattel's position towards contemporary French, Prussian and British politics can be reconstructed.

To speak of 'Vattel's position', however, is more complicated than might be expected. While Vattel became known in hindsight as a pro-British writer in relation to the eighteenth-century Franco–British political and economic rivalry, this was not how the *Law of Nations* was understood when it was first published. Vattel himself to begin with was extremely keen for his main work not to be interpreted or used as a pamphlet or text that was directly influenced by the polarised military politics of the Seven Years' War. Beyond its apparent contextual relevance to the military and diplomatic circumstances of the Seven Years' War, the *Law of Nations* masterly united political theory and philosophical conceptual innovation and reshaped the discourse of natural law in a manner that proved exemplary to later generations. Its stated aim, in the opening pages, to not primarily or exclusively address an academic audience but a wider public of educated functionaries, diplomats and other readers was reflected in the simple hierarchical structure and clear linguistic presentation of the text, simultaneously eschewing philosophical over-abstraction and indulgence in specific political and legal–diplomatic detail. In this way, the argument of the *Law of Nations* responded to a widely perceived urge to come to grips with the foundations of the eighteenth-century transformation of interstate political and economic relations.[1] That urge was also reflected in the immediate reception of the *Law of Nations*, which saw the book being appropriated by contemporary publishers, political writers and diplomats to serve a variety of political purposes. It is from the perspective of these appropriations that Vattel's own critiques of Frederick the Great, of British diplomacy and the various usages of the *Law of Nations* by political publishing campaigns can be aligned, so that the contours of Vattel's system of international law and political economy appear at the same time.

THE PUBLICATION OF THE *LAW OF NATIONS* AND ITS FIRST EDITIONS

For a text that was first published at the height of what in recent decades has been called the first actual World War, the *Law of Nations* is remarkably free from political and other judgements. The *Law of Nations* certainly was not a pamphlet. Yet, along with the relative absence of judgement, the book featured numerous specific examples and allusions to events in recent times. The meaning of these examples and, more generally, Vattel's relation to the context of the Seven Years' War has often eluded commentators in the past, but can in fact be squared with what we know about Vattel's authorial intentions and his concerns around the first publication of his main work.

When the *Law of Nations* was submitted for publication in France in late 1757, its political and religious character were assessed by the royal censor. Jean-Paul Tercier's advice characterised 'le sisteme de M. Vatel' as an attempt to derive the reciprocal duties of nations from first principles of natural justice and did not find fault with its contents despite the author's republican and protestant antecedents. The publication of the *Law of Nations* was duly approved by Malesherbes, the Director of the *Librairie*.[2] Yet, before Tercier's report was written and reached Malesherbes, Vattel himself had taken the initiative to directly contact Malesherbes in October 1757, plead

[1] What these transformations amounted to, and what theoretical and practical responses they generated is captured by Istvan Hont, *Jealousy of Trade. International Competition and the Nation-State in Historical Perspective* (Cambridge, MA, 2005), esp. 1–156.

[2] This and the following paragraph are largely based on Antonella Alimento, 'The French reception of Vattel's *Droit des gens*: Politics and publishing strategies', in Koen Stapelbroek and Antonio Trampus (eds.), *The Legacy of Vattel's 'Droit des gens'* (Basingstoke, 2019), 135–138.

orthodoxy and personally request permission to immediately publish separately the first volume of the *Law of Nations*, which had just been printed and of which he included a copy for Malesherbes. The reason for this unusual request, Vattel explained, was his suspicion that a 'Contrefacteur Hollandois' was preparing a pirate edition of his manuscript. Should the counterfeit edition appear before the French one was formally approved, this would not only cost Vattel dearly as an author, in case the 1,200 copies of his official edition remained unsold, but also spoil his attempt to promote himself in diplomatic circles, where he was seeking employment.[3]

As it happened, the *Law of Nations* received royal permission for publication in France in November 1757, ahead of the appearance in 1758 of Elie Luzac's edition. The latter bore the suggestive subtitle that promised the work was to 'guide the development of the true interests of states'.[4] Shifting from 'nations' to 'states' (or rather 'powers'), the subtitle Luzac added to the manuscript relegated the epigraph citing 'Scipio's Dream' in Cicero's *De republica* from the front page. More importantly, the subtitle indeed distorted the legal–political lexicon that Vattel very deliberately introduced and suggested that the *Law of Nations* could be read as a direct political scheme for stabilising the relations between states.[5] Yet, beyond the level of presentation, Vattel had been sufficiently concerned that Luzac might manipulate the content of the manuscript by cancelling and inserting bits and pieces, which could well have consequences for Vattel's political reputation. Addressing Malesherbes again, in December 1757, and voicing his lingering worry, he pleaded with him to withhold permission for the French publication of the Dutch edition of the *Law of Nations*, expressing urgent concerns that it would be all too easy for the Dutch pirate to insert ideas that he would not agree with or be unable to account for.[6]

A third edition of the *Law of Nations*, though not a complete one, was also published pretty much immediately. This edition was directly related to the

[3] See the autograph letter from Vattel to Malesherbes, Neuchâtel, 16 October 1757, in BN, NAF 3345, ff. 43-43v, included in the appendix to Antonella Alimento, 'Tra strategie editoriali e progettualità riformista: la circolazione in Francia del *Le droit des gens* di Emer de Vattel', *Rivista Storica Italiana* 129 (2017), 565–566.

[4] Elie Luzac, *Le droit des gens ou Principes de la loi naturelle appliqués à la conduite et aux affaires des nations et des souverains ouvrage qui conduit à dévoloper les véritables intérêts des puissances* (Leiden, 1758), 2 vols.

[5] For the lexicon developed by Vattel and the essential differences between 'nation', 'state' and 'power', see Gert-Fredrik Malt, 'Vattel's system for subjects in international law, and the establishment of Norway as a nation in 1814', in Koen Stapelbroek and Antonio Trampus (eds.), *The Legacy of Vattel's 'Droit des gens'*, (Basingstoke, 2019), 235–266.

[6] Alimento, 'The French reception of Vattel's *Droit des gens*', 138–141.

dynamic of the Seven Years' War and to what was at stake in this conflict. In its regular issue of 1758, the *Mémoires pour servir à l'histoire de notre tems*, which itself was the institutionalised sequel to an earlier pamphlet series, ostensibly written by *L'Observateur Hollandois*, announced to its subscribers the publication of a set of 'MEMOIRES POLITIQUES SUR LA GUERRE *où les Principes de la loi naturalle, & le Droit des gens, sont appliqués à la conduite & aux Affaires des Nations & des souverains*'. These memoires were promised to 'put the reader in a position to clearly judge everything related to the present war'.[7] The announcement framed the publication of these extra 'accompanying' *Mémoires politiques* as an extra service to the reader. 'Not wanting to omit anything in order to fulfil the given aim of these Memoires', the editor felt obliged to have the additional text printed and gave his audience their instructions on how to subscribe for the extra volumes at the Post Offices, along with the requisite price information.[8] The initiative was successful, as indeed a two-part extra publication of the series followed, still in 1758, containing an occasionally sloppy, but on the whole faithful early reproduction of books III and IV of Vattel's *Law of Nations*.[9]

The *Mémoires politiques concernant la guerre, ou principes de la loi naturelle*, as the latter books of the *Law of Nations*, were retitled for the occasion, were published without Vattel's full name on the cover, but simply gave the book as written 'Par Mr. de V.'. The text was preceded by a two-page introductory statement by the editor, the abbé Jean-Ignace de La Ville, which echoed Vattel's original preface. De La Ville mentioned that the message of the text was 'truly new and entirely different'. This was the case, because not the law of nations (which was not the primary concern of the republication),

7 Jean-Ignace De la Ville (ed.), *Mémoires pour servir à l'histoire de notre tems, contenants des réflections politiques sur la guerre présente, par l'Observateur Hollandois, redigez et augmentez par* M.D.V. (Frankfurt, 1758), 4: 'Ces *nouveaux Mémoires* mettront le Lecteur en état de juger sainement de tout ce qui se passe dans la presènte guerre'. There has been confusion among bibliographic scholars about the identity of 'M. D. V.'. Quérard and Barbier mistakenly imagined Vattel as the editor of the entire series. See also John Shovlin, 'Selling American empire on the eve of the seven years' war: The French propaganda cmpaign of 1755–1756', *Past & Present* 206 (2010), 136.

8 De la Ville, *Mémoires pour servir à l'histoire de notre tems*, 4.

9 Emer de Vattel, *Mémoires politiques concernant la guerre, ou principes de la loi naturelle* (Frankfurt, 1758), 2 vols. The words '*et la paix*' were inserted into the title of the second volume, coinciding with book IV of the *Law of Nations*. The edition was erratic in copying references to paragraphs from book I and II that were made in the original and occasionally left out an entire paragraph, forgot a paragraph marker or substituted a single word for another. I have not found an underlying 'political' motive for these errors.

but rather 'the Law of War is treated clearly there, and not drowned in a long deduction from Natural Law'.[10] Rather than a dry academic text, it 'spread pleasure, fire & interest in all the places that were susceptible to it', especially addressing those 'people who combined the politeness of the big world with the light of the Cabinet'.[11] After explaining the 'systématique' of the *Law of Nations* – the relationship between the notions of voluntary, arbitrary and conventional law – the editor stated that, alongside his maxims, the author frequently added 'examples that confirmed and clarified them' and which were not taken from the quaint humanist frame of reference of Grotius and his commentators, but instead 'regarded most of the Nations that were part of Modern History'.[12] Thus, the work furnished a carefully constructed legal–political analysis of the historically grown European states system and its 'consequences'. It clarified 'the resulting Laws ... by facts that relate to the history of our times'. By consequence, 'this work can be used as a key to the interpretation of the present events'.[13]

A further edition, also from 1758, was published as *Le droit de la guerre, ou principes de la loi naturelle, appliques a la conduite et aux affaires des nations et des souverains*. Although the title was slightly modified and Vattel's name was on the front page as the author (along with the places Amsterdam and Leiden, while sticking with the editorial designation 'Aux dépens de la compagnie'), this was in fact a straightforward copy of the 1758 spin-off from the *Mémoires pour servir à l'histoire de notre tems.*[14] In fact, the second volume gave up on the pretence, reverted to the original title page and restored Frankfurt and Leipzig as the (false) publishing places. Finally, the Dutch

[10] Ibid., 2: 'Cet ouvrage, déja annoncé au Public par un Programme, est véritablement neuf & tout diférent de ceux que l'on avoit jusques-ici sur la même matiére. Le Droit de la Guerre y est traité nettement, & non pas noïé dans une longue deduction du Droit Naturel'.

[11] Ibid., 2: 'Ce n'est point un livre de Collège, écrit avec la pesanteur & la sécheresse d'un stile purement didactique. L'Auteur y a répandu de l'agrément, du feu & de l'intérèt, dans tous les endroits qui en étoient susceptibles. Il a écrit pour les personnes qui joignent la politesse du grand Monde aux lumières du Cabinet'.

[12] Ibid., 2: 'L'Auteur a joint fort souvent aux Maximes, des Exemples capables de les confirmer, de les éclaircir, ou de délasser agréablement & utilement le Lecteur: Et pour ne point répéter ceux qui se trouvent dans GROTIUS & ses Comentateurs, il a pris la plus grande partie des Gens dans l'Histoire Moderne'.

[13] Ibid., 3: 'En un mot la matière y est traitée d'une façon nouvelle: Tout y est lié: Nulle ambiguïté de termes. Les Principes y sont établis avec toute la solidité possible: les Conséquences tirées avec une justesse d'esprit admirable; & les Loix qui en résultent sont éclaircies par des faits, qui ont rapport à l' Histoire de notre Tems. De sorte que cet Ouvrage pourra servir de clef à l'interprétation des Evénements présents'.

[14] The one difference to the text was that the last two short paragraphs of the 'Avis' with the pricing and printing information for subscriptions were dropped.

Royal library's copy of the exact same work has an extra front page with the differently subtitled *Memoires politiques concernant la guerre; pour servir d'eclaircissement à l'histoire de notre tems*, Par Mr. de V., with the places Frankfurt and Leipzig, even while it was directly followed by the just described front page of the *Le droit de la guerre, ou principes de la loi naturelle* (volume I, with places Amsterdam and Leiden) and again reverted to the original volume II title of the *Mémoires politiques concernant la guerre.*[15]

What actually happened in the process of the rapid republications by *L'Observateur Hollandois* was that Vattel's *Law of Nations* was assimilated into a highly politicised publishing agenda. The falsely titled journal *L'Observateur Hollandois* had been published from the summer of 1755 onwards as part of a French propaganda campaign to raise support for a colonial war effort in North American Acadia and to promote an expansive interpretation of the rights of neutrals, notably of Dutch merchants, to trade in wartime. Initially a news journal orchestrated by the French ministry, *L'Observateur Hollandois* edited by Jacob-Nicolas Moreau ran past its original publication span and ambition. Under the editorship of De la Ville and with funding from the French foreign ministry, it developed into a multivolume propaganda series of commentaries and republications of political texts on the ongoing war, notably on the history of Prussian conquests and the outbreak of the Third Silesian War.[16]

It is highly doubtful that Vattel, who was so anxious that his text might become appropriated for political purposes by the piracy of Dutch publishers, would have been happy with any of these republications. However, through the adoption of his text by *L'Observateur Hollandois*, it does become possible to appreciate some of Vattel's criticisms of British foreign politics at the time of the Seven Years' War, along with his critique of Frederick the Great's Prussia

[15] This publication history differs in some minor respects from the accounts by Elisabetta Fiocchi Malaspina, *L'eterno ritorno del Droit des gens di Emer de Vattel (secc. XVIII-XIX), L'impatto sulla cultura giuridica in prospettiva globale* (Frankfurt, 2017), 44–46; Stéphane Beaulac, *The Power of Language in the Making of International Law: The Word Sovereignty in Bodin and Vattel and the Myth of Westphalia* (Leiden, 2004), 244–245; and Emmanuelle Jouannet, *Emer de Vattel et l'émergence doctrinale du droit international classique* (Paris, 1993), 430–431.

[16] On Moreau, Dieter Gembicki, *Histoire et politique à la fin de l'ancien régime: Jacob-Nicolas Moreau, 1717–1803* (Nizet, 1979); Edmond Dziembowski, 'Les débuts d'un publiciste au service de la monarchie: L'activité littéraire de Jacob-Nicolas Moreau pendant la guerre', *Revue d'histoire diplomatique* 109 (1995), 305–322; and the chapters on the 'ideological arsenal' of Moreau in K. Baker, *Inventing the French Revolution: Essays on French Political Culture in the Eighteenth Century* (Ideas in Context) (Cambridge, 1990), 59–85. See also Gabriel-François Coyer, Jacob-Nicolas Moreau, *Écrits sur le patriottisme, l'esprit public et la propagande au milieu du XVIIIe* siècle, ed. Edmond Dziembowski (La Rochelle, 1997).

and his diplomatic connections to Saxony and Poland. With these elements in place, provided by the early publishing history of the *Law of Nations*, one can start to map the political context in which the work appeared and was held to represent a political meaning, however precise or narrowly circumscribed Vattel himself might have wanted that meaning to be.

THE BALANCE OF POWER AND THE SEVEN YEARS' WAR

When the Seven Years' War broke out, it was generally considered, by diplomats and political writers, to be a conflict about global hegemony and the future of the international order. Both focal points of the conflict, the Anglo–French opposition over their North American colonies and the central European war triggered by the Prussian occupation of Silesia, featured in the *Law of Nations*. Both were also central in the publication series started by Moreau, which would include the latter books of the *Law of Nations*. The mission of *L'Observateur Hollandois* was crystal clear. Commissioned from within the Ministry of Foreign Affairs, Moreau's job was 'to plead the cause of France against England, and [to] make all of Europe aware of the injustices and machinations of this power'.[17] Next to this international purpose, for which the false Dutch position was adopted, *L'Observateur Hollandois* domestically promoted French patriotism and a specific geopolitical strategy against British commercial–political hegemony.[18] Originally consisting of forty-six letters 'de M. Van** a M. H** de La Haye sur l'état présent des affaires de l'Europe', the magazine was published between the summer of 1755 and 1759.

Its main fundamental premise was that the Peace of Utrecht had not at all created a sustainable balance of power, but was an unacceptable settlement that had left space for elements within Britain to manipulate the entire global commercial system to their advantage. The fifth letter of *L'Observateur* explained that really there were two nations going behind the British constitution. One that deserved praise for being just, that lived according to the rule of law and that reflected upon and was considerate about the wider legitimacy of its actions in Europe and the world. Yet, there was also a wild and uncontrollably greedy England, which policies were inspired by different

[17] Jacob-Nicolas Moreau, *Mes Souvenirs*, 2 vols., ed. Camille Hermelin (Paris, 1898–1901), i: 59: 'de plaider la cause de la France contre l'Angleterre, et [de] mettre toute l'Europe au fait des injustices et des procedes de cette puissance'.

[18] Shovlin, 'Selling American empire', 145–147; Dziembowski, 'Les débuts d'un publiciste', 309–311, who also noted the opportunity seen by the French envoy to the Hague, Jean Louis d'Usson Marquis de *Bonnac*, to print *L'Observateur* in the Republic in order to work Dutch public opinion.

sentiments and that was easily enraged by ministerial power and spurred to action. This fanaticism should not be confused for love of country, as it was emotional, unreflected and primitive. Whereas British liberty was proud and false, French liberty was calm, rested on laws and a king protecting those same laws.[19] Rather than to settle for a balance of commercial emulative competition – Moreau copied Hume's terms – Britain was guided by jealousy and hate and through a system of public opinion attempted to turn itself into the sole ruler of the seas and arbiter of Europe.[20]

The balance of power needed to be restored, or rather remade in order to create a fair basis for global trade and sustainable peace. *L'Observateur Hollandois*, however, was not focused on promoting a vision for doing this, but on raising a politicised recognition of the British idea of the balance of power as false and deliberately hegemonic, while the British state itself was modern, commercial and constitutional. At that level, Vattel's was a welcome voice. The *Law of Nations* was reformist on constitutional principles involving economic aspects and political authority, but also featured a concrete political attack on Britain that was commonplace in *L'Observateur Hollandois*, which itself started being published in 1754 as a response to Anglo–French diplomatic struggles over Acadia. Vattel very specifically mentioned a particular outcome of the Utrecht settlement and, perhaps surprisingly, took the side of French diplomacy:

> If it be true that the boundaries of Acadia have always been uncertain, and that the French were the lawful possessors of it, that nation will be justified in maintaining that their cession of Acadia to the English, by the treaty of Utrecht, did not extend beyond the narrowest limits of that province. (*LN*, II-XVII-308)

More surprisingly still was that Vattel was close to Moreau in his suggestion that leaving the Acadia border a loose end, as an occasion for further warfare, had been a deliberate British policy, in the *Law of Nations*:

> Since the least encroachment on the territory of another is an act or injustice, – in order to avoid the commission of any such act, and to prevent every subject of discord, every occasion of quarrel, the limits of territories ought to be marked out with clearness and precision. If those who drew up the treaty of Utrecht had bestowed on so important a subject all the attention it deserved, we should not see France and England in arms, in order to decide

[19] Jacob-Nicolas Moreau, *L'Observateur Hollandois* (Paris, 1755–1756), letter 5, 42–43.

[20] Ibid., letter 4 and letter 5 *passim*, the paraphrases come from letter 4, 21 and 42 and letter 5, 24–25.

> by a bloody war what are to be the boundaries of their possessions in America. But the makers of treaties often designedly leave in them some obscurity, some uncertainty, in order to reserve for their nation a pretext for a rupture: – an unworthy artifice in a transaction wherein good faith alone ought to preside! We have also seen commissioners endeavouring to overreach or corrupt those of a neighbouring state, in order to gain for their master an unjust acquisition of a few leagues of territory [*quelques lieues de terrain*]. How can princes or ministers stoop to dirty tricks that would dishonour a private man? (*LN*, II-VII-92)[21]

This was exactly the field in which Moreau was operating when he started working on *L'Observateur Hollandois* and in 1756 published a separate *Mémoire contenant le précis des faits pour servir de réponse aux Observations envoyées par les ministres d'Angleterre dans les cours de l'Europe*.[22] The border dispute of Acadia in the 1750s was a heated subject in French politics and had triggered numerous publications, some based on diplomatic investigations and documents, others in the form of pamphlets of a more ideological nature. It was striking that Vattel in an otherwise not very politicised text weighed in on the topic.

Vattel's position on the Acadia issue was not lost on the French diplomats who, following the Diplomatic Revolution of 1756 and alongside Étienne François Choiseul's ongoing negotiations with Austria, treated it as a standard reference and normative source in their secret discussions with Britain to end their maritime war by settling the border dispute over the respective French and British territories in Acadia and Ohio.[23] Moreover, Vattel's scattered remarks in the *Law of Nations* on the French resistance to the accumulation of power by Charles V and the dynastic politics of the pragmatic sanction by

21 The chapter was entitled: 'Des effets du Domaine entre les Nations', which in English became more the direct and prescriptive: 'The limits of territories ought to be carefully settled'.

22 Jacob-Nicolas Moreau *Mémoire contenant le précis des faits pour servir de réponse aux Observations envoyées par les ministres d'Angleterre dans les cours de l'Europe* (Paris, 1756) translated into English as *A Memorial Containing a Summary View of Facts, with Their Authorities: In Answer to the Observations Sent by the English Ministry to the Courts of Europe* (1757), was an expression of the diplomatic warfare between teams of commissioners. The French commissioners de La Ville, Silhouette and de La Galissonière, who came from the same circles that Moreau moved in, in 1755 had issued a set of Mémoires des commissaires du Roi et de ceux de Sa Majesté Britannique sur les possessions et les droits respectifs des deux Couronnes en Amérique, avec les actes publics et pièces justificatives.

23 Shovlin, 'Selling American empire'; Alimento, 'The French reception of Vattel's *Droit des gens*'; Koen Stapelbroek, 'The foundations of Vattel's "system" of politics and the Seven Years' War: moral philosophy, luxury and the constitutional commercial state', in Koen Stapelbroek and Antonio Trampus (eds.), *The Legacy of Vattel's 'Droit des gens'*, (Basingstoke, 2019), 95–134.

Charles VI could be read as expressing support for the contemporary need to protect the liberties of small states in the Holy Roman Empire (*LN*, II-XVI-238; *LN*, III-III-42). It seems reasonable to suggest that Vattel was, in these passages, signalling both to Saxony statesmen and to circles surrounding the Duc de Choiseul in France what his legal-political vision of European peace amounted to: a system of alliances that revolved around France and that served to protect small states against the potentially hegemonic and belligerent impulses of, previously, Habsburg rule and, presently, Prussia under Frederick II.

VATTEL ON NEUTRAL TRADE AND THE DUTCH REPUBLIC

One of the favourite themes of *L'Observateur Hollandois*, in its posture of a series of letters written by a Dutchman, was to express concern for the rights of neutral trade. This topic had become an object of public diplomacy as well as French propaganda efforts during the War of the Austrian Succession. It was also included in Vattel's *Law of Nations*.

Vattel's discussion of commercial neutrality has gone down into history as the first modern treatment of the subject. Chapters 6 and 7 of book III of the *Law of Nations* tied in with the context of the Seven Years' War and were to influence political debates on neutral trade during later eighteenth-century wars. Vattel's chapters, however, formed a response to the issue as it appeared during the War of the Austrian Succession of the 1740s, where it particularly concerned trade carried by Dutch ships.[24] During this conflict – taking place in the aftermath of the renewal of the Franco–Dutch commercial treaty in 1739, which was first concluded at the Peace of Utrecht in 1713[25] – Dutch neutral trade benefitted France against its British enemy, but brought even more profit to its Dutch carriers. From the outbreak of the conflict in 1740, French writers and statesmen exerted pressure on Dutch neutral traders and statesmen to claim maximal freedom to exploit the benefits arising from the 'free ships, free goods'-clause, which had been included in the 1674 Anglo–Dutch Treaty of Westminster. This clause guaranteed either contracting party the enjoyment of neutral trade while the other party was at war.[26]

[24] Alice Clare Carter, *The Dutch Republic in Europe in the Seven Years' War* (London, 1971), chapter 6, esp. 90–91.

[25] Koen Stapelbroek, 'Reinventing the Dutch Republic: Franco–Dutch commercial treaties from Ryswick to Vienna', in Antonella Alimento, Koen Stapelbroek (eds.), *The Politics of Commercial Treaties in the Eighteenth Century, Balance of Power, Balance of Trade* (Basingstoke, 2017), 195–215.

[26] An example of such an extreme claim was Albertus Ploos van Amstel, *Verhandeling over het recht van commercie tusschen onzydige en oorlogvoerende volken: Uyt het Latyn vertaald en*

The feigned Dutch identity of the author of *L'Observateur Hollandois* was, in fact, a barely concealed aspect of a wider and consistent French campaign from 1740 until the end of the eighteenth century. During this period, a considerable number of anti-British pamphlets and magazines were published in the Republic with French financial support. These could be written by Dutch 'Patriots', often associated with Amsterdam merchants, or by French hired pens, like Moreau. Louis-Joseph Plumard de Dangeul's first writings, of 1741, for instance adopted the stance of a 'patriote hollandois'.[27] Likewise, in support of Danish neutral trade rights against British restrictions, Jean-Henri Maubert de Gouvest published *Le politique danois, ou, l'ambition des Anglais démasquée par leurs pirateries* under the false name of Martin Hübner, the Danish theorist of the law of nations and neutrality.[28]

Moreau's *L'Observateur Hollandois* thus was conceived as part of a combined domestic–European propaganda tool to support a specific French geopolitical commercial strategy. One that, beyond an abstract analysis of Britain's commercial empire and its constitutional make-up, aligned with the imperial interests of French financiers and American plantation holders.[29] This strategy entailed the creation of a French merchant fleet to replace the reliance upon Dutch traders for carrying French goods, while driving a wedge between what was left of the former Anglo–Dutch 'Protestant Alliance'. This was done by using profit from neutral trade as a 'bait' to stretch the exploitation of Dutch neutrality beyond what was acceptable for Britain.

In 1745, when the Dutch lent military succour to Britain in the War of the Austrian Succession, the French declared Dutch neutrality void, abolished the Franco–Dutch commercial treaty, and invaded the Republic, leading to the Siege of Bergen op Zoom in 1747 and the Treaty of Breda in 1748. With

vermeerderd met een aanhangzel over het nemen en verbeurdverklaren der schepen, en breedvoerige aanteekeningen (Amsterdam, 1760) [translation of *Specimen academicum inaugurale de jure commercii, quod gentibus in bello medii competit* (Leiden, 1759)], 35–42.

27 Louis-Joseph Plumard de Dangeul, *Lettre écrite à un Seigneur du gouvernement par un Patriote Hollandois, Au sujet des Conjonctures présentes contenant Quelques-uns des principaux Motifs qui doivent empécher les Provinces-Unies de prendre parti dans la présente Guerre de la Grande-Bretagne* (s.l., 1741). The pamphlet was translated and reprinted during the Seven Years' War and the War of the American Independence. See Koen Stapelbroek, 'Economic reform and neutrality in Dutch political pamphlets, 1741–1779', in Femke Deen, David Onnekink and Michel Reinders (eds.), *Pamphlets and Politics in the Dutch Republic* (Leiden, 2011), 196–200.

28 Martin Hübner [Jean-Henri Maubert de Gouvest], *Le politique danois, ou, l'ambition des Anglais démasquée par leurs pirateries* (Copenhagen [Paris], 1756). Gembicki, *Histoire et politique*, 202 notes that Moreau was the censor who approved this work for publication.

29 Shovlin, 'Selling American empire', 144 mentions Pierre Louis de Saintard, a staunch supporter of the most radical variation on French commercial Atlanticism that included a French Navigation Act.

neutral trade rights playing such a major role in international conflict, from the outset of the Seven Years' War the renewal of pro-French voices on neutral trade in the Dutch Republic, understandably, was fiercely opposed by a counter-campaign of British pamphleteering.[30] Moreover, the implementation of the doctrine of Continuous Voyage and what is known as the 'Rule of 1756' by the British prize courts created a 'neutral rights revolution'. Based on the ideas of the Dutch lawyer Cornelius van Bynkershoek, who had distinguished proper (and just) trade from the (unnatural) carrying trade, the British system restricted the proper realm of justified neutral commerce to 'trade *with* the enemy', as opposed to trade *for* the enemy, which was deemed contraband.[31]

Vattel's solution to the problem of how to separate legitimate trade from contraband differed from the 'Rule of 1756', as well as from the French emphasis on the 'free ships, free goods'-clause in the Anglo–Dutch treaty of 1674. Vattel's perspective was based on specific moral philosophical principles. It relied on a distinction between types of goods and their purpose in relation to human needs and desires. Goods that served the physical needs of humans should be allowed to freely cross between nations also in wartime, while trade in higher-order commodities could be subjected to politics and the dynamics of power between states. The specific characteristics of eighteenth-century rivalries, which often revolved around commerce, meant that trade policies could actually offer solutions to preserve international political stability and prevent war, or the escalation of conflict. In the face of potential hegemonic rule, for instance, a league of states could form a commercial alliance to oppose and dissolve the threat.[32]

Thus, Vattel offered an alternative outlook on the regulation of neutral trade to those that were proposed and implemented by European states in both the War of the Austrian Succession and the Seven Years' War. While Vattel did not choose a side in the conflict in this regard, his discussion of

[30] Anonymous, *Le véritable observateur, ou lettre d'un Anglois à un patriote* hollandois (London, 1756). See also William Kenrick, *L'observateur observé. Ou Lettre d'un Hollandois … dans laquelle on redresse l'Observateur Hollandois sur ce qu'il a avancé touchant le commencement des hostilités présentes entre les François & les Anglois* (The Hague, 1756).

[31] Tara Helfman, 'Commerce on trial: Neutral rights and private warfare in the seven years' war', in Koen Stapelbroek (ed.), *Trade and War: The Neutrality of Commerce in the Inter-State System* (Helsinki: Collegium for Advanced Studies, 2011), 14–41; Tara Helfman, 'Neutrality, the Law of Nations, and the natural law tradition: A study of the seven years' war', *Yale Journal of International Law* 30 (2005), 549–586; Koen Stapelbroek, 'The Dutch debate on commercial neutrality (1713–1830)', *Trade and War*, 114–142.

[32] Isaac Nakhimovsky, 'Vattel's theory of the international order: Commerce and the balance of power in the *Law of Nations*', *History of European Ideas* 33 (2007), 157–173, esp. 170.

neutrality was very much geared towards prevention or containment of conflict. It was no coincidence that Vattel discussed neutral trade alongside the legal restrictions that ought to exist with regard to (private) investment in foreign state debts by citizens of neutral states. The main investors in foreign debts were Dutch citizens. Such investments, Vattel emphasised, should not be politically interested (even if such investments led to spending on warfare). That is, interest rates had to reflect market conditions (*LN*, III-VII-110). Another was Vattel's opinion that fulfilling obligations emanating from long-standing defensive treaty alliances could be combined with the status of neutrality. The obvious precedent for this was the recurrent British appeal to the Dutch to provide 6,000 auxiliary troops to help to defend the British shores, and which had led to the collapse of Dutch neutrality in the War of the Austrian Succession (*LN*, III-VI-*passim*). Overall, Vattel deployed the experience of Dutch neutrality and actual problems that had occurred to determine the bandwidths within which a state could justify its status as neutral in eighteenth-century Europe.

Vattel's treatment of neutral trade and its implications for Dutch interests fit well with the views of the Dutch publisher and writer Elie Luzac.[33] The *Law of Nations* provided an outline of how the Republic could avoid breaking its ties with England, or be driven into the arms of the latest French political design. The *Law of Nations* was also relatively friendly towards Dutch privileged claims or a 'right to trade'.[34] This latter aspect would also be noted by its Venetian translator-publisher, who inserted long footnotes to correct and attack Grotius's ideas and the notion of the Dutch as benevolent neutral traders.[35]

Luzac's relationship with Vattel's *Law of Nations* had started in his capacity as a publisher. As is well known, Luzac was approached by Vattel through Johann Heinrich Samuel Formey in November 1755 to publish the *Law of Nations*. Although the negotiation collapsed, Luzac ended up publishing a

[33] Luzac joined the chorus of those who called the English rights discourses chimerical under the pseudonym of Reinier Vryaart, *Openhartige brieven, om te dienen tot opheldering en regte kennis van de vaderlandsche historie*, vol. 5 (Leiden, 1781–1784), 120–121. On Luzac's political economy see, W. R. E. Velema, 'Homo Mercator in Holland. Elie Luzac en het achttiende-eeuwse debat over de koophandel', *B⊠dragen en mededelingen betreffende de geschiedenis der Nederlanden* 100 (1985), 427–444, and W. R. E. Velema, *Enlightenment and Conservatism in the Dutch Republic. The Political Thought of Elie Luzac* (Assen, 1993), 115–143.

[34] See Alice Clare Carter, 'The Dutch as neutrals in the seven years' war', *The International and Comparative Law Quarterly* 12 (1963), 818–834, for a case-based insight into Dutch neutral trade issues during the Seven Years' War.

[35] Antonio Trampus, *Emer de Vattel and the Politics of Good Government. Constitutionalism, Small States and the International System* (Basingstoke, 2020).

pirate edition, while Formey took charge of comparing Luzac's version for authenticity in the *Bibliothèque Impartiale*, of January–February 1758.[36] Vattel had feared that Luzac was likely to spoil the message of the *Law of Nations*, which made perfect sense in the polarised context of the Seven Years' War. It was, however, not necessary because Luzac probably sufficiently liked what he saw in the *Law of Nations* as Vattel had written it.

To understand this, it is important to recognise Luzac's position vis-à-vis Dutch trade. In fact, Luzac's position was very similar to that of Jean Thomas La Fargue. La Fargue, in the 1740s, argued for a course of 'strict neutrality' [*stipte neutraliteit*], in contrast to the pro-French *neutraliste* position, and 'exposed' the previously mentioned publication by Plumard de Dangeul's false *patriote hollandais*, as seducing the Dutch into their own downfall along with that of Britain. La Fargue, instead, hailed the balance of 1717 that had ensued from the combination of concluded treaties and which prevented having to make a choice, as La Fargue put it, between 'onion soup or roast beef'.[37]

Following La Fargue, Luzac saw Vattel's *Law of Nations* as a sophisticated legal attempt to avoid that same political choice. Yet, Luzac, by the 1750s, did not have the luxury option of expressing nostalgia for the Triple Alliance of 1717. Instead of imagining a European balance of power where the Dutch sat prominently at the table, Luzac's more realistic priority was to support a political scheme of treaties that kept the Dutch off the menu of either of Europe's commercial monarchies.

The political scheme that Luzac needed was, however, not included in Vattel's *Law of Nations*, even if the subtitle of Luzac's edition instructed its readers to be guided to a better understanding of '*les véritables intérêts des puissances*'. Vattel both admired and criticised Britain, allocated France its role of balancer of Europe, supported the predicament of the Dutch trade republic and paved the way for the substitution of the Habsburg Empire with

36 Hans Bots and Jan Schillings, *Lettres d'Élie Luzac à Jean Henry Samuel Formey: regard sur les coulisses de la librairie hollandaise du XVIIIe siècle* (Paris, 2001), 290–291; Édouard Béguelin, 'En souvenir de Vattel', *Recueil de travaux offert par la Faculté de Droit de l'Université de Neuchâtel à la Société Suisse des Juristes* (Neuchâtel, 1929), 92–93. See André Bandelier, 'De Berlin à Neuchâtel: la genèse du Droit des gens d'Emer de Vattel', *Schweizer im Berlin des 18. Jahrhunderts* (Berlin, 1996), 45–56; and Frédéric Ieva, '"A poor imitation of Grotius and Pufendorf?". Biographical uncertainties and the laborious genesis of Vattel's Droit des gens', in Koen Stapelbroek and Antonio Trampus (eds.), *The Legacy of Vattel's 'Droit des gens'*, (Basingstoke, 2019), 53–76.

37 Jean Thomas La Fargue, Afscheid *aan de* nagtgedrochten met de ontleding van 't zeer aanmerkelijk Antwoord op zekeren (verdichten) brief van zijne Excellentie (The Hague, 1756), 28.

Frederick's Prussia, as the most likely threat to European peace. Yet, his sanctioning of the use of the voluntary law of nations to form commercial alliances did not add up to a concrete plan for stabilising European politics. Instead, such a political scheme for Europe that structurally engaged with commerce was developed from the time of the Seven Years' War under the leadership of Choiseul and most clearly expressed by Jacques Accarias de Sérionne in 1766.

Accarias de Sérionne's *Les intérêts des nations de l'Europe, développés relativement au commerce* presented a manifesto of Choiseul's scheme to orchestrate international peace through a bipolar hierarchy of states ,with Britain and France at the top connecting to each other with a commercial treaty.[38] Lower-level states in the hierarchy were to occupy themselves with providing agricultural supplies and support the manufacturing economies of the dominant states that competed with each other for market shares on a global level. As one of these lower-level economies, but with a different character, Accarias described the Dutch as the ideal carriers of the world's commerce (apart from Britain, which had isolated itself). This role, which created a wonderful match with the French interest in manufacturing and ignorance in trade, had been temporarily disfigured when the French had given the Dutch too good a fiscal deal on their carrying services. In the interest of global markets, it was important to restore the Dutch as the carriers of French trade, but also to let them compete with Hamburg and others to keep prices low. In addition, one ought to let them sustain their herring fishery, spice trade and protect the role of Amsterdam as a global financial centre.[39]

Developed in the Austrian Southern Netherlands and published in Leiden in the Dutch Republic by Elie Luzac, *Les intérêts des nations de l'Europe* was an invitation to all European states to join Choiseul's scheme for an interstate system based on the balance of trade. If each nation refrained from aspiring to a favourable balance, and trade in India were restructured according to the neutrality of European trade, Choiseul's plan could convert jealousy of trade into pacific emulation. According to Accarias de Sérionne, the quest for the balance of power thus far had caused rather than prevented conflict. The only way to establish a lasting equilibrium was to create an international economy in which states exploited their natural and cultural resources, which meant for

[38] Jacques Accarias de Sérionne, *Les intérêts des nations de l'Europe, développés relativement au commerce* (Leiden, 1766), 2 vols. On Accarias, Antonella Alimento, 'Raynal, Accarias de Sérionne et le Pacte de Famille', in Antonella Alimento and Gianluigi Goggi (eds.), *Autour de l'abbé Raynal: genèse et enjeux politiques de l'Histoire des deux Indes* (Ferney-Voltaire, 2018), 33–45.

[39] Accarias de Sérionne, *Les intérêts des nations de l'Europe*, I: 222–229.

instance that Spain and Portugal had to be agricultural economies and not attempt to be manufacturing exporters. Key to the realisation of the plan was the conclusion of a commercial treaty between the two main manufacturing economies that politically and economically topped each side, Britain and France.[40]

VATTEL VERSUS PRUSSIA'S FREDERICK II ON THE INTERNATIONAL ORDER

That the *Law of Nations* did not carry the same message as Choiseul's scheme was underscored by the lukewarm review of Vattel's work in the *Journal de Commerce*, the Brussels-based magazine edited by Accarias de Sérionne.[41] The *Law of Nations* might be read in support of a number of positions that were shared by Accarias and other writers endorsing Choiseul's scheme. Yet, its main selling-point within the French political faction struggle around the time of the Seven Years' War was its treatment of Frederick the Great and the Prussian threat to European stability.

As is well known, Vattel's portrayal of Frederick II's foreign policy and military campaigns is intrinsically related to his own life and career. Even if our current knowledge about Vattel's personal relation to the context of the Seven Years' War remains somewhat sketchy, what has become increasingly clear is that his professional links to Saxony and Poland are stronger and more varied than have been recognised until recently. It is also apparent that these political affiliations are an important key to placing the *Law of Nations* alongside Vattel's diplomatic career.[42]

Following his failed attempt at establishing a diplomatic career in Berlin in 1742, Vattel acted as a Saxony diplomat for Count Heinrich von Brühl in Neuchâtel from 1743 and was stationed as the Elector's minister-plenipotentiary in Berne between 1749 and 1759. It was the publication and reception of the *Law of Nations* that, in 1759, earned him his promotion to a post as political counsel at the court of Frederick Augustus II in Dresden,

[40] Ibid., *passim*.

[41] *Journal de commerce*, April 1759, 137–169 and May 1759, 35–63.

[42] Other than the standard work of Béguelin, 'En souvenir de Vattel', see Chapter 1, by Nadir Weber; Walter Rech, *Enemies of Mankind: Vattel's Theory of Collective Security* (Leiden: Martinus Nijhoff, 2013); Radoslaw Szymanski, 'Vattel as an intermediary between the economic society of Berne and Poland', in Koen Stapelbroek and Antonio Trampus (eds.), *The Legacy of Vattel's 'Droit des gens'*, (Basingstoke, 2019), 29–52; Ieva, 'A poor imitation of Grotius and Pufendorf?', and the important source edition of André Bandelier, *Emer de Vattel à Jean Henri Samuel Formey: correspondances autour du Droit des gens* (Paris, 2012).

which he retained (including a three-year period in Warsaw in 1760–1763) until his death in 1767. New research into the finer biographical details of Vattel's career and political networks will shed new light on the intricacies that bound him to various places and concrete policies. Yet, these basic facts already explain the U-turn from his dedication of his early work on Leibniz to Frederick II, to his allegiance in his career and writing to the cause of Saxony. Born in Prussian-ruled Neuchâtel, and moving between Dresden, Berne, Neuchâtel and Warsaw, Vattel's life and career were in large part dominated by the relation between Prussia and Saxony within the larger context of European politics. This was most clearly so during the Seven Years' War. Vattel's distrust of Frederick ran deeper, however. Already in 1747, in his 'application memorandum' to the Saxon court, Vattel made his case that the Principality of Neuchâtel ought to become a part of Saxony, while Frederick was distractedly busy with the annexation of Silesia.[43]

At the surface of the *Law of Nations*, not to be missed by any of its readers, especially those at the Saxon court, Vattel condemned Frederick's taste for territorial conquest and warfare (*LN*, III-IX-168; *LN*, III-IV-62).[44] While Vattel, famously, classified Frederick as an 'enemy of humankind', it has been asserted that Vattel saw the benefits of modern monarchy as a form of government and style of rule and administration in modern times. Likewise, it has been argued that Vattel rhetorically overstated, in his memorandum of 1747, the popular aversion against Frederick II's rule that existed in Neuchatel.[45] The major underlying point of difference between Vattel and Frederick was not a distaste of absolute royal government and its displays of military prowess, but Frederick's vision of the future of Europe and the international order. This difference came out very clearly during the Seven Years' War, and can be understood through the expression of support for Frederick's international vision by the political writer and loyal pamphleteer Johann Heinrich Gottlob von Justi.

Justi, from 1748, had sought to position himself as the leading political theorist of Frederick II's project to turn Prussia into a major power. In an essay of that year, he advised the Prussian court on maritime policy and identified

43 Tetsuya Toyoda, 'Vattel's doctrine of national sovereignty in the context of Saxony–Poland and Neuchâtel', *Theory and Politics of the Law of Nations. Political Bias in International Law Discourse of Seven German Court Councillors in the Seventeenth and Eighteenth Centuries* (Leiden, 2011), 161–190.

44 See, in particular, Emer de Vattel, 'Dialogue entre Pierre le Grand et Charles XII sur la gloire des conquérans', *Mélanges de littérature, de morale et de politique* (Neuchatel, 1760), 1–19; and Rech, *Enemies of Mankind*, chapter 4.

45 Rech, *Enemies of Mankind*, 201–202.

the Dutch Republic as an agent of unjust neutrality and disturbance of international order.[46] Following the abolition of the already mentioned preferential Franco–Dutch commercial agreement in 1745, Prussian diplomats made an effort to replace the Dutch, which resulted in a trade convention with France in 1753.[47] Justi was not obsessed with the Dutch Republic as such, but saw its rise as a historical problem. In Frederick's *Anti-Machiavel*, which was the backbone of a number of positions argued by Justi in his political theory, small states and republics were portrayed as antithetical to modernity and commercial order. The conditions of commercial competition in the eighteenth century, Justi echoed Frederick, made the monarchical form of government a requirement for order. European politics had converged on this following the Peace of Utrecht. No ruler could afford to lapse into Machiavellian policies. With the principle of civil liberty in monarchy solved, free governments had become redundant remnants of previous centuries that had become functionally extinct. The real origin of Holland's wealth lay not in Dutch virtue and commercial or seafaring talent, but in negligence by larger states to cultivate their proper interest. A concerted effort by Europe's commercial monarchies to displace small states and free governments was the appropriate remedy. This would result in a simpler and more solid international order.[48]

Frederick II in the *Anti-Machiavel*, thus, did not just, like many writers such as Hume, recognise the advantages of civil liberty under monarchical government, but saw a future of commercial modern monarchies squeezing small states and republics out of the political landscape.[49] It was this anti-small state idea of the history, present and future of Europe that fit tightly with Frederick's urge to reorganise the Holy Roman Empire, and which was both the cause of the escalation of Frederick's political aggression and the object of Vattel's

46 Ere Nokkala, 'Just and unjust neutrality: J. H. G. von Justi's defence of Prussian maritime neutrality (1740–1763)', in Koen Stapelbroek (ed.), *Trade and War: The Neutrality of Commerce in the Inter-State System* (Helsinki, 2011), 42–60.

47 See Marco Cavarzere, 'The rise of a trading nation. Prussia and the convention préliminaire de commerce with France (1753)', in Antonella Alimento, Koen Stapelbroek (eds.), *The Politics of Commercial Treaties in the Eighteenth Century, Balance of Power, Balance of Trade* (Basingstoke, 2017), 295–320; and in the same volume Stapelbroek, 'Reinventing the Dutch Republic', 195–215.

48 In the Dutch Republic, the vision of Frederick II and shared by Johan Heinrich Gottlob von Justi was taken up as a wake-up call that the Republic needed to be reformed, see Koen Stapelbroek, 'The international politics of cameralism: The balance of power and Dutch translations of Justi', in Ere Nokkala, Nicholas B. Miller (eds.), *Cameralism across the World of Enlightenment: Nature, Happiness and Governance* (London, 2019), 99–124.

49 Richard Whatmore, 'Vattel, Britain and peace in Europe', *Grotiana* 31 (2010), 85–107.

condemnation in the *Law of Nations*. If Vattel saw Europe as one large Republic that had emerged from post-Roman feudal Europe (*LN*, III-III-47), Frederick's anti-small state vision represented an attempt to break with that tradition and all of its legal and political customs and achievements.[50]

CONCLUSION

Compared with Frederick's overhaul of European history, Vattel's vision of a pacified European society offered an alternative prospect. One that was expressed through the notions of independence, the constituent body of the nation as the basis of the state, and legitimate sovereignty. This vision facilitated smaller states and republics in shaping their constitutional identity and dealing with the international legal, political and economic challenges (such as staying neutral in war, while maintaining commercial relations) that occurred in the turbulent contexts of the mid- and later eighteenth century. Rather than to regulate war and foreign interventions by great powers, the primary aim of the *Law of Nations* was to preserve the historically grown constitutional integrity, nationhood and autonomy of small states like Saxony within the Holy Roman Empire. It was for the same reason that it made sense for Luzac to publish Vattel, the *Law of Nations* could be read in support of a system of international peace and trade that preserved the political integrity of the Dutch state.

Vattel's *Law of Nations* considered in the context of the Seven Years' War and through the prism of its earliest editions, thus appears as a historically inspired guideline for the creation of an international order. To preserve Europe's historically grown order, the sovereignty of commercial territorial monarchies and smaller states were to be combined within one system, in which France appears as a natural arbiter, Prussia forms the current main threat to peace and the constitution of Britain acts as a model for modern monarchies. Acknowledging the recently emerged set of commercial challenges related to neutral trade and foreign investment that complicated the separation of war and peace, Vattel's system provided conceptual guidelines, yet neither offered a precise plan or diplomatic scheme for pacifying Europe nor took a clear side in the conflict amidst it was published. While the *Law of Nations* abounded with lightly concealed references to recent political events,

[50] On Frederick's vision as rejected by Vattel, see Rech, *Enemies of Mankind* and Isaac Nakhimovsky, 'The enlightened prince and the future of Europe: Voltaire and Frederick the Great's *Anti-Machiavel* of 1740', in B. Kapossy, I. Nakhimovsky and R. Whatmore (eds.), *Commerce and Peace in the Enlightenment* (Cambridge, 2017), 44–77.

Vattel made sure that the work never turned into a pamphlet. Amidst the military, diplomatic and propaganda confrontations of the time, Vattel's aim to steer clear of the tumults of warfare and great power rivalry naturally chimed with his role as a Saxon diplomat. Both his direct ambitions in that field and his future vision of a peaceful international order were served by the publication of the *Law of Nations*. Vattel very deliberately framed the *Law of Nations* as such and worked hard to protect its meaning in a context in which it was likely to take on other meanings, or be appropriated for aims contrary to Vattel's vision.

FURTHER READING

Tara Helfman, 'Commerce on trial: Neutral rights and private warfare in the seven years' war', in Koen Stapelbroek (ed.), *Trade and War: The Neutrality of Commerce in the Inter-State System* (Helsinki, 2011), 14–41.

Isaac Nakhimovsky, 'Vattel's theory of the international order: Commerce and the balance of power in the *Law of Nations*', *History of European Ideas* 33 (2007), 157–173.

Walter Rech, *Enemies of Mankind: Vattel's Theory of Collective Security* (Leiden, 2013).

Koen Stapelbroek and Antonio Trampus, *The Legacy of Vattel's 'Droit des gens'* (Basingstoke, 2019).

Tetsuya Toyoda, Theory and Politics of the Law of Nations. Political Bias in International Law Discourse of Seven German Court Councillors in the Seventeenth and Eighteenth Centuries (Leiden, 2011),

Antonio Trampus, *Emer de Vattel and the Politics of Good Government. Constitutionalism, Small States and the International System* (Basingstoke, 2020).

PART II

Concepts

6

Vattel, the Balance of Power, and the Moral Justification of War

CAMILLA BOISEN

INTRODUCTION

Vattel stands among the principal jurists of modern international relations. Yet the balance of power – a policy at the heart of the theory and practise of international relations, and which Edmund Burke, for example, declared central to the 'common law of Europe'[1] – hardly figures at all in Vattel's magnum opus. The question thus arises: why does it play a relatively insignificant role in his writings, and what role exactly does he think it plays? There is no doubt that he recognises it as an important element of policy in European relations. While the condition of a balance of power ideally maintains peace and harmony among states, it also carries within itself a powerful justification for preventive war. Balance of power is defined by the principle of collective security that prevents any states from attaining a preponderance of power and constituting a danger to the rest. Yet while this dynamic may ultimately limit the occurrence of war, as just war theory more generally seeks to do,[2] any attempt to wage war to preserve the balance of power is predicated on the institutionalisation of war as an instrument of policy. Vattel is thus sceptical of its efficacy as a reliable mechanism for the limitation of war. Whoever 'entertains a true idea of war . . . and considers its terrible effects', Vattel writes, would surely agree that it should not be undertaken unless for the best of reasons (*LN*, III-III-24). A justified reason for going to war is preventive warfare, and Vattel's remarks on the balance of power are often interpreted

I am sincerely grateful to Lucius Lambert for his research support in writing this chapter, and to David Boucher and Randall Lesaffer for comments made to an early draft.

[1] E. Burke *The Works of the Right Honourable Edmund Burke. World's Classics*, 6 vols., vol. VI, *Letters on a Regicide Peace*, III (London, 1907), 259.

[2] Unlike what Delahunty and Yoo claim that it does. R. Delahunty and J. Yoo 'From just war to false peace', *Chicago Journal of International Law* 13.1, Article 3 (2012), 1–47.

as giving justification to the use of force aimed against the aspirations of hegemonic powers.[3] However, Simone Zurbuchen has persuasively argued that Vattel ascribes the balance of power no role in the justification of preventive war, since, while threat of injury from an aggrandising power gives states a justified cause to make war, one cannot know if and when the affected state will be attacked.[4] Vattel is cautious because it is hard to determine when a state shows sufficiently present and imminent desire to attack its neighbours. The question is whether Vattel is uncomfortable with the inevitability of preventive war within a balance of power agenda?

In this chapter, I argue that we should not ascribe too much importance to Vattel's invocation of the balance of power as a mechanism for safeguarding the peace of Europe. Despite the longstanding scholarly practise of doing so,[5] Vattel says remarkably little about the concept of balance of power, only dedicating approximately five pages to it. Although Vattel tells us that the balance of power is one of the principles for '*estimating* the justice of a war' (*LN*, III-111-50; emphasis added), he is relatively unenthusiastic about its usefulness in doing so. In fact, as I demonstrate, Vattel does not think it a very consistent principle and, relatively speaking, it has only marginal importance in relation to the other principles of just war. His general position holds that while it is ideally possible to establish just cause, in practise it is very difficult, if not impossible. Invariably justice can be claimed on both sides, and the balance of power does not provide more than a rough-and-ready way out of that dilemma. The dilemma is not that justice is on both sides *per se* but rather a consequence, Vattel emphasises. The relations between sovereign states includes recourse to war. Thus, war as a means to pursue the interests of a sovereign state remained a realistic possibility and the right to wage war was actually an essential aspect of state sovereignty.[6]

More relevant to his theory is the role of subjective judgement, based to a large extent on what Burke called 'the manners of a gentleman' – it is the

3 Martin Wight understands Vattel's concept of the balance of power as producing a legal right in international law deriving from a principle of self-preservation. M. Wight, 'Balance of power', in Herbert Butterfield and Martin Wight (eds.), *Diplomatic Investigations* (Cambridge, MA, 1966), 149–176, at 153.

4 S. Zurbuchen, 'Vattel's *Law of Nations* and just war theory', *History of European Ideas* 35.4 (2009), 408–417.

5 See for instance, Richard Devetak, 'Law of nations as reason of state: Diplomacy and the balance of power in Vattel's *Law of Nations*', *Parergon* 28 (2011), 105–128; Evan Luard, *The Balance of Power – The System of International Relations 1648–1814* (London, 1992); Hedley Bull, *The Anarchical Society – A Study of Order in World Politics*, (New York, 1995).

6 I am grateful to Peter Schröder for clarifying this point. See also I. Hunter, 'Kant and Vattel in context: Cosmopolitan philosophy and diplomatic casuistry', *History of European Ideas* 39.4 (2013), 477–502.

inalienable prerogative of each sovereign to conduct his or her affairs as he or she sees fit. Vattel thinks that heads of state are not motivated by reason alone, and he distinguishes between justificatory reason and more individualistic motives, which seem to relate both to capabilities and expediency (*LN*, III-III-25). Although the balance of power encourages states to take the earliest possible justifiable instance to impede aggressive hegemons, Vattel sees the balancing mechanism imprecise at best and precarious at worst because we can rely neither on states being reasonable nor their intentions being honourable. A balance of power is always possible in a dishonourable and unvirtuous way; therefore, it can only be an element of maintaining peace if it is done the 'right' way. Establishing the moral justifications of war requires careful consideration, and the balance of power, when applied, is too fickle a political concept on its own to provide states with a good and morally reliable title to war; fickle because it can too easily be twisted into a pretext for an unjustifiable preventive war.

While Vattel's engagement with balance of power discourse evidences a deeply held concern for the collective security of states,[7] it also exposes a mistrust of the moral conduct of states. 'The right of making war', Vattel writes 'belongs to nations only as a remedy against injustice: it is the offspring of unhappy necessity' (*LN*, III-IV-51). This is an extraordinary passage because Vattel also thinks it is generally impossible to define what injustice is, let alone take up arms to correct it. That is, we cannot be certain whether an act lacks the virtue of being a pursuit of justice in every case because we cannot know all the cases to come (*LN*, III-III-44). Certainly, the balance of power is a questionable mechanism for doing so, even for preventive wars.

THE POLITICAL IDEA OF A BALANCE OF POWER

Whether as a moral proposition or a political device, the balance of power is inherently about order. It has taken on several meanings,[8] and gives rise to an array of competing interpretations. It is 'a concept riddled with ambiguity'[9] principally grounded in an inherent dualism of, on the one hand, common-interest ideas realised through preventive wars aimed to curb the hegemonic aspirations of any one state, and, on the other, states' self-interested motives to

7 See also W. Rech, *Enemies of Mankind: Vattel's Theory of Collective Security* (Leiden, 2013); R. Lesaffer, 'Aggression before Versailles', *The European Journal of International Law* 29.3 (2018), 773–808.

8 See M. Wight, 'The balance of power and international order', in A. James (ed.), *The Bases of International Order – Essays in Honour of C. A. W. Manning* (London, 1973), 85–115.

9 M. Sheehan, *The Balance of Power – History and Theory* (London, 1996), ix.

create balance of power imperatives to suit a particular political goal.[10] We should therefore question, as David Boucher has, whether or not eighteenth century Europe actually constituted a system of states seeking a common good by 'consciously acting in conformity with the mechanism of a system'.[11] Vattel is well aware of these ambiguities, of relying on balance of power mechanisms for the collective security of states and his short discussion of the balance of power in chapter III 'Of the Just Causes of War' demonstrates that it is flawed as a principle for establishing the just cause of war.

Although it was also criticised as a kind of Machiavellian reason of state pursuit of politics in interstate relations, by the mid-eighteenth century the balance of power had taken on an almost mythical status as a sort of natural law that could be invoked as a claim to just war or justify offensive alliances. The idea of a balance of power largely replaced the seventeenth century's model of universal monarchy as the best means to organise the European state system. The balance of power eclipsed ideas of universal monarchy, usually identified with aggressive Hapsburg or Bourbon domination, as a more 'neutral' organising concept and producer of peace that accommodated the liberty and independence of individual states.[12] The 'providentialism' of eighteenth-century balance of power politics was emblematic of a cosmological shift in natural philosophy that introduced Newtonian and 'scientific' materialist ideas about order. The balance of power was idealised, naturalised, explained, and articulated in mechanic terms as 'equilibrium'[13]: an essentialised good and producer of peace.

Nonetheless, leading intellectuals were sceptical. Abbé Saint-Pierre was the sharpest of critics, followed closely by Rousseau and Kant. Saint-Pierre believed that the balance of power obstructed the possibility of achieving a durable peace in Europe.[14] For Kant, the balance of power was too feeble an

[10] Moorhead Wright argues many of the theoretical explanations of the balance of power 'have been devoted to reconciling [these] two imperatives'. M. Wright, *Theory and Practice of the Balance of Power 1486–1914* (London, 1975), ix. The partitions of Poland (1772, 1793, 1795) are examples that can be accredited to this latter imperative.

[11] D. Boucher, *Political Theories of International Relations – From Thucydides to the Present* (Oxford, 1998), 308.

[12] For the changing strategies of international order between universal monarchy and balance of power, see P. Schröder, 'The concepts of universal monarchy & balance of power in the first half of the seventeenth century – a case study', in M. Koskenniemi and W. Rech (eds.), *International Law and Empire: Historical Explorations* (Oxford, 2016), 83–100.

[13] A. Benthley, *Scientific Cosmology and International Orders* (Cambridge, 2018), see chapter 3.

[14] P. Schröder, *Trust in Early Modern International Political Thought, 1598–1713* (Cambridge, 2017), 183–184.

institution to guarantee a long-lasting peace.[15] Rousseau noted that 'this much vaunted equilibrium has been established by anyone, and that anyone has done anything on purpose to preserve it: one finds that it exists; and those who do not feel themselves to have enough weight to break it, cover their particular intentions with the pretext of maintaining it . . .'[16] David Hume only agreed that the balance of power was beneficial in so far as it saved Europe from universal monarchy; preserving the balance of power was primarily an act of prudence. In his brief but influential essay, 'Of the Balance of Power' (1752), he states that 'the maxim of preserving the balance of power is founded so much on common sense and obvious reasoning . . .'[17] But as far as Hume was concerned, balance of power was not a natural and universal self-regulating feature of international relations but rather a political device to serve states' interest. More often than not, Hume warned, it is carried out with 'excess' and acts as a cause of war.[18] Vattel shared this scepticism about the balance of power as an efficient regulator of international order.

Thus, eighteenth-century balance of power ideas were far from unified. Recently, Bruno Arcidiacono has identified three different models of balance of power theorisation in the eighteenth century.[19] First, *équilibre sécuritaire*: a theory of security where survival relies on the ability to discourage attacks and repel them should they occur. Sovereigns must be vigilant of the power of their neighbours, and be cognisant that a winnable war today may provoke an unwinnable war tomorrow. Second, *anti-hegemonic equilibrium*: a condition that designates a global plurality opposed to the emergence of a hegemon, which is more powerful than any alliance of the rest of the system. Third, *pacifistic equilibrium*: an organising principle that assumes that multiple powers are pre-eminent powers such that no one actor could approach dominating the others or unifying them under their control, and no power could attack another, smaller state without imperilling the general state of liberty. In this case, the system would become a pacifistic one, which would dissuade and prevent any strong member from preying on a weaker one.

15 I. Kant, *Perpetual Peace: A Philosophical Essay*, translated by M. Campbell Smith (London, 1903).

16 J. J. Rousseau *The Plan for Perpetual Peace, On the Government of Poland, and Other Writings on History and Politics* (Chicago, 2005), 33.

17 D. Hume, 'Of the balance of power', in Knud Haakonssen (ed.), *Political Essays* (Cambridge, 1994), 154–160, at 157.

18 Ibid., 159–160.

19 B. Arcidiacono, 'De la balance politique et de ses rapports avec le droit des gens: Vattel, la 'guerre pour l'équilibre' et le système européen', in V. Chetail and P. Haggenmacher (eds.), *Vattel's International in a XXIst Century Perspective/Le droit international de Vattel vu du XXe siècle* (Leiden, 2011), 77–100.

Arcidiacono argues that these three interpretations of the balance of power invariably invoke different situations. For instance, the balance of power invoked at the Treaty of Utrecht 1713 was certainly not the political maxim of first category *équilibre sécuritaire*, but rather the second anti-hegemonic principle deployed to curtail the aggrandisement of the House of Bourbon.[20]

However practiced or theorised, by the eighteenth century, the balance of power was seen by most jurists and practitioners as integral to the rules that underpinned the law of nations, if not 'the necessary precondition to the existence of such a law'.[21]

THE NECESSARY AND VOLUNTARY LAW OF NATIONS

Vattel was intellectual heir to longstanding debates about the preservation of international order. In the sixteenth and seventeenth centuries, these debates fundamentally addressed endemic religious and cultural disputes that undermined the moral project of unified Europe. The challenge of defining a workable European order required a more systematic theorising of the law of nations and its relation to the law of nature. For instance, how were obligations arising from natural law norms about individual self-preservation and sociability to be effected in the law of nations once such individuals had formed social collectives? While Hobbes had made the controversial move of completely equating the two, most natural law theorists, Samuel von Pufendorf (1632–1694) excluded, believed that the natural law had to go through some transformation when applied to states. Yet Christian Wolff and Vattel thought Hobbes had been on to something important in arguing that the law of nations was in fact the law of nature applied to states rather than individuals.[22] Vattel acknowledges that in Hobbes' work we discover the 'hand of a master, notwithstanding his paradoxes and detestable maxims' (*LN*, prelim. 9). Even so, once men had been separated into corporate nations, natural law could never be applied directly and abstractly, but always indirectly through justice via the various civil laws, customs, conventions, institutions, and historical circumstances of each nation. Wolff and Vattel's

[20] See also R. Lesaffer, 'The peace of Utrecht, the balance of power and the law of nations', in A. Soons (ed.) *The 1713 Peace of Utrecht and Its Enduring Effects* (Leiden, 2019), 67–89.

[21] A. Vagts and D. F. Vagts, 'The balance of power in international law: A history of an idea', *The American Journal of International Law* 73.4 (1979), 555–580, at 555.

[22] Some of these ideas were laid out in C. Boisen and D. Boucher, 'Hobbes and subjecting international relations to law and morality', in R. Prokhovnik and G. Slomp (eds.), *International Political Theory after Hobbes – Analysis, Interpretation and Orientation* (London, 2011), 81–101.

separation of the two systems of law was not a disavowal of natural law as the moral basis of international justice, but rather an acknowledgement of the question of how best to articulate it.

Vattel expressly establishes the law of nations as a law between states, insisting on the perfect equality and independence of nations, regardless of size or strength (*LN*, prelim. 18). Nations are sovereign and politically self-determining (*LN*, II-IV-54). This strong emphasis upon sovereign integrity places the state, not individuals, at the centre of international law. In this sense, the state becomes the subject of rights and duties. Vattel took his lead from Jean Barbeyrac (1674–1744), Pufendorf's and Grotius' translator, in accepting that the law of nature required some modifications before it could be applied to the relationships between states, but contends that his predecessor did not go far enough in separating the two. Certain implications of a separate natural law of nations are obligatory to states and sovereigns (*LN*, prelim. 10). The conduct of states is different from that of individuals because it 'is not usually the caprice or blind impetuosity of a single person that forms the resolutions and determines the measures of the public: they are carried on with more deliberation and circumspection' (*LN*, prelim. 15). Vattel is thus adamant that a rule must be assessed and adapted according to its subject.[23] Vattel makes a threefold distinction of the law of nations: necessary, voluntary, and arbitrary. The first two, he contends, are derived from the law of nature. Necessary law is that which is internal and binding on one's conscience. It is just and good in itself, although there will be exceptions to and modifications of the rigour of the necessary law. The voluntary is that which is obligatory because it is conducive to the general welfare and safety of mankind. It further relies on the will of the sovereign and includes all the practical and prudential considerations in dealing with and alleviating the effects of war.[24] The arbitrary law of nations differs in kind from the other two in that it comprises those customs that have by tacit consent arisen from and bind only those nations who subscribe to certain maxims through common usage (*LN*, prelim. 17).

Two aspects of Vattel's concept of the law of nations needs further exposition to understand the restraints Vattel places on states' interactions: first, the necessary legal fiction of the moral person of the state to assume certain rights and duties and what those rights and duties are; and second, how and when they are discharged, especially duties relating to mutual assistance. With

[23] Zurbuchen, 'Vattel's Law of Nations', 409, see also Vattel, *The Law of Nations*, 5, 69.

[24] Vattel, *The Law of Nations*, 10a–11a; See also D. Boucher, *The Limits of Ethics in International Relations – Natural Law, Natural Rights and Human Rights in Transition* (Oxford, 2009), 140.

regard to the latter, we find Vattel to be over-cautious, even in service of the collective security of states. His prime concern is the irrational behaviour of states:

> How happy mankind would be, were these amiable precepts of nature every where observed! … [V]iolent methods of deciding contests would be no more heard of: all differences would be terminated by moderation, justice, and equity; men would live every-where like brothers, and each individual be a citizen of the universe. That this idea should be but a delightful dream! Yet it flows from the nature and essence of man. But disorderly passions, and private and mistaken interest, will forever prevent its being realised. (*LN*, II-1-16)

Vattel opposes an irrational actor discharging themselves of the duty that society places on them as discharging a duty presupposes rational judgement. If states aim towards peaceful living, the balance of power would ideally be the outcome of good faith discharging of duties. However, as will be apparent, balance of power can never be a reason to go to war by itself.

RIGHTS AND DUTIES OF STATES

Vattel, following Wolff, defines the nation or state as a body politic which has 'her affairs and her interest; she deliberates and takes resolutions in common; thus, becoming a moral person, who possesses an understanding and will peculiar to herself, and is susceptible of obligations and rights' (*LN*, prelim. 2). The rights and duties relating to each nation must be consistent with their distinct natures. Nations, he argues, can only be constructed as collections of so many individuals living in a state of nature, and therefore all the rights and duties ascribed to individuals must be ascribed to nations. Whatever their other differences, they share duties of self-preservation, self-promotion, and mutual assistance: '[A] moral being is charged with obligation to himself, only with the view to his perfection and happiness' (*LN*, I-11-14) and likewise for the preservation and happiness for other states (*LN*, I-11-17). The state has moral capabilities as a distinct deliberative agent with separate yet homologous rights and duties to those of the individual. The analogy between the moral person of the individual and the moral person of the state is a powerful fiction to clarify and legitimate certain duties to uphold justice. Nature has established a universal society among humankind derived from individuals' natural sociability. Natural societies, both between individuals and between states, are predicated on mutual assistance for their survival and development (LN, prelim. 12). 'Every nation', Vattel asserts, 'ought, on occasion, to labour for the preservation of others, and for securing them from ruin and destruction' (*LN*, II-I-4). In fact, he encourages states to undertake wars for the sake of mutual assistance, for example, assisting an oppressed people against tyranny (*LN*, II-IV-56; 61). Such cases are technically not a violation of states' liberty, as sovereignty is temporarily suspended (*LN*, II-IV-56), as is also the case in times when religious persecution is carried out with 'intolerable excess' such that 'all distinction of states and nations are to be disregarded, when there is question of forming a coalition against a set of madmen, who would exterminate all those that do not implicitly receive their doctrines' (*LN*, II-IV-62).

The duty to assist relies on a nation's own judgement of self-preservation and capabilities. In practice, this would mean that when a neighbouring state is attacked unjustly by a belligerent that threatens to destroy it, nations have a duty to assist on the condition that the duty can be discharged without exposure to 'great danger' (*LN*, II-I-4). We find the same duty of assistance in relation to famines (*LN*, II-I-5). Such duties to assist neighbouring states are imperfect. Nature has constituted a general society where humans require assistance from their fellow humans, even if nature cannot be said to have imposed or prescribed perfect obligations of uniting them together into civil society (*LN*, I-II-16). The reciprocal relationship between nations in terms of assistance, mutual intercourse, and communication can be sufficiently regulated by natural law.

Vattel divided the obligations nations have and the correlating rights that they produce into internal and external obligations. Internal obligations are what could be termed the conscience of each nation, deduced from the rules of their duty towards themselves and other nations. Nations may deduce the duties they have to one another through examining external obligations. These external obligations are divided into perfect and imperfect obligations. Vattel argues that the '*perfect obligation* is that which gives to the opposite party the right of compulsion; the *imperfect* gives him only the right to ask' (*LN*, prelim. 17). A nation is free to act as it wills as long as it does not violate the perfect right of other nations, and it acts under internal obligations without any perfect external obligation. If one state is to be subjected to another's authority, this requires consent.[25]

BALANCE OF POWER AS AN ESTIMATE OF JUST WAR

The fact that human society depends on observing justice is of even greater imperative for the society of states because war is so destructive (*LN*, II-V-63).

[25] Boucher, *Political Theories of International Relations*, 263.

However, nations are more self-sufficient than individuals and therefore not as vulnerable,[26] and when it comes to international justice, there is a strict hierarchy of duties that defines the extent of states' sociability. The voluntary law of nations is thus essential to promoting peace and happiness among the international society of states while recognising and maintaining states' reciprocal equality and independence. Because states are free and independent of each other, they themselves must serve as judges of what their conscience demands in relation to what they can or cannot do. For example, they must judge whether acting in solidarity with other states, such as coming to the aid of a neighbour threatened by an enemy, would prove a precarious business, for, Vattel warns, 'a nation ought carefully to avoid, as much as possible, whatever might cause its destruction' (*LN*, prelim. 19). This is especially the case if a neighbouring state would desire defence from a threatening neighbour who is growing in power. As we shall see, Vattel is unequivocal in his belief that invoking balance of power for distributive justice schemes designed to equalise the power of states is unjustified, and amounts to aggression.[27] Thus, the law of nations did not support this kind of 'international adventurism'.[28] However, we are advised to be vigilant against the rise of an aggrandiser. However, this vigilance presupposes knowledge about other states' capabilities and intentions that might be difficult to ascertain for the purpose of war; the principle of balance of power here is an unreliable mechanism to establish a title to just war.

A primary goal for Vattel, as it had been for the judicious Grotius, was always to warn against the effects of war, but if necessary ensure its expedience and prevent its recurrence through effective international corporation under the auspice of the law of nations.[29] The law of nations was not meant to establish just *causes* of war[30] but rather rules of just *conduct*. Similarly, Vattel's insistence on states' equal natural liberty meant that no one state could stand in judgement of another. In war, we have to assume justice residing on both sides of the warring parties, regardless of our judgement of the overall justice or injustice of their cause. Neither Grotius nor Vattel were primarily engaged in the moral struggle for the prevention of war, famously earning them the

[26] Ibid.

[27] See also ibid., 265.

[28] Zurbruchen, 'Vattel's *Law of Nations*', 2.

[29] H. Grotius, *The Rights of War and Peace*, bk III, chap. III, §1 (Indianapolis, 2005).

[30] Ibid., bk III, chap. III, §xi. As Grotius clarifies, the just cause of the war cannot be ascertained by its public declaration mainly because states' motives for engaging in war can never be properly established.

unkind epithet of 'miserable comforters' by Kant.[31] Yet while they certainly did not wish to undermine the nation's right to go to war as Kant tried to do, they did wish to subject it to the rule of law. War being so horrific, Vattel believed that recourse to it should be invoked only in extremity, and even then only 'as a remedy against injustice' (*LN*, III-IV-51). For Kant, *jus gentium* propositions conceptualised by the likes of Grotius, Pufendorf, and Vattel exposed an insincere commitment to a just international order as they continued to elevate war as a sacred and fundamental – that is to say *natural* – right of states.[32]

While Vattel preferred peace to war and frequently appealed to a universal society of states that might institutionalise conditions for peace more effectively, he was nevertheless deeply apprehensive of the sort of projects for perpetual peace that advocated either a 'benevolent hegemony or a European federation'.[33] Vattel recognised that the international society of states was not harmoniously united for the purpose of felicitous corporation (*LN*, I-II-16). He was never persuaded by his mentor Christian Wolff's grand scheme of a supreme-state based on the voluntary law of nations, *civitas maxima*, which he saw as a work of pure fiction (*LN*, prelim. 9). He was sceptical of the Holy Roman Empire assuming the place of role model for the necessary transformation and perfection of the European state system into a moral community of nations.[34]

Absent this harmony, Nicholas Greenwood Onuf finds that Vattel creates a problem for himself: while the natural society of states can remain as a foundation for the *necessary* law of nations, the *voluntary* law offers nothing comparable that guarantees states' compliance and adherence to peaceful and commodious living. Vattel's solution to this problem, Onuf argues, is the balance of power.[35] These important observations are misguided for two related reasons. First, they place too much faith in the balance of power as a promoter of international justice. Such a reading would inevitably presuppose a re-conceptualisation of Vattel's principle of mutual assistance, by changing the conditions under which obligations to assist might arise. Second, they

31 Kant, *Perpetual Peace*, 131.

32 Hunter, 'Kant and Vattel in context', 478.

33 B. Kapossy and R. Whitmore, 'Introduction', in *The Law of Nations*, ed. B. Kapossy and R. Whitmore (Indianapolis, 2008), xii–xiii.

34 I. Nakhimovsky, 'Vattel's theory of the international order: Commerce and the balance of power in the Law of Nations', *History of European Ideas* 33.2 (2007), 157–173, at 161.

35 Nicholas Greenwood Onuf, 'Civitas Maxima: Wolff, Vattel and the fate of republicanism', *American Journal of International Law* 88.2 (1994), 280–303, 301. Kapossy and Whitmore make a similar claim (see *supra* note 35).

would allow balance of power reasoning a more prominent place in the moral justification of war than what Vattel intended.

If war is truly horrific, and Vattel thinks 'it should never be undertaken without the most cogent reasons' (*LN*, III-III-24) such as to remediate injustices (*LN*, III-III-51), does the balance of power fulfil just war theory criteria? That is, can the defence of the balance of power morally justify taking up arms? Of course, all sovereign states have the right to go to war (and justice is on their side), but Vattel advises sovereign rulers to always caution themselves that unnecessary wars are unquestionable moral calamities that expose them to judgement – not punitively by other nations, but by God. What principles do we have to guide our estimation for when states are justified in using force? Vattel comments on three: injury; threat of injury; and the balance of power. He provides us with two levels of reasoning: justification and expedience. *Justificatory reasons* denote that an injury has taken place (*LN*, III-III-26). War is allowable, that is, justified under certain conditions: when states' immanent survival is threatened or the injury has already happened. As Vattel says, '[n]ature imposes no obligation on me, without giving them means of fulfilling them' (*LN*, II-IX-116). Use of force for reasons of self-preservation might necessitate pre-emptive strikes to anticipate an aggressor's intentions. The right to preserve oneself, or *right to security* as Vattel terms it, especially when used pre-emptively, is to be exercised with caution so as 'not to attack [an enemy state] upon vague and uncertain suspicions, lest she should incur the imputation of becoming herself an unjust aggressor' (*LN*, II-IV-50). Thus, force against 'those who spurn justice' (*LN*, III-III-25) is always to be used as a last resort. Expedience and capacity are the secondary reasons. These are what Vattel calls *motives* and 'determine whether it be expedient for the sovereign to undertake war' (*LN*, III-III-25). The justness of a war presupposes that we are able to ascertain whether an injury has been received or genuinely threatened with one. Only an injury to states' perfect rights gives rise to a just claim to war. The object of war is therefore always to avenge or prevent injury, seeking reparation, and if the damage done is too great, punish the offending party. Vattel deduces two kinds of just wars, offensive – 'to recover what belongs to us' and 'provide for our future safety' through punitive measures – and defensive – self-defence and 'repelling unjust violence' (*LN*, III-III-28).

Conditional upon the justified reasons for war are states' intentions. Vattel writes '[t]he proper motives shew that ... it is advisable and expedient' that a state makes use of its right to go to war. But states should not abuse their rights, and justification is relative to the reasons for defending them. We might be justified going to war, but if we undertake it for the *wrong* reasons (i.e. vicious motives), we are doing something immoral. Proper or commendable motives are those 'derived from the good of the state, from the safety and common advantage of citizens'. Vicious motives are those not drawn from a 'pure source' (motivation of charity), but instead by 'arrogant desires of command, the ostentation of power, the thirst of riches, the avidity of conquest, hatred and revenge' (*LN*, III-III-30). Vicious motives undermine claims to justice and dressing them up as honourable makes them mere pretexts (*LN*, III-III-32), which nonetheless, Vattel consoles, 'are at least a homage which unjust men pay to injustice' (*LN*, III-III-32). A special kind of enemy that deserves our condemnation are those states that would make war for no apparent reason or motives. They are 'public enemies' and '[a]ll nations have a right to join a confederacy for the purpose of punishing and even exterminating those savage nations' (*LN*, III-III-34). Public enemies are not merely a scourge of a less enlightened past. Even in more 'polished ages and among the most civilised nations' we find those 'supposed heroes whose supreme delight is battle' (*LN*, III-III-34).

Other cases are more doubtful, 'where the rights are uncertain' and ascertaining the justice of a cause questionable. Victory is no judge of right or justice, and neither is the voluntary law of nations. As Grotius also contended, it affords the warring parties with certain legal effects after taking up arms, not a justified reason for war.[36] The principle of sovereignty requires that we assume that states have just cause to war as neither can claim right of judgement over each other, even though '[w]ar cannot be just on both sides' (*LN*, III-III-39). In such cases, all nations can do is to judge for themselves and assist the party who appears to have justice on its side. 'Every free and sovereign state has a right to determine, according to the dictates of her own conscience, what her duties require of her, and what she can or cannot do with justice' (*LN*, III-XII-188; prelim. 16).

So far, we have explicated the principles for estimating the justice of war, which allows only the narrowest titles to war without violating states' liberties. Vattel curtails even punitive wars to punish serious breaches of natural law, which were favoured by his predecessor Grotius. Vattel stressed that Grotius' mistake lay in supposing that the freedom attributed to individuals and sovereign states somehow gave rise to a right to punish crimes against nature. To the contrary, a state's right to punish only existed against those who injured it. Any action beyond this maxim would violate the autonomy of the moral person of the sovereign state. Vattel warned that an unsubstantiated right to punish crimes against nature gave states ruled by ambitious men too easy a

[36] See Camilla Boisen, 'Hugo Grotius, Declaration of war and the international moral order', *Grotiana* 41.2 (2020), 282–303.

pretext for waging war and 'opens the door to all the passions of zealots and fanatics' (*LN*, II-I-7). States can promote alleged contributions to the common good, such as sending missionaries to preach religious ideals, but these humanitarian efforts are imperfect obligations, and nations cannot compel other nations to perform them, nor punish states who are in violation of them.

It is not without significance that Vattel introduces the balance of power in the context of denouncing punitive wars. Essentially, Vattel is interested in states' judgement of behaviours of other states and associated rights and duties. The indigenous nations in the Americas might have committed grave natural law violations, but they had committed none that affect Europeans so as to give just title to war (*LN*, II-I-7). Nations should, as far as possible, curb behaviours that might cause displeasure, but the fault (for being offended) lies with those who take offence (*LN*, II-II-19). Concerning judgements against states that fulfil their duty of self-perfection, Vattel asks whether the aggrandisement of a neighbouring power can authorise war against it (*LN*, III-III-42). Vattel cautions that, while adopting anti-hegemonic policies seems straightforward for politicians, 'it is more difficult of a solution to those who wish to see justice and prudence ever inseparably united' (*LN*, III-III-42). Vattel's subsequent discussion of balance of power reveals that in its interior logic, the balance of power did not hold a *casus belli*, but was simply a description of a desirable political circumstance. In fact, this was part of Vattel's line of defence to Frederick II's claim of having to take preventive action against an overbearing alliance from his manifesto of war of August 1756.[37] Vattel understands the balance of power as 'a disposition of things, as that no one potentate be able absolutely to predominate, and prescribe laws to others.' It has been established through '[t]he continual attention of sovereigns to every occurrence, the constant residence of ministers, and the perpetual negotiations, [which] make of modern Europe a kind of republic, of which the members – each independent, but all linked together by ties of common interest – unite for the maintenance of order and liberty' (*LN*, III-III-47). This common interest is to remain independent and is the source of the balance of power as essentially the disposition of things in which no power may be preeminent above the other. The situation where any power could 'prescribe laws to others' would be contrary to the *status juris*. Thus, prudence and justice should compel sovereigns to prevent the rise of a hegemon. The best way to maintain this state is to ensure the parity of all states, like Henry IV desired to do (*LN*, III-III-47), while another possibility would be for smaller

[37] See Lesaffer, 'Aggression before Versailles'.

powers all to unite to equal the power of the greatest among them. However, such parity is purely theoretical, inorganic, and impossible to maintain.[38]

Thus, Vattel bases the principle of the balance of power on the absolute right, especially of smaller states, to combine for the purpose of safeguarding their independence against the threat posed by their greater neighbours.[39] Nevertheless, the imprudence of states to remain passive spectators against aggrandised powers, Vattel counsels, does not give moral licence to war against the state that upsets the balance of power. War is only valid when it addresses an injury or responds to a real threat. Assessing what constitutes a real threat is a particular problem. Furthermore, all the commonplace requirements of just war are still in place. War has to be carried out honourably, only going so far as to proportionally address the injury or extinguish the threat. Any excess renders it invalid, and military action must be the last recourse.

Rather than a moral justification for war, the balance of power is a practical historical reality of European political life, with England traditionally holding the position of 'balancer'. England is 'attentive to preserve it in equilibrium: – system of policy, which is in itself highly just and wise, and will ever entitle her to praise, as long as she continues to pursue it only by means of alliances, confederacies, and other methods equally lawful' (*LN*, III-iii-47). Vattel seems unequivocal here: use of force is not a lawful method to maintain the balance of power, despite its contribution to the production of justice. Thus, the operationalisation of the balance of power is uncertain for Vattel exactly because he makes it conditional upon just and wise acts of policy. Working within the bounds of international law, England can maintain a European equilibrium, but as Peter Gellman rightly argues, Vattel's conceptualisation offers 'no rules of an operating balance of power, only a description of a particular state in a specific period committed to opposing imperialism through a program of countervailing alliance and naval mastery'.[40] As such, Vattel denies its efficacy as a guiding principle for assessing the justice of war.

Vattel's unenthusiastic account of the balance of power is somewhat glossed over by his recent commentators. Arcidiacono accounts Vattel's lack of enthusiasm for a confused and ambivalent engagement with the balance of power

38 See also Arcidiacono, 'De la balance politique'.

39 M. S. Anderson: 'Eighteenth-century theories of the balance of power', in Ragnild Hatton and M. S. Anderson (eds.) *Studies in Diplomatic History – Essays in the Memory of David Bayne Horn* (London, 1970), 183–198, at 190.

40 P. Gellman, 'The elusive explanation: Balance of power "theory" and the origins of World War I', *Review of International Studies* 15.2 (1989), Special Issue on the Balance of Power, 155–182, at 159.

that never settles on a single clear definition of 'equilibrium'. However, Arcidiacono argues that once we accept that Vattel engages with three distinct conceptual relationships to international law, his presentation of the idea of a balance of power becomes uniquely clear. The three workings of the balance of power (i.e. équilibre sécuritaire, anti-hegemonic equilibrium and pacifistic equilibrium) correspond to a more general usage of balance of power conceptual vocabulary in the eighteenth century. Arciadiancono argues that his threefold conception of balance of power clarifies Vattel's position. Arcidiacono's discussion of Vattel's invocation of anti-hegemonic equilibrium is of particular interest for present discussion. Here, he argues that Vattel attempts to combine the prudence of maintaining the balance of power with justice, that is complying with the necessary and voluntary law of nations. Arcidiacono is less interested in how this is done than in the discourse, that is, the exercise of putting the balance of power forward as an estimate of just title to war. However, as should already be apparent, Vattel is unable to reconcile the two. Nakhimovsky goes as far as collating the two criteria of prudence and justice.

Isaac Nakhimovsky claims that the balance of power constitutes for Vattel '[t]he most important institution described by the voluntary law of nations', whose operational purpose 'consists in the limitations that states may justifiably place on commerce in order to ensure their liberty'.[41] But as Zurbruchen correctly establishes, Vattel's doctrine of the balance of power specifically questions whether preventive warfare against an aggrandising power meets the *jus ad bellum* criteria.[42] On the balance of power, Vattel sets aside means for protecting the equilibrium that rely on violence and injustice and opines that '... force of arms is not the only expedient by which we may guard against a formidable power' (*LN*, III-III-46). Indeed, alliances, confederacies, and lawful methods 'of a gentler nature' are best suited to maintain the equilibrium. That said, diplomacy may not be sufficient. In reality, '[g]reat potentates ... are but too successful in gaining over partisans and allies, who blindly adopt their views' and risk being 'swallowed up' (*LN*, III-III-49). Vattel concedes that the community of states seize the 'first favourable opportunity ... to weaken the potentate who destroys the equilibrium' by means of force when this can be done 'consistently with justice' (*LN*, III-III-49). Vattel sees pre-emptive attacks as valid, as long as they are not based on vague and uncertain suspicions. It must follow a combination of the power of the would-be aggressor to domin-

[41] Nakhimovsky, 'Vattel's theory of the international order', 163.
[42] Zurbruchen, 'Vattel's *Law of Nations*', 413.

ate her neighbours and her clear disposition or desire to do so.[43] Even so, when a neighbour makes preparation for war, states should err on the side of caution. Whether states are allowed a preventive attack 'greatly depends on the manners and character of that neighbour' (*LN*, III-III-50). The appearance of danger does not give right and cannot be taken 'for a sufficient indication' (*LN*, III-III-44). Overtures and seeking clarification of intention is all states can hope to do for 'we ought not, without sufficient cause, to presume him capable of exposing himself to infamy by adding perfidy to violence' (*LN*, III-III-50). States should be vigilant, but to keep large standing armies for this end is to play into the hands of the would-be aggressor, in addition to being a financial and agricultural burden to the state and a threat to peoples' common liberties. Here Vattel commends both England and Switzerland in their long-standing mistrust of standing armies (*LN*, III-III-50). Thus, when applied, the balance of power is a precarious principle that entails vigilance through standing armies and armament, a necessary evil Vattel is unwilling to accept.[44]

Vattel saw the balance of power as an *ideal* that seeks to condition states toward more peaceful and commodious interactions, while encouraging collective vigilance over any aggrandiser, belligerent or peaceable. Invoking it as a principle of war is, however, unjustified. Europe by his day, Vattel noted, had become transformed from a 'confused heap of detached pieces' into an integrated 'political system' (*LN*, III-III-47), but the European society of states did not take on a greater moral value than the individual sovereign states that comprised it.

CONCLUSION

We are left to assess the remaining question, why did Vattel use the balance of power as an estimate of the moral justification of war? The answer is somewhat eclipsed by Vattel's own indoctrination into the eighteenth century thinking about the concept. The balance of power for Vattel is not an act or specific practice to be undertaken. Rather, it is a characteristic of peaceful coexistence. It has value as an assessment tool, but Vattel left its moral and political potentiality intentionally vague. Thus, Vattel used an established idea of how to think about order, but left it somewhat undefined and unexplored precisely because he thought the balance of power a concept of assessment

43 Ibid.

44 Vattel was in the service of the elector of Saxony and wrote a year after Frederick's 1756 invasion of Saxony under the claim that is was participant to a premeditated attack by Vienna and Petersburg on Prussia. See *supra* note 37.

and a characteristic of actions rather than a set of actions themselves. However, translated into practice, or operationalised, it is a policy that to a large extent rests upon the principles of reason. We cannot rely on states being reasonable even when they accept the same premise or follow established rules of conduct; it is rather the honour (or lack thereof) of their intentions that makes the balancing mechanism morally unreliable. As such, the balance of power cannot be a motivator or reason for conflict as at any moment the actor or state using it may be unreasonable. Instead Vattel sought to encourage states' good reflective practices when it comes to the discharge of their mutual rights and duties that could withstand changes in how that good was conceived or achieved. A state's duty is to reflect on the potentiality of an act and the duty to itself and how it affects others. The balance of power is part of a state's moral horizon, but attaining it does not follow a particular calculation or set of acts. Rather, it results from when these acts have been done correctly.

FURTHER READING

M. S. Anderson, 'Eighteenth-century theories of the balance of power', in Ragnild Hatton and M. S. Anderson (eds.) *Studies in Diplomatic History – Essays in the Memory of David Bayne Horn* (London, 1970), 183–198.

Bruno Arcidiacono, 'De la balance politique et de ses rapports avec le droit des gens: Vattel, la 'guerre pour l'équilibre' et le système européen', in Vincent Chetail and Peter Haggenmacher (eds.), *Vattel's International in a XXIst Century Perspective/Le droit international de Vattel vu du XXe siècle* (Leiden, 2011), 77–100.

Heinz Duchhardt, 'The missing balance', *Journal of the History of International Law* 2 (2000), 67–72.

Isaac Nakhimovsky, 'Vattel's theory of the international order: Commerce and the balance of power in the *Law of Nations*', *History of European Ideas* 33.2 (2007), 157–173.

Walter Rech, *Enemies of Mankind: Vattel's Theory of Collective Security* (Leiden, 2013).

Michael Sheehan, *The Balance of Power – History and Theory* (London, 1996).

Simone Zurbuchen, 'Vattel's law of nations and just war theory', *History of European Ideas* 35.4 (2009), 408–417.

7

Regular War, Irregulars, and Savages

PABLO KALMANOVITZ

One of the most appalling uses of standards of civilization in international legal history is the two-tiered construction of the laws of war in the nineteenth century. The international legal profession in Europe and other 'civilized nations' took 'savages' to be incapable of showing restraint in warfare, and as such beyond the pale of the limiting rules of civilized, regular warfare. International lawyers sanctioned the deployment of unlimited violence by European powers against non-Europeans in colonial wars; legal norms that were well established in European practice, such as giving quarter to combatants and sparing women and children from deliberate attacks, were deemed inapplicable in such radically asymmetrical wars.[1]

International legal scholars usually locate the historical roots of this particular form of civilizing brutality in the nineteenth century. While European imperial and colonial projects contributed decisively to the creation and development of the modern law of nations at least since the time of Hugo Grotius, the harshest forms of legally sanctioned imperial violence resulted from the radicalization of European ideals of progress, cultural superiority, and the 'civilizing mission' in the nineteenth century.[2] Legal treatises in the eighteenth century, by contrast, tended to embrace forms of universal

[1] F. Mégret, 'From "savages" to "unlawful combatants": A postcolonial look at the international humanitarian law's "other",' in Anne Orford (ed.), *International Law and Its "Others"* (Cambridge, 2006), 263–317; S. Scheipers, *Unlawful Combatants: A Genealogy of the Irregular Fighter* (Oxford, 2015), 146–187;S. Moyn, *Humane: America's Road to Endless War* (New York, 2021), chapter 4.

[2] As Mégret writes, 'the question of the position of non-European peoples in relation to the laws of war ... arose historically over only a small period of time during the second half of the nineteenth century (and only episodically after that), in situations in which savage peoples could still be considered to be relatively autonomous.' See Mégret, 'From "savages" to "unlawful combatants"', 270. On the colonial origins of international law, see generally M. Koskenniemi, *The Rise and Fall of International Law 1870–1960* (Cambridge, 2001), 98–178;

pluralism that were in principle open to recognizing non-European peoples as members in full standing of the community of nations and legitimate subjects of the law of nations. The laws of war in particular were in principle accessible to and binding on all sovereign peoples, not just on European states.[3]

This chapter examines the extent to which Emer de Vattel's work fits into this chronology and general picture of international legal history and the history of the laws of war in particular. Contemporary commentaries in this regard have diverged widely. Some commentators have highlighted the most universal and pluralist aspects of Vattel's work, noting in particular his condemnation of the Spanish conquest of America, his recognition of the sovereign rights of non-European peoples, and his rejection of Christianity as a criterion for membership in the society of sovereign nations.[4] Vattel wrote about the law of nations within the genre of the modern natural law tradition, which took universal reason to be the ultimate basis for legal validity and international rights and obligations. And while Vattel's pluralism was not unlimited, the conditions he set on membership to the community of nations were narrow and tied not to standards of civilization but to the pluralist principles he was so keen to defend. Only states that systematically failed to recognize the equal rights of other states put themselves outside the pale of the law of nations.[5]

Other commentators have highlighted the more parochial aspects Vattel's work, arguing that his apparent universalism is really a skillfully abstract rendering and defense of a highly particular and contingent state form, that is, the Protestant agricultural and militaristic republics of his Swiss

and A. Anghie, *Imperialism, Sovereignty, and the Making of International Law* (Cambridge, 2005).

3 See e.g. C. H. Alexandrowicz, 'The theory of recognition in Fieri', *British Yearbook of International Law* 34 (1958), 185, passim; C. H. Alexandrowicz, *An Introduction to the History of International Law in the East Indies* (Oxford, 1967); E. Tourme-Jouannet, 'Des Origines Coloniales du Droit International: À propos du droit des gens moderne au 18ème siècle', in P. Dupuy and V Chetail (eds.), *The Roots of International Law: Liber Amicorum Peter Haggenmacher* (Leiden, 2014).

4 Vattel defended the rights of China to forbid foreigners from entering its territory (*LN*, II-VII-94); rejected the thesis that international treaties could not be signed with non-Christian peoples (*LN*, II-XII-162); labeled the Spanish conquest of Peru and Mexico a 'notorious usurpation' (*LN*, I-VII-81, 130; II-I-7); and defended the right of the Aztec emperor Moctezuma to rebel against the Spanish conquerors (LN, IV-IV-37).

5 A. Hurrell, 'Vattel: Pluralism and its limits', in Ian Clark (ed.), *Classical Theories of International Relations* (New York, 1996); Tourme-Jouannet, 'Des Origines Coloniales du Droit International.' As Hurrell writes, 'Vattel tends towards an inclusive conception of international society, acknowledging the rights of political communities in many parts of the world . . . however, there may still be political communities whose refusal to accept the ground-rules of international society places them, quite literally, outside the pale' (p. 245).

homeland.[6] Vattel was not so much concerned with genuine questions of global ordering, in particular whether and how states could exist outside Europe, but rather with intra-European problems, in particular with the territorialization of state jurisdiction and the preservation of political autonomy for Protestant republics. According to this reading, the question of the scope of Vattel's universalism is misguided because it misses the actual purpose of his work and falls in the trap of his deceivingly abstract theoretical language.

Yet others have taken seriously Vattel's multiple references to non-European peoples but questioned the apparent universality of his pluralism. A central line of questioning has focused on Vattel's account of land cultivation as a natural duty of states and his defense of the occupation of and settlement in idle land. In virtue of this duty, nomadic peoples, such as the Tartars in Central Asia and indigenous tribes in North America, could not lawfully oppose the establishment of European colonies in the underexploited territories they roam (*LN*, I-VII-81, I-XVIII-209–210, but cf. II-VII-97). Similar to Locke before him, Vattel's account of the state and territorial rights produced a differentiated legal regime in which European nations in effect had a stronger immunity to intervention than non-European peoples deemed idle or wasteful, and in this way provided a powerful legitimization for European colonial projects in North America and elsewhere.[7]

In what follows I reconstruct and discuss another important instance of legal differentiation in Vattel's articulation of the doctrine of regular war. In general terms, Vattel presented his account of regular war as being applicable to any sovereign nation, regardless of its being European or not. He used the terms 'savage' and 'barbarian' to refer to agents of violence that seriously violated the rules of regular war, both European and non-European. He also said explicitly that non-European nations could fight war in a civilized manner, that is, in keeping with the rules of regular warfare (e.g. *LN*, III-VIII-158). However, I will show in what follows that Vattel did reserve to non-European peoples

[6] I. Hunter, 'Vattel's Law of Nations: Diplomatic casuistry for the protestant nation', *Grotiana* 31 (2010), 108–140; I. Hunter, 'The figure of man and the territorialization of justice in "Enlightenment" natural law: Pufendorf and Vattel', *Intelectual History Review* 23.3 (2013), 289–307; T. Toyoda, *Theory and Politics of the Law of Nations: Political Bias in International Law Discourse of Seven German Court Councilors in the Seventeenth and Eighteenth Centuries* (Leiden, 2011), 165–190.

[7] A. Anghie, 'Vattel and colonialism: Some preliminary observations', in V. Chetail (ed.), *Vattel's International Law in a XXIst Century Perspective* (Leiden, 2011); R. Tuck, *The Rights of War and Peace* (Oxford, 1999), 191–195; A. Fitzmaurice, *Sovereignty, Property and Empire 1500–2000* (Cambridge, 2014), 140–144.

the harshest forms of disciplinary response to violations of the laws of war. Only toward non-Europeans, and Muslims in particular, did Vattel defend extermination of whole nations as a permissible measure during war, and only in the case of savages did he admit despotic conquest and provisional enslavement as rights of the victor in the aftermath of war. This differentiated treatment was histroically influential and became further radicalized in nineteenth-century defenses of colonial warfare.

The chapter begins by reconstructing Vattel's articulation of ideals of limitation in regular war. These ideals reflected the progressively more restrained practices of civilized European warfare, as Vattel saw them, but they were defended within a general, indeed universal, account of state sovereignty and political prudence.[8] The second section turns to Vattel's discussion of irregulars in war. While Vattel did not actually use the term 'irregular' to refer to agents of force other than regular forces and disciplined state militia, he did discuss three separate categories of fighters – which I call regular forces, authorized irregulars, and non-authorized irregulars – and assigned to each different privileges and obligations in the law of nations. The third section looks closely at the class of non-European and non-authorized fighters, which were the object of the harshest forms of lawful violence contemplated in *The Law of Nations.* 'Savage' and 'barbarian' belligerents could be exterminated during war or conquered and ruled despotically in the aftermath of war. This special treatment for 'savages' foreshadowed and influenced nineteenth-century legal accounts of colonial warfare.

IDEALS OF LIMITATION IN REGULAR WAR

In Vattel's account of regular war, the most important principle for actualizing ideals of limitation in the conduct of hostilities is to restrict the use of military force only to designated combatants. Historically, the limit case of this form of convention was single combat, in which two appointed combatants fight each other under agreed conditions, and whoever wins gets to decide the stakes.[9]

[8] In terms of Jennifer Pitt's valuable characterization of the various modes of universalism one can find in Vattel, I will argue that, in the case of the laws of war, he created an 'aspirationally universal law' based on European principles and practices, rather than showing that European practices were compatible with an abstractly established natural law, or merely producing practical rules applicable in European diplomacy. See J. Pitts, *Boundaries of the International Law and Empire* (Cambridge, MA, 2018), 82.

[9] In *De iure belli ac pacis* Hugo Grotius discussed the practice in ancient Greece and medieval European warfare and rejected it on the grounds that its game-like nature could not reflect the seriousness of just warfare (LN, II-xxiii-10; III-xx-43).

While single combat may prove unfeasible in real politics, to the same class belongs the convention according to which only regular forces – or designated and well-disciplined militia – fighting on behalf of a sovereign state can legitimately engage in hostilities.

In modern times, probably the most famous formulation of this type of convention is J.-J. Rousseau's brief and suggestive account of war in *On the Social Contract* and his fragments on 'The State of War.' Central in Rousseau's account was the conceptual point that war can only take place among public powers, because only public powers can engage in the sustained relationship of enmity that constitutes a war. A war is legitimate among public powers, Rousseau argued, only when belligerents aim exclusively at their enemy's *res publica*, in particular enemy soldiers, public property, and public institutions. In principle, a war could be fought and won without killing a single member of the enemy state but by dissolving its constitution, laws, and government. On the other hand, if private individuals are deliberately targeted in war, or their property looted, that is not war properly speaking but rather brigandage and large-scale robbery. Even in the midst of war, Rousseau claimed, a just prince may well seize everything in enemy territory that belongs to the public, but he respects the person and the goods of private individuals; he respects the rights on which his own are founded.[10]

Vattel defended a superficially similar normative conception of war but for very different purposes. The sovereign power alone is possessed of the authority to make war, he wrote, and it normally makes war through the use of regular troops (*LN*, III-I-4, 471). 'At present, war is carried on by regular troops: the people, the peasants, the citizens, take no part in it, and generally have nothing to fear from the sword of the enemy . . . the country people come freely to the camp to sell their provisions, and are protected, as far as possible, from the calamities of war' (*LN*, III-VIII-147, 550). Ideally, in regular war the designated forces of each belligerent power fight each other, and private lives, goods, and transactions continue largely undisturbed. While in the past war could be made by 'anyone capable of carrying arms,' he wrote, in the present, 'a laudable custom, truly worthy of those nations who value themselves on their humanity,' had evolved in virtue of which war became the exclusive affair of designated soldiers (*LN*, III-VIII-147, 550). Vattel's implicit reference here to European nations becomes explicit when he notes that, among 'the

[10] See J.-J. Rousseau 'On the social contract', in *Rousseau: The Social Contract and other Later Political Writings* (Cambridge, 1997), 47 (book I, section iv), and see further his 'The State of War' in the same title, 171–172, 174–176.

polished nations of Europe,' it had also become common practice to spare women and children from captivity and to free officers made prisoners on parole (III-VIII-148, 551; III-VIII-150)

Vattel knew, however, that these limiting and humane customs were always fragile and precarious. They could be sustained 'provided the inhabitants submit to him who is master of the country, pay the contributions imposed, and refrain from all hostilities,' all of which often in fact did not happen during war (*LN*, III-VIII-147, 550). Vattel did not defend a strict immunity of private property during war, but he did impose some restrictions on pillaging and defended the making of sustainable requisition agreements. Vattel's justification for this and other legal limitations applicable in the conduct of hostilities was to make war a less destructive procedure for dealing with international conflicts. As Vattel's mentor Christian Wolff put it in his *Jus gentium*, in the actual practice of 'warlike operations' (*operationes vero bellicae*) military force is not always restricted to military force (*vim bellica*) – for force is not used against the enemy in all cases – but the principles of regular warfare do aim to restrict as much as feasible warlike operations to warlike forces.[11]

In a succinct statement of this limited war ideal, Vattel wrote in *The Law of Nations* that,

> should two nations encounter each other with the collective weight of their whole force, the war would become much more bloody and destructive, and could hardly be terminated otherwise than by the utter extinction of one of the parties ... It is therefore with good reason that the contrary practice has grown into a custom with the nations of Europe – at least with those that keep up regular standing armies or bodies of militia. The troops alone carry on the war, while the rest of the nation remain in peace. (*LN*, III-XV-226, 613)

The form of limitation that Vattel advocates here is drawn from the European practice of making regular troops or well-disciplined militia the sole instruments of sovereign powers at war. As we will see presently, however, Vattel's justification for the inclusion of these practices in the law of nations was made in a general and universal register. If ideals of limited war could be fully carried out in all wars, the valuable outcome would be that private individuals

[11] Wolff *Jus gentium*, §784, 405. Rousseau, by contrast, did not have much hope on the practical effects of the requirement that private goods and agents be left out of hostilities. States being artificial bodies, they can always enlarge and devour ever more resources in the pursuit of war. The existence of multiple sovereign states in a state of nature creates the conditions for violence of an intensity and duration that could not exist in the pre-civil condition of man. See 'The State of War', 169.

could go on with their lives and affairs – in particular trade – unaffected by war. And while this principle of limitation could always break down, in particular because states themselves could be tempted to bring irregulars to their wars if this appeared tactically advantageous, it was important for Vattel that rulers understood it was in their best interest to avoid this temptation and to include in the law of nations fitting deterring measures.

Vattel's defense of the ideals of limitation in regular war is indebted to Hugo Grotius' account of 'solemn war' (*bellum solenne*) in *De iure belli ac pacis*.[12] One of the central principles in Grotius' account is that only sovereign states should be entitled to the legal privileges associated with lawful war making. This restriction is rooted both in a general trust in the state as a jural community respectful of rights, and in the need to centralize the power of enforcement in states.

Grotius' discussion of solemn wars in *De iure belli ac pacis* begins with a contrast between sovereign states and groups of pirates and brigands, which was meant to show why a state should be recognized as having authority even if it commits wrongs, in particular the wrong of waging an unjust war. The crucial difference for Grotius is that pirates and brigands are 'banded together for wrongdoing,' while members of the state, 'even if at times they are not free from crime, nevertheless have been united for the enjoyment of rights, and they do render justice to foreigners.' A state remains a state for as long as it has tribunals running and other agencies necessary to administer justice to both citizens and foreigners. When violence and wrongdoing become widespread in a state, then it first becomes 'full of faults, and finally ceases to be,' and becomes in effect a band of brigands.[13]

Unlike pirates and brigands, Grotius further argued, states have by constitution a disposition to 'render justice to each other,' in particular during war, and as such can be trusted to compel their subjects to act in keeping with the law of nations.[14] Private agents do not deserve a similar trust. State courts are instituted precisely in order to avoid the pitfalls of private adjudication, in particular the excessive 'love of self or hatred of another' that lead to foreseeable miscarriages of justice.[15] Individuals associate in a state so that each can

[12] In Grotius' construction, however, solemn wars are legally equivalent to total wars. On Grotius' account of solemn wars and their influence on Vattel, to which the following is indebted, see P. Kalmanovitz, *The Laws of War in International Thought* (Oxford, 2020), chapter 2. See further P. Haggenmacher, *Grotius et la doctrine de la guerre juste* (Paris, 1983), 568–612; and S. Neff, *War and the Law of Nations: A General History* (Cambridge, 2005), 95–113.

[13] Grotius, *De iure belli ac pacis*, III-III-2, 631–632.

[14] Ibid., III-XXIII-10, 854.

[15] As Grotius wrote in *De iure praedae*, 130–133.

obtain protection for his rights 'through community of resource and effort.' Their association must include the power to use force to protect rights, just as individuals must be able to use force to protect their rights in the state of nature. But once political society is instituted, public magistrates must have the privilege of force, and individuals must give up their natural rights to administer justice.[16]

Equally for Vattel, just as within the state only public authority decides 'all the disputes of the citizens, represses violence, and checks every attempt to do ourselves justice with our own hands,' also outside the state only public magistrates can declare war, direct the conduct of hostilities, and negotiate transitions to peace (*LN*, III-I-4, 470; III-XV-223; IV-II-10). If private individuals had the power to wage war, there would be no way to preserve peace among nations. Furthermore, given the stakes behind the decision to wage war, only those public magistrates entrusted with the 'right of majesty' – that is, the sovereign representatives of the nation – can have the power to declare war, for only they should judge whether their nation has suffered an injury, whether a military response is justified, and whether it would be prudent to undertake war at all (*LN*, III-I-4).

In this conception of war and sovereignty, the military apparatus of the state appears as an instrument that sovereigns employ to 'prosecute' national rights (*LN*, III-I-1, 469; III-IX-164; III-XV-231). When a sovereign declares war, he defines the ends to be pursued by military means; generals, in turn, follow the sovereign's command in establishing the strategies to be pursued by subordinate officers and soldiers. Subordinate officers follow the generals' commands and soldiers the subordinate officers' commands. Within this strictly hierarchical system, Vattel wrote, 'fighting without orders is almost always considered as fighting contrary to orders' (III-XV-231, 615). Soldiers act pursuant of decisions that emanate ultimately from sovereign judgment, and must operate under the assumption that what is not ordered by superior authority is prohibited.[17] Just as strict hierarchy within the military is meant to secure that the conduct of war reflects sovereign decisions, it also excludes private individuals

16 Grotius, *De iure belli ac pacis*, I-II-1, 53, I-III-4.

17 The one exception to which Vattel hints in the passage just quoted is when soldiers take the initiative and perform acts of exceptional bravery and courage, but these, he argued, should in general be discouraged. Vattel's model here was probably Frederick II of Prussia, whose army famously operated like the works of a watch, 'the wheels of which by artful gearing produce an exact and regular movement.' See E. Robson, 'The armed force and the art of war', in J. Lindsay (ed.), *The New Cambridge Modern History: The Old Regime 1713–1763* (Cambridge, 1966), 176. On the crucial importance of discipline and sovereign control for the legitimacy of armed force during the Enlightenment, see also Scheipers, *Unlawful Combatants*, 51–53.

from taking the initiative and getting involved in hostilities. In general, only force authorized and overseen by sovereign powers should be recognized as lawful during war.

This interlocked conception of war and sovereignty has two distinctive aspects. The first is that regular forces are thought to be best positioned to act in keeping with the rules that govern hostilities. Such rules, in turn, are understood to reflect maxims of sound policy and good statesmanship, which enlightened rulers will want to follow and instruct their subordinates to follow as well. Secondly, regular state forces are not liable to punishment by their enemies for lawful acts of war (but irregular forces are, as we will see in the next section). Sovereigns may often think that their enemies are unjust, but this does not turn lawful acts of war by regular forces into crimes, for example, the killing of enemy soldiers into murder, the burning of enemy fields into arson, the taking of prisoners into kidnapping, and so on. In virtue of the principle of sovereign equality, sovereign belligerents are equals before the law that regulates their war, and their decisions in matters of *jus ad bellum* should (usually) be recognized as authoritative and valid, as long as they publish war manifestoes with plausible reasons for resorting to war.[18]

The reason for the immunity to punishment of regular forces is that no sovereign can pretend to have authority to stand as judge of another's decision to wage war. All states must be regarded as legal equals, even if from the standpoint of natural law, and before the eyes of God, at most one side can be truly just in war. As Christian Wolff put it,

> It would be absurd for an enemy to be appointed judge in his own case, who, since he would not confess that his cause of war is unjust, would declare all force used against him illegal. The question as to the abuse of law in war would always be in dispute between belligerents; therefore the decision cannot be entrusted to that one of the contesting parties who complains of the abuse.[19]

And yet, while regular wars are by construction less punitive than just wars, punishment could be inflicted against enemy soldiers or noncombatants when they violate the laws of war, that is, for violations of *jus in bello* but not of *jus ad bellum*. If the enemy 'has been guilty of some enormous breach of the law of nations,' Vattel wrote, 'and particularly when he has violated the laws of war,'

[18] The exception is when states altogether failed to publicly offer their reasons for waging war, in which case all other states are called to coordinate their military force to contain the aggressor. See P. Kalmanovitz, 'Sovereignty, pluralism and regular war: Wolff and Vattel's Enlightenment critique of just war', *Political Theory* 46.2 (2018), 230–233.

[19] *Jus gentium* §783, 404–405.

then punitive measures such as denial of quarter or refusal of capitulation during sieges, which normally would be unlawful, could be lawfully made (*LN*, III-VIII-141, 544).

Regular troops can be expected to comply with the laws of war to the extent that they operate as instruments of enlightened rule and are deterred by the prospect of punishment for legal breaches. This expectation applies in multiple areas of regular warfare, including the conventions of pitched battles; the conduct of orderly and limited requisitions of enemy property; the grant of capitulations during sieges; respect for the immunity of prisoners of war; and recognition of the rights and immunities of neutrals. In all these areas, legal norms reflect the long-term interest of states to minimize the destructive effects of war.[20]

Consider as an illustration, and to conclude this section, the regulation of requisitions during war. The historical background of these rules is the longstanding principle that all enemy property could be freely captured during war. Grotius included this principle in his account of solemn warfare when he held that enemy nations at war could treat each other's property as *res nullius*.[21] Vattel did not altogether reject this principle, nor deemed pillaging inherently illegal, but he introduced important limitations as a matter of both law and prudence (*LN*, III-IX-160–164, III-IX-171). These limitations he drew from the evolving practice in European warfare of requesting contributions in a centralized and disciplined fashion, instead of pillaging at each commander's or soldier's discretion, or ravaging a country like 'savage barbarians' do (*LN*, III-IX-167, 570).[22]

The prudential logic behind Vattel's account of the law of limited requisitions is straightforward. Instead of pillaging indiscriminately or destroying goods wantonly, each belligerent must negotiate 'contribution treaties' in

20 For a valuable discussion of the conventions associated with pitched battles in eighteenth-century European warfare, see J. Whitman, *The Verdict of Battle: The Law of Victory and the Making of Modern War* (Cambridge, MA, 2012). Whitman reconstructs and defends the limiting effects of these conventions, but does not discuss ideals of limitation beyond battlefields, which were also very important in both theory and practice.

21 *De iure belli ac pacis*, III-VI-8.

22 Vattel deemed the practice of Louis XIV a 'very commendable' model of 'humanity and moderation', as the French king's competent administrators criminalized 'freebooters' among their own forces, and brought the exploitation of enemy villages to unprecedented levels of efficiency (*LN*, III-IX-165, 569). The practice of rational requisitioning seems to have emerged during the Dutch Revolt against Spanish rule, but during the Thirty Years' War it became systematic, indeed the main source of revenue. See T. Piceu, '"Une oppression insupportable au Peuple": The impact of contributions on armistice, peace and truce negotiations', in R. Lesaffer (ed.), *The Twelve Years Truce (1609): Peace, Truce, War and Law in the Low Countries at the Turn of the 17th Century* (Leiden, 2014), 152–178.

enemy territory, which stipulate sustainable amounts to be paid in exchange for security and restraint. By so doing, the belligerent actor 'obtains a part of what is due to him; and the enemy's subjects, by consenting to pay the sum demanded, have their property secured from pillage, and the country is preserved' (*LN*, III-IX-165, 569). It was strategically crucial for military forces that contributions be 'supportable,' as they often lived off the land in occupied territories for long periods of time. The interests of belligerents to sustain their campaigns and discipline their forces, and of peasants and villagers to minimize the harm they could suffer, made the legal prohibition of pillaging, and the validity of contribution treaties, self-enforcing.[23]

REGULARS, IRREGULARS, AND BARBARIANS

Vattel's belief in the limiting power of regular armies stands in marked contrast to other Enlightenment theorists, including Rousseau, Montesquieu, and Kant, for whom the growing power of regular armies was bound to make the whole project of limited war collapse.[24] In *The Spirit of the Laws* Montesquieu deemed the spread and growth of regular troops in Europe a 'contagious disease' that would eventually lead to the 'common ruin' of Europe.[25] Regular troops were standing threats that would force all states to follow suit and invest heavily on armies, to their eventual ruin. Similarly for Rousseau, regular troops were the plague and depopulators of Europe, 'good for only two purposes, to attack and conquer neighbors, or to shackle and enslave citizens.'[26] Along these lines, in his essay on perpetual peace Kant famously called for the abolition of standing armies on the grounds that 'they constantly threaten other states with war by the very fact that they are always prepared for it.'[27] A shared worry of these Enlightenment thinkers was that the strategic dynamics of arms races and security dilemmas created by

[23] As Lynn remarks with reference to Louis XIV, for contributions to yield reliably over time, they had to function like a well-evolved parasite and draw sustenance from the host, not kill it. See J. Lynn, 'How war fed war: The tax of violence and contributions during the Grand Siècle', *The Journal of Modern History* 65.2 (1993), 297.

[24] This section draws from Kalmanovitz, *The Laws of War in International Thought*, chapter 4.

[25] C. L. S. Montesquieu, *The Spirit of the Laws* (Cambridge, 1989 [1748]), 224–225 (book XIII, chapter 17).

[26] 'Considerations on the Government of Poland,' in Rousseau and Gourevitch, *The Social Contract and other Later Political Writings*, 232–239. Rousseau's advise to Polish republicans was to set up small citizen militia following the Swiss model, rather than investing in regular troops to match their surrounding monarchies.

[27] Kant also admonished that, instead of creating regular standing armies, states should train voluntary citizen militia. See I. Kant and H. Reiss, *Kant's Political Writings* (Cambridge, 1970), 94.

standing armies would cause military life to spill over uncontrollably into all areas of society, and in the process undermine republican values and eat away at economic production and trade.

Like Rousseau and Kant, Vattel submitted that well-trained and disciplined citizen militia were better than standing regular armies (*LN*, III-111-50) – and equally apt embodiments of ideals of limited war – but he did not appear to worry about the spirilling growth of standing armies. Presumably, he thought states would not be so foolish as to allow themselves to collapse under the weight of their own regular forces. Thinking within the logic of ideals of limited war, for Vattel it appears more troubling that states would be tempted to breach the laws of regular war for short-term gain, and in particular enlist poorly trained and undisciplined irregulars to oppose their enemies. As a result of this, war would indeed fall into brigandage, unbridled cruelty, and wasteful barbarism.

This worry reflects a fundamental tension between two conflicting interests at the heart of the doctrine of *jus in bello* in regular wars. On the one hand, Vattel assumed that all states have an interest in limiting the destructiveness of their clash of forces. In virtue of this interest, they are taken to agree on general legal limitations applicable to the conduct of war. The Enlightenment publicist G. F. von Martens captured this aspect of the laws of war when he wrote that the civilized powers of Europe had, after slow and painful experience, come to understand that it was in everyone's best interest to avoid unnecessary violence and to diminish the scourge of war by observing legal limitations in the conduct of hostilities.[28] On the other hand, however, states are known to have short-term interests in using all available means to overcome their enemies, in particular illegal means if they provide tactical advantage. Such unlawful means may confer short time advantages, Martens cautioned, but they eventually backfire and ultimately undermine the progress of civilized Europe. While states may share a general and long-term interest in confining the use of force to regular forces or disciplined militia, they also have narrower and short-term interests in resorting to irregulars and half-organized citizen uprisings to resist their enemies.

Vattel claimed that in the practice of European warfare, authorizations to use force were usually confined to regular troops, but he conceded that sovereign rulers could also authorize irregulars to fight their wars, as it was

[28] G. F. Martens, *Précis du droit des gens moderne de l'Europe*, 2nd ed. (Göttingen, 1801), 398–399, 405–406. On the importance of G. F. von Martens for the Enlightenment project of international law, see M. Koskenniemi, 'Into positivism: Georg Friedrich von Martens (1756–1821) and modern international law', *Constellations* 15.2 (2008), 189–207.

their sovereign prerogative to do so (*LN*, III-xv-224–229; III-xviii-292). In fact, during the eighteenth century officers in regular armies often relied on irregulars because of their high mobility, efficiency, and ferocity. During the Seven Years War, the course of which Vattel followed closely, irregular troops were seen as indispensable supplements to regular forces. France and Britain recruited or rather brought as allies American Indian tribes to fight in North America. France may have fared much worse than it did in the war without its American Indian allies, even though irregular warriors were barely under effective French command and rarely played by the rules of regular warfare.[29] The Russians likewise brought Cossack, Tartar, and Kalmyk fighters to the War. They were deployed against other irregular forces – Poles, Turks, Tartars – but also against European regular forces and non-combatants. They attacked and preyed upon Prussian farmers and townspeople in reaction to their resistance and refusal to give supplies.[30]

It may appear surprising that Vattel did not deem the use of irregulars by states unlawful but, as in the case of the immunity of private property, he was pragmatic enough to realize that this would be an over-demanding legal requirement. It would not only diverge widely from actual practices of state violence, but also contradict the strong deference to state authority he was so keen to defend. Vattel's ambivalent position reveals a rather formidable obstacle in the project of limited war, because enlisting irregulars could lead to the unraveling of all war limitations.[31]

In response to this conundrum – the aspiration to articulate and defend the project of limited war while at the same time deferring to state practice – Vattel distinguished three types of agents of violence: regular forces, authorized irregulars, and non-authorized irregulars. Different legal norms apply to each, but the overall orientation of this three-fold distinction was to favor and privilege regularity.

Regular forces and state militia enjoy distinct privileges, as we have seen. They were entitled to be given quarter, that is, once they surrendered, they could not be killed, harmed, or punished (*LN*, III-viii-140). They could be

[29] M. Ward, 'Understanding Native American alliances', in M. Danley (ed.), *The Seven Years' War: Global Views* (Brill, 2012), 47–71. J. F. Witt, *Lincoln's Code: The Laws of War in American History* (New York, 2012), 88–93.

[30] M. Füssel, '"Féroces et Barbares?" Cossacks, Kalmyks and Russian irregular warfare during the Seven Years' War', in *The Seven Years' War: Global Views*, 243–262.

[31] Vattel's ambivalent position foreshowed the persistently contested legal standing of irregulars in the laws of war, which has been at the center of the construction of the modern laws of war up to the present. See E. Benvenisti and D. Lustig, 'Monopolizing war: Codifying the laws of war to reassert governmental authority 1856–1874,' *European Journal of International Law* 31 (2020), 21–28; Scheipers, *Unlawful Combatants*, 99–102; and G. Best, *Humanity in Warfare* (New York, 1980), 156–157.

held as prisoners and exchanged for ransom, but their captivity could not be punitive. They were immune to punishment, except possibly for serious violations of the laws of war, and only when this clearly served a deterring purpose (*LN*, III-VIII-141, 149).

Authorized irregulars, on the other hand, are agents of violence that are neither regular troops nor trained militia but are commissioned by the sovereign to engage in hostilities. The most important case is that of 'partisans,' which Vattel discussed in the context of foreign occupations (the term appears in *LN*, III-XV-224, 612).[32] Vattel took spontaneous uprisings against occupying powers to be implicitly, if not always explicitly, authorized by the displaced sovereign. And yet, 'if the peasants of themselves commit any hostilities, then the enemy . . . hangs them up as he would so many robbers or banditti' (*LN*, III-XV-226, 613). Martens likewise held that citizen militia could be treated more harshly than regular troops, as this was a powerful way to make war a contest between regular forces only.[33] While organized resistance to foreign occupation was legally permissible, the occupier nonetheless had a right to 'call in the aid of terror to a certain degree' against those who resisted and the occupied population at large (*LN*, III-XV-228, 614).

Somewhat paradoxically, then, both Vattel and Martens held that in order to preserve the limitations of regular war, authorized irregulars could be counteracted by 'very severe treatment' (*LN*, III-XV-228, 614), notwithstanding the existence of sovereign authorization and their own defense of the project of limited war. Permissible severe treatment exceeded what was lawful among regular forces, and could overflow virtually all limitations in war violence. In the case of belligerent occupation, since both irregular resistance to occupation and terror to suppress it were lawful, violence could escalate out of all bounds, without there being any actual breaches of law nor legal mechanisms available to restore limitations.[34]

Unauthorized irregulars were agents of violence that lacked authorization from a sovereign. They included 'predatory expeditions' and 'armies of banditti,' the sole purpose of which was to obtain 'spoil and plunder' in land

[32] The other important instance of authorized irregular is privateers, but these Vattel treated essentially as regular forces. Privateers are 'persons fitting out private ships to cruise against the enemy' that were authorized by the ruler to do so (*LN*, III-XV-229, 614). They operated as *ad hoc* navies for states lacking strong standing navies. In addition to the right to use force, Vattel recognized the right to capture enemy goods and persons, and immunity to punishment, which are distinct privileges of regular forces (see, respectively, *LN*, III-vii-132 and III-XV-229).

[33] Martens, *Précis du droit des gens moderne*, 271.

[34] On the challenges of governing belligerent occupations in the eighteenth and nineteenth centuries, and Vattel's path-breaking position for subsequent debates, see K. Nabulsi, *Traditions of War Occupation, Resistance, and the Law* (Oxford, 1999), 19–65.

warfare, as well as pirates and buccaneers in naval wars (*LN*, III-IV-67, 507). Properly speaking, Vattel argued, the violence caused by non-authorized irregulars could not be part of hostilities but was rather 'depredation,' lacking as they did any right or apparent cause, and consequently any lawful effects. "A nation attacked by such sort of enemies is not under any obligation to observe towards them the rules prescribed in formal warfare, and may instead treat them as criminals and punish them harshly" (*LN*, III-IV-68, 508).

Crucially for present purposes, in addition to bandits and pirates, Vattel included in this same class 'savage nations' (*nations féroces*), in particular the 'Barbary corsairs,' the 'nation of the Usbecks,' the Turks and other Tartars, Genghis-Khan, Timur-Bec, and Tamerlane (see, respectively, *LN*, III-VIII-141, 544; III-IV-67, 507; II-VI-78, 301; III-III-34, 487). While in some of these cases agents of violence could formally act as privateers under commission of their rulers, in fact they always lacked any presentable cause or pretext to justify their actions, and had no other motive than 'the lust of plunder' (*LN*, III-IV-67, 507). The irregularity of savage nations consists, for Vattel, both in their failure to observe the rules of warfare and in their lack of genuine authorization, which results from their lack of a proper war declaration or presentable cause for war.

Vattel distinguished on this basis 'two species of war' (*LN*, III-IV-67, 507). During regular wars, the specific privileges and limitations discussed in the previous section applied to all belligerent parties. 'Illegitimate wars,' on the other hand, were asymmetrical in the distribution of legal privileges and not oriented by ideals of limitation. On the contrary, since non-authorized irregulars could not be seen as instruments of a legitimate public power, Vattel took exception from constitutive principles of regular warfare and defended as legally permissible the recourse to the harshest possible forms of violence against them.

In regular wars, he argued, punishment should be used sparingly. Only 'enormous offences against the law of nations' and 'heinous outrages' in the conduct of hostilities could merit punishment, and only those guilty of such offenses should be targeted with punitive measures (*LN*, III-VIII-141, 544; III-IX-162, 567; III-X-173). Belligerents who punish their enemy for violations of the law of nations by vicariously targeting its innocent subjects should incur the reproach of cruelty, as there are always other ways of punishing a delinquent sovereign, including "depriving him of some of his rights, taking from him towns and provinces" (*LN*, III-VIII-141, 544). Furthermore, only punishment that directly contributes to the safety of the belligerent's forces or subjects is justified; not all serious violations of the laws of war deserve punishment but only those that are 'absolutely necessary' to restore legal compliance (*LN*, III-X-173, 575; III-IX-162).

None of this applies to savage nations. Since they 'observe no rules, and never give quarter, we may punish them *in the persons of any of their people* whom we take (these belonging to the number of the guilty), and endeavour, by this rigorous proceeding, to force them to respect the laws of humanity' (*LN*, III-VIII-141, 544, emphasis added). Savagery for Vattel justifies the punitive targeting of any subject, regardless of his capacity and will to use force, or of any responsibility in the violation of the laws of war.

Still more harshly, Vattel argued that in some cases it was permissible to 'totally ravage a country,' to sack towns and villages and deliver them to 'fire and sword,' in order to 'chastise an unjust and barbarous nation' (*une nation injuste et féroce*) (*LN*, III-IX-167, 570). Nobody would deny Spain and Italy the right to 'utterly destroy' such barbarous nations – 'those nests of pirates, that are continually molesting their commerce and ruining their subjects' (III-IX-167, 570). Against these 'African sea towns' (*villes maritimes de l'Afrique*), the object of violence is extermination, not punishment or reformation towards civilized statehood and legal compliance.

The license that Vattel gave European belligerents vis-à-vis such 'savage nations' ran not only against the limitations on punishment for violations of the laws of war that he defended in the case of European wars, but also against customary practices in Europe at the time and the modern tradition of natural law and the law of nations.[35] It also ran against a central principle governing the conduct of regular war, according to which those who refrain from all violence, and show no intention to use force, cannot be deliberately attacked.[36] What makes enemy subjects legitimate targets in regular wars is their will and capacity to resist by force. Not so, again, for members of savage nations, who could be attacked indiscriminately. The double standard here at play is made explicit in Vattel's discussion of the French king Louis XIV's authorization of indiscriminate bombing of cities. In the case of Algiers in 1682–1683, his conduct was praised by Vattel for its 'firmness and just resentment,' as its goal was to liberate enslaved Christians captured by Barbary forces, whereas in the case of the bombing of Genoa (in 1684), the purpose of which was to attack an important ally of Spain, the French king could rightly be accused of 'pride and inhumanity' (*LN*, III-IX-167, 570).

35 As Walter Rech shows, Vattel's position was inconsistent with the treatment of the Barbary nations given by Bodin, Grotius, Pufendorf, Samuel von Cocceji, and Bynkershoek, as well as customary practice in the Mediterranean. See W. Rech, *Enemies of Mankind: Vattel's Theory of Collective Security* (Leiden, 2013), 46–47, 112–125.

36 Wolff, *Jus gentium*, §792, 409, and *LN*, III-VIII-148.

'TO SUBDUE A FIERCE AND SAVAGE PEOPLE . . .'

It is important to be clear about the precise scope and nature of Vattel's double standards in war. Neither irregularity nor savagery was for him an exclusively extra-European phenomenon. On the contrary, the figure of the irregular is inescapable for the theory and doctrine of regular war, since for both tactical and logistical reasons sovereign states could always be expected to resort to agents of force beyond their regular troops or disciplined militia. Ideals of limitation through regularity, together with deference to state practice, force the theory of regular war to incorporate the figure of the irregular. Historically, irregular war was common practice in Europe before the famous *petites guerres* of resistance to Napoleon in Spain.[37]

On the other hand, Vattel used the labels of 'savage' and 'barbarian' to condemn serious breaches of the laws of war by European powers and agents of force. Such is the case of states that wage war without offering even a pretext for it, which includes, 'in polished ages and among the most civilized nations, those supposed heroes, whose supreme delight is a battle, and who make war from inclination purely, and not from love to their country' (*LN*, III-III-34, 487). Vattel probably had Frederick II in mind in this passage, but his approach to violations of *jus ad bellum* in European wars was not to call for the extermination of the aggressive nation but rather to call other nations to coordinate military counteraction to contain the aggressor (*LN*, II-IV-53; III-III-44–45). Likewise, while in a few instances Vattel did use the terms 'savage' and 'barbarian' to refer to European agents of violence who violated the laws of war (e.g. *LN*, I-XII-146; III-VIII-149; III-IX-166; III-XVIII-294), the punitive measures he advocated for such cases were accompanied by counsels of restraint and limitation, as we saw in the previous section. Vattel's calls for indiscriminate punishment and extermination applied only to non-European agents.

A further important differentiation in Vattel's treatment of Europeans and non-Europeans can be found in his discussion of the rights of the victor in the aftermath of war. He distinguished between wars fought against sovereign nations and wars fought 'to subdue a fierce and savage people'

37 The figure of the irregular does not entail the negation of regular war principles but is rather a consequence of the complex strategic practices associated with these principles. Contrast in this respect Carl Schmitt's commentary in his theory of the partisan, which treats irregulars as an anomaly and contradiction for the Enlightenment theory of regular war, in C. Schmitt, *Theory of the Partisan* (New York, 2007 [1963]), 6, 24, *passim*, and C. Schmitt, *The Nomos of the Earth in the International Law of the Jus Publicum Europaeum* (New York, 2003 [1974]), 152–171.

(*LN*, III-xiii-201, 599). In the latter case, he argued, the victor had the right to conquer and govern vanquished subjects despotically, and could even, 'if necessary, keep them for some time in a kind of slavery. But this forced condition ought to cease from the moment the danger is over – the moment the conquered people are become citizens' (*LN*, III-xiii-201, 599).

This, again, stands in marked contrast to his approach to intra-European wars. Vattel did defend conquest as a potential source of territorial rights, but not on whatever terms the conqueror chose to impose. When the defeated sovereign could no longer rule in his territory, the occupier 'acquires no other rights by his conquest than such as belonged to the sovereign whom he has dispossessed: and, on the submission of the people, he is bound to govern them according to the laws of the state. If the people do not voluntarily submit, the state of war still subsists' (*LN*, III-xiii-201, 599). The nation, which for Vattel is the constituent power that must appoint its sovereign ruler, is not dissolved through war but retains its sovereignty, in particular the right to use force despite its former ruler having been deposed in war. The terms of its political association, which bound the deposed ruler, now must bind the victor. Furthermore, the conqueror's right to rule on those terms is provisional and conditional on the eventual consent of the occupied nation, which is also necessary were the conqueror to undertake constitutional changes.

Now, it is true that Vattel's concerns in *The Law of Nations* were first and foremost intra-European. His account of the rightful use of violence by Europeans against non-Europeans constitutes a small fraction of his long discussion of the laws of war. It would be anachronistic and mistaken to label Vattel an apologist of colonial wars of extermination. And yet his two-tiered construction foreshadowed and directly influenced the diverging legal paths of the laws and customs of war among civilized states, on the one hand, and between civilized and 'barbarians,' on the other. The categories of 'savage nation,' lawful extermination, and civilization by conquest and despotic rule were appropriated and radicalized in the nineteenth century, as ideals of civilization and the European colonial project went into full force.

As an illustration of the tenor of nineteenth century legal approaches to colonial wars, consider the following passage from the influential British publicist John Westlake's treatise on international law:

> often the inroads or other outrages committed by savages or half civilised tribes can only be repressed by punitive expeditions, in which the whole population must suffer for want of a government sufficiently marked off from it. All civilized states which are in contact with the outer world are, to their great regret, familiar with such expeditions in their frontier wars, and the

> principle that to weaken the military forces of the enemy is the only legitimate mode of action can have no application to them.[38]

Already in Vattel, a century and a half before Westlake wrote this passage, we can find a similar differential treatment. There is also in Vattel already a sense that 'savage nations' cannot be equal members in the international legal community; that they are unwilling or unable to both justify resort to force and exercise restraint during war. These became commonplaces in nineteenth-century legal accounts of war with savages, and gained unprecedented practical relevance in the context of European colonial warfare.

As one of the last defenders of unlimited war against 'savage tribes' argued in 1927 – citing Vattel's authority – 'when you are dealing with opponents to whom the laws of war mean nothing, who respect no rights and know no wrong ... against such it is not only perfectly proper, it is even necessary, to take rigorous measures.' These included extermination and indeed any measure at the commander's discretion, which should not be bound by the limitations of regular warfare.[39] While historically irregular warfare occurred in both intra- and extra-European contexts, the tactics and practices of each differed in the perceived validity of exterminating or conquering enemy groups.[40]

FURTHER READING

A. Anghie, 'Vattel and colonialism: Some preliminary observations', in V. Chetail and P. Haggenmacher (eds.), *Vattel's International Law in a XXIst Century Perspective* (Leiden, 2011), 237–253.

G. Best, *Humanity in Warfare* (New York, 1980).

I. Hunter, 'Vattel's Law of Nations: Diplomatic casuistry for the protestant nation', *Grotiana* 31 (2010), 108–140.

P. Kalmanovitz, *The Laws of War in International Thought* (Oxford, 2020).

F. Mégret, 'From "savages" to "unlawful combatants": A postcolonial look at international humanitarian law's "other"', in A. Orford (ed.), *International Law and Its Others* (Cambridge, 2006), 265–317.

S. Neff, *War and the Law of Nations: A General History* (Cambridge, 2005).

J. Pitts, *Boundaries of the International: Law and Empire*, (Cambridge, MA, 2018).

[38] J. Westlake, *International Law*, vol. 2, 2nd ed. (Cambridge, 1913), 59.

[39] E. Colby, 'How to fight savage tribes', *American Journal of International Law* 21.2 (1927), 285–286 (citation in the text omitted). Colby cites Vattel's *Law of Nations*, III-VIII-141, where Vattel defends the permissibility of punishing any member of the savage nation for violations of the laws of war. On the context and significance of Colby's article, see Mégret, 'From "savages" to "unlawful combatants"', 289–292.

[40] Scheipers, *Unlawful Combatants*, 146, 178–179.

W. Rech, *Enemies of Mankind: Vattel's Theory of Collective Security* (Leiden, 2013).
S. Scheipers, *Unlawful Combatants: A Genealogy of the Irregular Fighter* (Oxford, 2015).
C. Schmitt, *The Nomos of the Earth in the International Law of the Jus Publicum Europaeum* (New York, 2003).
J. Whitman, *The Verdict of Battle: The Law of Victory and the Making of Modern War* (Cambridge, MA, 2012).

8

Constitutionalism

ANTONIO TRAMPUS

Was Emer de Vattel a constitutionalist? To what extent can the *Law of Nations* be considered a treatise on constitutional theory? To answer these questions, I will refer to several different case studies to illustrate and analyse the use of Vattel for the constitutional debate between the eighteenth and nineteenth century. In fact, as José M. Portillo Valdés wrote, sixty years before the Spanish constitution of June 1808, Vattel was the first who explained that only independent and sovereign entities could be labelled nations and his expression 'free and independent' would be used by many of the emerging republics in America and Europe.[1]

In the first half of the eighteenth century, the 1713 Peace of Utrecht and the 1718 Peace of Passarowitz had profoundly changed the international landscape, both through religious pacification, the weakening of the dynastic element and through the recognition that competition between states was by then more and more frequently of a commercial nature, rather than purely military. In consequence of this, the ancient moral code of conduct between states was gradually replaced by a system of legal norms based on the political will of the princes and nations. It was therefore necessary to look for the theoretical bases of this new system, and the philosophical texts of the past no longer provided satisfactory answers, nor did they use a language suited to the new times.

Vattel was aware of these changes and above all of the fact that in order to understand the new international order it was necessary to start from the point

[1] J. M. Portillo Valdés, *Early Constitutionalism in the Spanish World*, in S. Hensel, U. Bock, K. Dircksen and H.-U. Thamer (eds.), *Constitutional Cultures. On the Concept and Representation of Constitutions in the Atlantic World* (Newcastle, 2012), 48–49; A. Trampus, *Emer de Vattel and the Politics of Good Government. Constitutionalism, Small States and the International System* (Cham, 2020).

of departure, from the nature and function of the state and from the use of natural law to explain the mechanisms through which political relationships between single individuals and between the various communities of people are formed. As Martti Koskienniemi explained, during the eighteenth century we can find two types of narrative of constitutionalism. The first one, 'began to describe European politics in terms of a historical perspective on a "system" in which apparent diversity is reduced to the diplomatic practices that articulated Vattel's contemporaries' sense that, despite all the conflict, there was a historical and cultural unity that still bound European nations into a single commonwealth'.[2] The second one concerns a parallel and differently oriented stream of 'constitutionalism' from the catholic realm, in connection with the rationalism of St Thomas and the debates on divine-natural law. Christian Wolff's idea of *Civitas Maxima* represents a synthesis of this approach. But, as Koskenniemi observed, 'every commentary on Vattel begins by stressing his debt to the German rationalist philosopher Christian Wolff – and in the same breath highlighting his dissociation from Wolff's idea of the *Civitas Maxima*, "a supreme State" into which individual States have been combined "because they wish to promote the common good"'.[3]

Vattel dedicated the whole first part of his *Law of Nations* to the discussion of this problem, giving a long and detailed explanation of what exactly was meant by states, nations and constitutions, and also what was meant by sovereignty. The first book, in short, appeared more as a treatise on constitutional philosophy, which explained what the minimum criteria should be for achieving formal equality between states and which, in this sense, laid the foundations for modern constitutionalism.[4] At the same time, the pages which the *Law of Nations* dedicated to the internal constitution of states, to the subject of political consensus and the legitimacy of sovereignty indicated that to reach formal equality between the states it was necessary to study the mechanisms through which the political will of a nation was expressed, to study too the problem of the legitimation of sovereignty and, finally, to investigate the origins and the function of constituent power in line with a concept central in modern constitutionalism that Vattel, in 1758, was one of the first to define in this way.

[2] M. Koskenniemi, '"International Community" from Dante to Vattel', in V. Chetail and P. Haggenmacher (eds.), *Vattel's International Law in a XXIst Century Perspective / Le droit International de Vattel vu du XXIe siècle* (The Hague, 2011), 51–75.

[3] Ibid., 51.

[4] In this sense one can speak of Emer de Vattel's 'constitutionalism', and I am in agreement with the considerations expressed by Koskenniemi, '"International Community" from Dante to Vattel', 70–71.

THE GOOD GOVERNMENT AS CONSTITUTIONAL ENACTMENT

If one central political question was whether the rule of men or the rule of law was to be preferred, it had to be distinguished from the question of which was the best form of government. The concept of 'good government', which became central to Vattel's reflection on constitutionalism, was therefore known in the history of Western political culture from the classical to the modern age, but before the *Law of Nations* the term was used to describe a political practice, to denote a way of exercising sovereignty, and was not yet in itself a conceptual category. This concept, to which Vattel devoted many pages of the *Law of Nations*, is central to understanding the similarities and differences between the classical tradition, natural law and the birth of political modernity expressed in both the democratic and liberal experience of the nineteenth century. The concept of good government posited the primacy of the rule of law as the precondition for the 'good ruler', who governed by respecting laws that he could not freely control, either because they transcended him (such as those handed down by God), or because they were part of the natural order of things, or again because they were established collectively through the constitution of the state.[5] It is striking from this perspective to see that Vattel referred to Christian Wolff and the German cameralism and their State theory. From these sources Vattel drew a normative conception of the constitutional state and of good government. Good government, in this interpretation, consists of the principles and rules by which the internal security of the state is established and maintained. These are based primarily on the obedience of the people to government: compliance that can be spontaneous or result from the impossibility of resistance. Good government consisted of the principles by which the internal security and preservation of the state was established and maintained. According to Joseph von Sonnenfels (1732–1817), one of the most important interpreters in the eighteenth century of the idea of good government in State administration, it consisted principally in the observation of the law and of carrying out all the activities of state within the limits of the law.[6]

5 P. Costa, 'The Rule of Law: A Historical Introduction', in P. Costa and D. Zoro (eds.), *The Rule of Law: History, Theory and Criticism* (Dordrecht, 2007), 73–150.

6 K. Tribe, *Governing Economy: The Reformation of German Economic Discourse 1750–1840* (Cambridge, 1988), 55–90; E. Nokkala and N. B. Miller (eds.), *Cameralism and the Enlightenment. Happiness, Governance and Reform in Transnational Perspective* (London, 2019), chapter 12.

The latter concept, to which Vattel devoted many pages of the *Law of Nations*, is central to grasping the commonalities and divergences between the classical tradition, natural-law thinking and the transition to political modernity. Specifically, the concept of good government offered the possibility to contemplate the forming and reforming of new laws without the necessity to change the form of government.

Vattel's definition of constitution is found in Book I, *Of Nations considered in themselves*:

> The fundamental regulation that determines the manner in which the public authority is to be executed, is what forms the *constitution of the state*. In this is seen the form in which the nation acts in quality of a body-politic, – how and by whom the people are to be governed, – and what are the rights and duties of the governors. (*LN*, I-III-4)

According to Vattel, 'good government' is a corollary of this constitution and of 'the perfection of a state'.[7] Subsequently, 'its aptitude to attain the ends of society, must then depend on its constitution'. Chapter VI was dedicated to the *Principal Objects of a good Government; and first to provide for the Necessities of the Nation* and showed what was meant by a state being perfected constitutionally, and in its policies and laws. Here, Vattel stated that the 'first object of a good Government is to provide the necessities of the Nation'. It was the task of 'good government' to produce a 'happy plenty of all the necessaries of life' by managing the labour market, preventing emigration, fostering a healthy climate for industriousness in the fields of agriculture and domestic and foreign trade and in monetary policy (*LN*, I-IV-7).

The *Second Object of a good Government*, following Vattel, was *to procure the true Happiness of the Nation*, in other words was connected with how 'good government' went beyond the provision of physical needs. Vattel argued that the state had to 'instruct the people to seek felicity . . . in their own perfection'. Therefore the state had a duty 'to teach them the means of obtaining it', in much the same way as 'the education of youth'

7 At this point I take up the formulations that I have exposed in Trampus, *Emer de Vattel and the Politics of Good Government*, chapter 3.

deserved 'the attention of the government' given that 'literature and the polite arts' served to 'enlighten the mind, and soften the manners'. Moreover, it was 'necessary to inspire the people with the love of virtue, and the abhorrence of vice'. These feelings were the foundation of a perfect patriotism that kept the citizens of the nation united by being seen to be mutually advantageous to them all and thereby to the state: 'The grand secret of giving to the virtues of individuals a turn so advantageous to the state, is to inspire the citizens with an ardent love for their country' (*LN*, I-XI-110).

Then, in chapter XIV, Vattel rehearsed the same scheme, as he did several times in the *Law of Nations*, but replaced the discussion of good government in the internal constitution of the state with the concept of good government in the interstate system:

> The third Object of a good Government [is] to fortify itself against external attacks. One of the ends of political society is to defend itself with its combined strength against all external insult or violence. . . . To increase the number of the citizens as far as it is possible or convenient . . . The wealth of a nation constitutes a considerable part of its power, especially in modern times. (*LN*, I-XIV-177)

It was in this way that good government provided not only a solvent for the historical–political contradictions that eighteenth-century Italian political reformist thought ran into, but also provided a guideline for the reconsideration of the position of Italian small states in the competitive international arena of the time.

This process was accomplished, Vattel claimed, when, in order to become relevant on the international stage, a state or nation had to become a *constitutional state*, with all that that entailed. A constitution exists when there are laws made specifically with the public good in mind, such as those that relate to the body itself and the essence of society or the fundamental laws relating to the form of government and the organisation of powers: 'those, in a word, which together form the constitution of the state, are the *fundamental laws*' (*LN*, I-III-29).

CONSTITUTING AND CONSTITUTED POWER

The cornerstone of Vattel's political thought is the idea of legal autonomy, which connected his notions of individual self-preservation and perfection to the concept of the state. On this basis, each society of men that has united itself politically is, according to natural law, free and sovereign, irrespective of what degree of power or political and economic autonomy it possessed. Even when placed under the protection of another state, or in a situation of military inequality, a state remained free and sovereign. Vattel famously reasoned that states, as societies of men, stood in the same relation to one another with regards to their rights and obligations as individuals within any state[8].

Vattel also postulated – and was perhaps the first in Europe to do so – the distinction between *constituting power as political will* and *constituted power*. In fact:

> The consequences of a good or bad constitution being of such importance, and the nation being strictly obliged to procure, as far as possible, the best and most convenient one, it has a right to every thing necessary to enable it to fulfil this obligation. It is then manifest that a nation has an indisputable right to form, maintain, and perfect its constitution, – to regulate at pleasure every thing relating to the government, – and that no person can have a just right to hinder it. Government is established only for the sake of the nation, with a view to its safety and happiness. (*LN*, I-III-31)

The concept of a constituted power derives from the new government: 'they may quit a society which seems to have dissolved itself in order to unite again under another form: they have a right to retire elsewhere, to sell their lands, and take with them all their effects' (*LN*, I-III-33).

As a consequence, 'it essentially belongs to the society to make laws both in relation to the manner in which it desires to be governed, and to the conduct of the citizens: – this is called the *legislative power*'. Therefore 'a nation has an indisputable right to form, maintain, and perfect its constitution', while, as regards legislative powers, 'the nation may intrust the exercise of it to the prince, or to an assembly; or to that assembly and the prince jointly' (*LN*, I-III-34).

This type of constitutional state was therefore the real subject destined to act in international politics to safeguard the natural rights of society and of individuals from within the system that presupposed the attainment of formal equality of all states, large and small. Moderation in the conduct of war (*ius in bello*) ensues from this, as does the notable importance attributed to the purpose of neutrality. The state must first promote the common good of its citizens, basing its authority on the consent of the governed and recognising the right of people to choose their own laws without outside interference. Needless to say, these were arguments that could be adapted to serve the

[8] F. G. Whelan, 'Vattel's doctrine of the State', *History of Political Thought* 9.1 (1988), 59–90.

reform policies of eighteenth-century Europe, in particular those aimed at advancing general wellbeing and public happiness.[9] The common good of a nation, according to Vattel, was directly linked to the role of trade and political economy, which were not meant to support politics of power but to look after the primary needs of the population, and agriculture rather than manufacturing. He believed that domestic monopolies damaged the rights of citizens but accepted the use of monopolies at the international level – as a means of protecting a nation's trade – as long as they were restricted to the need of sustaining the life of a population.[10]

As we might note, this insistence on the relationship between state and nation and on the internal constitution of the states corresponded to the idea that the main aim of the *Law of Nations* was to provide a logic for the rationalisation of interstate conflict.[11] While this historiographical judgement of Vattel's *Law of Nations* is typical of the work's reception ever since its publication, it fails to do justice to Vattel's views on the resolution of interstate conflict. The solution to these conflicts, in fact, could only come after all the problems arising from the internal political organisation of the states had been resolved and clarified. In fact, Vattel directly engaged with the key political challenges of his time by very narrowly circumscribing war as a situation in which a state rightly pursued its laws by strength,[12] and he tried to align this notion of war as a sanction with a framework for the reform of European politics.[13] The reader's attention is directed on the parts of the work that deal with the constitutional dimension of the state and more specifically with the law of nations and of international society. This argumentative methodology demonstrate a clear interest in the theory of sovereignty outlined by means of the general layout of the work, as well as in the formation process of sovereign

9 J. C. Laursen, H. Blom and L. Simonutti (eds.), *Monarchism in the Age of Enlightenment. Liberty, Patriotism and Common Good* (Toronto, 2007), chapter 11.

10 I. Nakhimovski, 'Vattel's theory of the international order: Commerce and the balance of power in the *Law of Nations*', *History of European Ideas* 33 (2007), 157–173, 168–170.

11 I. Nakhimovsky, 'Carl Schmitt's Vattel and the *Law of Nations* between Enlightenment and revolution', *Grotiana* 31 (2010), 141–164.

12 For instance, *LN*, II-III-7. See S. Zurbuchen, 'Vattel's law of nations and just war theory', *History of European Ideas* 35 (2009), 408–417.

13 See Nakhimovsky, 'Vattel's theory of the international order', 157–173; K. Stapelbroek, 'Universal society, commerce and the rights of neutral trade: Martin Hübner, Emer de Vattel and Ferdinando Galiani', *COLLeGIUM: Studies Across Disciplines in the Humanities and Social Sciences* 3 (2008), 63–89. More reflections on Vattel's conceptions of war in I. Hunter 'Vattel's Law of Nations: Diplomatic casuistry for the protestant nation', *Grotiana* 31 (2010), 108–140 or P. Kalmanovitz, 'Sovereignty, pluralism, and regular war: Wolff and Vattel's Enlightenment critique of just war', *Political Theory* 46 (2018), 218–241.

authority with regard to the exercise of power by the prince and the rights of majesty (*LN*, I-I-45).

If we enter further into the text of the *Law of Nations* to analyse other traces of this reading, we may observe how the underscoring is particularly dense in the sections to do with the characteristics, rights and obligations of the nation, and also in the one which affirms the principle that all nations are free and independent in nature, just as men are (*LN*, prelim.). Vattel commented on the fact that there was a customary right of nations that competed with positive law (*LN*, I-I-27), that the nation was born out of a natural compulsion and could exist and survive independently of the state and its transformations (*LN*, I-II-14). Consequently, only the nation itself had the right to change its constitution and choose its form of government (*LN*, I-II-31), and a sovereign had a duty to understand the nation or nations within his state (*LN*, I-IV-44). The first book is also the book in which Vattel explained that, while the nation is *ipso jure* the founder of the constitution, exercising a right which is inherent and cannot be delegated, the legislative authority – as a constituted power – could only be entrusted to the prince, or to an assembly or to this assembly and prince together.

CONSTITUTIONAL EXPERIMENTS

Compared to the theoretical aspects of Vattel's *Law of Nations*, the constitutional debates and experiments in which Vattel's work was used are much less known. The Mediterranean area, and Sicily in particular, is one of the earliest occasions in which the *Law of Nations* was used in a debate on questions concerning the political and constitutional organisation of a state. After the death of Charles III of Bourbon, when Sicily faced the danger of reunification to the Spanish crown and thus needed to establish the legitimacy of its independence and sovereignty, Vincenzo Gaglio (1735–1777), a young jurist from Girgenti (now Agrigento), got to work using Vattel in support of his arguments.

The publication in 1759 of his *Saggio sopra il diritto della natura e delle genti e della politica* (*Essay on the Law of Nature and Nations and Politics*) was not therefore the result of an unconsidered decision by its author. Rather, Gaglio's aim was not only to intervene in the debate on the foundations of natural law and the relationship between law and morality, but also to reflect on the problem of sovereignty, on the relationship between the prince and the autonomy of the island and on the relationship between the law of nature and the royal right to administer the internal civil and political life of Sicily. As stated in his own account, his twin goal was to educate young people in the study of public law – a science still neglected in Italy – and to ensure the good government of cities, republics and societies. The final part of the work tackled the question of which was the best form of government.[14] While recognising that the most natural way to organise power was that of the monarchy, Gaglio claimed that natural law fulfilled the function of inspiring and guiding the authority of the prince and of subjecting this to limits and conditions by listing his duties towards his subjects. This preference for monarchy was justified by the fact that a democratic government could, in the normal way of things, raise to the highest offices citizens who enjoyed the highest level of support but who often turned out to be the least capable of governing. The intrinsic weakness of mixed governments, on the other hand, was the influence of external powers that laid bare their lack of stability.[15]

During the late eighteenth century, Vattel's *Law of Nations* came to be used and adapted also in the Grand Duchy of Tuscany. The book was pressed into the service of the process of constitutionalisation and state transformation carried out in the wake of the American Revolution, events that have up to now been little explored because of the scant attention paid to Vattel's work by the historiography.

Peter Leopold's constitutional project for Tuscany of 1779 clearly demonstrated that in order to tackle the crisis of the *ancien régime* it was no longer enough to institute partial reforms, but rather it was vital to take direct action on the state's constitutional composition. His plan indicated that all of this could be achieved through renewed collaboration between the ancient local communities and the intermediary powers. The objective was to bring in a model of a constitution of classes ('costituzione per ceti') established through clear agreement, to replace the dialectic between centralisation and decentralisation that characterised other European arrangements.[16] The project was thus based on the recognition of the role of institutions and local communities, on the duty of the peripheral government towards local agencies and on the network of judicial administrations which would enable all parts of society to participate in the programme of reforms.[17]

The project hinged on the adherence to a physiocratic form of economic policy that enabled the role and function of the communities to be enhanced while leaving the organisation of the territory almost intact, limiting itself in

[14] V. Gaglio, *Saggio sopra il diritto della natura e delle genti* (Palermo, 1759), 99–115.

[15] Ibid., 103–198, with reference to Bodin.

[16] B. Sordi, *L'amministrazione illuminata. Riforma delle comunità e progetti di costituzione nella Toscana leopoldina* (Milan, 1991); L. Mannori and B. Sordi, *Storia del diritto amministrativo* (Rome, 2003), 194–195.

[17] Sordi, *L'amministrazione illuminata*, 14–15.

fact to rationalising and optimising the existing structures. The decisive phase came in March 1779 when Peter Leopold began to reflect on the possibility of drafting a true and proper constitution for Tuscany. The moment was particularly delicate because it coincided with the aftermath of the American Revolution and the stiffening of the policies of his brother Joseph II of Habsburg, who was becoming increasingly despotic.[18] According to the interpreters, Peter Leopold's work proceeded more or less autonomously, at least initially, partly because his family experience had taught him that in Tuscany reformist propositions tended to succumb to conservative pressure.[19] Indeed, it was in the years 1778–1780 that he reordered all the early thoughts and ideas that had accumulated in his mind.

In the spring of 1779 Peter Leopold thus came to set out his first ideas on the project for the creation of the states.[20] This was a series of notes that he had developed step by step as the debate on the reform of the territorial administration progressed, and it was this that he used, soon afterwards, for the first draft for a planned constitution.[21] The text demonstrates his commitment to the rereading of the great tradition of European natural law which from Hobbes, Pufendorf, Locke and Wolff had reached Montesquieu, Rousseau and the Physiocrats, amongst whom was Turgot.[22] The echo of the teachings of Locke and natural law was clear, linked to an ever-growing concern to take into account all the needs of Tuscan society. Nevertheless, apart from these suggestions, it has been difficult for scholars to identify the sources that Peter Leopold drew on, apart from the Pennsylvania Constitution to which he referred explicitly.[23] Peter Leopold's project has echoes of the *Law of Nations*, especially where his concept of fundamental law seemed to evoke older pacts that were typical of the Germanic world, but no in-depth study has been made of this hypothesis. However, a more direct comparison with the *Law of Nations* makes it possible to discern Vattel's influence with some degree of precision. In particular, reference was made to Vattel's first book,

[18] A. Wandruska, *Leopold II* (Vienna, 1963). See also Peter Leopold, *Relazioni sul governo della Toscana*, vol. 1–3, ed. A. Silvestrini (Florence, 1969–1974).

[19] F. Diaz, *Francesco Maria Gianni. Dalla burocrazia alla politica sotto Pietro Leopoldo di Toscana* (Milan, 1966), 282.

[20] Florence, State Archive, Segreteria di Gabinetto, filza 167, ins. 21 'Idee sopra il progetto'.

[21] Florence, State Archive, Segreteria di Gabinetto. Appendice, filza 10, ins. 1.

[22] J. Zimmermann, *Das Verfassungsproject des Grossherzogs Peter Leopold von Toskana* (Heidelberg, 1901), 83; A. Wandruszka, 'Joseph II und das Verfassungsproject Leopolds II', *Historische Zeitschrift* 190 (1960); A. Wandruszka, *Pietro Leopoldo* (Florence, 1968), 387, 393.

[23] These documents are in Vienna, Haus- Hof- und Staatsarchiv, Familienarchiv, Sammelbände, Kart. 13, 'Fogli da aggiungersi alli Stati generali', ins. 10-11, 12, 'Constitution de la république de Pennsylvanie'.

in which one finds the first theorisations of the difference between constitution and fundamental law, and between constituent power and legislative power (*LN*, XXXI, XXIV). This is also the book in which it is explained that while 'the nation is *ipso jure* the founder of the constitution', exercising a right which is inherent and cannot be delegated, the legislative authority – as a constituted power – could only be entrusted 'to the prince, or to an assembly or to this assembly and prince together'.

The first lines of Peter Leopold's project openly declared that for him the state was a 'society of men grouped together under a government'[24] and in this sense there was clear agreement with Vattel, according to whom 'nations or states are the political corps, societies of men united together to gain their health and advantage' (*LN*, prelim.). In these lines there was a recognisable consonance with the *incipit* of the Pennsylvania Constitution and with the Declaration of Independence of the American colonies. Yet they also harkened back, in this case, to the words of Vattel (who had been an inspiration to the American revolutionaries) where he affirmed that: 'the Nations are free and independent of one another, because men are naturally free and independent; the second general law of their society is that each nation should be left to the peaceable enjoyment of this freedom, which is in its nature' (*LN*, I-ii-15). However, it was Peter Leopold's shift from the image of the 'states' towards the formulation of a 'management contract' which presupposed the idea of a constitution no longer only deducible from a pre-established order but conceived, following Vattel's example, as an expression of the freedom of a nation that was able to establish the rules of its own political existence.[25] Then, according to Peter Leopold:

> by fundamental law of the state one means the contract with which authority has been accorded to the social states, and which limits and prescribes the duties and obligations, the faculty and authority of subjects or of the members that make up society, towards their first magistrate or towards the one who is charged with executive power, be it a sovereign or a magistrate, and their duties and obligations towards the subjects.[26]

In this case, too, the agreement with the *Law of Nations* is notable, since Vattel had explained that:

[24] Florence, State Archive, Segreteria di Gabinetto, filza 167, ins. 21 'Idee sopra il progetto'.

[25] Sordi, *L'amministrazione illuminata*, 326–327; see also M. Valensise, 'La constitution française', in K. M. Baker (ed.), *The French Revolution and the Creation of Modern Political Culture*, vol. 1, *The Political Culture of the Old Regime* (Oxford, 1987), 445–446.

[26] 'Idee sopra il progetto', c. 11r.

> the fundamental rule which determines the way in which the public authority must be exercised is that which forms the constitution of the state. In it one sees the forms on which the nation acts in its qualities as a political body; how and by whom the people must be governed, what are the rights and the duties of those who govern. (*LN*, I-III-27)

Thus the solution seemed to him to be that of establishing 'a corps of public representation' that brought together the 'general deputies' who had been elected by all the provincial delegates to 'run the affairs of the whole country'.[27] Even here there is an idea of representation not dissimilar to that of Vattel (*LN*, I-III-34).

FROM THE AMERICAN CONSTITUTION TO THE FRENCH REVOLUTION AND CADIZ

For more than a hundred years Vattel's *Law of Nations* has attracted the attention of American historians, jurists and political philosophers. The uninterrupted discussion on Vattel's reception and success in American Revolution have been accompanied by discussions about the relevance of its author's ideas in the controversies within the framework of the British constitution. In recent years, renewed scholarship situates the Declaration of Independence in the context of Vattel's emerging structure of the international society as a society of independent states. Most of the documents written in preparation for the 1787 constitution contain suggestions or indirect references to the *Law of Nations*. Vattel's work was read as a guide for the creation of a new republic as glorious evidence of divine tolerance after wartime and as a point of constitutional and civil order for the reassertion of peace and progress.[28] As Max N. Edling wrote, 'if the peace pact was one purpose of the federal treaty, the other was to allow thirteen sovereign republics to act in unison as one nation against external powers'.[29] The law of nations established that all nations were equal. According to Vattel, 'A dwarf is as much a man as a giant; a small republic is no less a sovereign state than the most powerful kingdom' (*LN*, I-XVIII-VII). The equality of states extended beyond their size to apply also to their form. 'Whether they were democratic

[27] Ibid., c. 19r.

[28] J. M. Opal, *Avenging the People. Andrew Jackson, the Rule of Law and the American Nation* (Cambridge, MA, 2017). See also G. S. Wood, *Creation American Republic 1776–1787* (London, 1998), 273–276. Perhaps refer also to Chapter 10 by Mark Somos.

[29] M. N. Edling, 'Peace pact and nation: An international interpretation of the constitution of the United States', *Past & Present* 240.1 (2018), 267–303, at 291.

or monarchical, unitary states or federal republics, they were all *nations* in relation to each other'.[30]

Vattel's work was often referred in the American constitutional debate. Such as during the First and the Second Continental Congresses in 1774–1775 and 1781, the Committee of Foreign Affairs between 1777 and 1781 and the Confederation's Congress between 1781 and 1789. The most recent studies on the reception of Vattel's *Law of Nations* in the United States are based on intertextuality and 'silent intertextuality' through the analysis colonial source and different political documents. They focus their attention on the crucial period between 1762 and 1776 in order to demonstrate that Vattel's treatise was available to the American colonies and in the constitutional debate already in 1762.[31]

During his long journey through time, Vattel's treatise has been subjected to many processes that reflect the transformation of constitutional contexts and changes in international geopolitics. In the years between the French Revolution and the birth of the Napoleonic Empire, the European states took part in an intense constitutional debate linked to the possibility of adopting written constitutions based on the model of the French ones, giving thought both to that of the constitutional monarchy of 1791 and the republican constitutions of 1793 and 1795. At the same time, the problem for many states was that of distinguishing themselves from France in order to preserve and promote their legal and philosophical tradition. Thus, Vattel was once again at the centre of attention because the *Droit des gens* had been one of the sources and reference points for authors of the European Enlightenment (Beccaria, Blackstone) and therefore served as a cultural bridge via which they could acquire the basic principles for their new constitutional texts.[32]

To Italian eyes the *Law of Nations* offered a *trait d'union* between the Western natural law tradition and the republican conception of the constitutional state. It did so particularly in book one of the *Law of Nations*, where Vattel outlined the theory of the state and of constitutional sovereignty that

30 M. M. Edling, 'Peace pact and nation: An international interpretation of the constitution of the United States', *Past & Present* 240.1 (2018), 267–303. See also E. D. Dickinson, 'The Law of Nations as part of national law of the United States', *University of Pennsylvania Law Review* 101 (1952), 26–56.

31 A. J. Bellia Jr. and B. R. Clark, 'The Law of Nations as constitutional law', *Virginia Law Review* 98.4 (2012), 729–838; W. Ossipow and D. Gerber, 'The reception of Vattel's Law of Nations in the American colonies: From James Oatis and John Adams to the declaration of independence', *American Journal of Legal History* 57 (2017), 1–35.

32 For the systematic use of Vattel by Beccaria see *Des délits et des peins*, ed. P. Audegean (Lyon, 2009), 312–313, 317, 323, 330, 333, 352, 356, 361, 368, 377, 384, 388, 393.

had in those years been taken up in France by Sieyès. Even though it had not come into force, Sieyès's constitutional project was widely admired for the distinction it made between the various functions of the constituent power, which was responsible for determining the fundamental laws and functions of the constituted or legislative power that had to form the non-fundamental laws.[33] It is difficult to reconstruct with any precision all the genealogies through which the discourse on the natural rights of man moved, by way of the culture of natural law, to the written constitutions of the late eighteenth century.

Nonetheless, there is no doubt that the texts of the mid-century authors, including Vattel, played an important role within this heritage of the natural law culture. Not by chance, as it has been pointed out by other authors, it was Burlamaqui who coined the expression 'Droits de l'homme'" (1747) and hence the English 'rights of man', which came from the London translation of 1748.[34] Vattel – like most of his contemporaries – did not yet use the expression, but the *Law of Nations* contained a catalogue of those rights and the rights of the citizen, which reinterpreted the natural law tradition and which his contemporaries had no difficulty in interpreting in combination, together with the work of Burlamaqui and other authors.

The debate that took place in the Italian republics after Napoleon's army had entered Milan (1796) revolved around two crucial elements: the first was that of how to formulate the *Declarations of rights* (*Dichiarazioni dei diritti*) so as to avoid them being a simple copy of the French declaration of 1789. This concern explains why the declarations became statements about the *rights and duties* of man and citizen, thus exhibiting the influence of natural law. The other crucial element related to the list of rights and the choice of which of these to include in or to omit from the declarations and the constitutions. And it is in this debate that the contribution and practical use of the *Law of Nations* can be most accurately identified.

This reasoning applies in particular to the inclusion in the constitutions of the right of resistance and the right to asylum. The key text in the Mediterranean sphere was the *Progetto di costituzione per la repubblica napoletana presentato al governo provvisorio nel 1799*, which was important because it was made up of three parts: the report from the committee charged with drafting it, the declaration of rights and duties and the constitution.[35] The text was written in large part by Francesco Mario Pagano, one of the most

[33] O. Beaud, *La Puissance de l'État* (Paris, 1994), 206.

[34] L. Hunt, *Inventing Human Rights. A History* (New York, 2007), 231. Perhaps refer also to Chapter 11, by Nathaniel Boyd.

[35] F. Morelli and A. Trampus (eds.), *Progetto di costituzione della Repubblica napoletana presentato al governo provvisorio dal comitato di legislazione*, introduction by A. M. Rao (Venice, 2008), 66.

important men of Enlightenment in the Italian peninsula. Unfortunately the Neapolitan constitution never came into force because the republic was defeated by the Bourbons and their English allies and its protagonists were all hanged, but it is nevertheless possible to identify within it the legacy of the culture of the Italian Enlightenment and the influence of the natural law tradition handed down by Vattel.

The first point to which we must pay attention concerns the formulation of the right of resistance. The Neapolitan declaration of human rights is the only Italian text to define this as a right of man, since in general the other Italian declarations, modelled on the French constitution of the year III, only contained a definition of the arbitrary acts committed in violation of the rights of man, namely those carried out by the political authority outside of the examples and conventions established by the law. It is true that the Declaration of Independence of the United States of America had previously stated that one of the natural and imprescriptible human rights was the freedom to resist oppression, but the Neapolitan text went into greater detail, seeking to distinguish between man in the state of nature and man in the social state. Therefore, the natural right of resistance as a human right had to remain inactive as long as the man and the citizen acted independently, since otherwise the result would have been to encourage anarchy. The right of resistance was activated instead in the political sphere, when what was a natural law became a civil right and was exercised collectively by the entire population against any tyrannical authority that abused its constitutional powers.[36] Accordingly, in the Neapolitan declaration we find a typical formulation of the right of resistance that derives not so much from the revolutionary culture as from the natural law tradition, in the sense that it is not an expression and the consequence of the popular will, but, as it was for Vattel, the reflection of a natural right resulting from the abuse of power and the excess of tyranny that end up violating constitutional guarantees.[37]

The other point is that of whether the right to asylum was a human right, and through this we can again measure the use of the *Droit des gens* in the constitutional debates of late eighteenth-century. Traditionally, the granting of asylum was considered a means of asserting political power, given that it was born as a religious institution, in the form of a power and thus of a concession dependant – in Catholic countries – on the sovereignty and authority of the Catholic Church, first in the exercise of religious power and then of temporal

[36] Ibid., 123–124, 132.

[37] V. Chetail, 'Vattel et la sémantique du droit des gens: une tentative de reconstruction critique', in *Vattel's International Law in a XXIst Century Perspective*, 405.

power. The culture of European natural law reserved much attention to the right to asylum construed as a protection of foreigners, reflecting on its compatibility with the full exercise of sovereignty by a state and affirming the existence of a right of access for foreigners seeking refuge in the territory of another state on the basis of natural law and the *ius gentium*. Grotius had thus clarified the dual nature of asylum, as a natural law of the subject and as a prerogative of the sovereign in granting it. Pufendorf had studied the matter in depth, recognising the humanitarian and solidarity character of asylum, but without recognising the existence of a natural law obligation for the state to receive and grant shelter indiscriminately to all foreigners. On the one hand, therefore, hospitality became a common human duty, while on the other the interest of the host state was safeguarded for the sake of its particular interests. Wolff in turn had confirmed the imperfect nature of this right due to the fact that it was subordinated to the discretionary judgement of the sovereign.[38]

This picture was complicated further since Vattel linked the right to asylum to a series of other freedoms and rights that measured itself against political authority. Asylum as 'constitutional' right became a point of intersection between the problem of detachment from one's homeland (either voluntary, imposed or ordered) and that of arriving in other countries (expressed through asylum, but also through welcome and shelter).[39] The request for asylum could be the consequence of a judicial sentence (such as banishment and forced exile); or it could be a right of a person who left his country not as a result of a conviction, but as the voluntary exercise of a specific personal right that could be considered a form of passive resistance. From this derived the analysis of the duties of nations towards those who required asylum, and of the right to determine whether or not to accept a foreigner in one's territory. According to Vattel, a nation could not refuse, in the name of natural law, the even perpetual acceptance of a person expelled from his homeland, and if that person was denied entry it had to be for precise reasons that were carefully examined: among these could be the impossibility of being able to provide for the needs of both the nation and the foreigner at the same time.

Within the constitutional tradition and that of international law, the *Law of Nations*, in which the right to asylum was presented and discussed, continued to serve as an important cultural bridge, thereby facilitating the inclusion of

38 L. von Bar, *A History of Continental Criminal Law* (Boston, 1916), 88–92; G. Loescher (ed.), *Refugees and the Asylum Dilemma in the West* (Pennsylvania, 1992); F. Mastromartino, *Il diritto d'asilo. Teoria e storia di un istituto giuridico controverso* (Turin, 2012).

39 A. Carrera, 'The citizen's right to leave his country: The concept of exile in Vattel's *Droit des gens*', in K. Stapelnroek and A. Trampus (eds.), *The Legacy of Vattel's Droit des gens* (Cham, 2019), 77–93.

this right in the general category of human rights.[40] A demonstration of this, once again, was the draft Neapolitan constitution of 1799, in which the exercise of the right to asylum was reintroduced (albeit being confined to the general dispositions), in the wake of the provisions of the draft French constitution of 1793. Vattel's reflection on asylum would continue to be at the root of European political thought through the nineteenth century.[41]

The last great season of influence of Vattel's work on European constitutionalism was probably the experience of the Cadiz constitution. In Spain, the *Law of Nations* was banned by the Inquisition in 1779, but the work still circulated in private libraries and indirectly in university teaching. In the culture of the first liberals and in writing the Cadiz constitution (1812), Vattel's work explained a great influence and several articles of the Constitution (especially the third article) have been suggested or copied from the *Law of Nations*.[42] Though the *Droit des gens* was not a specific expression of the Enlightenment culture, but instead claimed continuity with the natural law tradition of previous centuries, it became associated with many of the works by eighteenth-century authors that to varying degrees were connected to constitutional debates. This happened because the *Droit des gens*, with a level of awareness on the part of its author that still remains difficult to determine, took as central elements of its entire reasoning certain problems, such as the function of the constitutional state in the interstate system and the relationship between the exercise of good government and the wellbeing of citizens, destined to be at the centre of modern political debate, along with the concepts of nation, homeland and citizenship.[43]

[40] M. R. García Mora, *International Law and Asylum as a Human Right* (Washington, 1956), 38–40; P. P. Remec, *The Position of the Individual in International Law according to Grotius and Vattel* (The Hague, 1960), 293; A. Grahl-Madsen, *The Status of Refugees in International Law: Asylum, Entry and Sojourn* (Leiden, 1966), vol. 2, 16.

[41] For a comprehensive discussion on this right with reference to Vattel, see L. Glanville, 'Historical thinking about human protection. Insights from Vattel', in B. J. Steele and E. A. Heinze (eds.), *Routledge Handbook of Ethics and International Relations* (London, 2018), 308–317.

[42] J. M. Portillo Valdés, *Revolución de nación. Orígenes de la cultura constitucional en España* (Madrid, 2000), 122–155; F. Tomás y Valiente, *Génesis de la Constitución de 1812. De muchas leyes fundamentales a una sola constitución* (Pamplona, 2012), 34–35; A. Fernández García, *Las Cortes y la Constitución de Cádiz* (Madrid, 2010), 47; E. Fiocchi Malaspina, 'Vattel's *Le droit des gens* and the Constitution of Cádiz', in D. Repeto García (ed.), *Las Cortes de Cádiz y la Historia Parlamentaria* (Cádiz, 2012), 33–40; E. González Diez, 'La monarquía constitucionalizada por la nación', in L. Palacio Bañuelos and I. Ruiz Rodríguez (eds.), *Cádiz 1812. Origen del constitucionalismo español* (Madrid, 2013), 139.

[43] More references in Trampus, *Emer de Vattel and the Politics of Good Government*, chapter 13.

FURTHER READING

A. J. Bellia Jr. and B. R. Clark, 'The Law of Nations as constitutional law', *Virginia Law Review* 98.4 (2012), 729–838.

M. Koskenniemi, '"International Community" from Dante to Vattel', in V. Chetail and P. Haggenmacher (eds.), Vattel's International Law in a XXIst Century Perspective / Le droit International de Vattel vu du XXIe siècle (The Hague, 2011), 51–75.

W. Ossipow and D. Gerber, 'The reception of Vattel's Law of Nations in the American colonies: From James Oatis and John Adams to the Declaration of Independence', *American Journal of Legal History* 57 (2017), 1–35.

K. Stapelbroek and A. Trampus (eds.), *The Legacy of Vattel's Droit des gens* (Cham, 2019)

A. Trampus, *Emer de Vattel and the Politics of Good Government. Constitutionalism, Small States and the International System* (Cham, 2020).

F. G. Whelan, 'Vattel's doctrine of the State', *History of Political Thought* 9.1 (1988), 59–90.

9

Vattel's Theory of the Social Contract

GABRIELLA SILVESTRINI

INTRODUCTION

At first glance, it seems that the theory of the social contract plays a highly enigmatic role in Vattel's treatise *The Law of Nations*. The 'very act of association' is undoubtedly a pivotal concept in the Swiss author's work, for it corresponds to the foundation of the nations, or states, which are the central protagonists of the drama. However, Vattel does not dedicate a chapter or even a paragraph to the theory of the contract, nor does he lay claim to any originality on the subject. This reticence is surprising given the space devoted to it by other authors of the contractarian tradition, such as Grotius, Hobbes, Locke, Pufendorf and Burlamaqui.[1] It is therefore understandable that scholars who have in recent years carried out a comprehensive re-evaluation of the importance of Vattel's doctrine of the state and domestic politics, recognising its independence from his more celebrated theory of international law, have stressed its relevance to the development of constitutionalism and the concepts of the representative government and inalienability of sovereignty, together with that of the moral person of the state.[2] Much less effort

[1] See J. W. Gough, *The Social Contract. A Critical Study of Its Development*, 2nd ed. (London, 1957); D. Boucher and P. Kelly (eds.), *The Social Contract from Hobbes to Rawls* (London, 1994). The research for the preparation of this article has been made possible by the PRIN 2015 fund 'Transformation of sovereignty, forms of "governmentality" and governance in the global era'. I would like to thank Matthew Armistead for the English revision of the text.

[2] See F. G. Whelan, 'Vattel's doctrine of the state', *History of Political Thought* 9 (1988), 59–90; E. Jouannet, *Emer de Vattel et l'emergence doctrinale du droit international classique* (Paris, 1998), 319–340; F. Mancuso, *Diritto, stato, sovranità. Il pensiero politico-giuridico di Emer de Vattel tra assolutismo e rivoluzione* (Naples, 2002); S. Beaulac, The Power of Language in the Making of International Law. The Word *Sovereignty* in Bodin and Vattel and the Myth of Westphalia (Leiden, 2004), 133–166; K. Stapelbroek and A. Trampus (eds.), *The Legacy of Vattel's Droit des gens* (Cham, 2019).

has been paid to explaining carefully his contract theory, often deemed confusing or even contradictory because of its failure to make a precise distinction between the act of association and the contract of government.[3]

In this chapter I aim to take a fresh look at Vattel's theory of the contract, not so much to verify its originality or coherence as to understand better its conceptual logic and function within Vattel's system of public and international law, as well as to clarify some points that, in my opinion, have so far been neglected. To this end, I must begin by briefly recalling Vattel's intense engagement with Christian Wolff. After that, I will carry out a conceptual analysis of the Swiss author's contract theory, showing how it is closely intertwined with his understanding of historical realities, especially Neuchâtel. I will then illustrate how the contractual conceptual tool functions inside the deductive system of the work, particularly as regards women and marriage. In my final remarks I will compare Vattel's contractual theory and Rousseau's political thought.

BETWEEN LOVE AND PHILOSOPHY: REDISCOVERING ONE'S VOCATION TOO LATE

As is well known, after abandoning his theological studies for philosophy, Vattel initially hoped to obtain a chair in philosophy and natural law in Neuchâtel.[4] During 1742 and 1743 he petitioned the Prussian king Frederick II to create an academy in that town. He presented his project as not only financially and politically advantageous but also as the fulfilment of a promise made by Frederick I in 1707, when he had obtained the title of prince of the city through a decree by the local Tribunal of the Three Estates that put an end to a crisis of succession.[5] The brilliant diplomatic career undertaken by Vattel after the publication of the *Law of Nations* was, in fact, the result of two disappointments: the unsuccessful attempts to become a professor or full member of the republic of letters, and the impossibility of crowning with marriage his ardent love for Esther Marguerite de Merveilleux, the daughter of

[3] According to Gough, *Social Contract*, 161, and Jouannet, *Emergence doctrinale*, 323, in Vattel's theory the contract of government disappears in favor of the contract of union; Mancuso, *Diritto, stato, sovranità*, 117, recognises a 'certain contradiction' in Vattel's formulations.

[4] For a brief presentation of Vattel's life and works see B. Kapossy and R. Whatmore, 'Introduction', in *LN*, IX-XXIX, along with Chapter 1 by Nadir Weber.

[5] *Emer de Vattel à Jean Henri Samuel Formey. Correspondances autour du Droit des gens*, ed. A. Bandelier (Paris, 2012), 11–15; E. Béguelin, 'En souvenir de Vattel', in *Recueil des Travaux offert par la Faculté de Droit de l'Université de Neuchâtel à la Société Suisse des Juristes* (Neuchâtel, 1929), 149–164.

a state councillor from Neuchâtel. The genesis of Vattel's main work, which can be construed as a repercussion of these failures, is crucial for understanding how the law of nations came to be a discipline in its own right.

Due to his lack of adequate financial means, the de Merveilleux family did not even grant Vattel permission to request an official engagement with Esther. The letters he wrote to Samuel Frédéric Ostervald and Jean Henri Samuel Formey attest to the extent to which his behaviour concerning his marriage aspirations was in keeping with the theories on engagement and on conjugal society he endorsed in his works. By the time Vattel began to write his commentary on Wolff's work his love had been defeated by the Merveilleux family's opposition, while his beloved was suffering from a disease that led to her death in 1756.

Vattel's long-running desire to settle in Neuchâtel with the woman he loved partly explains the lack of enthusiasm perceptible in his correspondence for a diplomatic career that required him to live far from his homeland. The suppression of Vattel's first love in late 1747 and the official ending of his courtship represent a watershed in his life. He now had the time to devote himself more systematically to philosophy and his earliest intellectual attraction, Wolff, whose metaphysical and psychological system had been of interest to him from as early as his articles written in 1737 for the journal *Mercure Suisse* and his first important work, *The Defence of système leibnitzien*, which he published in 1741.[6]

In March 1747, during his stay in Dresden, where he was forced to play the role of courtier and suppress his inner philosopher, Vattel expressed to Formey a desire to see the publication of an abridged French version of Wolff's philosophy, while also complaining about the growing length of *Jus naturae*, 'which is getting huge' at a rate that alarmed those interested in studying it.[7] A month later he enthusiastically approved Formey's plan for a French translation of Wolff's works, particularly the *Jus naturae*, and recommended that his friend dedicate much more time to a task whose completion would be of great value to the public.[8] Only after returning to Neuchâtel later in 1747 did he have the freedom for his favourite studies; the curbing of the

6 S. Zurbuchen, 'Die Schweizerische Debatte über die Leibniz-Wollfsche Philosophie und ihre Bedeutung für Emer de Vattel', in P. Coleman, A. Hofmann and S. Zurbuchen (eds.), *The Swiss Enlightenment: Reconceptualizing Science, Nature, and Aesthetics* (Geneva, 1998), 91–113.

7 Vattel to Formey, 27 March 1747, *Correspondances*, 67.

8 *Correspondances*, 80.

'impatient desire' to be with Esther gave him the peace of mind he needed to devote himself to letters and philosophy.[9]

The publication in 1749 of a new work by Wolff, the *Jus gentium methodo scientifica pertractatum*, offered the disillusioned lover the chance to fill the void of loneliness by producing a French version of Wolff's book suited to the taste of a public interested in its subject matter.[10] Initially Vattel considered his project to be a continuation of Formey's translation of the *Jus naturae* and, over the years, he persistently enquired about the progress of the work, which he would have liked to have read as a starting point for his own translation. In the absence of news, he began his journey alone, a journey which first led him to read the *Jus gentium* and then to face the immense mass of the *Jus naturae* in which Wolff had laid the foundations of the law of nations. When reading the *Jus naturae* he began to distance himself from his verbose teacher and to formulate his own views in the name of the truth pursued by philosophers.[11]

To avoid stepping on his friend Formey's toes, but perhaps also a little peeved by his lack of cooperation, Vattel began to write a commentary in which he highlighted the elements of Wolff's doctrine that he judged to be flawed, rectified the erroneous conclusions that the author had drawn from his principles and developed some of his arguments more convincingly. Eager to publish the initial fruit of his labour, Vattel sent a draft to Formey and Jariges, asking for corrections and advice, which, apparently, he received only from the latter.[12] The attempt to find a publisher for his commentary on Wolff's *Jus naturae* was doomed to failure, due to Wolff's poor reputation among the French public: the *Questions de droit naturel* would be published only after the success of *The Law of Nations* in 1762,[13] by which time Vattel had gained

[9] Ibid., 93. On the genesis of *The Law of Nations* see A. Bandelier, 'De Berlin à Neuchâtel: la genèse du *Droit des gens* d'Emer de Vattel', in M. Fontius and H. Holzhey (eds.), *Schweizer im Berlin des 18. Jahrhunderts* (Berlin, 1996), 45–56; P. Haggenmacher, 'Le modèle Vattel', in V. Chetail and P. Haggenmacher (eds.), *Vattel's International Law in a XXIst Century Perspective* (Leiden, 2011), 3–48; F. Ieva, 'A poor imitation of Grotius and Pufendorf? Biographical uncertainties and the laborious genesis of Vattel's *Droit des Gens*', in K. Stapelbroek and A. Trampus (eds.), *The Legacy of Vattel's Droit des gens* (Cham, 2019), 53–76. See also the letters exchanged between Vattel and Malesherbes in 1757–1758, published by A. Alimento, 'Tra strategie editoriali e progettualità riformista: la circolazione in Francia de *Le droit des gens* di Emer de Vattel', *Rivista storica italiana* 129 (2017) 536–574, at 565–573.

[10] *Correspondances*, 104.

[11] Ibid., 145: Vattel announces to Formey that he has written a work titled '*Observations sur le Droit nat[urel] de M. Wolf*'. In other letters the work is referred to as 'Commentaire de Wolf', and 'Remarques sur Wolff', ibid., 151 and 153. See also Chapter 3 by Ere Nokkala.

[12] *Correspondances*, 151.

[13] E. de Vattel, *Questions de droit naturel, et observations sur le Traité du Droit de la Nature de M. le Baron de Wolf* (Bern, 1762).

renown and had obtained a prestigious diplomatic position from the prince of Saxony.

It is important to understand the partly fortuitous and haphazard circumstances that led to the creation of Vattel's work, for these help explain how the independent discipline of the law of nations took shape. Wolff's treatise on *Ius Gentium* was the final part of a hierarchical philosophical system that had its starting point in logic and metaphysics. For it to be read and understood, knowledge of his earlier works was required.[14] Vattel was of this opinion and considered the law of nations to be a branch of practical philosophy, dependent on natural and universal public law. However, after realising that he could not rely on the previous translation of *Jus naturae* by Formey and refer readers to it, he tried his best to make his own work understandable as a self-sufficient text, while at the same time giving a new status to the discipline covered by the book.

It is therefore important to stress that Vattel's intention was not to create a new and independent science of the law of nations separate from the whole system but to make a clearer outline of its methodology, foundation and object. Following Wolff's footsteps, he aimed to criticise two erroneous ways of conceiving the subject: on the one hand, the conception of those such as Rachel, Textor and Bynckershoek, which had treated the law of nations as a mere positive and arbitrary law independent from natural law, and, on the other, that of those such as the Roman jurists, which had not adequately distinguished the natural law relating to individuals from the natural law relating to nations. The Moderns, starting from Grotius, Hobbes and Pufendorf, had begun to embrace the 'true idea' of the law of nations, but had not been able to clearly separate it from what was properly called natural law. According to Vattel, the glory of having first developed the true principles of the law of nations, correctly understood as the science of natural law modified so as to be applied to its subjects, the nations, belonged to Wolff (*LN*, preface). As we have already noted, the Swiss author's prime objective was to translate and adapt for a wider public the last part of Wolff's system of practical philosophy. When he realised that Formey was working alone, he took the editorial decisions that were needed to set his book apart from Wolff's previous works. Thus, taking it for granted that the reader already had some basic knowledge of natural law, he inserted in the first book of his 'translation' those parts concerning universal public law which Wolff had presented in book VIII of his *Jus naturae*. He also distanced himself from Wolff's ideas on

[14] J. H. S. Formey published a plan of the Wolffian system in the first volume of his translation, see C. Wolff, *Principes du droit de la nature et des gens* (Amsterdam, 1758), xlvi–xlvii.

some crucial points, especially the theory of patrimonial states, which involved equating political power with despotic power, freedom and property. Based on this criticism, Vattel developed the two fundamental ideas that distinguished his work from that of Wolff: the theory of the inalienability of sovereignty and the rejection of the idea of *civitas maxima* in favour of the concept of the 'society of nations'.

When working on his book Vattel become more aware of its value, and so grew in self-confidence to the extent that, without concealing his pride, he told Formey of his sincere regret that he had not undertaken the study of morality and the law of nature and nations sooner.[15] The enormous success of the *Law of Nations* enabled him to fulfil his desire to play an important role as advisor on foreign affairs at the court of the prince of Saxony. However, that position obliged him to abandon his philosophical career, leaving him with time for nothing more than the reworking of his earlier writings.

THE 'VERY ACT OF ASSOCIATION' AND THE CONTRACT THEORY

Depicting himself as an 'honest man' and a 'good citizen', at the end of the preface to the *Law of Nations*, Vattel stated that the book was inspired by the liberty that represented the soul of his country, the Swiss principality of Neuchâtel. This 'Swiss' perspective, embodied in the love for liberty, along with the elegant style and the clarity of the reasoning, undoubtedly contributed to distancing Vattel's work from Wolff's theory. However, it is important to bear in mind that the decision not to mention Wolff's name in the title of the new book was not unrelated to the failed attempt to publish the *Observations sur le droit naturel de M. Wolff*. It is not surprising, therefore, that the structure of the *Law of Nations* and most of its arguments follow the same lines of Wolff's treatise and bear some resemblance to the translating language used by Formey's *Principes du droit de la nature et des gens*, although the two works were developed independently.

As regards the theory of the contract and its crucial function in the conceptual framework of the law of nations, many of Vattel's arguments faithfully reflect Wolff's doctrine. The definition of the nation or the state is, therefore, the starting point of the *Law of Nations*: 'Nations or states are bodies politic, societies of men united together to promote their mutual safety and advantage by the joint efforts of their combined strength' (*LN*, prelim. 1; I-I-1).[16] The

[15] *Correspondances*, 188.

[16] C. Wolff, *Principes du droit de la nature et des gens*, VIII-I-4 and 7: 'Une multitude d'hommes associés en forme d'État, est dite Peuple, ou Nation … ce sont donc les fins de tout État,

formulation of the pact itself, which departs from previous theories such as that of Pufendorf's double contract, is taken from Wolff's *Ius naturae*.[17]

Pufendorf had long discussed and criticised the Hobbesian pact as a promise between individuals, 'each one with each other',[18] and, to solve the problems he had highlighted in the Hobbesian argument, he had proposed the theory of the double contract: the pact of association among individuals by which a first form of imperfect society without government was developed, followed by a decree on the form of government, and finally the pact of submission of each individual to the sovereign, be it a single person, an aristocratic body or a democratic assembly of the whole people. That being the case, only the pact of submission to the sovereign could bring to perfection the constitution of the commonwealth by producing effective political obligation. As it has been observed, in this way Pufendorf had simultaneously reinforced and weakened the original 'democratic moment' which was implied by the contractual theory contained in Hobbes's *On the citizen*: the indispensability of an assembled people at the beginning of political society.[19]

Wolff radicalised the democratic element of the social contract that gives rise to political society, as the democratic structure that characterises his *civitas maxima* confirms.[20] Following Wolff, Vattel presents the compact of society as a contractual act between each individual and the 'all' characterised, as a consequence, by reciprocity and mutual engagements: 'In the act of association, by virtue of which a multitude of men form together a state or nation, each individual has entered into engagements with all, to promote the general welfare; and all have entered into engagements with each individual, to facilitate him the means of supplying his necessities, and to protect and defend him. It is manifest that these reciprocal engagements can no otherwise be fulfilled than by maintaining the political association' (*LN*, I-II-16).[21] Vattel's

l'abondance, ou du-moins la suffisance et la tranquillité, ou la sûreté'. See also *LN*, I-II-14: 'A nation being a multitude of men united together in civil society'.

[17] On Wolff's political theory see M. Thomann, 'Christian Wolff', in M. Stolleis (ed.), *Staatsdenker im 17. und 18. Jahrhundert. Reichspublizistik, Politik, Naturrecht* (Frankfurt, 1977), 248–271.

[18] S. Pufendorf, *Of the Law of Nature and Nations*, 1672 (Indianapolis, 2015), VII-II-9; T. Hobbes, *On the Citizen* (Cambridge, 1998), VII-5-16.

[19] See G. Silvestrini, 'Neither ancient nor modern: Rousseau's theory of democracy', in K. Palonen, T. Pulkkinen and J. M. Rosales (eds.), *The Ashgate Research Companion to the Politics of Democratization in Europe* (Farnham, 2008), 55–73; L. Foisneau, 'La démocratie à rebours. Hobbes et la question de la règle de majorité', *Le philosophoire* 39 (2013), 147–162; R. Tuck, *The Sleeping Sovereign. The Invention of Modern Democracy* (Cambridge, 2015), 63–120.

[20] See S. C. Neff, *Justice among Nations. A History of International Law* (Cambridge MA, 2014), 187.

[21] For a very similar formulation see C. Wolff, *Principes du droit de la nature et des gens*, VIII-I-15: 'When a state is being formed each individual engages and commits himself to the whole

theory of the social compact thus merges association and submission into a single act: 'by the very act of the civil or political association, each citizen subjects himself to the authority of the entire body, in every thing that relates to the common welfare' (*LN*, I-I-1).[22] That being so, there is no need, in principle, to stipulate a second contract – the pact of submission – to produce sovereignty and political obligation which confer unity to body politics. On this point, Wolff's and Vattel's positions are very similar to the view that Rousseau had already propounded in the *Discourse on the Origin of Inequality* and *Geneva Manuscript*, whose first writing is dated 1756 and where we read: 'the primitive act of confederation includes a reciprocal engagement between the public and private individuals'.[23]

It is also worth noting that the ability of the nation to act as a unitary moral body derives from the conventional introduction of the majority rule which society requires in order to make collective decisions: the resolution of the greater number of the people must be accepted as the common will. It is by majority vote that the nation has the right to establish its constitution and to change it when deemed necessary (*LN*, I-III-33; *Questions*, VIII-91). By contrast with Grotius and Locke, but like Pufendorf and, later, Rousseau, Vattel does not consider majority rule to be a norm originated in natural law.[24]

In accordance with the perspective of *The Law of Nations*, Vattel does not discuss the different forms of government, because every nation or state is a member of the society of nations, independently of the particular constitution that regulates its internal organisation, whose merits it alone has the right to judge (*LN*, I-I-3; I-III-27–33).[25] The analysis of the different regimes does not pertain to the law of nations, but to universal public law. Nevertheless, the social compact certainly produces at first a democratic form of government because a popular government is nothing other than a product of the act of

society, promising that he will work with all his strength to obtain the common good; and society commits to each individual that it will bring about abundance and maintain security'.

22 See also *LN*, prelim. 11: 'having resigned their rights and submitted their will to the body of the society'.

23 J.-J. Rousseau, 'Geneva Manuscript" 1–3, in R. D. Masters and C. Kelly (eds.), *The Collected Writings of Rousseau* (London, 1994), vol. 4, 83. For the dating of *Geneva Manuscript*, see B. Bernardi and G. Silvestrini, *Introduction*, in J.-J. Rousseau, *Principes du droit de la guerre* (Paris, 2014), 12–14.

24 See also C. Wolff, *Principes du droit de la nature et des gens*, VIII-II-14. On the importance of Pufendorf's theory of *entia moralia* and the state as a moral person see Chapter 2, by Ben Holland.

25 In a footnote added to the posthumous edition of 1773, Vattel considers it important to specify: 'Nor shall we examine which of those different kinds of government is the best. It will be sufficient to say in general, that the monarchical form appears preferable to every other, provided the power of the sovereign be limited, and not absolute' (*LN*, I-I-2).

association: 'If the body of the nation keeps in its own hands the empire or the right to command, it is a popular government, a *democracy*' (*LN*, I-I-3). Only by a subsequent act of the common will can the nation 'entrust' one person or a collective body like a senate with the exercise of government, which by no means entails an alienation of sovereignty that always belongs to the body of the nation: as Vattel repeatedly affirms, the transfer of empire concerns exclusively its exercise and has the form of a repository ('dépôt'), without affecting the right of ownership (*Questions*, VIII-91).[26] Thus, while criticising Wolff's doctrine of patrimonial states, Vattel concludes that the power of the prince, even if it is not limited by fundamental laws, is always restricted at least by the tacit obligation to pursue the good of the people and to maintain the liberty of the nation (*Questions*, VIII-81, 126).

The creation of aristocratic and monarchical governments implies both a unilateral act of entrustment on the part of the nation and a mutually binding contract between the nation and the persons entrusted, even if Vattel, in fact, mentions the contract of government only in the case of a monarchy, when he speaks of the 'contract which bound the people' to the prince (*LN*, I-IV-51) and is the exact foundation of its power (*Questions*, VIII-59). Despite the numerous similarities between Pufendorf's double contract doctrine and Vattel's theory, the differences are much more significant and depend both on the declared 'republican' stance of the Swiss author and on the different theories of natural obligation, contrasting the emotional rationalism of the latter with the voluntarist position of the Saxon jurist. Whereas for the latter there can exist only one kind of political obligation, which results from the second compact and has its foundation in the will of a superior, Vattel admits a sort of plural political commitment: a general political one which implies a reciprocal bond between the individuals and the nation, and others which concern more specifically the historical actors involved in the transfer of public authority.[27] As Wolff had written, it is necessary to distinguish between

[26] It is worth noting that, even if they were written before *The Law of Nations*, the *Questions de droit naturel* had been revised by Vattel before their publication in 1762, as is clear at least from the two references to *The Law of Nations* (*Questions*, VI-494; VII-1080), along with the *Avertissement*. These two works were considered by Vattel as a unitary system concerning natural law and the law of nations, both natural and voluntary.

[27] This plural political obligation does not seem to contradict Vattel's statement in *LN*, I-II-21: 'Here the entire body of a nation, and each individual citizen, are bound by a double obligation, the one immediately proceeding from nature, and the other resulting from their reciprocal engagements'.

the contract which is 'constitutive' of civil society and other compacts that give order to the already constituted republic.[28]

Both the social contract and the other compacts between the nation and the prince correspond to historical realities and perform a fundamental logical function in the deduction of the principles of universal public law and the law of nations.

CONTRACTUAL ACTS IN THE LIGHT OF HISTORY AND REASON

As Vattel states, historical examples are useful not only to the author's discursive strategy, being used to capture the reader's attention, but also serve to make the doctrine more understandable, showing how sometimes the practices of nations conform to the principles set out in the work (LN, preface 19). Scholars have already demonstrated that the case of the principality of Neuchâtel is extremely relevant to an understanding of Vattel's *The Law of Nations* and his interpretation of the larger European context in which he operated and elaborated his thought.[29] It also helps to illustrate his contractual theory.

In the pages of the *Law of Nations*, the principality of Neuchâtel embodies the figure of the 'dwarf' *par excellence* among 'giants'. Attributing full sovereignty and the status of an autonomous nation to it is both a descriptive and a performative linguistic act. Before and after the Seven Years' War, Vattel was well aware of the precarious situation of his homeland under the hegemonic politics of its prince, Frederick the Great.

References to Neuchâtel seem to play a strategic role in Vattel's work, in the sense that they almost always appear when he criticises the application of private law to the public sphere and seeks to demonstrate that sovereignty is not a personal relationship concerning the private interests of the prince but corresponds to a representative function dependent on the consent of the nation. In other words, Neuchâtel is summoned as a witness in the trial against the patrimonial conception of the state and the critique of patrimonialism is also a defence of the full sovereignty of Vattel's homeland.

The first important reference illustrates at best Vattel's adopted dualistic conception of sovereignty, which was based on his plural conception of

[28] C. Wolff, *Jus naturae methodo scientifica pertractatum* (Leipzig, 1740–1748), VIII-i-16.

[29] On the importance of Neuchâtel politics and succession crisis, besides the contribution by Béguelin and Whelan, see T. Toyoda, 'La doctrine vattelienne de l'égalité souveraine dans le contexte neuchâtelois', *Journal of the History of International Law* 11 (2009), 123–124, and T. Toyoda, 'Vattel's doctrine of national sovereignty in the context of Saxony-Poland and Neuchâtel', in *Theory and Politics of the Law of Nations* (Leiden, 2011), 161–190.

political contracts. In the first chapter of book one, the principality of Neuchâtel is defined as a free and sovereign nation, although its prince had been, since 1707, the Prussian king. According to Vattel, this particular instance meant that the king had at least two political bodies, each carrying out one of two very different public roles that were separate and independent of each other: his function as king of Prussia was completely detached from his position as prince of Neuchâtel and Vallangin. As a consequence, in those communities, political obligation and submission were due only when the king was acting as the supreme magistrate of the principality and not as the Prussian king: in his role of prince he is 'incorporated' in the nation whom he represents. Three points are most relevant to Vattel: war, *interregnum* and domicile. Regarding war and exterior politics, the independence of Neuchâtel from Prussia is demonstrated by the fact that the subjects of the king are not obliged to serve in the event of a war fought by the king in the interest of Prussia (*LN*, I-1-9).[30] On the contrary, they can fight in the service of foreign powers at war with Prussia itself, as in the case of the Seven Years' War.

The entry 'Neuchâtel', published in the *Encyclopédie* edited by d'Alembert and Diderot and attributed to Frédéric Samuel Ostervald, tells of some Neuchâtelois soldiers serving in the French army who were captured by Prussians during the Battle of Rossbach in 1757 and were treated as prisoners of war and not as rebel subjects.[31] The same article includes a summary of the history and institutions of the principality and offers a 'popular' interpretation of the crisis of succession which took place in 1707 and ended by the decree of the Tribunal of the Three Estates, which recognised the rights of Frederick I of Prussia as the legitimate prince. The author suggests that the peoples of the principality 'took advantage' of the succession crisis to affirm their independence and to fix forever their rights and privileges. He presents the crisis in the light of the theory of a double contract, one which was possible because of the vacancy of the prince. At first, a new abridged code of public law – the General Articles – was elaborated and subsequently 'approved by the bodies and communities of the state, which were then united by an express act of general association guaranteeing the defence of their rights'.[32] Then, this

[30] See also *LN*, IV-v-60, on the right to deal with other sovereign powers. According to Vattel, the principality of Neuchâtel and Valangin is therefore sovereign because of its independence on issues relating to external politics.

[31] *Encyclopédie des arts et des métiers* (Paris, 1751–1780), XI (1765), 108–113. The article 'Neuchâtel', however, was signed by de Jaucourt, see P. Henry, 'Libertés neuchâteloises et liberté Suisse: regards étrangers sur les institutions de la principauté de Neuchâtel au XVIIIe siècle', *Musée neuchâtelois* (2002), 143–167, at 144.

[32] Art. 'Neuchâtel', 111.

'code of public law' was presented to all candidates as a condition to obtain sovereignty, and all of them agreed to sign it. After the pronouncement of the Three Estates in favour of the king of Prussia, the articles became the object of the reciprocal pact between the peoples of Neuchâtel and the king of Prussia, who was represented by his plenipotentiary, the count of Metternich. The latter contract is explicitly termed '*pacta conventa*', as a bilateral and mutual engagement between the nation and the king.[33] The same legal text is therefore considered under a double perspective: first, as the expression of the common will of the peoples united in a renewed act of association, and, second, as a fundamental law contracted with the new prince fixing reciprocal rights and obligations, as well as the liberties and privileges of the united communities.

This interpretation is not at odds with the documents written during the crisis of 1707. In the text of the decree of the Three Estates, defined as a 'sovereign and absolute sentence', we read that the king of Prussia received 'the investiture of this state and sovereignty, with its accessories, annexes, and dependencies, to be possessed by him as independent, inalienable and indivisible, preserving the Liberties, Franchises, Privileges, and Immunities'.[34] In the *Manifeste de S. M. le Roi de Prusse*, Frederick I accepted the General Articles that were drawn up in the name of the whole 'Body and Community of the Principality of Neuchâtel and Valengin' and, explicitly mentioning the theory that princes are made for their peoples and not peoples for kings, he promised to govern for the welfare of the state, while recognising the Canton of Berne as arbitrator of every contestation which should arise between him and the town of Neuchâtel, and to grant the 'liberties and franchises which are as old as your constitution'.[35]

A careful reading of Vattel's works shows how the language of constitution, as well as the concepts of inalienability and indivisibility of sovereignty, were familiar to the author before he engaged with Wolff's *Ius gentium*. Moreover, Neuchâtel illustrates well the case of *interregnum*, when the sovereign authority returns to the body of the nation, which has the right to decide the dispute

[33] On the General Articles as '*pacta conventa*', see M. de Tribolet, 'Chartes de franchises et "constitutions" neuchâteloises du moyen âge à la fin de l'ancien régime, XIIIe-XVIIIe siècle', *Musée neuchâtelois* (2002), 111–122; see also A. Bachmann, 'Les contrats de pouvoir de 1707', *Musée neuchâtelois* (2002), 125–141; A. Wyssbrod, *De la coutume au code. Résistances à la codification du droit civil à Neuchâtel sous l'Ancien Régime* (Neuchâtel, 2019, www.adrienwyssbrod.com), 53–58. On this point my interpretation differs from the one endorsed by Toyoda, 'Vattel's doctrine' and 'Theory and Politics'.

[34] *Supplément au corps diplomatique du droit des gens* (Amsterdam, 1739), II-II, 70.

[35] Ibid., II-II, 66.

concerning the succession (*LN*, I-v-66).[36] According to this, the fictive political body of the prince is bound to territorial public law and is required to domicile in the country because of its public representative function. Therefore, despite the fact that the prince is a foreigner, the representatives of the nation have to make their decision about succession by applying local public law (*LN*, II-VII-85). Vattel's arguments on succession are closely related to his criticism of patrimonial states. The laws regulating hereditary succession in a state are included in public law, whose source has to be considered the tacit or expressed will of the nation; they cannot be equated to private succession and matrimonial law, otherwise the people would be treated as property that could be divided between different heirs or even alienated to different dynasties.[37] In this context, it is clear that when Vattel speaks of the inalienability and indivisibility of sovereignty he is thinking first and foremost of the territorial and moral unity of a state or nation. Liberty remains in the background. Only in the *Questions de droit naturel* are the critique of patrimonial states and the theory of inalienability of sovereignty clearly deduced from the inalienability of freedom, both of nations and of individuals (*Questions*, VIII-81).[38] But how does this inalienability, inherent to the 'nature of sovereignty' itself, function in Vattel's thought? How strict are the limits set on contractual freedom?

The article 'Neuchâtel' throws light on the apparent overlap of the act of association with the contract that binds the prince and the people. A precise conceptual and historical sequence picks out the different moments: the gathering together of the bodies of the nation, which is considered as a renewal of the original act of association, then the elaboration of fundamental laws by a majority vote of the united communities and finally the contract of submission, which is, however, a mutual engagement that presupposes the previous existence of the sovereign nation and confirms 'the fundamental constitution'. Consequently, it is always assumed that the sovereignty of the

36 On the importance of *interregnum* in Pufendorf theory, see G. Silvestrini, 'Rousseau, Pufendorf and the eighteenth-century natural law tradition', *History of European Ideas* 36 (2010), 280–301, at 299.

37 Because of the public and representative function of the prince, the 'contract' binding him and the people has an extreme public function. Therefore, Vattel's theory of the distinction between the 'private' person of the 'prince' and his public and representative role does not have any correspondence in a presumed linguistical distinction between the terms 'compact', 'contract' and 'convention', which are employed as synonymous; see *Questions*, VIII-59: 'le pacte, ou le contrat' (with regard to the pact between the prince and the people); VIII-91: 'la convention des particuliers'; VIII-269: 'le contrat de société'. Vattel does not differentiate, as Locke did in his *Two Treatises*, between 'contract' and 'compact'.

38 On this point see Jouannet, *Emergence doctrinale*, 335.

state resides in the state itself but nevertheless, from a historical point of view, Neuchâtel's sovereignty is described as deriving from the powers of the prince.

In Vattel's perspective, the reading of history takes into consideration his method of rational deduction of consequences from 'principles'. From this point of view, the 'very act of association' and reciprocal engagements between individuals and the social body are the conceptual starting point of universal public law and the law of nations. Nonetheless, the original compact reappears in history when the nation exercises its right to modify or change its constitution. It is clear, however, that Vattel distinguishes two constitutional changes: a limited reform, as was the case for Neuchâtel, and a more radical transformation of the form of government itself. The distinction is based on the criteria established by the very act of association: if the modifications do not conflict with the original act of association and the intention of those who contracted the union, constitutional reforms can be passed by majority vote; otherwise, unanimity is required and the change corresponds to a renewal of the act of association (*LN*, I-III-33).

Considered in the light of a plural historical reality, Vattel's rational method of deduction, based on the concepts of the liberty and equality of individuals and nations, reveals a more fragmented 'modernity' in his conception of the moral person of the state.[39] His theory foresees a spectrum of differentiated conditions that limit contractual freedom and make pacts illegitimate and void. The first and most important condition is natural law, which imposes on every moral being the obligation to preserve and perfect himself. But natural law does not prohibit the creation of an absolute or even a despotic power and submission to it. It only protects individual liberty by limiting the obligation to submit to majority rule and by requiring unanimity for such a decision: if the greater part of a nation wished to relinquish its original freedom and submit to a monarch, as the Jewish people did at the time of Samuel, it may change the form of government, but the decision cannot bind the disinclined minority. The citizens who are unwilling to submit are entitled to leave the country with their property and families. The right to emigrate is one of the most important natural rights that cannot be surrendered by the original compact of association and indicates the unanimity implicitly required by the pact itself (*LN*, I-III-33; I-XIX-223–225).[40] Voluntary submission is not even excluded in

[39] H. Kalmo and Q. Skinner (eds.), *Sovereignty in Fragments. The Past, Present and Future of a Contested Concept* (Cambridge, 2011).

[40] On this topic, see V. Chetail, 'Sovereignty and migration in the doctrine of the Law of Nations: An intellectual history of hospitality from Vitoria to Vattel', *The European Journal of International Law* 27 (2016), 901–922.

the case of a despotic regime, which, according to Vattel, is not a 'civil government'. It is true that the 'contract of society' cannot give the majority the right to establish it, but the unanimous consent of the whole people creates a legitimate submission to a despot and voluntary slavery, which however binds only those who have willingly contracted it, and does not impinge on the rights and liberty of the next generation (*Questions*, VIII-269).

If natural law and natural rights are the conditions of Vattel's double contract, the contract itself constitutes a fundamental limit to the exercise of power, and its infringement authorises, on the one hand, emigration and, on the other, resistance and revolution.[41] From this point of view, the act of association and the contract between the nation and the prince, conceived both as historical facts and as scientific concepts, have to be explained according to the rules of interpretation of treaties, contracts and laws established in chapter XVIII, book II of *The Law of Nations*. One of the most important rules is the presumed intention or will of contractual parties – which is not so far removed from the method of deducing the voluntary law of nations from their presumed consent. Applied to the concept of the very act of association, this hermeneutic rule operates, together with the reference to natural law and rights, as a criterion of rational deduction to establish a legitimate code of public law. A most relevant example is to be found in the *Questions of droit naturel*, where Vattel criticises the practice of judicial torture. His main argument is based on the presumed consent of individuals at the origin of society: 'Where is the man who, by contracting a civil society, agreed to run the risk of ever being exposed to such cruel treatment? The public authorities have no rights other than those they derive from the express or tacit consent of citizens. Therefore, they have no right to expose an innocent person to infamous torture' (*Questions*, VIII-688). Undoubtedly, Vattel contributed to enlightened reforms of criminal law and inspired the works of the Milanese Academy of the Fisticuffs.[42]

THE SOCIAL CONTRACT, WOMEN AND CONJUGAL SOCIETY

Vattel's positions concerning women and marriage are significant and very useful in helping us to understand the interplay between natural law and contractual acts, which, according to him, is crucial in establishing the appropriate relationships between private law and universal public law.

[41] D. Armitage, *Civil Wars. A History in Ideas* (New York, 2017).

[42] Mancuso, *Diritto, stato, sovranità*, 88–95; E. Fiocchi Malaspina, 'The circulation of the École romande du droit naturel in eighteenth-century Italy', in S. Zurbuchen (ed.), *The Law of Nations and Natural Law 1625–1800* (Leiden, 2019), 304–325, at 313–314.

Hobbes had deemed the validity of contracts to be impossible in the state of nature and so had placed the analysis of family and property in the second part of his work *On the citizen* (the one dedicated to *imperium*), thereby signifying that private law was dependent on and subordinate to political law. Conversely, his successors – like Pufendorf, Locke, Wolff, and Burlamaqui – analysed the private law of contracts, property and family before the discussion of the birth of civil societies and public law. Kant, too, considered private law as natural law preceding the original contract and public law.[43]

However, despite this crucial divide, all authors conceive the institutions of private law as governed both by the law of nature and by contractual acts, which meet their limits precisely in natural norms: convergences and oppositions arise from the ways in which natural rules about contractual freedom and local customs and statutes are articulated. If we take the question of marriage and conjugal society as an example, we can observe that, in fact, the most important disparities derive from the various ways of interpreting the relationship between nature and culture, natural norms and consensual acts. As regards paternal power, Hobbes is the staunchest defender of the natural equality of the sexes, because males do not enjoy superiority over females thanks to a presumed excellence of their nature. While contesting any right arising from the simple fact of generation, he affirms that the mother is the original owner and the sovereign of her offspring. Women can indeed lose their natural power over children in four cases: negligence, conquest, local customs, and the contract of marriage. It nevertheless remains true that voluntary acts can establish societies dominated by women, as in the case of the Amazons, and that it is not against the law of nature for a queen to be the superior of her husband.[44]

In subsequent authors, such as Pufendorf, Sidney, Locke, and Burlamaqui, this essential natural equality between men and women is basically eroded: social peace, the unity of command required by every society, as well as the certainty of paternity of children nourished by the father, are the most common arguments that authors invoke to affirm that the contract of marriage of necessity involves the wife's subjection to her husband, especially her fidelity and domestic obligation.[45] In contrast, Wolffian doctrine appears

[43] I. Kant, 'The metaphysics of morals', in M. J. Gregor and A. Wood (eds.), *Practical Philosophy* (Cambridge, 1996), 353–604.

[44] N. J. Hirschmann and J. H Wright (eds.), *Feminist Interpretations of Thomas Hobbes* (Philadelphia, 2012).

[45] On Pufendorf, see S. Sreedhar, 'Pufendorf on patriarchy', *History of Philosophy Quarterly* 31 (2014), 209–227. On Locke, see N. J. Hirschmann and K. M. McClure, *Feminist Interpretations of John Locke* (Philadelphia, 2007). On Barbeyrac, who is more and more 'egalitarian' as

closer to Hobbes's position. According to the German philosopher, men and women are equal by nature and no particular essential differences in force, nor rationality, can legitimise a perpetual submission: only voluntary agreement – the contract of marriage – can introduce inequality and subordination, on one side or the other.[46]

In opposition to such Wolffian arguments, Vattel, in his *Questions de droit naturel*, takes a most critical stance. Although he concedes that procreation is the essential and natural purpose of marriage, he assiduously emphasises that it is not its one and only objective. In keeping with his previous writings,[47] he develops a theory of love marriage, based on mutual understanding and delight in living together, strengthened by the enjoyment of physical pleasure not necessarily aimed at procreation. In contrast to the canonical tradition and Wolff himself, Vattel contends that sexual relations are not per se sinful, as long as they are exercised in moderation and within the limits set by the matrimonial rules. As we can read in his correspondence, he insistently complimented his friend Formey for his marriage, wishing him full satisfaction with sexual acts, which he called '*Te Deum*'.[48] For his part, Vattel, although ardent, makes it clear that his desires could not be fulfilled with his beloved Esther, to whom he was never formally engaged; however, it seems that, after that relationship, he had some passing affairs with other women, before marrying Marie Anne de Chêne in 1764.[49] During his relationship with Esther, he worried about her education and asked his friend, Frédéric Samuel Ostervald, to provide her with readings suitable for the female sex, such as Cicero's moral treatises.[50]

It may, therefore, seem surprising that, despite his delicate views on love, the Swiss author rejects the idea of natural equality between man and woman

regards conjugal society, and Burlamaqui, who is closer to Pufendorf's positions, see A. Dufour, *Le mariage dans l'école romande du droit naturel au XVIII*^e^ *siècle* (Geneva, 1976), 39–82.

46 A. Dufour, *Le mariage dans l'école allemande du droit naturel moderne au XVIII*^e^ *siècle* (Paris, 1972).

47 E. de Vattel, Lettre à Mademoiselle de M… sur les sentiments délicats, généreux et désintéressés, and *Sur la nature de l'amour. A Mademoiselle de M…*, in *Le Loisir Philosophique, ou Pièces diverses de philosophie, de morale et d'amusement* (Dresden, 1747), 144–162 and 163–178. On the two editions of this work in 1746 and 1747, see Haggenmacher, 'Le modèle Vattel', 11.

48 *Correspondances*, 21.

49 Ibid., 210.

50 Ibid., 43. See also the list of readings for ladies who should be part of the 'elixir of books', *Projet pour la composition d'un elixir des livres, à l'usage des joueurs qui n'ont pas le temps de s'instruire*, in *Le Loisir Philosophique*, 199–225, at 220–223.

and affirms that, according to natural law, the conjugal relation is a hierarchical society in which the husband has superiority:

> However, it is apparent that nature has made men much better suited than women to many things. They are well-suited to important affairs, firmer, stronger and more courageous ... Such equality would make society ruinous and awash with quarrels; Natural Law cannot prescribe it. It seems to me, therefore, that this law establishes the husband as the head of the house. (*Questions*, VII-496, 261–263)[51]

Thus, a series of asymmetries regulates matrimonial relationships: natural law does not prescribe monogamic marriage, because it admits polygeny while condemning polyandry. Divorce is only legitimate once the educational duties of parents have been accomplished, but, in spite of his doctrine of love marriage, according to Vattel, a man has the right to divorce if he discovers that his wife is sterile (*Questions*, VII-507). Fidelity in marriage is expected of the wife, as a sure guarantee of paternity, and only mutual love can make it an obligation for the husband.

It is true that the *Questions* comments on the freedom of choice of individuals, who are not always and unconditionally bound by the natural obligation to marry and procreate; moreover, spouses are free to establish different conditions by their marriage contract (*Questions*, VII-497). However, a clear consequence emerges from Vattelian doctrine on marriage: women, because of their conjugal subordination, are excluded from the right to participate in political life and so cannot take part in the 'very act of association'. It is therefore possible to read in a different way what has been considered the 'modernity' of Vattel compared to Wolff, namely the more markedly individualistic perspective in his theory of the social compact, based on the rejection of the idea that states originate from the union of a plurality of families (*Questions*, VIII-4). On the one hand, as Vattel himself observes, in Wolff's text the actors of the pact of association are always individuals, even though the German philosopher, like Aristotle, Bodin, and Locke himself, thinks of political society as a union of several families. On the other hand, the Swiss author explicitly contests Wolff's argument against the exclusion of women from the exercise of political power: 'Can it be denied that in general women are much less suited to governing than men? I know that we have seen and still see great princesses who have governed well. But prudence conforms to what usually happens and not to rare examples, which are nothing but exceptions that confirm the rule' (*Questions*, VIII, 281, 355–356). It is obvious

[51] *Questions de droit naturel*, §496, 261–263. See Dufour, *Le mariage* (1976), 86.

that Elizabeth I of England, Catherine I of Russia and Maria Theresa of Austria are the most important exceptions. Marriage laws in civil society are therefore very important not only to avoid an illegitimate superiority of the clergy over civil authorities but also to prevent the crown from being passed on to foreigners, as well as to prevent the right of succession from being controlled by the pope and not by the nation itself (*LN*, I-v-67): the liberty and independence of the sovereign nations are once again Vattel's main concern.

Thus, it is evident that the very act of association, with Vattel's republican flair, reinforces with its 'modernity' the exclusion of women from citizenship: from this point of view Vattel's thought was not far from Rousseau's male citizenship model.[52]

CONCLUSIONS: VATTEL AND ROUSSEAU

Vattel's assertion of the inalienability of sovereignty has often been viewed as an anticipation of the theory expounded by Jean-Jacques Rousseau in his *On the Social Contract* published in 1762. However, the similarity is linguistic rather than conceptual. Although partly sharing the same conception of the social contract, construed as a mutual engagement between individuals and the community, the consequences drawn by the two writers are quite different. Vattel's 'very act of association' gives birth to the sovereignty of the nation, or their delegates, whose power is conceived as 'representative' but not necessarily derived from an elective procedure: from this point of view *The Law of Nations* cannot be considered as the first theory of modern representative democracies. In contrast, according to Rousseau, the contracting individuals become, by virtue of the contract itself, members of the sovereign body – the people's assembly – and precisely because of that membership, they acquire the status of citizens. Even if Rousseau does not employ the expression 'inalienability of sovereignty' in the first version of *Geneva Manuscript*,[53] the concept is there, implicitly linked to the theory of the general will.

52 For an apology of the Swiss model of citizenship based on women's exclusion, see B. Barber, *The Death of Communal Liberty: A History of Freedom in a Swiss Mountain Canton* (Princeton, 1974); for a criticism of this patriarchal 'communal freedom', see C. Pateman, 'Feminism and democracy', in G. Duncan (ed.), *Democratic Theory and Practice* (Cambridge, 1983), 204–217.

53 In the title of chapter IV, book I, of *Geneva Manuscript*, 'En quoi consiste la souveraineté et ce qui la rend inaliénable', the last part of the sentence is an addition to the first version: therefore, we cannot establish precisely when Rousseau made the correction to his draft. See Bibliothèque de Genève, Ms. fr. 225, f. 20.

As we have seen, Vattel defines himself as a 'good citizen', but this was a philosophical rather than a legal definition: there were no citizens in the principality of Neuchâtel and Valangin and the two upper classes were nobility and *bourgeoisie*. Vattel was a nobleman, a knight and a *bourgeois*, as well as a subject of the Prussian king. The Genevan institutional landscape was republican, not monarchical, but its complexity and hierarchical structure were not more egalitarian than those of Neuchâtel. Nonetheless, whereas Rousseau's political theory was also a critique of the increasing inequality threatening political liberty in his homeland and was mainly concerned about defending the people's assemblies against the government, Vattel was not so worried about inequality: his main concern was the independence of the sovereign nation and its defence against a prince in danger of becoming a tyrant.

What is more, while Rousseau's concept of the social contract definitely excludes the possibility of a mutual contract between the people and the government, Vattel maintains a doctrine of the double contract, albeit one intrinsically different from Pufendorf's theory. From Rousseau's social contract theory there derives an institutional right to check government by the regularly assembled people, thus precluding the conceptual possibility of a 'right' to resist. Conversely, Vattel's double contract is the very foundation of a right of resistance as a right of war.

But despite their different positions both authors combine, each in his own way, natural law and contractualism. The fact that their works retained their vitality long after their death helps explain why, far from waning at the end of the eighteenth century, natural law and contractualism were still widespread theories during the nineteenth century. It is no coincidence that Nietzsche, in his *On the Genealogy of Morals*, felt it necessary to refute the theory of the contractual origin of the state.

FURTHER READING

Writings by Vattel

Vattel, E., *Emer de Vattel à Jean Henri Samuel Formey. Correspondances autour du Droit des gens*, ed. A. Bandelier (Paris, 2012).

Le Loisir Philosophique, ou Pièces diverses de philosophie, de morale et d'amusement (Dresde, 1747).

The Law of Nations, ed. B. Kapossy and R. Whatmore (Indianapolis, 2008).

Questions de droit naturel, et observations sur le Traité du Droit de la Nature de M. le Baron de Wolf (Berne, 1762).

Selected Secondary Literature

Beaulac, S., *The Power of Language in the Making of International Law. The Word* Sovereignty *in Bodin and Vattel and the Myth of Westphalia* (Leiden, 2004).
Gough, J. W., *The Social Contract. A Critical Study of Its Development*, 2nd ed. (London, 1957).
Pateman, C. and Mills C. W., *Contract and Domination* (Cambridge, 2007).
Stapelbroek, K. and Trampus, A. (eds.), *The Legacy of Vattel's Droit des gens* (Basingstoke, 2019).
Weatherall, T., *Jus Cogens. International Law and Social Compact* (Cambridge, 2015).

PART III

Receptions

10

Vattel's Reception in British America, 1761–1775

MARK SOMOS

Vattel's influence on the American Revolution is often mentioned but rarely discussed in detail. Most historians of the American Revolution do not consider him at all. Those who do, in a routine gesture 'piously transmitted',[1] invoke one of the most memorable vignettes in the history of international law: Charles W. F. Dumas (1721–1796) sending three copies of *Le droit des gens* to Benjamin Franklin (1706–1790) in 1775. In a 9 December 1775 letter, Franklin thanked Dumas and assured him that the copies 'came to us in good season, when the circumstances of a rising state make it necessary frequently to consult the law of nations' and the copy assigned to Congress 'has been continually in the hands of the members of our congress, now sitting'.[2] Franklin gave the other two copies to the Library Company of Philadelphia and Harvard College.[3] This episode is often mentioned to prove that the founders understood that they must justify secession under international law, and they saw Vattel as one of their chief authorities for doing so. The pre-1775 reception remains almost entirely unnoticed.[4]

The reception stories that begin in 1775 are also unsatisfying. Franklin's remark and the significance of Vattel's reception for the American Revolution,

1 William Ossipow and Dominik Gerber, 'The reception of Vattel's Law of Nations in the American colonies: From James Otis and John Adams to the Declaration of Independence', *American Journal of Legal History* 57 (2017), 521–555, at 523, where the authors also list major historians who ignore Vattel.

2 9 December 1775, Papers of Benjamin Franklin, *Founders Online*, National Archives, https://founders.archives.gov/documents/Franklin/01-22-02-0172.

3 Library Company, Rare E Vatt 303.Q. Houghton, *AC7.F8545.Zz775V. David Armitage, 41.

4 Ossipow and Gerber summarise and rightly criticise current historiography for fixating on Dumas's package to Franklin and missing or even explicitly denying Vattel's pre-1775 reception in the American colonies. Ossipow and Gerber, 'Reception', 523–536. For the reception after 1775 see Charles G. Fenwick, 'The authority of Vattel, Part I', *American Political Science Review* 7.3 (1913), 395–410.

and for the combination of the thirteen colonies into the new United States, have been asserted continuously for at least a century; but the assertions of influence are non-specific and unsupported. The majority of references to Vattel in the secondary literature on the American Revolution either simply lists him alongside Grotius and Burlamaqui as one of the founding generation's sources on international law, or they rely on assumptions, not evidence. Admittedly, assumptions are hard to resist, because Vattel's influence seems palpable in many revolutionary texts.

However, even hard-to-resist assumptions can be wrong. We read that Vattel inspired the founding generation's 'democratic principles'.[5] Others assume that Vattel must have been the founding generation's chief or even sole authority for theories of secession, as no one else treated the topic in detail.[6] Close inspection shows that Vattel's treatment was very brief and, unlike Vattel's, Frances Hutcheson's (1694–1746) equally desultory discussion in his 1747 *Short Introduction to Moral Philosophy* was developed and taught to the revolutionary generation in colonial colleges in detail and at length that steadily increased throughout the 1760s.[7] There is, at present, more evidence to support the influence of Hutcheson's commentators than Vattel's. The language of Vattel's formulation feels instinctively present in early revolutionary texts – but feeling is not proof. Similarly, it feels irresistibly evident that the federal structure of the early United States was inspired by Vattel.[8] However, evidence is lacking and other guides to federations, such as Pufendorf, who actually featured on colonial curricula, are better attested.

The shallowness of our knowledge of Vattel's impact is partly due to the gap between evidence and historical imagination and partly due to a textually faithful but methodologically uncritical reflection on primary sources. The founding generations would mention Vattel in lists of writers on constitutional and international law, without identifying the passage they had in mind. His name became a short-hand and *locus* for propositions, such as popular sovereignty and armed neutrality, that remained often unsubstantiated in

5 E.g. Williem Theo Oosterveld, *The Law of Nations in Early American Foreign Policy: Theory and Practice from the Revolution to the Monroe Doctrine* (Leiden, 2015), 34.

6 Ossipow and Gerber, 'Reception'.

7 E.g. Jasper Yeates, student notes on 'a brief compendium of the law of nature,' University of Pennsylvania, Kislak Library Special Collection, Ms. Coll. 600. Yeates went on to serve as justice of the Pennsylvania Supreme Court.

8 Vincent Chetail, 'Vattel and the American dream: An inquiry into the reception of the Law of Nations in the United States', in Vincent Chetail and Pierre-Marie Dupuy (eds.), *The Roots of International Law/Les fondements du droit international* (Leiden, 2013), 251–300, at 261. The Founders' view of human rights is similarly attributed to Vattel here, without any evidence.

revolutionary pamphlet wars, and allowed fellow American opponents to cite Vattel's authority for the contrary proposition. There is also the matter of second-hand reception, citing Vattel from newspaper reviews and extracts or lifting increasingly inchoate paraphrases from other pamphlets. This paper focuses on explicit references in order to start addressing this gap in our evidence and understanding.[9] Even before investigating paraphrases and indirect reuses, we can safely say that Vattel was more read, discussed, thought about and made more of an impact than current scholarship is aware.

One way in which focusing on the 1761–1775 period corrects existing literature relates to Vattel's reception and international law. It has been often and rightly noted that the legal theory and practice of the American Revolution must be understood in the context of international law. Intention and reasoning in documents such as the 1776 Declaration of Independence or the 1793 Proclamation of Neutrality cannot be understood without the legal education and practice of the founders who penned them. The sources surveyed in this chapter show some of Vattel's influence on the Revolution in the context of international legal history.

But this is not all we find. The primary sources show that from the early 1760s, soon after the publication of *Le droit des gens* (1758), Vattel inspired non-international legal theory and constitutional innovations among the colonists, ranging from adaptations of his views on popular sovereignty as something that the people inherit from the state of nature, through the development of a distinctly American doctrine of judicial review, to American proposals to reform the British Empire from within. Retracing Vattel's influence requires moving beyond international legal historiography and recognising Vattel as more than an international law authority.

Alongside the founders' realisation that they must justify American independence in international law, or risk losing support and credibility, another point often made is that the colonists did not so much as consider

[9] Ossipow and Gerber, 'Reception', offer twenty-nine citations in nineteen texts to Vattel between November 1762 and February 1776, hoping their work 'paves the way for inquiry into Vattel's intellectual authority in the revolutionary context' (521). Though an important survey, it has limitations. One of their nineteen texts is an advertisement for Vattel's book (F1), one is from 1776 and thus beyond the scope of this paper, and nine are based on questionable hypotheses concerning paraphrasing and unacknowledged borrowing, for instance taking the use of the phrase, 'free and independent states' as evidence of Vattel's influence (542). Moreover, Ossipow and Gerber miss at least twenty-six explicit references to Vattel in this period (all discussed throughout this chapter). Discounting the 1776 reference and the speculative ones, Ossipow offer nine for the 1762–1775 period. This paper describes thirty-five.

independence until 1775.[10] Existing accounts miss the earliest and in many ways most important part of his American reception because historians retrospectively misread Vattel as chiefly an international law authority in the colonies, and accept other historians' claim about the pre-1775 lack of any thought about independence. These two points combined go a long way towards explaining blind spots in current views on Vattel's early American impact.

A review of the primary sources shows that the founding generations' engagement with Vattel was not limited to international law. In fact, he was first cited as an authority on domestic constitutional norms and procedures. One of the earliest references to Vattel comes in the diary of John Adams (1735–1826), who castigated himself on 1 February 1763 for not spending enough time thinking and reading about Vattel's work.[11] I suggest that Adams was reading Vattel at the time in order to discuss judicial review with James Otis, Jr. (1725–1783). To understand why, we need to go back two years, to February 1761.

For over fifty years, John Adams repeatedly described James Otis's concluding speech in the 1761 *Paxton's Case* as the beginning of the Revolution. In a letter, one in a series he sent in 1816–1819 to William Tudor, his former clerk who was preparing a biography of Otis, Adams assessed the significance of Otis's speech as, 'Then and there, the child Independence was born. In fifteen years, i.e. in 1776, he grew up to manhood and declared himself free'.[12] Perhaps because most recent secondary works on the American Revolution begin with 1763, the end of the Seven Years' War, Adams's own assessment remains largely ignored.[13]

The background to Otis's speech can be summarised briefly. Smuggling was rampant in the colonies. One attempt to curtail smuggling involved

[10] E. S. Morgan, *The Birth of the Republic, 1763–89* (Chicago, 1956, rev. ed. 1977); M. Jensen, *The Founding of a Nation: A History of the American Revolution, 1763–1776* (New York, 1968, reprinted 2004); G. Wood, *The Creation of the American Republic, 1776–1787* (North Carolina, 1969); J. P. Reid, *Constitutional History of the American Revolution, vol. 2: The Authority to Tax* (Wisconsin, 1987); J. P. Greene, *The Constitutional Origins of the American Revolution* (Cambridge, 2011); S. Pincus, *The Heart of the Declaration: The Founders' Case for an Activist Government* (Yale, 2017).

[11] John Adams, *Works*, ed. Charles Francis Adams (Boston 1850), II.141.

[12] 'Child independence': Adams to Tudor, 29 March 1817, in Charles F. Adams (ed.), *Works of John Adams* (Boston, 1850–1856), 10, 247–248. Also see Adams's letter to his wife, Abigail, on 3 July 1776 concerning the causal link between Otis's 1761 speech and the Revolution; and Adams to William Wirt, 5 January 1818, in *Works*, 10:272.

[13] Jensen, *The Founding of a Nation*; Morgan, *Birth of the Republic*; Greene, *The Constitutional Origins of the American Revolution*, chapter 2; Pincus, *The Heart of the Declaration*.

issuing writs of assistance that allowed customs officers to search ships, shops and houses without giving a reason and without liability for damage. In August 1760, William Pitt the Elder (1708–1778), at the time Secretary of State for the Southern Department and leader of the House of Commons, instructed colonial governors to clamp down on contraband naval stores that could aid Britain's enemies. Francis Bernard (1712–1779), the new Governor of Massachusetts, who arrived in Boston only that month, assured Westminster that no smuggling took place in the province. Bernard appointed Thomas Hutchinson (1711–1780) as Lieutenant Governor, although the post had been promised to James Otis, Sr.

George II died in October 1760. Writs of assistance had to be reissued under the new royal authority within six months. News of the king's death reached Boston in December, and a group of sixty-three merchants instructed Oxenbridge Thacher (1719–1765) and the disgruntled James Otis, Jr. to challenge the writs in court. The dispute came to be known as *Paxton's Case*, after the British customs agent who obtained such a writ in 1755 and now filed a countersuit.[14] Otis's speech turned *Paxton's Case* into one of the most defining moments in pre-revolutionary America. Among other things, Otis argued that even though writs of assistance carry both the monarch's and Parliament's authority, all writs of assistance are void, because they violate natural and English rights, and judges must accordingly vacate them. Understandably, Otis's speech in *Paxton's Case* is often described as a landmark in the emergence of the American doctrine of judicial review. In preparing it, Otis relied on intense and detailed discussions with Adams.[15] As far as we can reconstruct Otis's speech and the preparatory work he did with Adams, Vattel played no part in this early formulation of the American judicial review doctrine.[16] The surviving documentation on the arrival of physical copies of Vattel's book in the colonies supports this conclusion, though it is possible

[14] Maurice H. Smith, *The Writs of Assistance Case* (Berkeley, CA, 1978); William J. Cuddihy, *The Fourth Amendment: Origins and Original Meaning, 602–1791* (Oxford, 2009), chapter 17. For a brief overview of the history and types of writs of assistance, see Horace Gray in Josiah Quincy Jr., in Samuel M. Quincy (ed.), *Reports of Cases Argued and Adjudged in the Superior Court of Judicature of the Province of Massachusetts Bay, Between 1761 and 1772* (Boston, 1865), Appendix I, section A, 395–400.

[15] Mark Somos, *American States of Nature: The Origins of Independence* (Oxford, 2019), 57–62.

[16] For the most complete reconstruction of Otis's speech see ibid., appendix 1. Wroth and Zobel, editors of the previous authoritative reconstruction, postulated that Otis already used Vattel in 1761. L. Kinvin Wroth and Hiller B. Zobel (eds.), *Legal Papers of John Adams* (Cambridge, MA, 1965), introduction, 106–123. However, Otis began this appropriation in 1761, and Vattel does not appear in his writings until 1764.

(albeit unlikely) that advertisements by a book trader appeared in a colonial newspaper now lost.[17]

Though all the evidence suggests that, *pace* current scholarship, Otis had not read Vattel yet by 1761, Vattel plays a key role in Otis's next, more mature formulation of colonial grievances and the doctrine of judicial review. In his 1764 *The Rights of the British Colonies Asserted and Proved*, Otis drew on Vattel's authority to make multiple points, starting with the origin of government.

Otis rejects four common opinions concerning the origin of government: religion, force, contract and property. He summarily dismisses the first two as obviously unacceptable. Otis's account of the third theory of government, based on contract, is entertaining and instructive. It is essentially five pages of questions. Is the original contract historical or analytical? Does it bind posterity? What are the justifications and ramifications of the transition from the pre-contract to the post-contract condition? Are women as free as men in the pre-contract stage? What conditions must be met to justify returning to, renegotiating or abrogating the original compact? Can one extrapolate these conditions from the legal principles in current use, for instance when equity overrides the letter of the law? Otis builds up a sequence of these provocative questions, only to put them aside with the instruction that those who wish for answers should consult Locke, Vattel, and their own conscience.[18]

[17] As Ossipow and Gerber note, the first surviving advertisement for Vattel's book in the colonies is by the New York bookseller and teacher, Garrat Noel, who offered copies for sale in the 29 November 1762 *New York Gazette*. Ossipow and Gerber's list of references to Vattel misses another nineteen advertisements, which add up to a useful pattern. Noel advertised in the same paper again on 31 January and 14 March 1763. The bulk of trade during the 1761–1775 period seems to have been done by partners of James Rivington, a London bookseller. Rivington had not moved to the colonies, but he partnered with William Miller in Boston and 'Rivington & Miller' advertised Vattel's book in the 6 December and 13 December 1764 *Boston News-Letter*; the 10, 17 and 31 December 1764 and 21 January and 4 February 1765 *Boston Gazette*; the 31 December 1764 and 7 January 1765 *Boston Post-Boy*; and the 18 February 1765 *Boston Evening-Post*. The partnership ended when Miller died in November 1765. After a long silence in Boston, advertisements for Vattel's book began to appear again in the *Boston Gazette* (24 December 1770, 10 and 17 June 1771) in the shop of John Langdon III. Rivington distributed the book in Philadelphia via Brown, another associate, and they advertised it in the 8 November and 6 December 1764 and the 10 October 1765 *Pennsylvania Gazette*. On 16 June 1768, John Elliott advertised copies for sale in the *Pennsylvania Gazette*.

These data points confirm that Vattel's early reception concentrated in New England; that copies were probably hard to come by before 1762; and that Boston and Philadelphia saw a huge surge of interest in late 1764 and early 1765.

[18] J. Otis, Jr., *The Rights of the British Colonies Asserted and Proved* (Boston, 1764), 6. Also see 118–120.

Evidence of close collaboration between Adams and Otis from 1761 on suggests that Adams was reading Vattel in February 1763 to help Otis prepare this section of *Rights*.[19] Otis's and Adams's choice of Locke and Vattel as the two and twinned guiding authorities on the origin of government is a strong signal that by 1764 Vattel was already relied upon for constitutional innovations that had, at least in this text, little to do with international law. Furthermore, *pace* the seminal historians John Philip Reid and Jack Greene, the decision to combine Locke and Vattel moved the legal discourse towards natural law, beyond the realm of the common law.[20]

The colonists' reliance on Vattel was no mere theory. As an Appendix, *Rights* reprints a memorandum that was drafted by Otis but formally approved and sent by the Massachusetts Assembly to Jasper Mauduit, the colony's agent in London.[21] When published, such memoranda were not only instructions to the agent, but also clear messages to Westminster. In the memorandum, the Massachusetts Assembly musters legal authorities for the opinion that statutory laws are invalid if they violate the harmony of laws that makes the English legal system exceptional.

> The judges of England have declared in favour of these sentiments, when they expresly declare, that *acts of parliament against natural equity are void*. That *acts against the fundamental principles of the British constitution are void*. This doctrine is agreeable to the law of nature and nations, and to the divine dictates of natural and revealed religion.[22]

The Assembly's footnote cites *Bonham's Case* and a long passage from Vattel in English, without identifying book, chapter or verse. In the long cited passage, Vattel argues that the legislative cannot change the constitution at will, and that colonies are integral parts of the state.[23] The memorandum in

[19] Close collaboration: Somos, *American States of Nature*. For Adams' role in drafting *Rights*, see John Philip Reid (ed.), *Briefs of the American Revolution* (New York, 1981), 119–125.

[20] Others have interpreted this key passage as drawing on Vattel for the very notion of the constitution as fundamental law. Charles Grove Haines, *The American Doctrine of Judicial Supremacy* (New York, 1914), 36–41, 46–47.

[21] Drafted by Otis: Adams, letter to William Tudor, 31 August 1818, proceeding to cite the whole text (though with variations, e.g. lifting footnotes in the appendix to *Rights* into the running text). Ossipow and Gerber posit that the 1775 *Declaration by the Representatives* ... was 'a significant turning point' in early American uses of Vattel as 'for the first time, his authority is no longer confined to theoretical debates or pamphlets, but came to influence a political message'. The Assembly's 1764 memorandum had done the same.

[22] J. Otis, Jr. and the Massachusetts House of Representatives, 'Memorandum to Jasper Maudit', in Otis, *Rights*, appendix, 72–73.

[23] Otis, *Rights*, 109–110. On *Bonham's Case* and judicial review see Glenn Burgess, *Absolute Monarchy and the Stuart Constitution* (New Haven, CT, 1996), 173–194. Daniel J. Hulsebosch,

fact intercuts *LN*, I-III-34, where Vattel makes the first point, with *LN*, I-XVIII-210, where he makes the second. Unnoticed in existing secondary literature, the main text of the memorandum after this footnote is a paraphrase of the rest of Vattel's *LN*, I-III-34, where Vattel chooses England as an example of a country where it would be absurd and unthinkable if the legislative tried to alter the constitution. Then the Assembly adds to Vattel's text that even if Parliament offered to make the King an absolute despot, the King would be unwise to accept it, since the people did not entrust Parliament with the power to exchange their liberty for slavery. Massachusetts is citing Vattel as an authority, then rephrasing his text as their own to point out the King's responsibility and adding slavery to the language.

Immediately after this hybrid passage, the Assembly inserts another long Vattel citation in a footnote, from *LN*, III-XIII-201, to show that even the conqueror of a whole state has limited rights over the conquered. This point seems to me incongruous to the Assembly's arguments, unless they posited the scenario of full conquest as an extreme case to prove that their point applies to the milder problems of intra-imperial constitutional interpretation. In any case, it is clear from the scope and variety of citations that the drafters of the Assembly's 1764 memorandum were intimately familiar with the whole of Vattel's text. (The citations also reveal that the Assembly was not using the 1760 English translation.)

Following Wroth and Zobel, editors of Adams's legal papers and Otis's 1761 speech, scholars had thought that Otis used the same two sources, *Bonham's Case* and Vattel, to formulate his influential judicial review doctrine in *Paxton's Case*. The discovery of a new manuscript shows that this is not the case: in 1761, Otis did not cite Vattel yet.[24] Bailyn argued that Otis cited Vattel decoratively and ignored Vattel when he formulated the American judicial

Constituting Empire: New York and the Transformation of Constitutionalism in the Atlantic World, 1664–1830 (Chapel Hill, NC, 2005), 30–31. Other positions reviewed in R. H. Helmholz, 'Bonham's case, judicial review, and the Law of Nature', *Journal of Legal Analysis* 1.1 (2009), 325–354.

24 Wroth and Zobel, commenting on *Rights*: 'In all probability he cited the same authorities and made the same appeal to higher law before the Superior Court in 1761'. *Legal Papers of Adams*, 119. The newly discovered manuscript of Otis's speech proves otherwise: Somos, *American States of Nature*, appendix 1. Moreover, it is generally accepted that Adams helped Otis draft the 1761 speech, as well as *Rights*. Adams's Diary details his readings throughout the 1760s, but he first mentions Vattel only in 1763. This also points to the conclusion that Vattel was absent from the 1761 speech. It is probable that in 1761 neither Otis nor Adams had read *Le droit de gens*, unless extracts in popular reviews.

review doctrine.[25] Otis's use of Vattel in his 1764 *Rights* disproves this, as well. This first use was certainly genuine and substantial. Otis, Adams and the Assembly were not carelessly multiplying sources. The combination of two passages from Vattel as if they were one allowed them to address the legislative's authority over the colonies in a way that *Bonham's Case* did not. More importantly, by adding Vattel to *Bonham's Case* they moved beyond the scope of the common law to argue that reason, natural law, and equity, not only Bonham's precedent, set limits on Parliament's authority.[26]

The Massachusetts Assembly's criticism of Westminster in the 1764 *Rights* signified heightening tension and discontent. Soon after, in March 1765, Parliament passed the Stamp Act, which stipulated that a range of documents, including pamphlets and newspapers, court documents, professional licenses and playing cards, be printed on paper manufactured in London and carry an embossed stamp. Colonial resistance became wider and deeper. A recurring colonial objection was that no one can be taxed without their consent, which in the British Empire meant suffrage and parliamentary representation – something the colonists were denied. The colonists protested the 1764 Sugar Act on the same grounds. However, as the Stamp Act also affected court documents, the colonists argued that Westminster effectively ceased to provide judicial services. Those who did not wish to pay sugar tax could find an alternative, for instance cut down on sugar or rum (a chief use for sugar), or buy smuggled sugar at added risk and cost. But there was no alternative to transactions involving court documents and licenses approved by the mother country. Britain put the colonists in a situation where they had to choose between accepting taxation without representation or the cessation of all legal services.[27]

When Otis, Adams and other eminent lawyers formulated the colonists' constitutional objections to the Stamp Act for Governor Bernard on 5 December 1765, they argued that 'The King is always presumed to be present in his Courts, holding out the Law to his Subjects; and when he shuts

[25] Bernard Bailyn, *The Ideological Origins of the American Revolution* (Cambridge, MA, 1967), 178–179.

[26] This adds to other criticisms of the position, promulgated by scholars such as John Philip Reid and Jack Greene, that natural law had little significance for early American thought, which operated mostly within the confines of the common law. Ossipow and Gerber, 'Reception', 525. Justice Gray represents the mainstream opinion when he argues that by the time Otis stood up in court in February 1761, there was an English tradition that built on *Bonham's Case* to argue that the judiciary had the power, even the duty, to declare unconstitutional statutes void. *Quincy's Reports*, Appendix 1, 520–527.

[27] Somos, *American States of Nature*, chapter 4.

his Courts, he unkings himself in the most essential Point'. According to *Quincy's Report*, the sources they cited in support were '18 E. 3, ch. 1. 1 H. 4. 20. E. 3, ch. 2. 4 H. 4, ch. 1. Vattel, p. 20'.[28] Once again, the addition of Vattel to a conventional common law chain of sources is striking. Remarkably, just as the colonists mobilised Vattel's authority to support American judicial review over Parliament in the 1764 *Rights*, a year and a half later we find them adding Vattel to common law reasoning against the King. On 27 December 1765 Adams, returning to the topic of judicial review, cited in his diary three passages from Vattel's II.xvii on the interpretation of laws.[29] The three elements of Vattel's procedural hermeneutics that Adams noted were interpreting laws according to legislator's intention to events that the legislator could not have foreseen (*LN*, II-xvii-297), cases where interpretation leads to absurdity must be rejected (*LN*, II-xvii-292), and that interpretations leading to impossibility, whether moral or physical, constitute absurdity (*LN*, II-xvii-282).

A prominent rejoinder to Thacher's 1764 *Sentiments* and Otis' 1764 *Rights* was *The regulations lately made concerning the Colonies*, published anonymously in London in 1765.[30] Often ascribed at the time to Grenville himself, it was written by Thomas Whately, secretary to the Treasury under Grenville, later the author of pamphlets defending Grenville's financial schemes.[31] A widely read and cited colonial rejoinder to Whately was penned by Richard Bland (1710–1776). His *An Inquiry into the Rights of the British Colonies* has been appreciated as an unusually astute argument ever since it first appeared in the week of 7–14 March 1766.[32] By then, Bland had served in

28 *Quincy's Reports*, 205. This reference to Vattel is missing from Ossipow's and Gerber's list. Ossipow and Gerber theorise that Oxenbridge Thacher's 1764 *Sentiments of a British American*, written against the Sugar Act, contains a Vattelian reference. Equally tenuously, they read a Vattelian paraphrase into the 1768 *Massaschusetts Circular*.

29 John Adams, *Works*, II.166. Adjacent passages relevant to judicial review are Vattel, *LN*, II-xvii-300, 307.

30 These texts were Whately's main target according to Ian R. Christie, 'A vision of empire: Thomas Whately and the regulations lately made concerning the colonies', *The English Historical Review* 113.451 (1988), 300–320, at 303–304.

31 Thomas Whately, *Remarks on The Budget; or a Candid Examination of the Facts and Arguments Offered to the Public in that Pamphlet* (London, 1765); and *Considerations on the Trade and Finances of the Kingdom and on the Measures of the Administration since the Conclusion of the Peace* (London, 1766). Sometimes attributed to Whately but probably written by William Knox: *Present State of the Nation* (1768; appendix, 1769), and *The Controversy between Great Britain and her Colonies Reviewed* (1769). Whately's authorship of *Regulations* is interesting but does not mean that he did not reflect Grenville's position accurately; see the citations and summaries in Reid, . . . *Authority to Tax*, 16.

32 Kevin J. Hayes, *The Road to Monticello: The Life and Mind of Thomas Jefferson* (Oxford, 2008), 153.

the Virginia House of Burgesses for 24 years. As it was formally a response to Whately's counterattack, Bland restated some of the Bostonians' arguments, but gave them his own twists. He also added original arguments of his own, and brought new issues into the debate, further widening its scope. To explain people's natural liberty in the state of nature, Bland referenced 'Vattel's Law of Nature. Locke on Civil Govern. Wollaston's Rel. of Nat.'. The combination of Vattel and Locke is as noteworthy as the addition of Wollaston; and the reference to Vattel's work as *Law of Nature*.

The shift from using Vattel in constitutional frameworks to international law frameworks signals the (pre-1775) moment when the colonists effectively declared independence. In the 13 June 1771 *Massachusetts Spy*, 'Centinel' insists in letter VII that George III has no right to send troops to the colonies, because when the first settlers left Britain, they became independent. As *LN*, I. XIX indisputably established, according to Centinel, citizens have an absolute right to leave when the monarch breaks a compact or violates their freedom of conscience.[33] Centinel continues to apply Vattel's clause to the settlers: '[t]he connection between them and the sovereign is broke, and consequently they fall into a state of nature which preceeded government'. In that American state of nature the settlers created their own constitution and bought land from the Native Americans, after which they had 'all those titles to an absolute sovereignty any nation can vouch'. Sovereign and independent in intention and fact, they applied to Britain for protection. In Centinel's application of Vattel's categories, the approach to the mother country was therefore not a domestic matter but a relationship between sovereign states. Centinel explains Vattel's view that in these situations the applicant state does not surrender its sovereignty and the sovereign state that offers protection must observe the conditions under which obedience had been offered. To this Vattelian principle, Centinel adds that this relationship is analogous between states and private individuals in a state of nature, because when the monarch fails to provide protection, his subjects relapse into a state of nature, as well.[34]

The theme of a permanent break with England was picked up and further developed by 'Valerius Poplicola' (probably Samuel Adams, 1722–1803) who, in between long citations from Locke's *Second Treatise*, inserted a reference to Vattel's *LN*, I-XIX-223 in the 28 October 1771 issue of the *Boston Gazette* concerning citizens' 'absolute right' to leave their country if they do not like it, for instance because 'the sovereign, or the greater part of the nation will

33 Also Vattel, *LN*, I-XII-128.

34 This direct use of Vattel is also missing from Ossipow and Gerber's list of nineteen. Centinel could have also used *LN*, II-IV-50 on how lack of protection produces the right to resist.

permit the exercise of only one religion in the state'. This, according to Poplicola, is what happened to the first settlers, ancestors of the current generation of colonists. While Centinel merely hints at the reasons why the first American settlers left the old world, and attributes the first settlers' independence and sovereignty to the physical facts of distance from the mother state, which made government impossible, Poplicola argues that the first settlers left with the pre-existing and causative intention to become independent.

Centinel's XXIII essay appeared in the 28 November 1771 *Massachusetts Spy*.[35] Centinel restates that the first settlers became independent and, though they sought Britain's protection, Vattel's authority sufficiently demonstrates that Britain acquired no rights other than what the settlers may have explicitly surrendered. When Britain claims further rights, for instance to tax the colonies without their consent, they are illegally using force.

'Agricola' penned a wonderful essay for the 22 October 1772 issue of the *Massachusetts Spy*. The piece begins with the author announcing her or his fear of offending the government. Having recently bought copies of Vattel and Mably on Romans, and subscribed to Montesquieu, the author intends to send extracts or snippets in the (pretended) hope that the government would take no offence. Then follows an extraordinary selective paraphrasing, entirely from Vattel. Agricola reviews the origin of society, the natural obligations of states toward one another and the equal sovereignty of states ('a dwarf is as much a man as a giant'), which includes the right to determine its own actions. Other states may disagree, may pursue their own interests, but they may not pretend that sovereign states have no right to set their own course. The only exception is when a prince attacks the fundamental laws of his own country and provokes justified resistance from his subjects, who call in foreign assistance. So far, Agricola has selected passages from *LN*, prelim. 5–8, 13, 15, 18, 21, and II-IV-56, in this order. Next, Agricola cites Vattel on society's obligations toward itself to choose the best possible constitution and 'constantly to suppress' violations of the constitution. Again, if the prince violates it, the contract with his subjects is broken and the people can request foreign intervention. Finally, Agricola reprints passages from Vattel that describe patriotism, love of oneself and love for one's society, and the particular obligations and high standards that this love imposes on the sovereign – and on the patriots who resist an unjust and tyrannical sovereign. To assemble this train of thought, Agricola intercuts passages from *LN*, I-III-29-31, I-IV-51 and I-XI-120–121 and 123–124, in this order.

35 Missing from Ossipow and Gerber.

Agricola removes Vattel's warnings about the public's proneness to error, normal lack of complete information, and Vattel's exhortations for the people to exercise the utmost possible patience. Instead of reproducing Vattel's meaning, Agricola pieces together an extraordinary and creative 'remix' in which Vattel appears to call upon the people to constantly monitor the constitution's integrity and resist any encroachment, much more so than Vattel's own text does. Vattel's exceptional criteria for convening a global federation to fight an unjust prince, who proved himself to be an enemy of humanity, is similarly transformed from a very high threshold to an ongoing, normal obligation to monitor princes' fidelity to their states' constitution and an active obligation to correct them through foreign assistance.

In the 30 November 1772 *Boston Gazette*, 'A Tenant' cites the republican statesman and theorist Algernon Sidney, Locke and Vattel in support of popular sovereignty, against 'A Landlord' who objected to people assembling to voice their grievances.[36] The Tenant drew on Vattel's formulation of popular sovereignty to defend freedom of assembly (and the right to petition?). Once again, it is striking that Vattel is inserted into a common law chain of reasoning.

'The votes and proceedings of the freeholders and other inhabitants of the town of Boston, in town meeting assembled, according to law,' better known as part of *The Boston Pamphlet*, is one of the founding documents of the first committee of correspondence, effectively shadow governments in the thirteen colonies. The *Pamphlet* begins with a short account of the meetings on 28 October and 2 November 1772, when the Committee of Correspondence was established. Samuel Adams, James Otis, Jr. and Dr. Joseph Warren (1741–1775) were instrumental in its formation and in shaping its mission to co-ordinate resistance to Britain. The *Pamphlet*'s discussion of rights is divided into three sections: on the natural rights of colonists, on their rights as Christians and concerning their rights as subjects. The last section begins with a definition of the state as 'a Body politick or civil Society of Men, united together to promote their mutual Safety, and Prosperity, by Means of their Union'. The authorities cited, without reference to a passage, are Locke and Vattel.[37] *The Boston Pamphlet* ends with the Committee's address to 240 towns to join the cause in the Massachusetts Bay Colony.[38] At least 144 replied by the

36 Missing from Ossipow and Gerber.

37 P8. Missing from Ossipow and Gerber.

38 The arrangement of *The Boston Pamphlet* shows an understanding of what Putnam calls a two-level game, between domestic politics and external diplomacy. Robert Putnam, 'Diplomacy and domestic politics: The logic of two-level games', *International Organization* 42 (1988), 427–460. *The Boston Pamphlet*'s petition section is moderate, and expresses hope for

end of summer 1773; the *Pamphlet* launched an extraordinarily discussion about independence throughout the colonies.

Largely reacting to *The Boston Pamphlet* in a famous speech on 6 January 1773, Governor Thomas Hutchinson cited Vattel, *LN*, I-XVIII-210 to the Massachusetts Assembly to show that they had no right to pass resolutions challenging Westminster. The passage concerns a new colony which, 'though separated from the principal establishment, or mother country, naturally becomes a part of the state, equally with its ancient possessions'. As we saw, the Assembly cited the same passage in their 1764 memorandum appended to Otis's *Rights* to claim that the colonists had the same rights as residents of the mother country. Nine years later, in a far more tense situation, Hutchinson cites this Vattel passage back at the Assembly in order to show that they also had the same obligations. The first settlers continued to owe allegiance to Crown and Parliament, and their descendants inherited the same rights and obligations. Hutchinson holds that Vattel's point applies to all imperial constitutions, not only Britain's.[39]

The Council and the House wrote separate replies. The House replied on 26 January 1773. They rejected Hutchinson's premise and argued that settlers of charter colonies owed no obedience to Parliament. To show that Hutchinson's construction was untenable, they invoked Vattel's principles of interpretation. Given geographical distance, everyone understood that the first settlers would not be represented in Parliament; therefore the privileges that the charters bestowed upon them were and remain effective and non-derogable.[40] The House's account of the consequences of geographical separation alluded to another vital argument frequently drawn from Vattel, namely that separation is justified when the mother country could not protect the colonies (*LN*, I-XVII-200–202).

For the 11 November 1773 *Massachusetts Spy*, Britannus Septentrionalis composed a long essay that drew heavily on Vattel.[41] He or she confesses to being born in Britain, having moved to Massachusetts, never giving up her or his individual rights and being shocked at the British government's violation of

reconciliation with Britain. By contrast, the letter to other towns justifies independence based on British tyranny and despotism. Evidence of reception and reaction shows that London, the colonists, and the writers all understood that the *Pamphlet* used the threat of independence to bargain for better terms.

39 Thomas Hutchinson, 'Speech to the two houses, 6 Jan. 1773', in A. Bradford (ed.), *Speeches of the Governors of Massachusetts from 1765 to 1775* . . . (Boston, 1818), 336–342, at 337.

40 Ibid., 351–365, at 356. Otis wrote for the Council, so this riposte was probably suggested by Samuel Adams, Major Hawley, Thayer or another House writer.

41 Missing from Ossipow and Gerber.

the charters which, given that the first settlers created an independent state, are in fact interstate treaties, best understood from Vattel. In quick succession and integral to her or his train of thought, Britannus cites from the 1760 English edition *LN*, II-XII-191 on treaties, *LN*, II-IV-54 on the equality of states, *LN*, I-II-9 on the situation in which two independent states have the same prince, *LN*, Prelim. 1 and 18 on the definition, generation and equality of states, *LN*, I-I-4 on the equality of states, *LN*, II-IV-54 again and *LN*, II-IV-57 on the restraints upon the state affording protection to another, and several paraphrases.

Daniel Leonard (1740–1829), King's Attorney and wealthy member of the Massachusetts House of Representatives and of the Boston Committee of Correspondence, is usually labelled a Loyalist. He was not, at first. Historians cite Leonard's exchanges with John Adams, with Leonard signing as Massachusettensis, and Adams as Novanglus, as a classic clash of Patriot and Loyalist views. This is a mistake. When he published 'To All Nations of Men' under the pseudonym, Massachusettensis, in the 18 November 1773 *Massachusetts Spy*, Leonard was still active on the Boston Committee of Correspondence. Instead of a continuous staunch Loyalist position, the Massachusettensis letters show Leonard changing sides in response to, arguably, Adams's increasing radicalism, which also alienated hitherto revolutionary representatives in Congress. This early Massachusettensis letter is still written by Leonard as a Patriot.

In the first half of the essay, Leonard cites Burlamaqui, Hobbes and Locke to argue that taxation without representation is unjust, and resisting it even with force is a just course of action. However, things probably would not go that far, because open war would turn Britain into an enemy of all humankind.

> It is highly probable our oppressors will withdraw their hand when they find our resolution, and consider how fatal it must be to themselves to drive things to extremity. Great-Britain at war with her colonies would be in the condition of a trunk deprived of its members. Besides the foundation of the dispute being an effort of her ministers to diminish the sovereignty of so great a number of free self governing states, and erect an absolute despotism over them, must give umbrage to every other power in Europe, this being an open violation of the law of nations, and punishable by all as Vatell [sic] B II. C. IV. § 53 declares in these words, 'If then there is any where a nation of a restless and mischievous disposition always ready to injure others, to traverse their designs, and to raise domestic troubles; it is not to be doubted but all have a right to join in order to repress, chastise, and put it ever after out of its power to injure them.' And in the next paragraph the interference with their

government and diminution of their sovereignty is declared to be capital injuries.[42]

The passage is remarkable for several reasons. Leonard already allows the British empire to be legitimate only if it is a Vattelian federation of 'free self governing states', with the law of nations, not municipal or constitutional, regulating relations between them. Moreover, Leonard stipulates that violence by Britain would make it a rogue nation, punishable by all.[43] The Boston Tea Party, one of the best-known episodes of the American Revolution, took place less than a month later, on 16 December 1773. It was followed by punitive laws from Westminster, passed between March and June 1774 and known collectively as the Coercive Acts in Britain, or the Intolerable Acts among revolutionaries. Fifty-six representatives gathered in Philadelphia at the First Continental Congress in September 1774 to consider their options.

The records of the Boston Committee of Correspondence attest to a remarkable continuity between *The Boston Pamphlet* and the meeting of delegates from twelve of the thirteen colonies in Philadelphia in September and October 1774. The continuity is both organisational and substantive. Many of the committees of correspondence, and the towns, counties and provinces they reported to, were increasingly excited about the prospect of a colonial congress. Every topic mentioned before appears in the intense exchange among the towns, and between the colonies.[44] The Congress chose William Bradford (1719–1791) as their official printer, responsible for producing the definitive version of the resolutions and documents, including (eventually) the Declaration of Independence. Bradford's son, William Bradford Jr. (1755–1795), lawyer, later judge and second US Attorney General, was a friend of the young James Madison. In a 17 October 1774 letter, Bradford informed Madison,

42 Missing from Ossipow and Gerber. Leonard could have also used *LN*, II-v-70, 77.

43 In a later, 9 January 1775 Massachusettensis essay in the *Massachusetts Gazette*, Leonard would cite Vattel *LN*, I-xviii-210 to argue, as Hutcheson did, that the colonies owe allegiance to Britain. 'The colonies are a part of the British empire. The best writers upon the law of nations, tell us, that when a nation takes possession of a distant country, and settles there, that country though separated from the principal establishment, or mother country, naturally becomes a part of the state, equal with its ancient possessions. Two supreme or independent authorities cannot exist in the same state. It would be what is called imperium in imperio, the height of political absurdity.' Adams replied directly to Leonard's argument in a 6 March 1775 essay in the *Boston Gazette*, citing Vattel's passage and adding: 'there is nothing in the law of nations, which is only the law of right reason, applied to the conduct of nations, that requires that emigrants from a state should continue, or be made a part of the state.'

44 Boston Committee of Correspondence records, NYPL MssCol 343.

> The Congress sits in the Carpenter's Hall in one room of which the City Library is kept & of which the Librarian tells me the Gentlemen make great & constant use. By which we may conjecture that their measures will be wisely plan'd since they debate on them like philosophers; for by what I was told Vattel, Barlemaqui Locke & Montesquie [sic] seem to be the standars [sic] to which they refer either when settling the rights of the Colonies or when a dispute arises on the Justice or propriety of a measure.[45]

Unnoticed in the secondary literature that cites Franklin's December 1775 letter, Franklin was politely disingenuous when he thanked Dumas for sending French copies of Vattel for Congress; for more than a year, Congress had already been using Vattel as their 'standard'.

Vattel's impact on the early American Revolution is rarely discussed. When it is, it is treated in vague terms, with no or flawed evidence. To my knowledge, the 2017 article by Ossipow and Gerber is the only systematic attempt to date to quantify reception and pave the way for a proper understanding. They identified nine explicit references to Vattel in colonial sources between 1762 and 1775. This paper presented thirty-five, and began to broach qualitative issues, such as the fact that Vattel was first read and used in the colonies as a constitutional authority whose authority and compelling force rested on natural law, not common, divine or international law. Vattel played a formative role in the evolution of the American doctrine of judicial review. When he was invoked as an international lawyer from 1771, the founding generation used his authority to effectively declare their independence and to portray Britain as a rogue state against which confederations should be formed.

FURTHER READING

Chetail, Vincent, 'Vattel and the American dream: An inquiry into the reception of the Law of Nations in the United States', in Vincent Chetail and Pierre-Marie Dupuy (eds.), *The Roots of International Law/Les fondements du droit international* (Leiden, 2013), 251–300.

Hulsebosch, Daniel J., *Constituting Empire: New York and the Transformation of Constitutionalism in the Atlantic World, 1664–1830* (Chapel Hill, NC, 2005).

Ossipow, William and Gerber, Dominik, 'The reception of Vattel's Law of Nations in the American colonies: From James Otis and John Adams to the Declaration of Independence', *American Journal of Legal History* 57 (2017), 521–55.

[45] 'To James Madison from William Bradford, 17 October 1774', *Founders Online*, National Archives, https://founders.archives.gov/documents/Madison/01-01-02-0036.

11

Tradition and Revolution

Eighteenth-Century German and French Contexts and Vattel's *Law of Nations*

NATHANIEL BOYD

The present chapter focuses on the *Law of Nations* (1758) and its relation to the political tradition and to modern ideas of constitution and nation – taking Germany and France as objects of study. On the one hand, it takes up Vattel's interpretation of the structure of the Holy Roman Empire and the threat posed by Frederick II to the society of nations; on the other, it focuses on elective affinities, examining the correspondence between certain of Vattel's ideas and the new constitutional doctrines in revolutionary France. These are two strikingly different contexts. The first perhaps best represents the pinnacle of the early modern princely territorial state, albeit clothed in the ideas of the Enlightenment. By contrast, the second is nothing other than the dramatic destruction of the *ancien régime* – establishing a new constitution and idea of the nation.

The chapter is structured in three sections. First, I analyse Vattel's thought in relation to the political tradition. Here I explore the significance of the tension between subjective right and objective law and his doctrine of the constitution. The purpose of this initial discussion serves as an entry point to the different contexts that will then be examined. With this in mind, I then study the imperial constitution in Vattel and his attack on the politics of Frederick II and his threat to the society of nations. Lastly, I investigate Vattel's constitutional thought – his idea of the body of the nation as a collective will forming the constitution – and its proximity to the later political doctrines of Emmanuel Joseph (Abbé) Sieyès in revolutionary France and its founding document, the Déclaration des droits de l'homme et du citoyen (1789).

THE POLITICAL TRADITION AND VATTEL'S *LAW OF NATIONS*

Vattel makes no secret of the fact that he sets out from Christian Wolff's philosophy.[1] Nevertheless, there are great differences between the two thinkers. Wolff had attempted to reveal to humanity the true foundation of law, which he subordinated to philosophy.[2] Vattel, on the other hand, took law away from both the jurists and the philosophers and put it in the hands of the sovereign and his ministers, with the aim of enlightening the practice of eighteenth-century politics and diplomacy. The rational method of deduction that had preoccupied both Leibniz and Wolff and which aimed to demonstrate the certainty of both natural and positive law was of little concern for Vattel in the *Law of Nations*. In contrast to these advocates of the mathematical, rational method of finding justice, which saw the world as created by God and in a harmonious order recognised through enlightened reason, Vattel's approach was much more inconsistent – even if purposively so. Ian Hunter has revealed this to be part and parcel to a form of casuistic argumentation. The apparent duality between the nation-state's self-assertion and the normative law of nations is intrinsic to Vattel's world of politics and diplomacy, which is far more unsettled and does not lay claim to a philosophical foundation.[3]

At the centre of the *Law of Nations* there seemed to be a conflict or ambiguity between the universalist claims of the society of nations, which Vattel drew from equating the individual in the natural state – 'capable of doing so little by themselves, that they can scarcely subsist without the aid and laws of civil society' (*LN*, preface 15) – and the national interest of particular states. At the individual level, association was necessary for survival: 'But it is easy to perceive that the civic association is very far from being equally necessary between nations, as it was between individuals' (*LN*, preface 15). Thus, while Vattel adopted from Wolff the distinction between the necessary and voluntary laws of nations, he rejected 'the idea of a great republic (*civitas*

1 See F. Ieva, '"A poor imitation of Grotius and Pufendorf?" Biographical uncertainties and the laborious genesis of Vattel's *Droit des gens*', in K. Stapelbroek and A. Trampus (eds.), *The Legacy of Vattel's Droit des gens* (Cham, 2019), 53–76, for more details on the complex development of Vattel's *Law of Nations*.

2 See Chapter 3, by E. Nokkala; M. Thomann, 'Die Bedeutung der Rechtsphilosophie Christian Wolffs in der juristischen und politischen Praxis des 18. Jahrhunderts', in H. Thieme (ed.), *Humanismus und Naturrecht in Brandenberg-Preussen: Ein Tagungsbericht* (Berlin, 1979), 121, 126; Christian Wolff, *Vernünftige Gedanken von dem gesellschaftlichen Leben der Menschen, und insonderheit dem gemeinen Wesen, 'Deutsche Politik'*, ed. H. Hoffmann (Munich, 2004), 57f.

3 See I. Hunter, 'Vattel's Law of Nations: Diplomatic casuistry for the protestant nation', *Grotiana* 31 (2010), 108–140, at 109, 114.

maximae)' (*LN*, preface 15). Or at least that is the way he claimed to do. Yet Vattel attributed a great deal of weight to the community of nations to act collectively when a single state infringes its laws. Hence, his attempt to distinguish himself from Wolff in this respect needs to be nuanced. After all a 'republic of sovereigns' (*LN*, IV-v-59) will play a central role in proceeding against belligerent states.

Natural law, since Hobbes, began from the idea that right was subjective. Once objective law was established in the interests of self-preservation, however, the subjective character of right lost most of its significance. From a contemporary perspective, this division between right and law appears anachronistic: in the post-revolutionary epoch, law is often little more than the positivisation of individual, human rights. At the outset of the *Law of Nations*, Vattel made explicit reference to this dimension in Hobbes as founding the very basis of the distinction between the law of nature, which concerned the individual, and the law of nations (*LN*, preface 8), which involved 'societies of men united together for the purpose of promoting their mutual safety and advantage by the joint efforts of their combined strength' (*LN*, prelim. 1–2). For Hobbes, natural rights were the property of the individual prior to what he discussed in *De Cive* as a 'transfer of right'.[4] In Wolff's philosophy this led to a logic of accommodation. Whereas at first glance it appeared that Wolff saw basic rights as innate and integral to the person, which could in no way be taken away, they could be given away.[5] Natural liberty was reduced to the right to make contracts that revoke that very same said liberty. This was thus very different from the modern idea of human rights. It was to this extent that Wolff could consider patrimonial kingdoms and slavery as founded on an originary right, each of which for Vattel went against the 'reason and sentiment … of every true citizen' (*LN*, preface 13). Hence the individual subject, for Vattel, could in no way be considered the property of the sovereign. All of this marks a change in Vattel's conception of the state and a break from the political tradition.

If the state is no longer the private property of a possessor who, at a whim, determines the limits of its activity, where does its power lie and who or what possesses sovereignty? To answer such questions, it is necessary to discuss some of the most innovative aspects of the *Law of Nations*. Objective law in Wolff's philosophy was established in the best interests of the subjective rights and

[4] See T. Hobbes, *On the Citizen*, ed. and translated by R. Tuck and M. Silverthorne (Cambridge, 1998), 34–35.

[5] See K. Haakonssen, 'German natural law', in M. Goldie and R. Wokler (eds.), *The Cambridge History of Eighteenth-Century Political Thought* (Cambridge, 2008), 271ff.

'happiness' or 'bliss' [Glückseligkeit] of its subjects. There was no division here between the welfare of the state and the citizen. Such happiness was not self-determined, but dictated by power. The ruler, according to this long established tradition, was like a father to his subjects who were his children. Every aspect of life was organised for the same end, whether that be in marriage, paternal society, the society of rule or the house – 'to promote the happiness of the human race'.[6]

By contrast, for Vattel, the people or the social body of the nation invest the sovereign and his ministers with power. Yet, in so doing, their sovereignty is no way rescinded. In this respect, the subjective right of the nation is retained as the formative power underlying all objective law. Thus, Vattel makes an important distinction between sovereignty and the sovereign. This has been rightly considered a central step in modern constitutional theory.[7] The sovereign 'represents the nation' which has intrusted authority 'to a senate or a single person' for the safety and preservation of the state (*LN*, I-IV-38). Hence this power is derived from the subjective right of the nation, the *body* of political society, which has united for its own happiness, advantage and safety. But Vattel goes further: 'The perfection of a state, and its aptitude to attain the ends of society, must then depend on its constitution' (*LN*, I-III-28). The prince or senate invested with sovereign power may indeed possess legislative authority, but the latter also stops at the constitution and the fundamental laws that govern the nation (see *LN*, I-IV-45). The sovereign is the guardian of the constitution, the defender of its laws, but is not above the laws (*legibus solutus*). Through reference to the sovereignty of the nation and 'the safety of the people as the highest law' (*salus populi suprema lex*) (*LN*, I-V-61), Vattel resolved a longstanding problem: the law of succession (the Salic Law) (*LN*, I-V-58). Upon the death of a sovereign, power returned to the people or the body of the nation who were always its true possessors. Thus, the constitution implied both the establishment of the state *and* its essential organisation. Arguments over the throne and rightful succession need not disrupt the essential character of sovereignty. As a concept, the state was present as both a foundation and as an object open to modification for the preservation or perfection of the nation.

6 Wolff, '*Deutsche Politik*', §§210ff., 16ff., 80ff., 160ff., 192ff.

7 H. Mohnhaupt, 'Verfassung I', in O. Brunner, W. Conze and R. Koselleck (eds.), *Geschichtliche Grundbegriffe: Historisches Lexikon zur politische-sozialen Sprache in Deutschland, Volume* 6, (Stuttgart, 2004), 859; compare D. Grimm, 'Verfassung II', in the same title, 867–868.

Vattel's understanding of the law of succession reveals both the novelty of his conception of sovereignty and idea of the constitution. In breaking with the notion that the state can be a hereditary acquisition or possession, it becomes an expression of the purely collective – and thus public – power of the nation. In this way the prince and his patrimony are inverted (LN, I-v-61): succession merely 'a law of the state' (*LN*, I-v-62). The sovereign, government or public administration is 'established only for the sake of the nation, with a view to its safety and happiness' (LN, I-III-31). Additionally, it is only the nation that can resolve problems in the functioning of these powers and in so doing alter the very constitution: 'if any disputes arise in a state respecting the fundamental laws, the public administration, or the rights of the different powers of which it is composed, it belongs to the nation alone to judge and determine them conformably to its political constitution' (*LN*, I-III-35). In every other respect, the constitution and its fundamental laws must be considered sacred to assure the stability of the state. Moreover, the sovereign can in no way alienate sovereignty as it is retained by the nation, who alone possesses this right (*LN*, I-v-69). The modernity of the constitution as Vattel conceives it can be observed here, which presupposes that it is essentially at the behest of the nation: 'This constitution is in fact nothing more than the establishment of the order in which a nation proposes to labour in common for obtaining those advantages with a view to which political society was established' (*LN*, I-III-27).

Even if still co-existing alongside more traditional descriptions, such as the (Aristotelian) best form of constitution, the *salus publica*, body politic and the *leges fundamentales* (LN, I-III-28–29), Vattel's discussion provides what the historical literature has argued is the first fully independent concept of the constitution of the state.[8] Moreover, this constitution, as we have seen, is intrinsic to the 'novel superior authority' of the nation, which, as Vattel put it, is 'a moral person, who possesses an understanding and a will peculiar to herself, and is susceptible of obligations and rights' (*LN*, prelim. 1–2). Consequently, the nation is a self-determining entity possessing the juridical attribute of sovereignty.

The question seems to remain rather open as to whether Vattel simply anticipated ideas that later came into circulation in revolutionary France or if the very reception of his thought was in fact central. In his description of the foundational unity of political rule through the concepts of state, nation and political society, he has been seen as forging a path to the radical political

[8] Mohnhaupt, 'Verfassung I', 859; compare Grimm, 'Verfassung II', 867–868.

thinking of 1789.[9] For other commentators, however, Vattel was still too closely tied to the tradition and, above all, Wolff's philosophy, to have a fully developed doctrine of rights. This meant that such rights were relinquished or sacrificed to whatever society required following the dictates of the moral law of perfection.[10] Yet given the fact that the body of the nation invests the public authority, which is to make laws for 'the welfare of the state and of the citizens' (*LN*, I-III-29), it would seem that Vattel's constitutional conception opens the door to positive codification and thus to the concordance of subjective right with objective law, which is indeed amenable to the republicanism that came later into political existence. On the other hand, if we look to the different contexts that will concern the remainder of this chapter it may perhaps be this interpretive tension that attests most strongly to the reason Vattel's *Law of Nations* had such a wide field of application.

THE IMPERIAL CONSTITUTION AND THE PRUSSIA OF FREDERICK II

The influence of Vattel's ideas in the German-speaking territories or the Holy Roman Empire remains somewhat underexplored and for good reason. In comparison to the number of English editions, which even surpassed the French, only one German translation and edition was published in the period (1760).[11] Considering that French was often the official language of politics, this does not really attest to the extent of Vattel's impact. The case of Montgelas can be taken as representative here. He took the idea of a sovereign state from Vattel for Bavarian reform and studied the *Law of Nations* exhaustively, but wrote and published primarily in French. From Montgelas, the influence of Vattel can be felt on the later Prussian reform – the 1807 *Nassau Memorandum* of Stein.[12]

The very idea of the sovereign state that Montgelas took from Vattel and applied to the Bavarian position has, for one modern commentator, been seen as precisely the reason why his work had only a minimal or largely negative

9 U. Dierse and H. Rath, 'Nation, Nationalismus, Nationalität', in J. Ritter, K. Gründer and G. Gabriel (eds.), *Historisches Wörterbuch der Philosophie, Band 6* (Basel, 1984), 408.

10 See Haakonssen, 'German natural law', 278.

11 See A. de Lapradelle, 'Introduction', in E. Vattel, *Le droit des gens, ou Principes de la Loi Naturelle, appliqué à la Conduite et aux Affaires des Nations et des Souverains Vol. III*, translated by G. D. Gregory (Washington, 1916), lxi.

12 See H. Quaritsch, *Souveränität: Entstehung und Entwicklung des Begriffs in Frankreich und Deutschland vom 13. Jahrhundert bis 1806* (Berlin, 1986), 106, who references the Montgelas biography by E. Weis, *Montgelas 1759–1799: Zwischen Revolution und Reform* (Munich, 1971), 266ff.

impact on German scholarship in the eighteenth century.[13] From this perspective, by giving the imperial estates 'international legal status' Vattel showed only a 'superficial' grasp of the imperial state form.[14] Yet arguably Vattel was simply following what had been passed into law after the treaties of Munster and Osnabruck, which were not only peace settlements and imperial laws, but also part of the constitution.[15] Despite all attempts to the contrary, Vattel concluded that the emperors had to concede 'to the princes and states of Germany', 'the right of treating with foreign powers and contracting alliances with them', which also gave 'the right of embassy' (*LN*, IV-v-59). In this way, as he saw it, 'the empire is now considered a republic of sovereigns' (*LN*, IV-v-59). Due to its great popularity, the *Law of Nations* thus promoted, as Helmut Quaritsch put it, 'the acceptance of legally dubious passages' such as this.[16] Since Vattel's work appeared in a period of imperial decline, which only worsened during the course of the late eighteenth century, the actual political situation did little to refute his interpretation, but confirmed it. On the other hand when he discussed states that were inimical to the society of nations and its security, Vattel gave the international legal order of the Holy Roman Empire surprising legitimacy. His idea of a 'republic of sovereigns' recalls Wolff's *civitas maxima* here. Ultimately, Vattel supported the international and confederate character of the imperial constitution in the post-Westphalian order. It was in this community of nations or greater republic that states were assured their freedoms and could pursue their common aims.

Vattel's interpretation of the empire as 'a republic of sovereigns' should be sought first in his understanding of the Swiss model of confederacy. It was here that he undoubtedly was able to draw a parallel with the Holy Roman Empire and the German territories (*LN*, II-XII-154; IV-v-60): public treaties and treaties of alliance as well as the rights of embassy and contract were as essential to Swiss confederacy as they were to the imperial constitution after 1648, which from that moment onwards assured the quasi sovereignty of the estates guaranteed by foreign powers such as France and Sweden. When Vattel extrapolated the principle of the equality of nations from the natural equality of human beings in the state of nature, 'Power or weakness does not in this respect produce any difference. A dwarf is as much a man as a giant; a

[13] Quaritsch, *Souveränität*, 105.

[14] Ibid.

[15] See R. Lesaffer, 'The Westphalian peace treaties and the development of the tradition of great European peace settlements prior to 1648', *Grotiana* 18 (1997) 71–95, at 71.

[16] Quaritsch, *Souveränität*, 105.

small republic is no less a sovereign state than the most powerful kingdom' (*LN*, prelim. 18). In this way Vattel spoke of the right of treating with foreign powers in his native *Neuchâtel*, even if this city came under the dominion of a foreign prince (*LN*, IV-v-60). Comparatively, 'the princes and free cities of Germany, though dependent on the emperor and empire, have the right of forming alliances with foreign powers' (*LN*, II-XII-154). This was enforced not only by custom, but also by the imperial constitution. For a direct model in the empire, Vattel needed to look no further than his employer, Saxony.

The second aspect to consider in Vattel's interpretation of the Holy Roman Empire is the rise of Prussia to the status of a great power, which set the bar for the other princes and cities in Germany to acquire the title of 'royalty', as he quotes from the *Memoirs of the House of Brandenburg* of Frederick II (*LN*, II-III-41). Not only is Vattel's interpretation here directly connected to historical developments, it also gives new meaning to the importance of the imperial structure as a society of nations. For Vattel, the fabric of the imperial international order, composed of different jurisdictions, rights and obligations, precisely led to its 'republican' character. When the security of this order was threatened, when rights were left unfulfilled and obligations unperformed or a prince arbitrarily attacked its neighbour, imperial institutions allowed for legal reciprocity and in the extreme case war, as a tactic to pursue the satisfaction of a right infringed or the lawlessness of an aggressor. Moreover, depending on the greater power of the house of Austria or its rival Prussia, the smaller states in Germany were allied with one or the other, which led to 'that balance of power, the object of perpetual negotiations and wars' (*LN*, II-XII-179). Hence, Vattel's position affirms both the juridical sovereignty of the territories in the imperial constitution as well as the importance of territorial confederacy in the overarching structure of the Holy Roman Empire.

In a letter to an unknown correspondent dated 26 May 1757, Vattel wrote despairingly over the Third Silesian War (1756–1763).[17] Part of expansive international hostilities, Austro–Prussian dualism in the Holy Roman Empire was definitively established in this period. Being a citizen of Neuchâtel, Vattel was also a subject of Prussia. His early extensive *Défense du système leibnitzien* (1741) had been dedicated to Frederick II in an attempt to attain a post in Berlin, with little success.[18] But by the time Frederick II invaded neighbouring Saxony in the Third Silesian War, Vattel was in the employ of Count Brühl, Saxony's prime minister, and King Frederick August II (August III, elective king of Poland). As he put it to his employer, the *Law of*

[17] See E. de Vattel, quoted in Lapradelle, 'Introduction', iii.
[18] See Lapradelle, 'Introduction', iv.

Nations would in part prove the invalidity of the Prussian assault and the cause of Saxony.[19] But Vattel went further, condemning Frederick II's actions openly when discussing the First Silesian War (1740–1742). The later Prussian invasion in 1758 ended in the plundering of Saxony's riches and, undoubtedly, the destruction of 'those edifices which do honour to human society' (*LN*, III-XIX-168).[20] Both of these wars were unconscionable acts of aggression and threatened the very fabric of the society of nations and the delicate balance of power in the empire and in Europe. When waging war Frederick II did not conform to its laws. For Vattel, the empire ought to punish him collectively in order to preserve the freedom and security of its members.[21]

When Vattel wrote his Défense, Frederick II had only recently become King of Prussia. There were promising reasons to expect some sort of patronage from the new monarch who set out to distance himself from his predecessors. On the occasion of his coronation in 1740, he had a medal embossed with the inscription 'Fridericus rex natura'.[22] Thus he began by basing his rule on the principles of enlightened natural law that had determined the philosophical education of his youth and not on divinely ordained dynastic succession.[23] Hence, the *ancien régime* under Frederick II received a new form of enlightened legitimation. This was meant to give a new authority to the state, henceforth founded on the idea of the contract and the preservation and happiness of its subjects. It transformed the notion of the sovereign into the 'first servant of the state', a formulation that can already be discovered in Frederick II's Réfutation du Prince de Machiavel (1739), popularly known as the 'Antimachiavel', published just before he ascended the throne.[24] Such ideas went against the mixing of sovereignty with private property, that for

[19] See B. Kapossy, 'Introduction: Rival histories of Emer de Vattel's *Law of Nations*', *Grotiana* 31 (2010), 5–21, at 5, who has also raised the 'interpretive value' of these letters for understanding the intentions of the *Law of Nations* (ibid., 6). For a contrast, see W. Rech, *Enemies of Mankind: Vattel's Theory of Collective Security* (Leiden, 2013), 144–149.

[20] See K. Stapelbroek, 'The foundations of Vattel's "system" of politics and the context of the seven years' war: Moral philosophy, luxury and the constitutional commercial state', in Stapelbroek and Trampus (eds.), *Vattel's Droit des gens*, 95–133.

[21] See R. Whatmore, 'Vattel, Britain and peace in Europe', *Grotiana* 31 (2010), 85–107, which makes similar arguments with respect to imperialist France and the capacity of Britain to maintain the independence of smaller sovereignties that I am making here with the aggressive imperialism of Prussia and the Holy Roman Empire as a catalyst for confederacy.

[22] P. Baumgart, 'Naturrechtliche Vorstellungen in der Staatsauffassung Friedrichs des Großen', in Thieme (ed.), *Humanismus und Naturrecht*, 143.

[23] Ibid.

[24] Frédéric II, 'L'Antimachiavel, ou examen du prince de Machiavel', in J. D. E. Preuß (ed.), *Œuvres de Frédéric le Grand, Tome 8* (Berlin, 1846–1856), 168.

Frederick II tainted dynastic rule. In the *Law of Nations*, Vattel would undoubtedly agree; there he stated that 'the prince, or the superior of the society' is 'naturally no more than the administrator, and not the proprietor of the state' (*LN*, I-XXI-260).

For many scholars, the reign and personality of Frederick II represent a conflict between enlightened morality, on the one hand, and the reality of mundane politics and state interest on the other – of the notion of the political ideal of the state where the assertion of its power and glory had become the essential aim. From this perspective, there is supposedly a 'tragic dualism' at the core of the enlightened project.[25] Whereas in his 'Antimachiavel' Frederick II rejected the notion of a war of conquest under the guise of humanity insofar as the conquering nation in no way profits from it and the occupants of a given territory are indifferent as to which state they happen to be ruled by,[26] in 1775 he asserted that 'the interest of the state must serve as a rule for the conduct of sovereigns', which retrospectively justified his own actions when breaking the treaties of Breslau and Dresden and occupying Saxony, beginning the Third Silesian War.[27] In order to make space for the moral progress of the individual, the preservation and even expansion of the Prussian state now first had to be assured. Consequently, during his reign, the welfare of the nation and the happiness of its population came to rely on a model of predation.

This brings us to a tension or conflict that continues to be at the centre of much debate over the *Law of Nations*: Vattel's principle that it 'exclusively belongs to each nation to form her own judgement of what her conscience prescribes to her . . .', 'a consequence of that liberty and independence' of nations (*LN*, prelim. 16). In this way, it has been claimed that Vattel's natural law between nations is essentially flawed due to the predominance of state interest and political utility.[28] On the one hand, Vattel claimed 'that the best and safest policy is that which is founded on virtue' (*LN*, preface); on the other, he confessed that 'the question of expediency belongs to politics'

[25] See F. Meinecke, *Machiavellism: The Doctrine of Raison d'État and Its Place in Modern History*, ed. W. Stark and translated by D. Scott (New Brunswick NJ, 1998), 272–339; R. Koselleck, *Critique and Crisis: Enlightenment and the Pathogenesis of Modern Society* (Cambridge, MA, 1988), 117, n 49; V. Sellin, 'Politik', in *Geschichtliche Grundbegriffe, Band 4*, 838–840.

[26] See Frédéric II, 'L'Antimachiavel', 171.

[27] Frédéric II, 'Histoire de mon temps', in Preuss (ed.), *Œuvres, Tome 2*, xvii–xviii.

[28] R. Tuck, *The Rights of War and Peace: Political Thought and the International Order from Grotius to Kant* (Oxford, 1999), 191–196.

(*LN*, I-III-35).[29] Frederick II also paid tribute to this dichotomy in a passage from Histoire de mon Temps: 'I hope that posterity [will] know to separate the philosopher from the prince and the man of virtue from the politician'.[30]

What we discover here is something we already encountered in terms of subjective right and objective law. Rather than dealing with the individual in the state of nature and the establishment of the state and its civil laws, however, what we see here is the tension between the state individual and the objective laws of the society of nations. Vattel's efforts are simultaneously directed to the maintenance of state right as a subjective power *and* objective international law: 'Nations owe to each other the same assistance, the same respect, the same friendship, as individuals living in the state of nature' (*LN*, II-XII-178). For his argument, the individuality, subjective right or sovereignty of the state is best preserved within an overarching legal structure that leads to the regularisation of conduct and politics between nations. Here the constitution of the Holy Roman Empire can be taken as representative: it preserves state rights since it is a 'republic of sovereigns' and provides for legal reciprocity and arbitration between its nations, even those outside of its structure, such as Sweden and France. This involves 'the faith in treaties' – such as the treaties of Munster and Osnabruck – that are 'to be held sacred and inviolable between the nations of the earth, whose safety and repose it secures' (*LN*, II-XV-220). Hindering the rise of Prussia, Frederick II, on the contrary, enumerated reasons for breaking both contract and treaty, ultimately stating that 'Princes are the slaves of their means . . ., the interest of the state serves them as law, and this law is inviolable'.[31] The difference is thus insurmountable: Vattel attempted to resolve the tension between law and politics by reviving Cicero's *honestum = utile*, while, for Frederick II, politics and state interest are the only laws applicable to the nation.

In this context, given his biography, it should come as no surprise that Vattel explicitly mentions the First Silesian War (1740–1742); it served him as a negative example of how nations were not to behave in their relations to other states. Frederick II deployed strategies of dissimulation that feigned good intentions and friendship. Furthermore, he did not issue a public declaration of war and fought irregularly, which put the very principles of a 'war in due form' (*jus in bellum*) that Vattel held up as an ideal and rational achievement

[29] This is at the centre of Sellin's analysis; see Sellin, 'Politik', 839–840.

[30] Frederich der Grosse, 'Geschichte meiner Zeit', in G. B. Volz (ed.), *Werke, Band 2* (Berlin, 1912), 2. I take this quote from Sellin, 'Politik', 839; it is not in the original French version.

[31] Frédéric II, 'Histoire de mon temps', xviii.

of European humanity at risk.[32] Moreover, it was precisely due to this irregularity that the nature of the threat to the society of nations was absolute.[33] This society, founded squarely on the basis of regular legal and political norms, was nothing other than an agreed upon code of conduct, a prevailing consensus in both times of peace and war. Were this to come under attack or be subject to the arbitrary will of sovereign command, the entire society was imperilled. The 'war in due form' was the very expression of regularity and perhaps the most exemplary of all norms, given that it conformed to the ideal of unanimity even in the most extreme case. By contrast:

> It is the sovereign who violates his engagements on pretences that are evidently frivolous, or who does not even think it worth his while to allege any pretence whatever, to give a colourable gloss to his conduct, and cast a veil over his want of faith, – it is such a sovereign, who deserves to be treated as an enemy of the human race. (*LN*, II-XV-222)

For Vattel, the politics of Frederick II expressed nothing other than this want of faith – imperilling balance in the empire and Europe at large. Silesia, that populous and industrious neighbouring region of Prussian Brandenburg, was of strategic importance as a conduit for troops lying on the north-eastern frontier of the Holy Roman Empire. Prussian claims to the region were justified, if only after the fact, on the basis of a revoked inheritance treaty by Frederick William I, which went back to 1537.[34] When he drew up his justification 'at the head of sixty thousand men', Frederick II was most likely 'guilty in the sight of his own conscience, and very unjust towards him whom he attacks' (*LN*, II-XVIII-335). Moreover, 'it is not allowable to take up arms in order to obtain possession of a thing to which the claimant has but an uncertain and doubtful right (*LN*, II-XVIII-337). As Vattel went on, what may indeed be 'sufficient at the tribunal of the voluntary law of nations', which operated under the dictates of necessity and preservation, 'may be found unjust in itself' (*LN*, II-XVIII-335). Frederick II abusing the liberty of this law 'gives all nations cause to hate and suspect him; he authorises them to confederate against him; and thus, while he thinks he is promoting his interests, he sometimes irretrievably ruins them' (*LN*, II-XVIII-335).

32 See the discussion in Chapter 7, by Pablo Kalmanovitz.

33 See C. Schmitt, *The Nomos of the Earth in the International Law of the Jus Publicum Europaeum*, translated and annotated by G. L. Ulmen (New York, 2006), 160ff; G. Silvestrini, 'Justice, war and inequality: The unjust aggressor and the enemy of the human race in Vattel's theory of the law of nations', *Grotiana* 31 (2010), 44–68.

34 For more details, see Rech, *Enemies of Mankind*, 138.

The lasting importance of the imperial constitution for Vattel appears here; it can act unanimously as a confederation of sovereign states, including both France and Sweden, to punish the unjust aggressor who threatens the balance of powers and the very principles of international law or the society of nations. In this sense, Vattel constructed his doctrine of international law and its enforcement on the basis of how the imperial constitution proceeded when peace and security were threatened.[35] This was founded on medieval precedent, but was actualised during the Silesian Wars and the War of Austrian Succession in an attempt to punish Prussian aggression and re-establish 'collective security' that could only be carried out through consensus or common endeavour.[36] Historically this entailed not only smaller states like Saxony and the Protestant imperial estates supporting the Austrian cause, but also France and Sweden, given that they were guarantors of peace and protection in the empire since 1648. The imperial framework was, moreover, worth protecting against Prussian aggression as Frederick II set a dangerous precedent with his new form of irregular and illegal war, aiming simply to further his own glory and power.

When outlining the *jus in bellum*, Vattel 'carefully distinguished' it from 'predatory expeditions', like Frederick II's, which were undertaken 'without apparent cause' (*LN*, III-v-67). If the unjustness of wars waged simply for ambition were to become the norm, as Vattel insightfully noted, 'it will become necessary to always continue in a military posture' (*LN*, III-v-62). The law of nations and the ideals of its society as such would be put in danger. In order to avoid this situation, it was necessary to distinguish the legitimate from the illegitimate, 'to recollect the nature and object of lawful war', which 'is only as the last remedy against obstinate injustice' (*LN*, III-v-68). Illegitimate war, by contrast, is undertaken 'without any right' and 'can be productive of no lawful effect, nor give any right to the author of it' (*LN*, III-v-68) For Frederick II, as he remarked on 7 November 1740 at the beginning of the First Silesian War, the legal issue of the conflict and its justification was really a question for diplomats and ministers – the troops after all had already received their orders.[37]

FROM CONSTITUTION AND NATION TO REVOLUTION

The importance of the *Law of Nations* is central to the conceptual history of constitution and nation. Vattel provided the theoretical material necessary for

35 Ibid., 132.

36 Ibid., 137–138.

37 See Meinecke, *Machiavellism*, 299.

a 'philosophical break' with the *ancien régime* that would be carried out in the French Revolution. Insofar as the unanimous consent of all citizens was required when changing the fundamental laws, Vattel is essential reading in modern constitutional theory.[38] Without this new conceptual understanding of nation and constitution, the Déclaration des droits de l'homme et du citoyen by Marquis de Lafayette and the Abbé Sieyès would most likely not have been possible. Important here was Vattel's distinction between the form-giving power of the nation and its constitution and government or public administration. Hence, for Vattel a constitution is no longer restricted to the form of government. In this way – even though he does *not* do it (*LN*, I-I-3) – it could be argued that all constitutions are, at their foundations, *republican*.[39] Nation and constitution are logically prior to the offices they invest. Is it any wonder then that Vattel is the first to give the word 'nation' an explicitly political meaning in the French language?[40]

For Vattel, there was really no opportunity to appeal to a revolutionary situation such as that which had occurred in France. When he discussed William of Orange and his landing in England to assist the nation against James II, who had violated the fundamental laws providing his subjects with the legal right to resistance (*LN*, II-IV-56), the restoration of the constitution symbolised the preservation of the ancient privileges and rights of the estates. In a similar context, Vattel considered 'the fundamental laws of England' that had established the House of Lords and the House of Commons: 'if the two houses should resolve to supress themselves, and to invest the king with full and absolute authority, certainly the nation would not suffer it' (*LN*, I-III-34). In this way, the limits of the sovereign, government and public administration are exposed. For Vattel, the form-giving power of the nation is determinative and it must have ultimate recourse with respect to the constitution and its fundamental laws when a threat to them is posed. That being said, Vattel's reference to England here is a comment on a *particular* constitution and he denied the possibility of a universal: 'the laws and constitutions of different states must necessarily vary according to the disposition of the people, and other circumstances' (*LN*, I-III-29). Yet it would be a mistake to interpret Vattel's conception of the constitution directly here with that of Montesquieu or Rousseau, each of whom, as well known, set out from the idea of mores or

38 See P. Bastid, *Sieyès et sa pensée* (Geneva, 1978), 580.

39 For this innovation, see J. J. Rousseau, *The Social Contract*, ed. S. Dunn (Binghamton, 2002), II.7, 179.

40 See Dierse and Rath, 'Nation', 408.

customs as constitutionally determinative.[41] By contrast, Vattel's argument is more formal and logical in character: he is the first to harmonise '*the constitution of the state*' with the binding effect of a legal norm, a 'fundamental regulation that determines the manner in which the public authority is to be executed' (*LN*, I-III-27).[42] Significantly, the latter can only emanate from the body of the nation itself. Beyond the reach of government, the constitution emerges from and essentially belongs to the nation and its sovereignty (*LN*, I-I-2). In so doing, the contract that bound the people was broken and resistance became possible when the sovereign attacked the constitution (*LN*, I-V-51).

In stark contrast to the Glorious Revolution, the French Revolution had as its object the complete dethronement of the *ancien régime*. Sieyès, its prophet, proclaimed that 'the Third Estate thus encompasses everything pertaining to the Nation, and everyone outside the Third Estate cannot be considered to be a member of the Nation. What is the Third Estate? EVERYTHING'.[43] In Sieyès's identification of a single estate with the nation, the very principle of a differentiated hierarchy of orders dissolved. The consequences of Vattel's 'fundamental regulation' are carried to their logical conclusion here. For Sieyès, the constitution is likewise separate and independent of its form and content and it too is established on the basis of the sovereignty of the people. The Déclaration des droits de l'homme et du citoyen made Sieyès's proposals into positive law: the ruling estates along with the provinces, parishes and corporations lost their authority and privileges, while the underprivileged strata gained rights and recognition. Political entitlement disappeared. This was contained in Articles 1, 3 and 6 as well as in the French constitution of 1791, which refers once more to the abolition of the *ancien régime* and all of the rights and privileges its society entailed.[44]

The role Vattel had to play in this discussion can only be a matter of speculation. Even so, he was the first to put forward the idea that the constitution was a construction. Given the fact that it was something made, it too could be changed or modified according to the legal norm or 'fundamental regulation' that brought it into being (*LN*, I-III-27). By identifying the latter with the nation, Vattel could easily have provided the conceptual ballast for

[41] See C. L. de S. Montesquieu, *The Spirit of Laws*, ed. and translated by A. M. Cohler, B. C. Miller and H. S. Stone (Cambridge, 1989), III.19, 308–333; Rousseau, *The Social Contract*, II.12, 191–192.

[42] Original emphasis.

[43] E. Sieyès, 'What is the third estate', in *Political Writings: Including the Debate between Sieyès and Tom Paine in 1791*, ed. and translated by M. Sonenscher (Indianapolis, 2003), 98.

[44] M. Riedel, 'Gesellschaft, bürgerliche', in *Geschichtliche Grundbegriffe, Band 2*, 763.

1789 through his identification of state, nation and political society, which were the basic political units forming the constitution. This marks a shift from the construction of rule by contract, predominant in the early modern period and in early modern natural law that legitimised the political order on the basis of an originary consensus, to the plausible positivisation of equal natural rights in the constitution and international law through the form-giving power and 'synonymity' of people, nation and state (*LN*, I-I-1; I-III-27). The *Déclaration des droits de l'homme et du citoyen* set out from this uniquely Vattelian principle. From here the distinction between the necessary and voluntary law of nations is drawn, the first 'always' binding in conscience, the second being composed of both 'the *conventional* and the *customary* [that] together constitute the *positive law of nations*' (*LN*, prelim. 27).[45] The latter was not a moral but rather a political argument insofar as it proceeded 'from the will of nations' (*LN*, prelim. 27). A generation later, it allowed the fellow Swiss jurist and politician Johann Caspar Bluntschli to conclude that Vattel was to be ranked among the authors and promoters of positive international law.[46] Connected to the historical process involved in the centralisation of power, the right of the nation to institute, change and perfect its constitution could thus logically become a driving force for positive codification, both at the domestic level and in the international society of nations.

What is missing from Vattel's discussion is a strict emphasis on the *written* form of the constitution as a document that founds the state.[47] In view of the instituting document of 1789, such a theoretical shift would have a more practical basis. Nevertheless, for Vattel, the position of the nation had become autonomous.[48] Already by the middle of the eighteenth century, then, the Swiss privy councillor was aware of the fact that the constitution is precisely a means to legitimise and legally secure state power: 'The constitution and laws of the state are the basis of public tranquillity, the firmest support of political authority, and a security for the liberty of citizens' (*LN*, I-III-30). In the same context it was the task of the nation to guard against any infringement of the constitution, Vattel having in mind here both the governing and the governed. In this sense governing was authorised only on the basis of the constitution,

45 Original emphasis.

46 See J. C. Bluntschli, *Le droit international codifié*, 5th ed., translated by M. C. Lardy (Paris, 1905), 39. I owe this reference and discussion to M. Senellart, 'La qualification de l'ennemi chez Emer de Vattel', *Astérion* 82 (2004), 1–16, at 4.

47 See O. Beaud, 'L'histoire du concept de constitution en France. De la constitution politique à la constitution comme statut juridique de l'état', *Jus Politicum: Revue de Droit Politique* 3 (2009), 1–29, at 22ff.

48 See Mohnhaupt, 'Verfassung I', 859.

whereas obedience fell into the remit of what was legally defined. This theory has been rightly viewed as an essential step in the subordination of legislative to constitutional power.[49] Put in the language of Sieyès, the 'national will' was 'prior to any constitution' and founded the fundamental laws that bound the legislature and representative government. The 'special representative will' and 'all the parts of a government are thus answerable to and, in the last analysis, dependent upon the nation'.[50] Thus, Sieyès politicised constitutional law and the French Revolution led to a fusion of the political and juridical concept of the constitution.[51]

For Sieyès, the third estate, which was the nation, had the function of founding the constitution; he thus set out to elucidate a new political paradigm that legalised political rule by replacing the sovereignty of the monarch with the sovereignty of the nation. Vattel already intuited such ideas in his very distinction between the sovereignty of the nation and the sovereign as *legislative power.* Moreover, there was no insurmountable gap separating the idea of the nation in Vattel as a body politic that determines how the people are to be governed and the rights and obligations of the governing from Article 3 of the Déclaration ('The principle of any sovereignty resides essentially in the Nation. No body, no individual may exercise any authority which does not proceed directly from the nation'). If Sieyès spoke of the 'extraordinary representation' of the nation, which has 'no similarity to an ordinary legislature',[52] Vattel too had recourse to 'the body of the nation' as having the 'right to check those at the helm when they abuse their power' (*LN*, I-III-32). As Sieyès had defined it after transforming the Estates General into the National Assembly, the latter could 'give itself the organization and procedural formalities appropriate to the functions that it will be called upon to exercise'.[53] What this did *not* mean, however, was 'that at bottom any ordinary legislature can be responsible for giving itself its own constitution. There must not be any confusion between a constituting power and a constituted power'.[54]

In Vattel's discussion, whereby the nation possesses all public power and is formative of the state and government (*LN*, I-III-27), an inkling of Sieyès's later innovative differentiation between constituting and constituted power can be observed: 'a nation has an indisputable right to form, maintain, and

[49] See Beaud, 'L'histoire du concept de constitution en France', 23.
[50] Sieyès, 'What is the third estate', 136.
[51] See Beaud, 'L'histoire du concept de constitution en France', 28, 29.
[52] Sieyès, 'What is the third estate', 139, 140.
[53] E. Sieyès, 'Views of the executive means available to the representatives of France in 1789', in *Political Writings*, 34.
[54] Ibid.

perfect its constitution, – to regulate at pleasure everything relating to the government . . .' (*LN*, I-III-31). Yet, if Vattel in the *Law of Nations* 'intuited' the idea of constituent power, he did not succeed in 'systematising' it. By contrast, Sieyès had the advantage of being fully aware of the concept and thus could set it in relation to a new theory of how the constitution was formed.[55] Nevertheless, for Vattel, the fundamental laws and the constitution of the state were beyond the jurisdiction of the legislative power. When Sieyès reflected on similar issues in revolutionary France, his political conception of the constitution thus had a close affinity to Vattel. Perhaps this is even more so the case than to Montesquieu, who still worked within the conventional pre-revolutionary tradition or appealed to the English model in order to justify the intermediary powers of the estates against monarchical 'despotism', or to Rousseau who rejected representation *tout court* in *Du contrat social*.[56] For Vattel, the estates may be the legislative, sovereign power, but they are not sovereignty – this resides alone in the body of the nation.

The elective affinities between Vattel and the revolutionary tradition in France comes down to the conception of a power that constitutes rule and the legal order through an act of will, the repository of the nation, which produces the very legitimacy of the state. This move ultimately lays the basis for the political sanction of rule and government in favour of the freedom of society, the equality of individuals before the law and the individual pursuit of happiness. Hence Vattel breaks with the mere popularisation of the *ancien régime*, whether in England or elsewhere. In his attack on luxury and the promotion of agriculture and commerce as the true wealth of a nation, he moves within the sphere of a Protestant liberal-bourgeois ideal, which also goes against the superfluous expenditure of the aristocracy and court culture (*LN*, I-VI, I-VII, I-VIII).[57] Furthermore, if an 'unfortunate monarch' has been deposed – however justly or unjustly – and a new sovereign established through the will of the nation, other powers are forced to recognise the legitimacy of the new regime no matter if they had originally been at odds with it, for 'to oppose these domestic regulations, or to dispute their justice or validity, would be interfering in the government of a nation, and doing her an injury' (*LN*, II-XII-197). Such an insight would no doubt play out well for 'one of the oldest nations on earth, which for 1400 years has given itself its own form

[55] See O. Beaud, *La puissance de l'État* (Paris, 1994), 223–243.

[56] See Beaud, 'L'histoire du concept de constitution en France', 21.

[57] See I. Nakhimovsky, 'Vattel's theory of the international order: Commerce and the balance of power in the Law of Nations', *History of European Ideas* 33.2 (2007), 157–173.

of government',[58] and had done so once again with the French Revolution, dissolving all intermediary powers between the individual and the state.

CONCLUSION

The *Law of Nations* broke from the political tradition, the constitution and its identification with the binding effect of a legal norm innovation. Possessing all public power, the nation created both constitution and government. Vattel's conception opened the door to positive codification and the concordance of subjective right with objective law and was, thus, amenable to revolutionary republicanism. Yet the tradition also appeared with new force in Vattel's thought. Far from neglecting the institutions of the Holy Roman Empire, Vattel demonstrated how the imperial structure as a theatre of war and diplomacy maintained the delicate balance of powers in Europe. In this instance, the imperial constitution was given renewed significance as a 'republic of sovereigns'. The dynamic between subjective right and objective law also emerged here, but under the guise of sovereign states and the society of nations.

FURTHER READING

I. Hunter, 'Vattel's Law of Nations: Diplomatic casuistry for the protestant nation', *Grotiana* 31 (2010), 108–140.

N. G. Onuf, 'Civitas maxima: Wolff, Vattel and the fate of republicanism', *The American Journal of International Law* 88.2 (1994), 208–303.

G. Silvestrini, 'Justice, war and inequality: The unjust aggressor and the enemy of the human race in Vattel's theory of the law of nations', *Grotiana* 31 (2010), 44–68.

S. Zurbuchen, 'Emer de Vattel on the society of nations and the political system of Europe', in S. Kadelbach, T. Kleinlein and D. Roth-Isigkeit (eds.), *System, Order, and International Law: The Early History of International Legal Thought from Machiavelli to Hegel* (Oxford, 2017), 263–282.

[58] G. du Motier de La Fayette, quoted in J. Habermas, 'Natural law and revolution', in *Theory and Practice*, translated by J. Viertel (Boston, 1974), 82–120, at 90.

12

Vattel's *Law of Nations* in Late Eighteenth- and Early Nineteenth-Century Greece and Italy

ELISABETTA FIOCCHI MALASPINA

INTRODUCTION

The circulation of the *Law of Nations: or, Principles of the Law of Nature Applied to the Conduct and Affairs of Nations and Sovereigns*, which began immediately after its publication in 1758 through the various editions and the first eighteenth-century translations, allowed Vattel's thinking to spread in a juridical–political context that went beyond time and space.

The impact of the *Law of Nations* was extremely versatile, given the dissimilar ways in which it was received in the various political environments, in historical–juridical contexts and in attempts to implement its practice and doctrine. In fact, between the eighteenth and nineteenth centuries, many jurists, and politicians too, looked on Vattel's book as their point of reference – an indication of the special authority acquired by the work.[1]

The purpose of this chapter is to analyse, on the one hand, how the decision to translate the *Law of Nations* served a political–constitutional purpose in the case of Greek independence between 1821 and 1832; and to examine, on the other hand, how Vattel's treatise was used during the Italian Risorgimento, and the motives that led Terenzio Sacchi to translate part of the *Law of Nations* in the mid-nineteenth century.

We shall reconstruct the diffusion of the *Law of Nations* in Greek and Italian contexts, not so much from an exegetical point-of-view, but rather through an overall survey of the dynamics that actually drove the treatise's use, with particular attention to its influence both in the internal affairs of states and in international relations.

[1] See E. Fiocchi Malaspina, *L'eterno ritorno del Droit des gens di Emer de Vattel (secc. XVIII–XIX). L'impatto sulla cultura giuridica in prospettiva globale* (Frankfurt am Main, 2017).

'THE DIRECT RELATION WITH THE NEEDS AND AFFAIRS EXISTING IN OUR NATION': THE *LAW OF NATIONS* IN GREECE (1821–1832)

From 1821 until 1832 Greece fought a war of independence against the Ottoman Empire, which four centuries earlier, after the fall of Constantinople, had seen the gradual conquest of Greek territory by Ottoman Turks. Constantinople had been taken in 1453 after a very long siege. In 1456 Athens fell and in 1460 the Ottomans conquered all of continental Greece. As Richard Clogg has written, between the eighteenth and nineteenth centuries something changed radically in the Greek people, laying the political and social foundations for achieving independence. The uprisings that had taken place in previous centuries had been sporadic and usually badly planned but, at the beginning of the nineteenth century, a coordinated revolution began to take shape. This was the direct result of efforts by the Greek *intelligentsia* to help their fellow-countrymen 'rediscover' a national consciousness.[2]

This *intelligentsia* had been fascinated and influenced by the upheavals of the French Revolution and had allowed a strong sense of national consciousness, cultural identity, traditions and politics to begin to develop in the Greek people.[3]

The political and social revolution of Greece took its course, accompanied by a real 'moral revolution', which was shaped in part by translations of European Enlightenment texts into the Greek language.[4] This was a true transfer of thought that allowed greater assimilation of Enlightenment ideas from Europe, which gained a stronger hold through translation work done by Greeks who had studied in France or Italy.

Already at the end of the eighteenth century, at the time of the French Revolution, Greece saw an increase in translated texts and a commitment to the ideological instruction of compatriots. Adamantios Koraïs translated into Greek and annotated the work of Cesare Beccaria.[5] Treatises on the

[2] R. Clogg, *Storia della Grecia moderna dalla caduta dell'impero bizantino a oggi* (Milano, 1996), 49.

[3] A. Sfoini, 'Transfert des idées par la voie de la traduction pendant l'ère révolutionnaire grecque (1797–1832)', *The Historical Review/La Revue Historique* 12 (2015), 47.

[4] For the use of 'moral revolution' see: Sfoini, 'traduction pendant l'ère révolutionnaire grecque', 53; A. Sfoini, 'Loyaume and Nomarchie: Keywords of the French revolution in the Greek vocabulary', *The Historical Review/La Revue Historique* 11 (2014), 127–138.

[5] About the translation of Cesare Beccaria: Sfoini, 'traduction pendant l'ère révolutionnaire grecque', 55.

relationship between politics and morals also had great success. In 1813 Ioannis Kaskabas published in St. Petersburg his translation of the famous text by Mably *Entretiens de Phocion sur le rapport de la morale avec la politique* (1763), since it contained 'lofty beliefs that should be read and understood by Greeks, so they might remember their ancient homeland and valiant men'.[6]

Such were the works translated before the Greek revolution. Those translated during the revolt had another significance. It is true that there were fewer translations compared with the previous phase, but it can be said that they were more specialised.[7] Political events were increasingly intertwined with the work of translating the more modern constitutions. Anastasios Polyzoïdis translated those of England and France, so they might serve as models for drawing up their own Greek constitution. But there were also Greek versions of works on military equipment and strategy, especially for naval warfare, and, of course, on the law of nations.[8]

Part of Vattel's *Law of Nations* was translated by Spyridon Skouphos, who signed himself with initials only and the pseudonym 'a patriot'. The task, completed in just twenty days and titled *Excerpts on Vattel's Law of Nations*, which was published in Nafplio in 1825. The choice of the excerpts from the *Law of Nations* is very interesting – to address the needs of revolution, Skouphos chose certain chapters and paragraphs from the treatise.[9] In his introduction dedicated to the Greek people he had no hesitation in declaring the importance of the work and the value of the translation. Skouphos claimed that the passages chosen were 'directly connected with the current needs' and 'affairs of his country'.[10]

Skouphos does not indicate either in the notes or in the text exactly to which chapters and sections of the *Law of Nations* he refers, but reading the titles, one can easily trace the source: he translated a large part of chapter VII of book III dedicated to neutrality. In particular, he chose paragraphs 103 to 118, relating, for example, to the passage of troops through a neutral state, with particular regard to the conduct that must be observed by the latter (§104); to trade with warring states (§§111 et seqq.); to smuggled goods (§112); to neutral ships, to their trade and to goods belonging to the enemy aboard them (§115); to the impartial duties of neutral nations (§118). Swiftly skipping in his

6 Sfoini, 'traduction pendant l'ère révolutionnaire grecque', 58.

7 Ibid.

8 Ibid.

9 On Skouphos, see: N. Andriotis, ''Ενα υπόμνημα του 1829 περί στατιστικής. ΚαταΘολές και επιδράσεις', *Μνήμων* 18 (1996), 181–190, at 181–182.

10 S. Skouphos, *Απόσπασματα εκ των του κυρίου Βαττέλλου περί Δικαίου των Εθνών* (Nafplio, 1825), προς τους Έλληνας.

translation the next sections, Skouphos began again from §132, concerning the prohibition of exercising any hostility in a neutral country. He continued and concluded his selection of passages on neutrality with §133, according to which a neutral country cannot lend itself to receiving troops from a warring state in order to attack their enemy.[11]

The second part chosen by Skouphos included some paragraphs from the next chapter, chapter VIII, dedicated to the very delicate matter of treatment of the enemy in war and, therefore, the legitimate, correct way of acting. The Greek translator focussed on §138, regarding the right to debilitate the enemy in all permissible ways; rights over the person of the enemy (§139) and on its limits, with particular attention to the proscription of killing him when he ceases to resist (§140); on one case in which he may be killed (§141); on retaliation (§143) and on the possibility that the enemy might kill a commanding officer who puts up resistance. The next parts addressed by Vattel and considered by Skouphos concerned certain categories of persons: §144 deals with the treatment of refugees and deserters; §145, of women, children, the elderly and infirm; §146, of ministers of religion and intellectuals; §147, of farmers and in general of all unarmed persons; §148 concerns the right to take prisoners of war, which leads to a series of other principles, such as: the proscription of killing them (§149), their treatment (§150), the legality of killing them when they cannot be detained or nourished (§151); the possibility of enslaving them (§152); their ransom (§153); the State's obligation to liberate them (§154), concluding with §158, which dictates the way of communicating with the enemy. It is highly significant that Skouphos ended with such a passage. In this paragraph, in fact, Vattel reminded readers that enemies are still human beings and 'constrained by painful necessity to defend our rights by the use of force and of arms' the charity that binds all mankind cannot be ignored. The rights of one's country may be defended but without offending the rights of humanity (*LN*, III-VIII).

The translating undertaken by Skouphos in the early years of the Greek revolution was not an isolated episode, indeed it developed greatly at the end of the war. *Law of Nations* was published in 1831, again in Nafplio, in two volumes, translated by a well-known Greek advocate and politician, Georgios Rallis (1804–1883). Rallis's father, Alexandros, a diplomat in the Ottoman Empire, had been hung by the Ottomans after revolution broke out in 1821. After his father's death, Georgios Rallis studied law in both Paris and Vienna. He returned to Greece in 1829 to pursue his previous career as a magistrate,

[11] Ibid., 1–35.

becoming president of the Supreme Court (1849–1861), and also as an academic. In 1837 he was appointed professor of commercial law at the faculty of law in Athens, where he was rector for two terms from 1838 to 1841 and from 1867 to 1869.[12] In addition to devoting himself to commercial law, he was particularly interested in bankruptcy law and the law of nations, becoming a central figure for Greek legal and institutional theory.[13]

History, context and political ideas are vital in understanding the Vattel-project undertaken by Rallis. He dedicated his translation work to Ioannis Kapodistrias, first head of state of independent Greece, dating it 20 April 1831, seven months before the violent assassination of that statesman in Nafplio on 9 October of that year. As far as the revolutionary process was concerned, in 1827 England, France and Russia signed the Treaty of London, imposing on the Ottomans an armistice and the recognition of Greek independence. The Sultan refused and a war ensued which saw the three powers engaged against the Ottomans and ended with the Peace of Adrianople (1829). Meanwhile Kapodistrias, a minister at the Russian court, had been appointed by the National Assembly of Troezen in April 1827 as Governor with executive power for a seven-year term and in February 1828 assumed that office of government in Nafplio.[14] On 3 February 1830 the Conference of London confirmed the sovereignty of Greece as a monarchy and offered the crown to Prince Leopold of Saxe-Coburg. Leopold declined the crown and Kapodistrias – suspected of aspiring to the Greek throne – was accused of having engineered the prince's decision. Suddenly a civil war broke out against Kapodistrias. This was soon quelled, but when he had the Maniot prince Petros Mavromichalis arrested, he was assassinated by the prince's brother and son in Nafplio.[15]

The translation of Rallis is very interesting because in 1831 it was not sufficient to translate just a few fragments dedicated to warfare, as Skouphos had done in 1825. Now there was a need to translate the entire first book, dealing with nations, because in Greece the phase of national (re)-birth was

[12] S. Petmezas, 'From privileged outcasts to power players: The "romantic" redefinition of the Hellenic nation in the mid-19th century', in R. Beaton, Roderick and D. Ricks (eds.), *The Making of Modern Greece* (Oxon, 2009), 126–139, at 126; also M. Sotiropoulos, European Jurisprudence and the Intellectual Origins of the Greek State: The Greek Jurists and Liberal Reforms (ca 1830–1880), PhD in Philosophy (Queen Mary, University of London, London, 2015), supervised by Varouxakis, Georgios and Maurizio Isabella, https://qmro.qmul.ac.uk/xmlui/bitstream/handle/123456789/9111/Sotiropoulos_Michail_PhD_270215.pdf?sequence=1, accessed 17 February 2020, 277.

[13] Sotiropoulos, *Greek jurists and liberal reforms*, 41.

[14] Clogg, *Storia della Grecia moderna*, 68 ff.

[15] P. Poleme (επιμ.), *Φίλιππου Ηλιού Κατάλοιπα: Ελληνική Βιβλιογραφία του 19ου αιώνα. Βιβλία-Φυλλάδια. Τόμος Β'* (1819–1832) (Athína, 2011), 68 ff.

beginning. The new nation required all aspects to be disciplined, particularly constitutional and internal aspects. So Rallis translated the twenty-three chapters of the first book and the second book dedicated to relations between nations.[16] The translation opened with the dedication to Kapodistrias and, like Vattel, Rallis focused his work on nations and on those who govern them. Next came the *Prolegomena* in which, after briefly illustrating the life of Vattel, Rallis specified that the idea of a Greek translation had come to him while studying in Paris,[17] thus confirming, once again, that the treatise also circulated in academic environments. He then considered the work done for the 'partial' edition of Skouphos, and argued that these kinds of translation were useful in encouraging and disseminating the language and theories of the rights of nations.[18]

As Michail Sotiropoulos wrote: 'The reception and dissemination of Vattel's translation was the first among many to show that Greece was touched in these years by emerging global currents of liberal thought'.[19] The *Law of Nations* itself is a possible connection between the Greek and Italian revolutions, as it was a point of reference for Italian exiles too, and in particular for Count Alerino Palma, who was politically and intellectually involved in the Greek uprisings.

PUBLIC AND CONSTITUTIONAL LAW IN ITALY: THE *LAW OF NATIONS* IN THE RISORGIMENTO

As Eugenio di Rienzo maintains, between 1820 and 1830 there was a 'Vattel Renaissance' not only in Europe, but also in Italy. Vattel's theories had considerable influence on the thinking of some Italian jurists and patriots during the Risorgimento.[20]

The discontent of the order restored by the Congress of Vienna manifested itself in the form of secret societies that spread throughout Europe. These included the Carboneria, which acquired numerous followers in Spain, in the kingdom of Savoy, in the Lombardo-Veneto kingdom and also in London,

[16] Ibid., 512–513.

[17] Sfoini, 'traduction pendant l'ère révolutionnaire grecque', 69. See: G. Rallis, 'Προλεγόμενα', in E. de Vattel (ed.), *Το Δίκαιο των Εθνών, ή αρχαί τού φυσικού νόμου, Προσηρμοσμένου εις τήν διαγωγήν και εις τά πράγματα τών Εθνών καί τών Κυριαρχών* (Napflio, 1831), vol. I.

[18] Rallis, 'Προλεγόμενα'.

[19] Sotiropoulos, *Greek jurists and liberal reforms*, 41.

[20] E. Di Rienzo, 'Decadenza e caduta del cosmopolitismo: Francia/Europa, 1792–1848. Note per una ricerca', in L. Bianchi (ed.), *L'idea di cosmopolitismo: circolazione e metamorfosi* (Napoli, 2002), 419–458, at 449.

where Luigi Angeloni and Giovanni Battista Marochetti were among the founders of the 'Carboneria Association of Italian refugees by the Thames'. This association was immediately put under close surveillance by the English authorities, which obliged its members to publish on 17 June 1823 a declaration aimed at denying the rumours spread about them. In this programmatic document, the ideas and political thought of Angeloni and Marochetti on the question of nationhood were visible, both being firm supporters of the creation of an Italian state with a federal structure.[21]

Angeloni (1758–1842) was a key figure among exiled Italians and Mazzini remarked on his 'faith in life, in the capacity and the strength of his nation'.[22] Before moving to London, in 1814 in Paris, together with Buonarroti he had played a very special role. His republican intransigence and his connections with all the major European liberal exponents made him the rallying point and moral guide of the entire Italian liberal movement in the French capital.[23] And it was in Paris that he wrote and published *Dell'Italia, uscente il settembre 1818*, in which he openly denounced the betrayal of promises made to the Italians by the allies and the Holy Alliance and claimed Italy's right to independence and freedom, based on two examples: the United States, of which he always declared himself a great admirer, and Switzerland.[24] Angeloni, in fact, returned to considerations made in his previous essay, *Sopra l'ordinamento italiano che dover avrebbero i governi d'Italia* (Paris 1814). He expounded his federal thesis with renewed force and greater arguments, allowing that an Italian confederation could be of a mixed nature, and therefore could include both monarchist and republican states.

In the *Dedication* he proposed the territorial strengthening of the Kingdom of Sardinia and safeguarding the requirements of the papacy, urging Italians to take action to obtain their independence.[25]

He then added, to claim this independence, that Vattel – in his beautiful work, with great sagacity – stated 'firstly, that Nature has given (men) a freedom and an independence that they cannot lose . . . and then, that nations

[21] E. Morelli, 'Gli esuli italiani e la società inglese nella prima metà dell'Ottocento', *Rassegna Storica del Risorgimento* 66 (1979), 3–13.

[22] G. Mazzini, 'Luigi Angeloni', *Apostolato popolare* 1 (1840), 40–41.

[23] B. Di Sabantonio, 'Luigi Angeloni tra liberalismo e democrazia', *Rassegna Storica del Risorgimento* 64 (1977), 3–21, here 3 ff.

[24] D. Ricciotti, *In ricordo di Luigi Angeloni: scrittori e pensatori politici dell'Ottocento frusinate* (Frosinone, 2009).

[25] L. Angeloni, *Dell'Italia, uscente il settembre 1818, ragionamenti IV, di Luigi Angeloni Frusinate, dedicati all'Italica Nazione* (Parigi, 1818), vol. I, Dedicatoria, I–II.

are therefore naturally equal, just as men are alike, towards each other.'[26] He also addressed Vattel's theory of the state, and the idea of sovereignty as the key principle of nationhood, supporting his arguments by quoting entire paragraphs from the *Law of Nations.*[27]

The position of Angeloni was not an isolated one. References to and citations from Vattel's work by exiles became increasingly frequent in that period. Maurizio Isabella points out that these patriots referred to Vattel as if he were 'an advocate of a liberal international order'.[28]

Very close to Angeloni was Giovanni Battista Marochetti (also Marocchetti). Born in Biella in 1772, he was a fine jurist and lawyer, and participated actively in the Jacobin insurrection in Val d'Ossola. After the uprising that broke out in Turin on 12 March 1821, when some army units conquered the Citadel and asked the king to grant the Constitution, the government junta nominated Marochetti political head of the town of Biella.[29]

There, he organised an uprising, convinced that it was supported by large sections of the population. He replaced monarchist town councillors with other liberals and purged the state administration of employees contrary to the new policy. But after the rebels were defeated at Novara, the majority of Piedmont's constitutionalists went into exile. Marochetti fled to Switzerland using a false passport, whence he joined Angeloni in London.[30]

In the meantime, however, on 3 September 1821 he was publicly sentenced to death in his absence.[31]

Political activism is also reflected in his writings. Like Angeloni, he recommended a federal solution for Italy. In *Le congrès bienfaisant* (Paris 1826), republished a few years later in 1830 under the title *Indepéndance de l'Italie, moyen de établir dans intérêt général de l'Europe, considéré spécialement sous le point de vue de l'équilibre politique, ou Partage de la Turquie*, he addressed the Italian problem in the context of a new European equilibrium, calling for

[26] Ibid., 90: 'innanzi tratto ch'essi hanno dalla natura una libertà ed una indipendenza che essi non possono perdere . . . e poscia che le nazioni sono così tra loro naturalmente eguali, come sono gli uomini gli uni verso gli altri' (author's translation).

[27] Angeloni, *Dell'Italia, uscente*, vol. II, Ragionamento III, 90 ff.

[28] M. Isabella, *Risorgimento in Exile. Italian Émigrés and Liberal International in the Post-Napoleonic Era* (Oxford, 2009), 99–100.

[29] M. Novarino, 'Marochetti Giovanni Battista', *Dizionario Biografico degli Italiani* 70 (2008), 637–640.

[30] Ibid., 637–640.

[31] P. Torrione, 'L'autobiografia di Giovanni Battista Marochetti il più grande rivoluzionario biellese', *Rivista Biella* 4 (1968), 21–32, at 26.

Austria to renounce its claim to Lombardo–Veneto and instead, exploiting the crisis of the Ottoman Empire, to shift its interests to the Danube–Balkan area.

In Marochetti's opinion, Lombardo–Veneto and the duchies of Parma and Modena could be annexed to the Kingdom of Savoy, which in exchange would cede Sardinia to France and Savoy to the Swiss Confederation, obtaining the canton of Ticino.[32] Out of the ruins of the Ottoman Empire a new European order would arise. Then Bulgaria, Serbia, Bosnia, Croatia and Albania would be assigned to Austria, Russia's full sovereignty over Moldova and Wallachia would be recognised and a kingdom of the Bosphorus would be created for the Duke of Modena.[33]

While, like Angeloni, for Italy he preferred unification, in order to avoid international opposition he proposed a federal system with three states: the Kingdom of Northern Italy, the Kingdom of the Two Sicilies and the Papal State, with strong hegemony of the Savoy dynasty and the papacy limited to exercising temporal power over Rome. This project could only take shape if France agreed to lead a programme of European renewal.

In Europe, Marochetti noted, the principle of balance of power had been truly destroyed, starting with Napoleon and continuing with the results achieved by the Holy Alliance. He saw the latter as a group of dominant states, in which the smaller states, defined as being of the second and third order, such as Piedmont, Bavaria and the kingdom of Naples, had no part.[34]

According to Marochetti, these marked differences between states should not exist, nor should some states have to submit to the decisions of others. This contravened the fundamental principle argued by Vattel on which all international law rested: all states are equal, without any kind of distinction and have the same rights within the international community.[35]

Also in Piedmont, on the occasion of the uprisings of 1821 in which, we have seen, Marochetti played an active part, Alerino Palma, count of Cesnòla, published his *Difesa dei Piemontesi inquisiti a causa degli avvenimenti del 1821*.[36] Palma (1776–1851), appointed commissioner extraordinary in Vercelli

32 Novarino, 'Marochetti Giovanni Battista', 637–640.

33 Ibid.; G. B. Marochetti, *Indépendance de l'Italie, moyen de établir dans l'intérêt général de l'Europe, considéré spécialement sous le point de vue de l'équilibre politique, ou Partage de la Turquie* (Paris, 1830), Avant-Propos, V ff.

34 Marochetti, *Indépendance de l'Italie*, 108 ff.

35 Ibid.

36 On the political situation and events refer to: P. Colombo, 'I presupposti dello Statuto albertino. Dai moti del 1821 alle riforme del 1847', *Historia Constitucional (revista electrónica)* 3 (2002), 147–170, www.historiaconstitucional.com/index.php/historiaconstitucional/article/view/174, accessed 17 February 2020.

under Napoleon, was a magistrate in Ivrea and a fervent revolutionary, so much that he governed Ivrea during the uprising of 1821. On the failure of the revolution he fled first to Spain, then to London and finally to Greece.[37] He was politically and intellectually involved in the Greek revolution and subsequently became a magistrate there.[38] *Difesa dei Piemontesi* was published in 1826 and divided into three parts. In the first, the author intended to demonstrate how the imputation of *lèse-majesté* to those who took part in the events of March 1821 was illegal both from a civil and a political viewpoint, 'both in the forum of honesty and common sense, and in that of written law'.[39] In the second part, he maintained that the sentences against these men were not only unjust 'but also flawed by total nullity because of the same laws of Piedmont'.[40] Finally, in the third section, he explained that 'refugees from Piedmont have the right to ask for honest welcome and assistance in every place with a constitutional government, and as they may rightly expect their cause of their homeland, at the same time, they may also rightly expect to have protection'.[41]

Palma introduced this latter part with words of solidarity and support for those who had received the death sentence.[42] He supported the Turin uprisings, whose aim was to overturn the Savoy monarchy and win adoption of a constitutional charter inspired by that of Cadiz, with greater rights for the Piedmontese people and less power for the sovereign.[43] It is in this context that Palma forcefully cited Vattel, translating the entire passage in the *Law of Nations* where Vattel maintained that: 'a nation has every right to rebellion and every foreign power has the right of aid when it asks for help: all this is simply justice, to assist a brave people who are defending their freedom'.[44]

37 R. Damilano, 'Palma di Cesnola Alerino', *Dizionario Biografico degli Italiani* 80 (2014), 586–588.

38 E. Pinoli Maritano, *Ivrea e il Canavese nella Rivoluzione Piemontese del 1821* (Ivrea, 1975), 80 ff.

39 A. Palma, *Difesa dei piemontesi inquisiti causa degli avvenimenti del 1821 con un'invocazione ai ministri costituzionali* (Bruxelles 1829), 7'presso il foro dell'onestà e del buon senso e appò quello della legge scritta' (author's translation).

40 Ibid., 7: 'ma viziate eziandio di nullità radicale a forza delle legge medesime del Piemonte' (author's translation).

41 Ibid., 8: 'i riffugiti Piemontesi han diritto a richiedere onesta accoglienza e soccorso in ogni contrada governata con ordini costituzionali, e come giusta sia in essi l'aspettazione, che ivi la causa propria della loro patria ad un tempo, sia per avere protezione' (author's translation).

42 Ibid., 70.

43 Ibid., 78.

44 Ibid., 78: 'una nazione può con tutta giustizia ribellarsi ed ogni potenza straniera ha diritto di soccorso quando questa chieda aiuto: tutto ciò è mera giustizia il sovvenire ad un popolo prode che difende la propria libertà' (author's translation).

In the light of this, we might make three observations: the constant reference to Vattel's theories by the writer Angeloni, the lawyer Marochetti and the judge Palma enables us, firstly, to understand the dynamics governing the circulation of Vattel's text in this delicate phase of Italian history; secondly, it offers a precise picture of the type of reflections made by some Italian patriots and by the use of sources that include Vattel; thirdly, it paves the way for examining the reception of the *Law of Nations* in southern Italy, in the Kingdom of the Two Sicilies, which will feature the translations of Terenzio Sacchi.

IN THE KINGDOM OF THE TWO SICILIES: TERENZIO SACCHI REVISITS THE *LAW OF NATIONS* (1854)

In Italy the *Law of Nations* was popular not only with patriots and constitutionalists like Angeloni and Marochetti, but also with conservatives like Terenzio Sacchi, who translated it into Italian in 1854 with the title *Il diritto delle genti di E. de Vattel applicato allo stato attuale delle nazioni*. Terenzio Sacchi (1809–1865) was a member of the Accademia Pontaniana and an official of the Ministry of Internal Affairs of the Kingdom of the Two Sicilies.[45]

In 1846 he took part in a Conference of Italian Scientists held in Naples, being described as 'secretary in charge of the Section of the Two Sicilies, of the General Shipwreck Association'.[46]

Sacchi focused his attention on the institutions governing the Kingdom of the Two Sicilies, with particular regard to international relations with other states in the form of peace and trade treaties, then to the internal structure of the state, the subdivision between individual rights (civil equality, civil liberty and property) and public interest (religion, education, industry, agriculture, trade).[47]

A strong supporter of the Bourbon monarchy, he lived through the Sicilian independence revolution of 1848 when King Ferdinand II tried to stem liberal requests by granting a constitution, under a royal decree of 29 January 1848.

It was following this and subsequent revolts that Sacchi wrote *Delle istituzioni di governo del reame delle Due Sicilie, ragionamenti* (Naples, 1849), in

45 R. Cotugno, *Tra reazioni e rivoluzioni. Contributo alla storia dei Borboni* (Lucera, 1860), 96.

46 Atti della settima adunanza degli scienziati italiani tenuta a Napoli dal 20 di settembre al 5 di ottobre del 1846 (Napoli, 1946), parte seconda, 35: 'segretario in capo della Sezione delle due Sicilie, della Società generale de' naufraghi' (author's translation).

47 T. Sacchi, *Delle istituzioni di governo del reame delle Due Sicilie, ragionamenti* (Napoli, 1849), 55–56.

which he contested the right to revolution.[48] For Sacchi, in fact, the revolutionary wave that was 'breaking' over most European states was the result of 'an illusion of an idea and not a true idea'.[49] Sacchi was clearly pro-monarchy: the sovereign Ferdinand II was worthy of honour on two counts. Firstly, 'for the improvements made in the years of his reign to the institutions themselves, and even more to the conditions of the Kingdom'; secondly, 'for the wisdom and strength with which he has saved our institutions and our conditions from the violations and ruin suffered especially by other Italian states, and which he has shown in the relations and complications of foreign policy'.[50]

The insurrections of the Kingdom of the Two Sicilies thus became the occasion for reflecting on the concept of sovereignty, on the principle of nationality and on the political balance of states, through a historical *excursus* and a comparison between the different European states,[51] concluding with a fiercely drastic stance against the revolutionaries.[52]

In 1854 he published *Diritto delle genti*, which is a partial translation of Vattel's first book, concerning the principles that govern a nation. Sacchi illustrated the method and approach used in translating Vattel's work, saying that to 'rectify these theories, by bringing the principles back to their elements, and applying them to the current state of nations, that is, to the degree of civilisation now reached, is a work worthy of our age'.[53] The result of his effort was to apply, but at the same time to correct, Vattel's *Law of Nations* in the light of the current state of nations, revisiting the various developments of the treatise and the annotations made by some jurists, especially during the nineteenth century. And it was on this aspect that he disagreed with the commentary of Pinheiro Ferreira, published as a third volume to the *Law of Nations* in 1838.

48 Cotugno, *Tra reazioni e rivoluzioni*, 96.

49 Sacchi, *ragionamenti*, 61: 'venisse neutralizzata l'azione di questo prestigio, sì che non torni più a turbare le condizioni e la pace de' popoli, e di fare una prova generosa dei fatti che ha prodotto' (author's translation).

50 Ibid., 4–5: 'a' miglioramenti che negli anni decorsi del suo regnare hanno ricevuto le istituzioni medesime, e più ancora le condizioni del Reame; … 'alla saviezza e alla forza con che ha salvato le nostre istituzioni e le nostre condizioni dai violamenti e dalle ruine che han sofferto specialmente gli altri stati d'Italia e che ha mostrato fra le relazioni e le complicazioni della politica estera' (author's translation).

51 Ibid., 46–47.

52 Ibid., 52.

53 T. Sacchi, 'Alla sacra real Maestà di Ferdinando II. Re del Regno delle Due Sicilie', in E. de Vattel (ed.), *Il diritto delle genti di E. de Vattel applicato allo stato attuale delle nazioni* (Napoli, 1854), [6]: 'rettificare coteste teoriche, con riportare i principî a' loro elementi ed applicarli allo stato attuale delle nazioni, ovvero al grado di civiltà a cui sono pervenute, è opera degna dell'età nostra' (author's translation).

Not only did he disagree with Pinheiro's method of working, especially with his intention of completing Vattel's work, but he also felt it necessary to modify Vattel's order of writing. For Sacchi, the division into four books and the insertion of the *Preliminari* were wrong and required drastic revision of the order and importance of the subjects to be addressed. He likewise analysed Vattel's thinking and gave his criticisms on certain points.

Sacchi pointed out the similarity of the *Law of Nations* to the work of Wolff, 'his [Vattel's] treatise being to some extent a compendium of the earlier philosopher's law of nature and of nations; which school fell into the error of considering men in the so-called state of nature, which is an ideological hypothesis where they compare the nature of human life and the elements of the relations of men and nations'.[54]

For Sacchi, Vattel's theories lacked 'greater insights, which science, if indeed the principles we deal with and their applications can be reduced to a single science, has added as the last century developed.'[55] However, Sacchi also disassociated himself from the claims of completeness of Pinheiro Ferreira who, in order to 'justify' Vattel's theories, which he himself defined as generic, had resorted to the positions of some internationalists, above all to the Bentham's school, which Sacchi criticised.[56]

He also analysed the *Avertissement* of Pinherio Ferreira to Vattel's *Law of Nations*. He agreed with the Portuguese jurist in considering this text a classic work, saying that in fact 'it is still cited as a text for doctrines, especially in defining the rights of nations and the means of experiencing them';[57] he argued that obviously political and commercial relations between nations had changed compared with the previous century when Vattel had published his treatise, but unlike for Pinheiro, for Sacchi this change did not affect the elements of the political state of the nations, or the constitutive principle of governments which, in his opinion, remained unchanged.[58]

[54] T. Sacchi, 'Prefazione', in E. de Vattel (ed.), *Il diritto delle genti di E. de Vattel applicato allo stato attuale delle nazioni* (Napoli, 1854), 15–29, at 18: 'essendo il suo trattato in certa guisa un compendio del diritto di natura e delle genti di questo capo-scuola; la quale scuola cadeva nell'errore di considerare gli uomini nel così detto stato di natura, ch'è una ipotesi ideologica cui contrastano insieme la natura della vita umana e gli elementi delle relazioni degli uomini e delle nazioni' (author's translation).

[55] Ibid., 20: 'de' maggiori lumi, di che la scienza, se pure ad una scienza unica possano essere ridotti i principî di cui trattiamo e le loro applicazioni, è stata cresciuta nel volgere dell'ultimo secolo' (author's translation).

[56] Ibid., 20.

[57] Ibid., 20: 'è ancora citata come testo di dottrine, specialmente nel diffinire i diritti delle nazioni ed i mezzi per sperimentarli': (author's translation).

[58] Ibid., 21.

So Sacchi not only distanced himself from Pinheiro's theories, but actually 'distrusted and began to despise them'.[59] In this long and interesting preface, he tells the reader that the main sources used by him in commenting on the *Law of Nations* were the writings of François Guizot.

Sacchi referred chiefly to the ideas of Guizot contained in his fourteen lessons on the general history of civilisation in Europe. These conceived civilisation as an unstoppable destiny, which since the collapse of the Roman Empire had shaped the history of the world, regardless of transitory events. For him, civilisation followed two courses, 'social development' and 'moral development', which he proclaimed to be intimately and necessarily correlated.[60]

Sacchi, however, added to these considerations some others that were necessary, following recent historical events (including those in the Kingdom of the Two Sicilies), to clarify and justify the elaboration of the new version of Vattel's *Law of Nations*. Sacchi pointed out that, at the time Guizot had published his work, Europe had not yet undergone the great trials and the great internal upheavals that were to arrive a few years later, in France, as well as in central-northern Italy, in southern Italy, in the Habsburg Empire and in the German Confederation.

'Our age is unjustly burdened with accusations, as if the disorders it has seen and the evils provoked were truly its fault.'[61] Echoing the words of Guizot, Sacchi firmly maintained that science and reality, theory and practice, law and fact should be considered as one, avoiding falling into general and philosophical questions because a principle 'can never be rational if it is not based on elements of the truth in which men have faith'[62] and, were it to be demolished and destroyed by the force that dominates all historical events, it certainly 'cannot fail in itself and in its own action'.[63]

In addressing Vattel's text, however, he made some changes to the order of the chapters and paragraphs 'according to what will be necessary' and placing of the observations, 'in order to reduce the one and the other theories to elements of truth, for which only the principles of science can be certain'.[64]

[59] Ibid., 21: 'le diffidava e cominciava a disdergnarsene' (author's translation).

[60] R. Pozzi, 'Guizot, o dell'Europa una e molteplice', *Cromohs* 15 (2010), 1–8, www.istitutodatini.it/biblio/riviste/a-c/cromo.htm, accessed 17 February 2020.

[61] Sacchi, 'Prefazione', 26: 'L'età nostra è ingiustamente sopraccaricata di accuse, come se fossero veramente sue colpe i disordini di cui è stata tratta, ed i mali cagionati' (author's translation).

[62] Ibid., 25: 'non può essere mai razionale se non è basato con elementi del vero in cui gli uomini abbiano fede' (author's translation).

[63] Ibid., 25: 'non può mancare a se stesso ed alla propria azione' (author's translation).

[64] Ibid., 28: 'nel fine di ridurre le une e le altre teoriche agli elementi del vero, pe' quali unicamente possono essere certi i principi della scienza' (author's translation).

The choice of Naples as the place of publication for Sacchi meant that 'in this Kingdom people live and are inspired by a faith in the Catholic–Apostolic–Roman Church, which for us is inviolable; so we will exclude from the theories of Vattel and the Portuguese jurist those that might attack or oppose the inviolability of the Religion we profess'.[65]

The modification of the *Preliminari* shows the extent of Sacchi's intervention on the structure and form chosen by Vattel. While Vattel introduced his work with a definition of the state, Sacchi began by defining the rights of nations, added the opinion of Pinheiro, who accused Vattel of being simplistic and exclusively philosophical, and then concluded with his reflections.[66] Sacchi wondered whether Vattel's treatise clearly set out the obligations and rights of nations, or if it explained how states should regulate their actions; he also asked whether the law of nations was a legal science or if it only established the principles of natural law for the conduct of sovereigns.

In a long philosophical dissertation, while stating that Vattel's theory was 'luminous' and 'reaches in "possible morality" the principle of law both for men and for nations',[67] he dissociated himself from the position of Pinheiro, who had argued, in line with Bentham's theories, that the principle of every right and every duty was nothing other than the principle of what is right, and 'nothing is right except that which produces the greatest sum of good for all'.[68]

From these considerations and by illustrating some passages commented upon by Sacchi, the following observations may be made. Firstly, Sacchi, precisely as he anticipated in his preface, had no hesitation in presenting Vattel's doctrine in a more markedly Catholic light, from which he then derived principles regarding both human and international relations. Secondly, his was a very philosophical approach, paradoxically lacking references, including historical ones, to the period in which he was translating the *Law of Nations*. The result was therefore to somehow distort the form and substance of Vattel's text. Regarding the form, paragraph orders were changed, notes that had been footnotes were translated and placed in the main text, while Pinheiro's *Notes* were interspersed within Vattel's text. Regarding the substance, Sacchi almost seemed to force, by virtue of his Catholic inclination and 'search for the elements of truth', a reading of Vattel's text in a 'modern'

65 Ibid., 28: 'in questo Reame le genti vivono e s'inspirano nella fede della Chiesa cattolico-apostolica-Romana, ch'è per noi inviolabile; sì che escluderemo dalle teoriche di Vattel e del giurista portoghese, quelle che mai attentassero o contrastassero alla inviolabilità della Religione che professiamo' (author's translation).

66 Ibid., 35–36.

67 Ibid.

68 Ibid., 37.

key, one therefore likely to be well accepted by the institutions and government of the Kingdom of the Two Sicilies.

We do not know why Terenzio Sacchi abandoned his translation work. However, without straining a point, we may posit that Sacchi had sensed his attempt to modernise the *Law of Nations*, especially from a constitutional point of view, did not fit well with the requirements and historical facts of the period, which later led to the decline of the Kingdom of the Two Sicilies.

While this was the only Italian edition of the treatise during the nineteenth century, one might briefly mention the opinions expressed on Vattel by Italian scholars of international law. Niccola Rocco (1811–1877), professor of commercial and international law at the University of Naples, gave a significant boost to the systematic exposition of private international law.[69] In his works, his attention to Vattel's thought was equivocal and ambiguous, and changed over the course of his career. At first, he described him as an author of extreme lucidity in explaining, in particular, issues concerning the discipline of immunity of public ministers in foreign states; the rules to be observed towards foreigners who are passing through or resident in another country, focusing on disputes that may arise between a foreigner and a citizen.[70] Later, however, he did not hesitate to paint Vattel as an outdated jurist, relegated, together with Grozio and Pufendorf, to history, whose theories were defined as 'dry' and no longer useful in an ever-changing international community.[71]

Other illustrious Italian jurists and experts in international law also shared the ambivalent attitude of Rocco. They recognised that, in their time, Vattel still enjoyed considerable authority, especially in the diplomatic and political sphere. But, as was happening in German territories, his thinking was increasingly being placed in the history of the law of nations, thus favouring an autonomous development of international law, practically devoid of Vattel's influence.

Massimo Panebianco has rightly noted that, in Italy, works on international law paid more attention to historical events in which the countries played a leading role.[72] In *Lezioni del diritto internazionale*, Ludovico Casanova saw 'history as the source of international law' to justify a tradition that was continued by other jurists, for example in the writings of Luigi Olivi and of

[69] On Rocco see: E. Zaniboni, 'Rocco Nicola', in I. Birocchi, E. Cortese, A. Mattone and M. N. Miletti (eds.), *Dizionario Biografico Giuristi Italiani* (Bologna, 2013), vol. II, 1709–1710.

[70] N. Rocco, *Dell'uso e autorità delle leggi del Regno delle Due Sicilie considerate nelle relazioni con le persone e col territorio degli stranieri* (Napoli, 1837), XVII, 88, 109, 142, 151–157, 166–167, 177–178, 196, 256, 273–275.

[71] Ibid., XXXI.

[72] M. Panebianco, *Ugo Grozio e la tradizione storica del diritto internazionale* (Napoli, 1974), 167–168.

Giovanni Lomonaco.[73] In this context, therefore, we can well understand the criticisms of many Italian jurists, experts in international law, against Vattel's work. They clearly tended to cite the *Law of Nations*, but in a purely historical perspective, reserving Vattel's authority exclusively to a practical and diplomatic context.

Pasquale Stanislao Mancini (1871–1888), referring to Vattel, wrote that he was considered a sort of oracle only valid for men of government, and although jurists such as Heffter and Wheaton were inspired by his system, he was no longer considered by academics.[74]

For Giuseppe Carnazza Amari (1837–1911), Vattel was simply an imitator of Wolff,[75] while Pasquale Fiore (1837–1914) referenced Vattel's theories, specifying however that his starting point were the theories so well expressed in Bluntschli's treatise.[76]

In support of the limited influence of Vattel on the thought of the major Italian internationalists, one might recall the words of Augusto Pierantoni (1840–1911), who was even more incisive and pungent towards Vattel, Pufendorf and Wolff, but perfectly in line with the thought of Mancini. He maintained that 'scarce was the influence of their works, which were written less for the people than as manuals for men in offices'.[77]

In light of these considerations, one might argue that in Italy the development of international law coincided with the awareness of national identity and independence at all levels. Vattel was an author by now too distant for Italian expectations, which instead required an international law closer to the needs of the time and which would be shaped by jurists such as Rocco, Mancini, Pierantoni and Fiore.

CONCLUSIONS

Emer de Vattel wrote the *Law of Nations* fully aware that there was a tension between domestic and international law, focusing attention on the concept of

[73] Ibid., 167–168.

[74] P. S. Mancini, *Della nazionalità come fondamento del diritto delle genti. Prelezione al corso di diritto internazionale e marittimo pronunziata nella R. Università di Torino nel dì 22 gennaio 1851* (Torino, 1851), 19.

[75] G. Carnazza Amari, *Prelezione al corso di diritto internazionale letta nella Regia Università degli studi di Catania* (Catania, 1865), 15.

[76] P. Fiore, *Trattato di diritto pubblico internazionale* (Milano, 1865), 29.

[77] A. Pierantoni, 'La riforma del diritto delle genti e l'istituto di diritto internazionale di Gand', in D. Dudley Field and A. Pierantoni (eds.), *Prime linee di un codice internazionale del giurista americano Davide Dudley Field*, (Napoli, 1874), 1–86, at 6: 'scarsa fu la influenza delle loro opere dettate men per il popolo che per essere i manuali degli uomini di gabinetto' (author's translation).

nation and outlining all the requirements for achieving its conservation, perfection and happiness, through promulgation of a constitution. Dialogue between nations took place within a community of independent states and sovereigns, understood as subject to the law of nations. What emerged during the first half of the nineteenth century was a reinterpretation of the treatise, which oscillated between constitutional and international law and which was clearly shown in the cases of the Greek war of independence and the Italian Risorgimento.

During the Greek revolution, there was an initial approach to Vattel's treatise through the partial translation of Skouphos of 1825, which concentrated on the themes of neutrality and treatment of the enemy, in order to satisfy 'the needs and affairs' of the nation. Then followed Rallis's translation of the first two books of the *Law of Nations* in 1831, after the appointment of Kapodistrias as the first president of independent Greece.

In Italy in the first half of the nineteenth century, Vattel's *Law of Nations* was the reference treatise for the spirit of the Risorgimento, both for constitutional and for international law. In the Kingdom of the Two Sicilies, Sacchi's partial translation modified the *Law of Nations* according to political needs, criticising Vattel's thought in an attempt to update it to the historical context of Naples at that time.

Translation, understood in its broadest meaning, not only of formulating an original text in another language, but also of 'carrying beyond', certainly played an important role in the circulation of the *Law of Nations*. Traditionally relegated to prefaces, introductions or translator's notes, translation was instead a link in the process of professionalisation of international law. Translators, just like jurists, can be portrayed as mediators and diplomats because they are called upon to solve problems of enormous distances in culture, language, time and space. They were the key transmitters of legal ideas and values in Europe.[78]

The intertwining of revolutionary events and the use of the *Law of Nations* was ever-present throughout the nineteenth century. The political thought it contained, the possibility of the translator selecting parts relevant to the current historical moment and the contents well suited to a heterogeneous and multiform range of political and diplomatic situations ensured that the treatise remained almost 'above history' and 'timeless', permitting it to return again and again.

[78] L. Liu, *Tokens of Exchange: The Problem of Translation in Global Circulations* (Durahm, 1999), 128.

FURTHER READING

Writings by Vattel

Skouphos, S., *Απόσπασματα εκ των του κυρίου Βαττέλλου περί Δικαίου των Εθνών* (Nafplio, 1925).

Vattel, E., *Το Δίκαιο των Εθνών, ή αρχαί τού φυσικού νόμου, Προσηρμοσμένου εις τήν διαγωγήν και εις τά πράγματα τών Εθνών καί τών Κυριαρχών*, translated by Georgios Rallis (Nafplio, 1831).

Il diritto delle genti di E. de Vattel applicato allo stato attuale delle nazioni ad opera del napoletano Terenzio Sacchi (Napoli, 1854).

The Law of Nations, ed. B. Kapossy and R. Whatmore (Indianapolis, 2008).

Selected Secondary Literature

Greppi, E., 'The Risorgimento and the "Birth" of International Law in Italy', in G. Bartolini (ed.), A History of International Law in Italy (Oxford, 2020), 79–108.

Jouannet E., *Vattel and the Emergence of Classic International Law* (Oxford, 2019).

Petropulos, J. A., Politics and Statecraft in the Kingdom of Greece, 1833–1843 (Princeton, 1968).

Pitts, J., *Boundaries of the International Law and Empire* (Cambridge, 2018).

Pizanias, P., The Greek Revolution of 1821: A European Event (Istanbul, 2011).

Sereni, A. P., *The Italian Conception of International Law* (New York, 1943).

Stapelbroek, K. and Trampus, A. (eds), *The Legacy of Vattel's Droit des gens* (Basingstoke, 2019).

13

Reception of Vattel in Eighteenth- and Early Nineteenth-Century England and Scotland

MARCO BARDUCCI

In his *Examination of the British doctrine which subjects to capture a neutral trade not open in time of peace* (1806), the would-be fourth president of the United States, James Madison, affirmed that '[t]he reputation that Vattel enjoys in Great Britain, greater perhaps than he enjoys anywhere else, requires that he should be particularly consulted on this subject'. Madison did not stress the 'originality of his plan, or his matter', which he suggested Vattel had derived from the German philosopher Christian Wolff, but rather the way in which the Swiss jurist 'in many instances, improved the doctrines of all his predecessors'.[1] Madison's consideration about Vattel's reputation in Britain is confirmed by the numerous references to the author of the *Law of Nations* in late eighteenth and early nineteenth-century English and Scottish journals. In 1814, the *Morning Chronicle* announced the auction of *Clarke's Bibliotheca Legum, or complete catalogue of the common and statute law and prices of the United Kingdom*, in which the only foreign title listed was Vattel's *Law of Nations*.[2] Vattel was acknowledged to be 'the greatest authority of the day' on the law of nations, and his name often appears cited next to those either of 'the best writers upon the Law of Nations, Grotius, Burlamaqui'[3] or of Heineccius, Martens and Bynkershoek.[4] At the same time, concepts and doctrines drawn from the *Law of Nations* were utilised either in parliamentary debates, in the administration of colonial affairs and in the proceedings of the Courts of Admiralty or discussed by intellectuals engaged in debates on issues of

1 I would like to thank Knud Haakonssen, Diego Quaglioni, Peter Schröder and Elisabetta Fiocchi Malaspina for their comments on a draft of this chapter.

J. Madison, *An Examination of the British Doctrine which Subjects to Capture a Neutral Trade not Open in Time of Peace* (London, 1806), 25.

2 *The Morning Chronicle* (22 January 1814).

3 *The Morning Post* (20 October 1804).

4 *The Aberdeen Journal* (1 November 1809).

international politics, ethics and law, such as William Cobbett, Edmund Burke, Thomas Reid and Adam Smith.

From this introductory outline, at least five considerations about the reception of Vattel in England and Scotland emerge. Vattel as a leading authority on matters concerning international law; Vattel as the continuator of the continental natural law tradition; Vattel as a *trait-d'union* between this continental strand of thought and British legal and intellectual culture; Vattel as an author known not just to a specialist audience, but also to a wider constituency of informed public opinion; finally, unlike other authors with whom his name was often associated in the period here considered, such as that of Hugo Grotius, whose religious and hermeneutical works had been very influential on English and Scottish culture, the reputation of Vattel primarily lied on his magnus opus the *Law of Nations*. However, the analysis of the circulation and interpretation of Vattel in the British Atlantic world between 1758 and the early decades of the following century shows the existence of distinct although overlapping strands of reception, which emerged from the re-adaptation of the *Law of Nation* to a plurality of contexts including the British colonies of North America, England and Scotland. Recent studies have demonstrated that the *Law of Nations* circulated on American soil since at least 1762. In this relation, William Ossipow and Dominik Gerber have argued that, due to Thomas Jefferson's familiarity with the work of the Swiss jurist, 'the first, second, and fifth paragraphs of the Declaration [of Independence] can be robustly shown to contain both immediately Vattelian hypotext and Lockean hypotext mediated by Vattel.'[5] Therefore, there was a British colonial strand of reception of Vattel, which eventually became a component of the intellectual history of the newly formed United States of America. This topic is more thoroughly examined by Mark Somos in Chapter 10. A second distinction, and one relevant to the subject of the present essay, has to be traced between the English and the Scottish dimension of the reception of Vattel. The two nations shared a king since 1603, but they became formally united with the Acts of Union of 1707, which sanctioned the unification of both parliaments into the Parliament of Great Britain. Before 1707, England and Scotland had different legal systems (the former based on common law, the latter on a combination of Roman law and Scottish common law), different legal

[5] W. Ossipow and D. Gerber, 'The reception of Vattel's Law of Nations in the American colonies: From James Otis and John Adams to the Declaration of Independence', *American Journal of Legal History* 57 (2017), 521; see also V. Chetail, 'Vattel and the American dream: An inquiry into the reception of the *Law of Nations* in the United States', in V. Chetail and P.-M. Dupuy (eds.), *The Roots of International Law. Liber Amicorum Peter Haggenmacher* (Leiden, 2013), 251–300.

education and different propensities to shipping, trade and colonialism. With this regard, it is just worth mentioning that, during the period 1670–1730, Scotland's main economic, intellectual and religious partner was the Dutch Republic, which was probably one of the fiercest rivals of England.[6] Notwithstanding that nearly a half century separated the Acts of Union from the publication of Vattel's *Law of Nations*, some differences persisted between England and Scotland in terms of legal systems and intellectual culture, which inevitably affected the way in which Vattel was read and used between the late eighteenth and the early nineteenth century. Furthermore, given the different contribution of the two nations to the British Empire and the related preponderance of the English fleet in international shipping and trade, differences also existed in the utilisation of Vattel in the proceedings of maritime courts such as the Admiralty courts.

Due to his combination of natural law and the law of nations with reason of state and casuistry in the *Law of Nations*, Vattel has been regarded either 'as a statist or internationalist, as a "realist" or an "idealist", as an heir to the *ius gentium* tradition or the initiator of legal positivism'.[7] In this chapter, I will identify and examine two interconnected strands of reception of Vattel in England and Scotland: the first regarded Vattel as the heir to and systematiser of the continental tradition of natural law and *ius gentium* harking back to Grotius, Pufendorf and Barbeyrac. Such a strand originally consolidated itself among international lawyers practicing in the Courts of Admiralty, and successively propagated itself both within academia, as in the case of Reid's lectures on practical ethics at Glasgow, and beyond, thanks to the periodical press and to the writings of Cobbett. The second strand emerged from the engagement of authors such as Burke and Smith with Vattel's application of reason of state and casuistry to international relations. The attitude of Burke and Smith towards Vattel's reason of state was not identical, as it differently reconnected to existing traditions of thought in England and Scotland. The two strands that I have identified in the reception of Vattel do not necessarily involve the existence of an original contradiction between the principles of 'modern natural law' tradition and reason of state, in that the universal principle of self-preservation and the calculation of which actions or goods

6 E. Mijers, 'Scotland, the Dutch Republic and the union: Commerce & cosmopolitanism', in A. Macinnes and D. Hamilton (eds.), *Jacobitism, Enlightenment and Empire, 1680–1820* (London, 2014), 93–109.

7 L. Cello, 'The legitimacy of international interventions in Vattel's *The Law of Nations*', *Global Intellectual History* 2 (2017), 106–107.

were consequentially necessary to preserve it actually dovetailed within the theory and practice of the modern state.[8]

The reception of Vattel in England and Scotland was influenced by important contextual factors that need to be examined in more detail. The Acts of Union basically preserved the Scottish legal system, although they attributed to the House of Lords at Westminster jurisdiction to hear Scottish civil appeals. The process of unification of the English and Scottish legal systems progressed especially during the second half of the eighteenth century, when Scottish jurists increasingly accepted English influences particularly in the application of the principles drawn from modern Continental international law.[9] The relationship between the law of nations and 'the law of the land' or 'municipal law' (i.e., the law of a particular sovereign) as rules of decision in English courts is of particular relevance in order to understand the reception of Vattel in England. In the late eighteenth century, prominent English judges, legal thinkers and treatise writers, including William Blackstone (1723–1780) in his *Commentaries on the Laws of England* (1765), introduced the idea that the laws of England incorporated certain parts of the law of nations, such as the maritime law, which operated independently of municipal law.[10] Maritime law, but also merchant law, pertained to the jurisdiction of the Courts of Admiralty. The common law defined the prerogative of Admiralty courts in England, and 'the lawes of the realme' allowed them to apply the maritime law to disputes within their jurisdiction.[11] English Courts of Admiralty frequently applied the law of nations in their prize jurisdiction and recurred to Vattel's concept of 'perfect right' in a number of cases. Bellia and Clark have demonstrated that the concept of 'perfect rights' and the justification of just war in case of their violation was well recognized in England, where it was used in conjunction with theories drawn from Pufendorf and Burlamaqui to describe either cases of prizes, seizures and treaties, or the origins and principles of the war against France.[12] The *Reports of Cases Argued and Determined in the High Court of Admiralty* describe numerous episodes of seizures and prizes in neutral territories such as the case of the Dutch ship 'The Twee Gebroeders' captured by a Prussian vessel. The

8 D. Armitage, 'Edmund Burke and reason of state', *Journal of the History of Ideas* 61 (2000), 619–620.

9 D. Scullion, 'The union of 1707 and its impact on Scots law', *Aberdeen Student Law Review* 1 (2010), 111–114.

10 A. J. Bellia & B. R. Clark, 'The federal common law of nations', *Columbia Law Review* 109.1 (2009), 22–23.

11 Ibid., 17.

12 Ibid., 19.

matter of dispute was whether the capture took place in a neutral territory or in an enemy territory, and Grotius and Vattel were cited to defend the neutral state's right to give free passage to troops on land and water.[13] Vattel was cited also in relation to cases of confiscation of goods from ships and contraband, such as the so-called "Maria's case". This was the case of a vessel of Swedish merchantmen 'carrying pitch, tar, hemp, deals, and iron, to several ports of France, Portugal and the Mediterranean; and taken, Jan. 1798, sailing under convoy of a ship of war, and proceeded against for resistance of visitation and search by British cruisers.' Here Vattel is referred to as an authority on 'the law of nations', who justifies confiscation of neutral ships resisting visitation and search in times of war.[14]

Admiralty courts also existed in Scotland until 1830 and, although they claimed independent jurisdiction, they were in fact subordinated to the civil Courts of Session.[15] From the seventeenth to the nineteenth century, Scottish Admiralty courts increasingly adopted English cases concerning merchant law and maritime law, in which the name of Vattel was frequently cited. Meanwhile, Scottish jurists like John Millar (1735–1801), Regius Professor of Civil Law at the University of Glasgow from 1761 to 1800, acknowledged the derivation of English cases directly from the Continental tradition of the law of nations.[16] Even though more extensive research is needed on this point, with due precaution it is possible to affirm that while the name of Vattel was frequently cited in the proceedings of English Admiralty courts, there is less evidence of the presence of the Swiss jurist in the proceedings of the Scottish Courts of Admiralty. In her study on shipping and trade in Scotland, Susan Mowat examined records of proceedings of the Scottish Courts of Admiralty from the seventeenth to the nineteenth centuries. Mowat has shown that after the Acts of Union, the small Scottish fleet was incorporated with the British fleet and that the Courts mainly heard cases of mercantile nature involving merchants, masters and crews, with the notable exception of wartime, when the Courts were involved in cases of prize taking of enemy vessels.[17] Vattel's work therefore circulated both in England and in Scotland, but it is most likely that English cases facilitated the reception of his concepts in Scottish

[13] C. Robinson (ed.), *Reports of Cases Argued and Determined in the High Court of Admiralty* (London, 1853), IV, 353–354.

[14] C. Robinson (ed.), *Reports of Cases Argued and Determined in the High Court of Admiralty* (London, 1812), I, 343.

[15] A. R. G. McMillan, 'Scottish Court of Admiralty: A retrospect', *Juridical Review* 34 (1922), 39–42.

[16] Scullion, 'Union of 1707', 114.

[17] S. Mowat, 'Shipping and trade in Scotland, 1556–1830', *Mariner's Mirror* 83 (1997), 14, 17.

legal culture and practice. A certain pre-eminence of the English reception of Vattel with respect to the Scottish one was determined also by economic and commercial factors, relating, in the first instance, to the different preponderance of shipping and trade in the two British nations. In this respect, it is fair to argue that the difference between English and Scottish uses of Vattel in the proceedings of maritime and merchant law was rather quantitative than qualitative.

So far we have seen how the name of Vattel was recurrently invoked by jurists specialised in the law of nations to settle cases of seizures and prizes in neutral territories or in territories claimed to be under the jurisdiction of a state. However, the reputation of Vattel as an authority providing arguments which were instrumentally deployed in a political and legal contest was not circumscribed to lawyers and academics, in that some of his doctrines and concepts had been made accessible to a wider constituency of informed public opinion through the periodical press. The interest of public opinion in questions pertaining to the law of nations and, consequently, in the doctrines of Vattel, grew between 1803 and 1815 in consequence of the involvement of Britain in the war against Napoleonic France and its allies. In January 1805, *The Morning Post* reported the case of a pamphlet written by an anonymous author to defend the decision of British authorities to seize some Spanish vessels in the absence of a formal declaration of war with Spain, which had been allied with France since the Treaty of Alliance of 1790. The author justified the seizure – which somebody at the time had reputed 'an act of robbery' – by relying on Vattel's 'book 2, ch. 18 sect 353', in which the Swiss jurist justifies seizures or reprisals as acceptable expedients for the sovereigns to secure justice for their nation while avoiding waging a war.[18] In 1809, *The Aberdeen Journal* published an article on 'Maritime Laws' which was a defence of the 'right of search', that is of the right of a belligerent nation to seize neutral vessels doing commerce with hostile nations and with their colonies. England was accused of this by its enemies, when instead, the article affirmed, France habitually put in practice this principle by relying on the authority of Bynkershoek, Heineiccius and Vattel,

> a French [sic] writer, who has been considered not only as the text-book for the modern French civilians, but has even been quoted in this country; and he says 'We cannot prevent the conveyance of contraband goods without searching neutral vessels that we meet at sea; we have therefore a right to

[18] *Morning Post* (9 January 1805).

search them. A neutral ship refusing to be searched, would for that proceeding alone be condemned as a lawful prize'.[19]

MP and journalist William Cobbett (1763–1835) made extensive use of the *Law of Nations* in his famous *Political Register* (1802–1836). In an article on the 'Gum trade', Cobbett engaged in a dispute with the author of *Eight Letters on the Peace and on the Commerce and Manufactures of Great Britain* (1802), Frederick Morton Eden (1766–1809), who had affirmed that the Treaty of Paris of 1783 – which acknowledged the independence of the United States of America, and signed separate peace treaties between Britain and the nations that had supported the American Revolution, that is, France, Spain and the Dutch Republic – would 'throw commerce into infinite confusion'. Focusing in particular on the passage of the Treaty concerning the abolition of existing treaties, Eden criticized the words of those English MPs who took it as involving that the right to gum trade had been fully ceded to France. Eden therefore invoked the authority of Martens and Vattel to claim that the right to gum trade still belonged to Britain in virtue of the conquest of Senegal in 1758, sanctioned by the Treaty of Paris of 1763.[20] Cobbett responded to Eden that, in consequence of the Treaty of 1783, the right to gum trade actually ceased. To this end, he cited the same passage that Eden had previously quoted from Martens, to demonstrate that treatises cease to be obligatory when one of the sovereign powers which have stipulated them ceases to exist, changes constitution, passes under the dominion of another power or 'always when a war, on whatever account, breaks out between the contracting parties, except it may be such provisions contained in them as have been made in the case of war'. Cobbett then cited Vattel to conclude that '[a]ll things not mentioned in the treaty, remains as they were at the conclusion of it'.[21]

Cobbett's writings contributed to the diffusion of Vattel's concepts and doctrines in British legal and political language and culture. With this regard, it is worth mentioning a few examples which concern the utilisation of Vattel's notion of 'sovereignty'. In his *Complete Collection of State Trials and Proceedings for High Treason and Other Crimes and Misdemeanors* (1814), Cobbett published the report of a case of 1775 between 'Mr. Macdonald for the plaintiff vs Mr. Hargrave for the defendant' concerning the recovery of a sum levied by the defendant in Granada as a duty and paid by the plaintiff without consideration. The discussion concentrated on how, after the Treaty

[19] *Aberdeen Journal* (1 November 1809).
[20] W. Cobbett, *Political Register* (London 1802), I, 545–548.
[21] Ibid., 550.

of Paris of 1763, Granada had become a territory under the sovereignty and jurisdiction of the king of Britain. The island's new governor imposed by prerogative a tax on commodities exported, which was levied by the defendant and paid by the plaintiff. The question at stake here was whether the tax that the governor imposed was for his own benefit or on behalf of the state. The issue was a complex one and its origins harked back to at least the early phases of English colonialism and to the related controversy between King and Parliament on jurisdiction over extra-European settlements. Concisely, English common law was a prerogative of the 'King-in-Parliament', but since the latter did not hold jurisdiction over extra-European settlements, these actually fell under the prerogative rule of the king. In order to exert their authority over an empire that extended over extra-territorial dominions, since at least the seventeenth century, English kings drew on the principles of natural law and the law of nations contained in Roman law. Before the publication of Grotius' *De Iure belli ac Pacis* (1625), English civil lawyers dealing with matters relating to international affairs and the occupation of extra-European territories mostly relied either on the chapter 'Acquisition of ownership of things' of Justinian's *Digest* or on the doctrines of Francisco Vitoria (1483–1546) and Alberico Gentili (1552–1608). However, since Roman law was not originally intended to regulate colonial affairs, its adaptation to the administration of extra-European territories was subject to conflicting interpretations during negotiations with other European nations. A century and half later, as problems relating to jurisdiction over extra-European settlements persisted, Macdonald posed the question of whether, when the sovereign conquers, he does so in the interest of the state or for himself. To respond, he recurred to Vattel's doctrine according to which if 'an inhabited country be planted by British subjects, all the English laws which are there immediately; but if it be a conquered state which has laws of its own, those laws remain there until others are provided.'[22] It is within the context of this discussion that Macdonald faces the problem of how to align the terms 'state' and 'sovereignty' to the organisation of English mixed government.

This problem had been tackled before by those, like Andrew Tooke (1673–1732), who attempted to re-adapt Continental ideas of state and sovereignty to the English context. When Tooke undertook the English translation of Pufendorf's *De Officio Hominis et Civis* with the title of *The Whole Duty of Men According to the Law of Nature* (1691), he avoided using the term state 'as a supreme and unified political authority' in the 'context of a temporary

[22] T. J. Howell, W. Cobbett and D. Jardine (eds.), *A Complete Collection of State Trials and Proceedings for High Treason and Other Crimes and Misdemeanors* (London, 1814), v.20, 289

equilibrium in the unfinished contest between crown and parliament for the rights and powers of sovereignty'.[23] In dealing with the same problem, Macdonald explained that the use of 'king or sovereign' in treatises of general law adapts to the general context to which it applies: in Grotius 'rex et regnum' means the States General in Netherlands, and 'king and parliament' in England.[24] However, what the plaintiff contended in this case report was that the king's prerogative was valid only during wartime, but not when a country (i.e. Granada) had surrendered, in which case the imposition of taxes required the consent of Parliament. A similar case in which the authority of Vattel was invoked to deal with the relationship between sovereignty and taxation was that reported by the *Caledonian Mercury* of 13 July 1805, concerning a request of account by the House of Lords of the revenue and expenditure in the Isle of Man from 1798 to 1805. The matter of controversy about the financial management of the island mainly concerned the issue of sovereignty, and specifically the request of the island's governor, Duke of Athol, to pass a bill to increase his revenues. Lord Ellenborough opposed this bill before the House of Lords on the ground that it contained a false proposition, that is that Athol was sovereign, while 'Vattel defined sovereignty to consist in a State's governing itself by its own laws', which meant that the administration of the island was subject to the authority British Parliament. A century or so after Tooke's translation of Pufendorf, Cobbett had contributed to consolidate the association between the continental concepts of sovereignty and state exemplified by Vattel, with the British constitution of 'king-in-Parliament'.

Cobbett was therefore one of the main promoters of the circulation of the concepts and doctrines of Vattel in England, and the fact that his portrait is exhibited in the Scottish National Portrait Gallery suggests that he might have contributed to their reception also in Scotland. Cobbett, in fact, not only 'Translated from the French' and published a *Summary of the law of nations ... By Mr. Martens, professor of law in the University of Gottingen*, but in 1797 he probably (the edition was anonymous) published a revised edition of a previous English translation of Vattel's *Law of Nations* dating to 1760.[25] Cobbett's version was then corrected and improved by Joseph Chitty the elder (1775–1841), a barrister and one of the most prolific legal writers of his day, who also mentored some of the most influential lawyers of England. First

[23] D. Saunders and I. Hunter, 'Bringing the state to England: Andrew Tooke's translation of Samuel Pufendorf's *De Officio Hominis et Civis*', *History of Political Thought* XXIV (2003), 234.

[24] Howell et al., *State Trials and Proceedings*, 289.

[25] J. E. G. de Montmorency, 'Émerich de Vattel', *Journal of the Society of Comparative Legislation* 10 (1909), 17–39; J. Macdonnel and E. Manson (eds.), *Great Jurists of the World* (Boston, 1914), 477.

published in 1834, Chitty's version revised and expanded the explanatory notes, adding in particular legal citations 'based on the case law of the sea that emerged in the Napoleonic era'.[26] Many of these comments concerned differences and similarities between English common law and international law. According to Ian Hunter, Chitty's 'Anglicization' of Vattel's understanding of international law through 'a web of case-law citations taken from the Court of Admiralty and the King's Bench' was used by British colonial officials and jurists in colonial context. However, as Hunter convincingly argued, Chitty's 'anglicised' Vattel 'was thus not really a source of ideological justifications for the exercise of English sovereignty over colonial territories … but rather as a means for receiving English law in colonial territories whose British sovereignty was treated as a military-political presupposition of legal order'.[27]

Despite the reports of Admiralty courts and case reports published in newspapers which may suggest a certain uniformity in the reception of Vattel's natural law and international law theories in England and Scotland, the overall picture is further complicated by the different influence of Vattel on legal education in the two nations forming Great Britain. As Richard Devetak has explained, the *Law of Nations* was originally intended as a contribution to the understanding of the international environment which, in the course of the eighteenth century, increasingly depended 'on appreciating the centrality of war, diplomacy, and the balance of power'. Seen in this context, Vattel's work was essentially 'an intellectual response to Europe's changing political and diplomatic milieu, the aim of which was to provide statesmen and diplomats with a broad normative programme'. From the early eighteenth century onwards, diplomacy became viewed as a vital instrument of state, 'and contributed to the establishment of foreign ministries and the institutionalization of regular diplomacy across Europe'.[28] With this purpose, the French foreign minister Marquis de Torcy established in 1712 a Political Academy for the professional training of French diplomats and foreign ministry administrators, which devised a curriculum based on the study of the law of nations and nature, particularly on Grotius's *De Jure Belli ac Pacis*. Also Great Britain established a foreign ministry in 1782, but it is not in the context of diplomatic training that we must look for the diffusion of Vattel in England

[26] Vattel, *The Law of Nations*, xxii.

[27] I. Hunter, 'Global justice and regional metaphysics', in S. Dorsett and I. Hunter (eds.), *Law and Politics in British Colonial Thought: Transpositions of Empire* (Basingstoke, 2010), 23.

[28] R. Devetak, 'Diplomacy and the balance of power in Vattel's *Law of Nations*', *Parergon* 28 (2011), 124–125.

and Scotland, but rather in the curriculum of moral philosophy in Scottish universities, on the one hand, and in the legal education curriculum of English advocates and academics engaged in both legal practice and legal theory, on the other.

Since the late seventeenth century, Scottish law students used to enrol in Dutch universities where they were introduced to the natural law and international law theories of Grotius and Pufendorf. The development of Scottish law during the eighteenth century reflected this engagement with continental legal theories. This process was solicited by the work of scholars such as Gershon Carmichael (1672–1729) who particularly used Pufendorf's *De Officio* to establish the natural law tradition in the teaching of moral philosophy in Scottish universities. John W. Cairns has demonstrated that, by the 1760s, the theories of Grotius, Pufendorf and Barbeyrac were commonly used in faculty of law curricula and deployed in the construction of arguments before superior courts.[29] However, Cairns never mentions Vattel, and a similarly striking absence of any reference to the Swiss jurist is in Bruce Buchan's essay on the Scottish Enlightenment and international relations, which explores the ways in which David Hume (1711–1776), William Robertson (1721–1793), Adam Smith (1723–1790) and Adam Ferguson (1723–1816) framed their understanding of the civilizing process in Europe.[30] The only extensive discussion of Vattel's natural law and international law theories during the Scottish Enlightenment was in Reid's lectures on practical ethics.[31]

After some years spent teaching natural philosophy, mathematics and moral sciences at King's College in Aberdeen, in 1764 Reid (1716–1794) succeeded Adam Smith to the chair of moral philosophy at Glasgow University. Reid did not show any particular interest in natural law during his period at Aberdeen, while his engagement with natural jurisprudence was solicited by the requirement to teach a two-month course on natural law at Glasgow, which had been the central theme of Smith's lectures. To make up for such a gap on relatively short notice, in his opening lecture Reid asked his students for notes of the lectures of his predecessor.[32] Furthermore, in his lecture on 'Natural law and

[29] J. W. Cairns, 'Legal theory in the Scottish Enlightenment', in A. Broadie and C. Smith (eds.), *The Cambridge Companion to the Scottish Enlightenment* (Cambridge, 2019), 221.

[30] B. Buchan, 'Civilisation, sovereignty and war: The Scottish Enlightenment and international relations', *International Relations* 20 (2006), 176.

[31] From now on, I will refer to Knud Haakonssen's impeccable edition of Thomas Reid's *Practical Ethics* (*Thomas Reid on Practical Ethics: Lectures and Papers on Natural Religion, Self-Government, Natural Jurisprudence and the Law of Nations* (Edinburgh, 2007, online edition 2015)).

[32] K. Haakonssen, 'Introduction', to *Thomas Reid on Practical Ethics*, xxxii–xxxiii.

natural rights' Reid recommended to his students a list of authors on 'natural jurisprudence', which included 'Grotius, Hobbes Selden Puffendorf. Barbyrack upon Grotius & Puffendorf. Carmichael upon Puffendorf. Locke. Hoadly. Hutcheson Burlamaqui Vattel. Cocceij'.[33] While Reid did not make use of all these authors in his lectures, his most immediate sources were Hutcheson's *Short Introduction* (originally published in Latin in 1745, translated into English in 1747) and *System of Moral Philosophy* (1755), both of which appeared earlier with respect to Vattel's *Law of Nations*.[34] Furthermore, in his lectures on jurisprudence ('Jurisprudence is that science which inquires into the general principles which ought to be the foundation of the laws of all nations'), Smith mainly engaged with the work of Hobbes, Pufendorf, Barbeyrac and Grotius, all of whom he regarded as 'casuists'.[35]

Colin Heydt has recently demonstrated that Pufendorf's practical ethics, with its emphasis on rights and duties over Aristotelian virtues, dominated moral philosophy curricula in Scottish universities.[36] Haakonssen has confirmed that by the end of the 1760s Reid had essentially completed his *Practical Ethics* 'on lines taken over from Hutcheson and his Pufendorfian systematics'[37] and that he conventionally dealt with rights and obligations between states as part of natural jurisprudence. It was in this latter context that Reid extensively relied on Vattel.[38] In his 'Lecture XVII. Rights and Duties of States' Reid explained that 'Political jurisprudence regards first the mutual rights and obligations of the supreme power and the subject … secondly. The rights of a political body or state both in relation to other states and in relation to individuals. This second part of political jurisprudence is that which [is] properly called the law of nations as distinguished from the law of nature.' This paragraph was followed by a reference to 'Addit Extracts from Vattel' and by the analogy between a 'nation incorporated and united into one political body' and a 'moral person'.[39] While Reid generally followed the Pufendorfian taxonomy and reserved the label 'political jurisprudence' for the political relations of the individual, due to the influence of Vattel's 'pursuance of the analogy between the individual and the state', in this passage

33 Reid, *Practical Ethics*, 96.

34 Haakonssen, 'Introduction', lxxix.

35 K. Haakonssen, 'The *lectures on jurisprudence*', in R. P. Hanley (ed.), *Adam Smith: His Life, Thought, and Legacy* (Princeton, 2016), 51–52.

36 Colin Heydt, *Moral Philosophy in Eighteenth-Century Britain* (Cambridge, 2018), 6–8.

37 Haakonssen, 'Introduction', xxiii.

38 Ibid., lxxx; lxxviii.

39 Reid, *Practical Ethics*, 153.

he made it cover 'both individual and collective political relations'.[40] Also, the notion of the state as a corporate moral personality, which Reid had already mentioned in his lecture 'Duties to Others: States', although very much in the natural law tradition of Hobbes, Locke and Pufendorf, was most likely drawn in the first instance from Vattel's 'Preliminaries' to the *Law of Nations*.[41] Reid used Vattel also in dealing with aspects of the law of nations concerning the causes and conduct of war, and he did so often in conjunction with other modern natural law authors, Grotius in the first instance, but also Pufendorf and Heineccius.[42]

This brief overview raises a question about the specific contribution of Vattel to Reid's *Practical Ethics* with respect to other authors of natural jurisprudence. Reid's relatively late approach to natural jurisprudence as primarily occasioned by the fulfilment of his teaching obligations at Glasgow; his adoption of arguments, such as the analogy between individuals and states, which were in line with the natural law and international law tradition; and finally, his decision to follow convention when dealing with rights and obligations between states, seem to suggest that Reid used Vattel either as a source on or as a compendium of existing literature on natural law and state practice, and that he aligned him to the doctrines of Hutcheson and Pufendorf. This vision of Vattel as a 'transitory thinker' rather than as an author who had a distinctive impact on Reid's moral philosophy is only partially mitigated by the analysis of the possible impact on Reid's notion of moral community of the ethical assumptions about 'the natural society established between all mankind' underpinning the *Law of Nations*. Central to the argument of some of the Scottish thinkers who influenced Reid's moral science, such as Turnbull and Hutcheson, was the 'providentialist' idea of a moral community or system and that human perfection could be achieved through the teaching of moral philosophy (including natural jurisprudence) rather than through the enforcement of justice. Such an idea occasionally assumed in Reid the character of a utopian vision of a moral commonwealth.[43] These moral aspirations to human perfectibility were not entirely absent from Vattel's treatment of the state as a 'moral person'. In a passage of the 'Preliminaries' to the *Law of Nations* Vattel affirms: 'the object of the natural society established between all mankind is that they should lend each other mutual assistance in order to attain perfection themselves and to render

[40] Ibid., 153, n1.
[41] Ibid., 81, n2.
[42] Ibid., *passim*.
[43] K. Haakonssen, 'Natural jurisprudence and the theory of justice', in A. Broadie and C. Smith (eds.), *The Cambridge Companion to the Scottish Enlightenment* (Cambridge, 2019), 195–197; 204.

their condition as perfect as possible'. It follows that the first general law 'that we discover in the very object of the society of nations, is that each individual nation is bound to contribute everything in her power to the happiness and perfection of all the others'.[44] However, as Ben Holland has pointed out, in the same passage Vattel argued that the perfection of a nation primarily concerned the perfection of her own faculties rather than the attainment of individual and/or civil perfection.[45] This overlay of 'self-perfection' and 'self-interest' reflected on Vattel's critique of Wolff's postulate of a *civitas maxima*, and underpinned his vision of a sort of (European) Republic centred on the actual practice and interest of independent sovereign states as developed around the distinction between 'voluntary law' and 'necessary law'.[46] The distinct way in which Vattel intended to develop the precedent tradition of natural jurisprudence apparently did not contribute to open up new avenues for the development of Reid's moral philosophy. In his *Essays on the Active Powers of Man* (1788), in dealing with system of morals that established 'a close relation of right to duty', Reid referred to Grotius as 'the capital work' on natural jurisprudence, while he did not mention Vattel.[47]

With the notable exception of Reid, then, the name of Vattel only occurs marginally, if at all, both in law curricula and in the writings of other exponents of the Scottish Enlightenment, while his doctrines were mentioned in newspapers and, in all probability, in Scottish Admiralty courts. There are at least two main reasons which may help to explain the dynamics of the reception of Vattel in Scotland at the end of the eighteenth century. The first relates to the fact that, after 1707, Scottish lawyers and journalists increasingly imported from England concepts and doctrines pertaining to the law of nations, which English lawyers and journalists (like Cobbett) had in turn borrowed from continental authors, including Vattel. A second reason was the way in which the engagement with natural jurisprudence had developed in Scotland by the time of the publication of the *Law of Nations*. Also as a reaction to ethical rationalism and natural law theories which were still so influential on the Continent, a new historical approach to legal theory influenced by the historical analysis of legal systems borrowed from Montesquieu, was developed by John Millar, Smith and Lord Kames (1696–1782).[48]

44 Vattel, *LN*, prelim. 73.

45 B. Holland, 'The moral person of the state: Emer de Vattel and the foundations of international legal order', *History of European Ideas* 37 (2011), 443.

46 G. Cavallar, 'The Law of Nations in the age of enlightenment: Moral and legal principles', *Jahrbuch für Recht und Ethik* 12 (2004), 222–223.

47 T. Reid, *Essays on the Active Powers of Man* (London, 1788), 393.

48 Cairns, 'Legal theory in the Scottish Enlightenment', 222–224.

The development of the English approach to the law of nations in the eighteenth and nineteenth centuries differed from that occurring in Scotland. As Michael Lobban explained it, in the early nineteenth century, international lawyers in England 'formed part of a closed professional elite: civilian lawyers, who were members of the College of Advocates and Doctors of Law, known as Doctors Commons'. The latter did not practice in the courts of common law but rather in a number of non-common law jurisdictions, such as the Courts of Admiralty. They studied at Oxford and Cambridge, and their curriculum mostly included Roman law, although they 'largely spoke the same languages of their continental counterparts'. After the 1830s, international law was taught also at London University, where J. T. Graves, who held the chair of jurisprudence and the law of nations from 1838 to 1843, lectured on Vattel.[49] From the middle of the nineteenth century onwards, English approaches to international law distinguished themselves from continental ones in two respects. The first was practical: 'in the 1870s, in a number of high profile international disputes, English common lawyers stressed the nature of international law as a matter of practical politics and negotiation rather than as a matter for jurists' speculation'. It followed that international law was to be found 'in state practice, and in the consent of nations as manifested in positive agreement or established usage'. The second was intellectual, and related to the diffusion of the writings of John Austin (1790–1859), who questioned if international law could be denominated law at all.[50] These developments in English approaches to international law theory eventually transcended the strand of reception of Vattel as the heir to and systematiser of the continental tradition of natural law and *ius gentium*, harking back to Grotius, Pufendorf, and Barbeyrac.

The second strand of reception of Vattel emerged because of his application of reason of state and casuistry to international relations, as can be seen in the engagement with Vattel by Edmund Burke and Adam Smith, respectively.

Edmund Burke (1729–1797) used Vattel to justify a military pre-emptive intervention to halt France's Revolutionary expansionism as an act of 'necessity'. Burke's *Thoughts on French Affairs* (1791) reveal a profound knowledge of the work of Vattel and of other international jurists. Furthermore, in 1793, he prepared extracts from Vattel to be published in an appendix to his *Remarks on the Policy of the Allies*, with a view to justifying English military intervention

[49] M. Lobban, 'English approaches to international law in the nineteenth century', in M. C. R. Craven, M. Fitzmaurice and M. Vogiatzi (eds.) *Time, History and International Law* (Leiden, 2007), 67, 70–71.

[50] Ibid., 66, 73.

against France.[51] In order to justify, before an English audience, a foreign intervention in a civil war already started, Burke assimilated the French Revolution to the Glorious Revolution of 1688 as both 'just wars' waged between two *de facto* independent sovereign authorities.[52] Drawing on 'Vattel, b.ii.c.4.sect.56 and b.iii. c18 sect.296', Burke affirmed that '[i]n this state of things (that is in the case of a divided kingdom) by the law of nations, Great Britain, like every other Power, is free to take any parts she pleases.'[53] Against non- interventionists in the House of Commons he relied on Vattel to justify a preventive aggression against the expansionist dimension of the French Revolution, in that it endangered the balance of power established by the Treaty of Utrecht. Yet, the idea of European balance that underpinned Burke's claims for a leading role of England in the anti-revolutionary crusade against France was different from that proposed by the Swiss jurist, in that Burke was aware that this legal maxim actually allowed a discretionary power to states to intervene in civil wars regardless of their being on the 'just side'.[54]

As well as many eminent continental thinkers before him, from Voltaire to Montesquieu, Vattel expressed his praise for the English constitution and laws, and for the concern of English Kings with the common good of society (*LN*, I-IV-39). Vattel ascribed to England a leading role in the balance of Europe. 'Europe' – says Vattel in an often cited passage 'forms a political system, an integral body, closely connected by the relations and different interests of the nations inhabiting this part of the world'. England 'has the glory of holding the political balance. She is attentive to preserve it in equilibrium: – a system of policy, which is in itself highly just and wise, and will ever entitle her to praise, as long as she continues to pursue it only by means of alliances, confederacies, and other methods equally lawful' (*LN*, III-III-47). However, notwithstanding that his familiarity with Vattel was such that in a letter concerning 'America', Cobbett proposed to envoy him along with other men 'deeply read in Vattel and Pufendorf' to deal with Napoleon's expansionist claims,[55] Burke did not rely on the Swiss jurist when formulating his own version of a 'Commonwealth of Europe'. According to Camilla Boisen, Burke's vision of a European international society was traceable to the English tradition of common law and to the related assumption that what

[51] E. Burke, *Further Reflections on the French Revolution*, ed. D. Ritchie (Indianapolis, 1992), 207, n2.

[52] Armitage, 'Edmund Burke', 696.

[53] Burke, *Further Reflections on the French Revolution*, 207.

[54] J. Welsh, *Edmund Burke and International Relations* (Basingstoke, 1995), 128–129.

[55] W. Cobbett, *Letters on the Late War between the United States and Great Britain* (New York, 1815), 157.

really assimilated European countries were 'common customs, legal heritages, and "manners"'. The 'common law of Europe', which lays at the core of Burke's notion of balance of power, constituted the shared heritage of a customary society springing from a common appurtenance to Christian European civilisation, which was endangered by the modern doctrines underpinning the French Revolution.[56]

However, in stressing how the analogy between civil laws and international laws was vital to his justification of the war against France 'as a matter of moral prudence',[57] Boisen implicitly reconnects Burke to the English tradition of 'good' reason of state as distinct from Machiavellian 'false' reason of state. This tradition harked back to at least the early Stuart period, when it merged into terms such as 'laws of state', 'state necessity' and '*salus populi*' and culminated, through the mediation of the Whig tradition, in Burke's own engagement with the concept of 'moral necessity'.[58] The discretionary, voluntarist, casuistic dimension of Vattel's reasoning, exemplified in England by the reception of Burke, made its way also through Scotland, where it was discussed in the work of Adam Smith. Ryan Walter has studied Smith's uses of casuistry in his treatment of the exceptions to the policy of free trade, which Smith justified in terms of 'higher principles' such as security and justice. Notwithstanding Smith's low opinion of casuistry as a moral system in *The Theory of Moral Sentiments* (1759),[59] as many other eighteenth-century thinkers including Burke, he used casuistry in terms of both 'historical contextualization of principles' and 'balancing conflicting principles'. In his *Inquiry into the Nature and Causes of the Wealth of Nations* (1776), Smith adopted a casuistical approach to conflicting principles in relation to free trade, that is, 'a policy that best promotes wealth, but one that should be sacrificed to the higher tasks of defence and justice as occasion required'.[60] Drawing on Ian Hunter's study of Vattel's development of a diplomatic casuistry targeted at statesmen and diplomats who needed practical principles to promote wealth in the context of competing national interests and superior state objectives,[61]

56 C. Boisen, 'The law of nations and the common law of Europe: The case of Edmund Burke', in I. Van Hulle and R. Lesaffer (eds.), *International Law in the Long Nineteenth Century (1776–1914)* (Leiden, 2019), 36–37.

57 Ibid., 40.

58 M. Barducci, *Anthony Ascham and English Political Thought, 1648–1650* (Manchester, 2015), 99; Armitage, 'Edmund Burke', 622.

59 See Haakonssen, '*Lectures on jurisprudence*', 51–52.

60 R. Walter, 'Adam Smith's free trade casuistry', *Global Intellectual History*, 1.1 (2016), 62.

61 See I. Hunter, 'Kant and Vattel in context: Cosmopolitan philosophy and diplomatic casuistry', *History of European Ideas* 39 (2013), 477–502.

Walter argues that Smith was indebted to Vattel's *Law of Nations*. However, 'unlike Vattel's justice and national interest, Smith's conflicting principles – defence, justice, and health – were not equal but hierarchically ordered'.[62]

Reconnecting by way of conclusion to James Madison's introductory statement, it is possible to affirm that, notwithstanding his great reputation, Vattel did not become, as Grotius did before him in the German-speaking lands (thanks mainly to the work of Pufendorf) the founding father of a new strand of thought about international law in England and Scotland. The transformation of moral-sense theory solicited by the encounter with 'a theory of development derived and adapted from Montesquieu',[63] on the one hand, together with the mounting dissatisfaction with natural law-related arguments and the development of distinct practical and positive approaches to international law, on the other, eventually determined the end of his intellectual 'moment' in both nations.

However, probably the main stumbling block to the late implementation of Vattel's doctrine of interstate relations as relations between moral persons equally endowed with 'perfect rights', was the practice of British imperialism. As Casper Sylvest has pointed out, during the second half of the nineteenth century British international lawyers increasingly approached this subject 'within a specific, and specifically progressive, temporality that cultivated a constant expansion of civilised international legal relations in quantitative, qualitative, and geographical terms'.[64] Drawing on the analysis of examples relating to British imperialism in Africa, Sylvest argued that the expansion of international law did not involve a concomitant expansion of the notion of international society as formed by equal subjects. British imperialism operated, instead, through the application of hierarchical principles to nations deemed uncivilised and therefore unable to adopt international law principles.[65] The notion of universal justice underpinned by an 'explicit Protestant moral-republican argument that political rights are grounded in the cultivation of civic virtues', which Vattel had originally developed with a view to securing a balance of power between European states,[66] proved difficult to adapt to a global context increasingly dominated by imperial rivalries and by hierarchical and, successively, evolutionist conceptions of the international society.

62 Walter, 'Adam Smith⊠s free trade casuistry', 63.
63 Cairns, 'Legal theory in the Scottish Enlightenment', 222.
64 Casper Sylvest, 'Our passion for legality', international law and imperialism in late-nineteenth century Britain', *Review of International Studies* 34 (2008), 406.
65 Ibid., 409
66 Hunter, 'Global justice and regional metaphysics', 20.

FURTHER READING

Cairns, J. W., *Enlightenment, Legal Education, and Critique* (Edinburgh, 2015).

Haakonssen, K., 'Natural jurisprudence and the identity of the Scottish Enlightenment', in R. Savage (ed.), *Religion and Philosophy in Enlightenment Britain* (Oxford, 2012), 258–277.

'Natural rights or political prudence? Toleration in Francis Hutcheson', in J. Parkin and T. Stanton (eds.), *Natural Law and Toleration in the Early Enlightenment* (Oxford, 2012), 261–289.

McNair, A. D., Fitzmaurice, G. G., de Murray, S. C. B., de Freitas, G. and Harvey Moore, W., 'The debt of international law in Britain to the civil law and the civilians', *Transactions of the Grotius Society* 39 (1953), 183–210.

Stapelbroek, K. and Trampus, A. (eds.), *The Legacy of Vattel's Droit de Gens* (Cham, 2019).

Van Hulle, I. and Lesaffer, R. (eds.), *International Law in the Long Nineteenth Century (1776–1914)* (Leiden, 2019).

14

Receptions of Vattel in Nineteenth- and Twentieth-Century International Law

THEODORE CHRISTOV

INTRODUCTION

The turn of the nineteenth century is widely seen in histories of international law as a watershed moment, when the naturalism of the eighteenth century paved the way for legal positivism in the nineteenth and twentieth centuries. Intellectual historians and legal theorists have generally hailed Vattel as the truly decisive break from the earlier tradition of jurisprudence associated with Gentili and Grotius. The natural law framework of his predecessors relied on universally recognizable principles based in reason, whereas Vattel's emphasis on consent and voluntarism oriented 'international law ... on its positivist career' and infused it with 'wholesome realism.'[1] His work is widely seen as one of the first to 'elevate positive law as the basis for a nation's duties under international law' and prepare 'the ground for the era of uninhibited positivism,' although its 'principles became accepted only in the nineteenth century.'[2] Detached from the naturalism from Grotius and Pufendorf, Vattel is still considered formative in the evolution of legal positivism.

The view of Vattel's positivist orientation persisted in the twentieth century with the revised English translation of the *Law of Nations*. The legal scholars, associated with the Carnegie Institute of Washington around World War I, included the work in a series of translations of classics on the laws of war and

[1] Wolfgang Friedmann, *Legal Theory* (London, 1949), 116; C. van Vollenhoven, *The Three Stages in the Evolution of the Law of Nations* (The Hague, 1919), 27, respectively.

[2] Jules Lobel, 'The limits of constitutional power: Conflicts between foreign policy and international law', *Virginia Law Review* 71.7 (1985), 1113; Leo Gross, 'The peace of westphalia, 1648–1948', *The American Journal of International Law* 42.1 (1948), 36; Ronen Palan, 'Tax havens and the commercialization of state sovereignty', *International Organization* 56.1 (2002), 165, ff. 64, respectively.

peace.[3] Subsequent generations of scholars continued to characterize Vattel as laying the ground for positivism: in their attempt to 'uncover' the positivist turn in the history of international law, they saw him as contributing to the deepening gulf between natural law and positivism. His reception has tended to emphasize the social construction of international norms, rather than their derivation from natural law. In his definitive study of war, Quincy Wright even concludes that Vattel 'adhered to the atomistic theory which holds that international law is *merely* a series of contracts between wholly independent states.'[4] Interpreters have been less interested in the question of how the law of nature informs the Vattelian model of the international system and subsequently focused on its contractual scope.[5] One influential study of the history of the law of nations asserts that 'the survival of Vattel's influence' in the early twentieth century 'has been a disaster for international law ... by cutting the frail moorings which bound international law to any sound principle of obligation he did it an injury which has not yet been repaired.'[6] The 'inconsistencies' between the sources of nature and of consent, some have argued, have been the very reason he has appealed to scholars of international law, which itself is a field that straddles the line between unwritten norms and consensual customs.[7]

Part of the reason why the reception of Vattel as a naturalist or a positivist has been so contested has to do less with 'inconsistencies' in his own writing and more with external debates about the status of law among nations, in which he was co-opted. His authority has remained preeminent, particularly in debates over the meaning of the – misleadingly and anachronistically termed – 'Westphalian' model of sovereignty in the evolution of international law, and whether we should see the law as simply a function of social practices, as positivists do, or that law has a moral element at its very core, as naturalists believe. Naturalism and positivism (law should be described *as it is* as opposed to *what it should be*) have subsequently emerged as major competing approaches to sources of international law, in which Vattel has been received as a champion on either side, depending on how he fits in already

3 Emer de Vattel, 'The Law of Nations' [1758], in James Brown Scott (ed.), *Classic of International Law* (Washington, DC, 1916).

4 Quincy Wright, *A Study of War* (Chicago, 1964 [1942]), 230.

5 For a critique of these interpretations, see Theodore Christov, *Before Anarchy: Hobbes and His Followers in Modern International Thought* (Cambridge, 2015), 234–268.

6 J. L. Brierly, *The Law of Nations: An Introduction to the International Law of Peace* (Oxford, 1963), 40.

7 Stephane Beaulac, 'Emer de Vattel and the externalization of sovereignty', *Journal of the History of International Law* 5 (2003), 237–292.

established discourses: naturalism was the dominant jurisprudential thought of the Enlightenment, whereas positivism supplanted it later in the nineteenth century.

This chapter reassesses such a linear transition narrative from naturalism to positivism by tracing the reception and use of Vattel, particularly in the international law literature and practice. It argues, first, that the ambiguities of Vattel's' position on international intervention anticipate our own puzzle about intervention and, second, that his writing may also offer one possible corrective to the dominant view of formal sovereign equality. By tracing his reception since the nineteenth century, the chapter examines three major themes in the field of international law that have not only made use of Vattel but have also been defined by his lasting legacy. The first theme, the equality of states, argues how Vattel's legacy influenced the equivalence between sovereignty and equality in international law, which, while lofty in theory, has remained a tool of submission in the hands of the more powerful states. Migration across borders forms the second theme, which examines the movement of people in a world of states. Vattel's defense of the primacy of self-determination has been largely used instrumentally to establish the right to exclude those described as 'outsiders.' International intervention, the third and final theme, focuses on the ambivalent stature of Vattel in the history of just war theories and lays out the conditions for when states may intervene in the domestic sovereignty of another state. It concludes that as long as we are prepared to radically re-envision the firmly established Vattelian framework of equal state sovereignty (which has sometimes served normatively but hardly ever descriptively), we may be able to address the entrenched power imbalance in institutionalized global political and economic structures (by using some of Vattel's own prescriptions). The changing reception of Vattel's *Law of Nations* (*Droit des Gens*) of 1758 over the course of the past two centuries illustrates his enduring authoritative status not only in the academic community but also in the jurisprudential practice of lawyers. A re-evaluation of the use and misuse of his core views may help us understand some of the limitations of – what has come to be known today as – the Vattelian international system. It also raises some serious questions about the authoritative status of central concepts we have come to take for granted in international legal thought and practice and about the ambiguous status of reception more generally.

SOVEREIGN EQUALITY

Contemporary debates about the normative concept of state sovereignty have inherited a uniquely Vattelian tension between *de jure* equality of sovereign standing and *de facto* inequality of power imbalance. The Janus-faced feature of sovereignty, bearing the opposing aspects of equality and inequality at the same time, has come to define the central ingredient of modern statehood. The United Nations 'Organization is based on the principle of the sovereign equality of all its Members,' as Article 2(1) of the UN Charter stipulates, and its reference in international law has kept the normative vitality of sovereign equality to the present day. The value of the norm, however, is particularly dubious from the point of view of the more powerful states, as the history of international relations has shown. Few scholars and practitioners of international law would disagree on regarding Vattel as the originator of the idea of sovereign equality, but almost universally they all diverge in their interpretations of what he took that to mean and how we should receive these interpretations.

A major strand of scholarly consensus holds that Vattel 'began to elevate positive law as the basis for a nation's duties under international law' and 'prepared the ground for the era of uninhibited positivism,' although its 'principles became accepted only in the nineteenth century.'[8] His emphasis on 'the independence rather than the interdependence of states,' reads the Introduction to the *Classics of International Law* commissioned by the Carnegie Institution of Washington in 1916, transformed the natural law of duties and obligation into an 'international law of political liberty.'[9] Similarly, generations of international legal thinkers over the last century read Vattel as highly ambiguous, who skillfully 'disguised his evil intentions through words of sublime charity' despite his defense of sovereign equality.[10] Rather than read him as a critic, these thinkers instead regard him as a defender of any potential power imbalance in the international system, and one side effect of these interpretations is that sovereign equality serves as a mere fig leaf concealing a basic imbalance among states. Despite Vattel's own defense of state equality, the idea that not all states were created equal (or at least, not equal in all respects) took a life of its own, and various misinterpretations (and in

[8] Jules Lobel, 'The limits of constitutional power: Conflicts between foreign policy and international law', *Virginia Law Review* 71.7 (1985), 1113; Leo Gross, 'The peace of westphalia, 1648–1948', *The American Journal of International Law* 42.1 (1948), 36; Ronen Palan, 'Tax havens and the commercialization of state sovereignty', *International Organization* 56.1 (2002), 165, ff. 64, respectively.

[9] Albert Lapradelle, 'Introduction' to Emer de Vattel, *Law of Nations* [1758] (Washington, DC, 1916), lv.

[10] C. van Vollenhoven, *The Three Stages in the Evolution of the Law of Nations* (The Hague, 1919), 27.

some cases, repudiations) of juridical equality have emerged over the last century and a half.[11]

Georg Friedrich von Martens, a German jurist and one of the earliest leading authorities in the early nineteenth century, endorsed Vattel's view in his multi-volume work published at the turn of that century.[12] 'Vattel regarded states as equal by nature because they were composed of men who were equal by nature,' he argued, 'and consequently could be considered as so many free persons living in a state of nature.' The idea of sovereign equality rested on the analogy between persons and states in a state of nature, which Vattel himself invoked throughout his *Laws of Nations*. 'Since men are by nature equal, and their individual rights and obligations the same, as coming equally from nature,' he asserted, 'Nations, which are composed of men and may be regarded as so many free persons living together in a state of nature, are by nature equal and hold from nature the same obligations and the same rights' (*LN*, I-XI). The relative strength or weakness of a state makes no difference in its juridical status internationally, and a dwarf is as much a person as a giant is, as Vattel famously claimed.

The essential analogy between the state of nature and the international arena lies at the heart of Vattel's project: his natural persons *are* indeed states, who exhibit the central features we associate with nation states. As artificial persons, states acquire the moral status of free and autonomous natural persons, whose obligations to other sovereign states are merely derivative of the duties they owe to themselves. Persons, whether natural or artificial, are virtually indistinguishable with respect to their juridical standing in a domain without an overarching international authority, and for that reason they are both sovereign *and* equal. To understand how states stand in relation to one another, we only seemingly need to reflect on how individuals themselves interact outside politics, with the requisite qualification that – and Vattel insisted on this point – such an analogy between persons and states falls short of the creation of a world state. What enabled the conjunction of 'equality' and 'sovereignty' was the application of the analogy to the realm of international relations, particularly in the first half of the nineteenth century, and the invocation of Vattel in the growing literature on international law, in the second half of that century, firmly established his authority on the subject.

[11] Hans Kelsen, a prominent legal positivist, without mentioning Vattel by name, argued that 'equality does not mean equality of duties and rights,' as Vattel had formulated them, 'but rather equality of capacity for duties and rights': see Hans Kelsen, 'The Principle of Sovereign Equality of States as a Basis for International Organization', *The Yale Law Journal* 53.2 (1944), 207–220 at 209.

[12] Georg Friedrich von Martens, *Recueil des traits* (Göttingen, 1791–1801).

'The equality of states,' according to one influential account of the concept's history, 'came down to the nineteenth century grounded upon the natural law, the state of nature, natural equality, and the analogy [between persons and states].'[13]

The last three decades of the nineteenth century saw a proliferation of textbooks on a new discipline of – what would come to be called – international law. The authority of Vattel in support of the discipline's basic tenets was quickly established, and his work was used 'to justify and give conclusiveness and force to statements as to the proper conduct of a state in its international relations.'[14] As law schools in the United States began to emerge in the nineteenth century, intellectual debates over the nature of juridical equality of states entered the legal academy and university faculty used Vattel in their syllabi as the 'chief basis of lectures on the law of nature and nations.'[15] As a chief contributor to American jurisprudence, whose work was heavily used in law school curricula, John Norton Pomeroy opened his major work on international law (written in the immediate aftermath of the Civil War in the United States) with long quotations from Vattel (followed by no fewer than forty references to him throughout the book).[16] Vattel was quickly being turned into a shorthand for an entire way of thinking about state sovereignty that gained much prominence in the first two decades of the twentieth century.

The authority of Vattel was further widened in debates over transformations of the very concept and practice of sovereignty in the twentieth century, particularly around the time of the founding of the League of Nations. The birth of sovereign equality as a distinct juridical category, infused with a Vattelian pedigree, unleashed a rich discourse, specifically, on the legal scope of sovereignty and the nature of world politics, more generally. How can the practice of sovereignty be accommodated in a world of international institutions? The Westphalian model of sovereignty – anachronistically and rather inaccurately used – with its rigid view of Vattelian pedigree as absolute and infringeable has in fact done more damage to those 'in need' than any tangible good. That view of sovereignty – as juridical equality – with Vattel as its champion, has come to dominate international affairs globally.

[13] Edwin DeWitt Dickinson, *The Equality of States in International Law* (Cambridge, MA, 1920), 99.

[14] Charles G. Fenwick, 'The authority of Vattel', *The American Political Science Review* 7.3 (1913), 395–410, at 395.

[15] Anna Haddow, *Political Science in American Colleges and Universities, 1636–1900* (New York, 1939), 74.

[16] John Norton Pomeroy, *Lectures on International Law in Time of Peace* (Boston, 1886).

The renowned German jurist Lassa Oppenheim turned to Vattel in his 1905–1906 treatise on international law and relied on his authority in an extensive section.[17] Borrowing from Vattel, Oppenheim elaborated an international jurisprudence based on specific agreements and customs among nations rather than on theoretical prescriptions. Although he emphasized the supremacy of national laws and national sovereignty over international law, he came to recognize the need for the League of Nations, especially in the aftermath of World War I. While broad support for sovereign equality of the kind defended by Vattel had been in place at the turn of the twentieth century, there was much less agreement over its precise meaning and practice. Oppenheim was conceptually indebted to Vattel for treating sovereignty as equality only in the legal, rather than the political sense of it. The balance of power was merely a description of the reality of international politics and Oppenheim was not committed to sovereignty of power.[18] Nevertheless, the Vattelian principle of sovereign equality had already started its firm grounding in the international legal system. Through its written constitution, the League of Nations acquired an organized status and came to be seen as possessing some kind of legal personality. As a community of self-governing political entities, the organizing principle behind the League of Nations allowed for the idea of legal personhood to be later applied to sovereign states.

In an influential study on the prime characteristics of sovereign statehood, W. W. Willoughby formulated an essential analogy between a legal person and a sovereign state, where every state 'may be regarded as a person in the legal sense of the word.' His juristic conception of the state with a will that is 'legally supreme' made a state's 'juristic nature' coterminous with sovereign authority domestically and states' 'equality of status' as 'generally accepted' internationally. Sovereignty and equality could now be regarded as two sides of the same coin, and Willoughby essentially paraphrased Vattel almost word for word without any attribution: 'sovereignty has no connection whatever with material or physical power … [and] is an attribute of the smallest and weakest of states as fully as it is of the mightiest empire.'[19] The intellectual grounds for the equivalence of sovereignty and equality had been laid, and from then on Vattel's doctrine of state equality – with or without attribution to his metaphor that 'A *dwarf* is as much a man as a *giant*; a small republic is not

[17] Lassa Oppenheim, *International Law: A Treatise* (New York, 1905), Vol. I, 196–203.

[18] Benedict Kingsbury, 'Sovereignty and inequality', *European Journal of International Law* 9.4 (1998), 599–625.

[19] W. W. Willoughby, 'The juristic conception of the state', *American Political Science Review* 12 (1918), 192–208, at 194, 193, and 202.

less a sovereign state than the most powerful kingdom' – has come to dominate discussions on sovereign equality in international law. 'Among later publicists,' a major historian of international law wrote around the time of the Treaty of Versailles, 'we find no one who bases his derivation and definition of the doctrine of equality so firmly as Vattel' on the basic political concept of 'the social compact.'[20] The equality of citizens before the law in a state serves as the basis on which sovereign equality can then be conceptualized as the condition where every sovereign state possesses the same legal rights as any other sovereign state in international law.

MIGRATION ACROSS BORDERS

Now that he has established a state's basic right to self-determination as a right to self-rule domestically, Vattel considers the role sovereign states play in the regulation of the movement of people. The basic premise is that, in times of peace, '[e]very man has a right to quit his country, in order to settle in any other, when by that step he does not endanger the welfare of his country.' The freedom of emigration is derived from the voluntary nature of the social contract between a citizen and a state, so that in cases where a state fails in its obligations 'a citizen has an absolute right to renounce his country, and abandon it entirely' (*LN*, I-XIX-223). The freedom of emigration is universal and based in the laws of nature, rather than secured through any positive law. The admission of emigres, in contrast, is at the discretion of the country host and limited by noninterference with its welfare.

Are there any circumstances that might justify states in restricting the free movement of people across international borders? While the modern debate over restrictions on migration has featured extensively since at least the end of the nineteenth century (*LN*, I-XIX-220), it has oscillated variously between what makes international migration morally permissible and the practical role of state authority in granting such permissibility. Regardless of whether the open borders or restrictive borders arguments prevail, three distinct questions have guided the debate: about whether border restrictions are permissible in the first place, about under what circumstances they are permissible, and about who gets to decide which are permissible. In all cases, these discussions revolve around the regulatory powers of states in the movement of people as,

20 S. W. Armstrong, 'The doctrine of the equality of nations in international law and the relation of the doctrine to the treaty of Versailles', *The American Journal of International Law* 14.4 (1920), 540–564, at 542.

prior to Vattel, control of immigration had not been considered as the exclusive right of states.

While most public debates about immigration today axiomatically grant the assumption that it is a state's prerogative to control its own borders, the view that immigration control proceeds from state sovereignty is just over a century-old and owes its justification to arguments first advanced by Vattel. Some of the formative decisions in early American immigration jurisprudence to accord discretion to states in excluding foreigners were informed by his views.[21] 'Every nation has the power, as inherent in sovereignty, and essential to self-preservation,' the United States Supreme Court declared in 1892, 'to forbid the entrance of foreigners within its dominion, or to admit them only in such cases and upon such conditions as it may see fit to prescribe.'[22] Responding to challenges of the constitutionality of some of the provisions of the Immigration Act of 1891, the following year the Supreme Court sided against the Japanese litigant Nishimura Ekiu and decided in favor of the government in upholding the law. Passed in 1882 as a way to add restrictions to – what had been until 1875 – an essentially unrestricted immigration to the United States, the Chinese Exclusion Act became the first immigration law that excluded an entire group of nationals based on their ethnic origin. In rejecting open borders claims in favor of state-sanctioned limitations, the Supreme Court cited the work of Vattel on the state's right to decide whom to admit based on the long-standing influence that his canonical authority had acquired even prior to the adoption of the Declaration of Independence.[23]

As the leading thinker featured in the earliest immigration law cases in US history, Vattel was widely considered 'the favorite authority in American theory of international law' that continued well into the nineteenth century.[24] Such a wide acceptance should not be seen as surprising from the position of a large international actor, such as the United States, seeking to accommodate its nascent immigration law to emerging practices of international law and establish its dominant place on the global stage. In asserting that 'the rights of

[21] Sarah Song, 'Why does the state have the right to control immigration?', in Jack Knight (ed.), *NOMOS LVII: Migration, Emigration, and Immigration* (New York, 2017), 3–50.

[22] *Nishimura Ekiu* v. *United States*, 142 U.S. 651, 659 (1892), citing Emer de Vattel, *Les droit des gens* [*LN*, II-VII-94 and II-VIII-100].

[23] Theodore Christov, 'Emer de Vattel's *Law of Nations* in America's independence', in Glenn Moots and Phillip Hamilton (eds.), *Justifying Revolution: Law, Virtue, and Violence in the American War of Independence* (Norman, OK, 2018), 64-82; William Ossipow and Dominik Gerber, 'The reception of Vattel's Law of Nations in the American colonies: From James Otis and John Adams to the Declaration of Independence', *American Journal of Legal History* 57 (2017), 521–555.

[24] Arthur Nussbaum, A *Concise History of the Law of Nations* (New York, 1954), 160–161.

domain and sovereignty' determine that the 'sovereign may forbid the entrance of his territory either to foreigners in general, or in particular cases, or to certain persons ... as they may think it advantageous to the state,' the Supreme Court relied heavily on Vattel – reading him both impartially and selectively – to articulate an entirely novel position.[25] It essentially set a precedent by expanding the proper powers of the federal government under the Constitution when it comes to immigration control. The power to exclude foreigners was firmly established as plenary and neither local nor state government could claim what now firmly falls under the jurisdiction of the federal government.

It is hardly incidental that the Supreme Court chose to invoke Vattel as a major authority in the legislation of immigration powers, particularly in a case involving immigration from China. In that same paragraph, cited by the Supreme Court, Vattel approvingly makes an example of the Chinese, who 'forbade all people entering the empire' for fear that 'intercourse with strangers' would 'corrupt the manners of a nation, and impair the maxims of a wise but singular government.' Such a prohibition 'was not at all inconsistent with justice' but even laudatory for its approach to 'the duties of humanity,' which 'permit us ... to prefer ourselves to others' (*LN*, II-VII-94). The reception of Vattel by the Court was not merely political in its use to solve a specifically political problem (how to establish Congress's power to control immigration). It was also moral in its appeal to 'justice' and 'humane assistance' in providing the state with a normative justification to control immigration. In following his predecessor Christian Wolff, Vattel simply applied the law of nature of individuals in the state of nature to that of states: such an analogy conferred the state with the status of moral personhood endowed with 'an understanding and a will of which it makes use for the conduct of its affairs' (*LN*, I-IV-49).

In defending the federal government's right to decide whom to admit inside its borders, the Supreme Court closely followed Vattel's distinction between a state's decision to admit a foreigner and the moral constraints on such a decision. His insistence that the presence of state authority does not entail the absence of moral consideration and constraint introduced the basic differentiation between perfect and imperfect rights of states. Throughout the twentieth century, the distinction would remain central to debates over the state's authority to control immigration and the limits, if any, on the

[25] *Nishimura Ekiu* v. *United States*, 142 U.S. 659 (1892), citing Emer de Vattel, *The Law of Nations*, II-VII-94.

exercise of that authority.[26] While the right to admit is 'necessary and perfect in the general view of it,' it remains 'imperfect with respect to each particular country' and 'every nation has a right to refuse admitting a foreigner into her territory, when he cannot enter it without exposing the nation to evident danger, or doing her a manifest injury' (*LN*, I-XIX-230). The changing scope of moral permissibility of the United States federal government's power to exclude foreigners has continued all the way to the present day,[27] but the terms of the debate were already set in motion with the reception of Vattel's argument.

The proposition that a state has a plenary right to exclude foreigners is of uniquely late nineteenth-century US origins. Not incidentally, it arose during a time when the westward dispossession of native lands had been mostly completed and the country faced a wave of immigration from Europe. As a means to provide for greater judicial latitude in a largely new legal terrain, the use of Vattel by the courts made sense, even more so in light of positivist tendencies of particularizing law to sovereign commands. In contrast, European and Latin American jurists – who also made extensive references to Vattel – have largely sought to distance themselves from the US's exclusionary proposition and assert the principles of interdependence and freedom of movement instead.[28]

Moreover, the use of Vattel in the US jurisprudential tradition has tended to obscure his distinction between rights and duties of states and instead focused on the former at the expense of dismissing the latter. His reception has been generally less favorable with respect to the observance of their duties, which may lead to states' abuse of an external right and amount to a breach of law.[29] Even if the sovereign yields the inherent power to exclude, they also need to decide what principles (humanitarian, for example) may limit such an

[26] Some landmark Supreme Court cases include the following: *Arizona* v. *United States*, 567 US (2012) ('That power to exclude has long been recognized as inherent in sovereignty'); *Landon* v. *Plasencia*, 459 U.S. 21, 32 (1982) ('[T]he power to admit or exclude aliens is a sovereign prerogative'); *Fiallo* v. *Bell*, 430 U.S. 787, 792 (1977) ('Our cases "have long recognized the power to expel or exclude aliens as a fundamental sovereign attribute ..."'); *Harisiades* v. *Shaughnessy*, 342 U.S. 580, 588–589 (1952) (the 'traditional power of the Nation over the alien' is 'a power inherent in every sovereign state').

[27] The most recent case concerned two successive executive orders (the second revising and replacing the first) issued by President Donald Trump that, in their revised form, seek to deny entry temporarily to foreign nationals from six predominantly Muslim countries and to all refugees, subject to limited waiver.

[28] For a detailed discussion, see Richard Plender, *International Migration Law* (Leiden, 1972).

[29] James Nafziger, 'The general admission of aliens under international law', *American Journal of International Law* 77.4 (1983), 804–847.

exclusion, and the US tradition stands out as having been less receptive of Vattel's qualified duty to admit some foreigners on grounds consistent with general obligations to humanity.

Over the course of the twentieth century, international law further qualified the power to control immigration by granting authority over the right to exclude foreigners to states themselves (and by affirming the special case of diplomats, for example, who not only retain immunity in the host country but also whose rights as 'ministers,' as Vattel describes, 'are to be held sacred and inviolable among all nations' (*LN*, IV-VII-81)). The invocation of Vattel, in Europe and beyond, was seen largely as a source to support not only states' rights to exclude foreigners, but also to highlight their special duties towards migrants and exiles.[30] Early American jurisprudence, in contrast, established the federal government's immigration power and continued to pave the way for far stricter juridical grounds for exclusion – firmly solidified in the national origin quota of the Immigration Act of 1924 – that persisted in the United States all the way until the passage of the Immigration and Nationality Act in 1965, which removed *de facto* origin and ethnicity from the US immigration policy.

Curiously, the reception of Vattel in the twentieth century – in Supreme Court citations, for example – diminished in comparison to the nineteenth century but the essentially dualistic use of his writings remained broadly unchanged.[31] Depending on judicial preference, his writings were invoked either in support of a strict immigration policy designed to exclude outsiders, or in favor of espousing their admission not merely as an obligation but, above all, as a strict duty. That states have 'common duties to humanity' alongside 'the care of self-preservation' would become a hallmark of Vattel's thought and open up a firm distinction, and a permanent dissonance, between the outside and the inside (*LN*, II-I-18; II-IV-49). One version of the tension between outsiders and insiders – those who prize inclusion and those who privilege exclusion – can be seen in the moral and political dilemmas of international intervention.

INTERNATIONAL INTERVENTION

Vattel's predecessors Gentili and Grotius were some of the first to sanction warfare in the name of protecting 'innocent Subjects' against 'wicked Men'

30 Vincent Chetail, 'Sovereignty and migration in the doctrine of the law of nations: An intellectual history of hospitality from Vitoria to Vattel', *European Journal of International Law* 27.4 (2016), 901–922.

31 Brian Richardson, 'The use of Vattel in the American law of nations', *The American Journal of International Law* 106.3 (2012), 547–571.

and punishing and restraining the wrongdoing of a state.[32] While their arguments operated from the 'primitive notion' of 'a single fabric of morality and law' that allowed for a broadly interventionist policy, the *Law of Nations* was arguably the first major work that introduced the recognizably modern terms of the debate about intervention.[33] Under what conditions, if any, does an international system of legally equal and independent sovereign states allow for any interference from outside, so that they may still fulfil their duties of humanity and mutual assistance?

Vattel's response to this question is itself fraught with tension and for that reason his legacy throughout the nineteenth and twentieth centuries has similarly been received as double-faced: on the one hand, his unambiguously firm commitment to non-intervention, and his sanctioning, on the other hand, of 'a mischievous nation' that violates the law of nations.[34] While equal sovereignty demands upholding the principle of inviolability and non-intervention, such a principle may seem to be compromised under certain conditions. By defending a right of punishment in cases of 'grievous' violations of the law of nature and nations as well as a right to assist foreign subjects 'injured' by their rulers, Vattel's model of equal and inviolable sovereignty becomes potentially subject to external scrutiny and appears strikingly close to Grotius's.[35] Such a link should not be seen as surprising, after all, in light of the imperial expansionist policies of the time aimed at advancing European interests overseas.[36] What does seem undeniable is that Vattel set the stage for one of the most extensive discussions of international intervention long before such debates blossomed in the middle of the twentieth century and continue to be debated to the present day. His view of the equal sovereignty of states has been incorporated into the traditional model of Westphalian sovereignty to produce a 'Vattelian/Westphalian sovereignty' that closely captures not only equality, but also externalization and inviolability of sovereignty.[37]

[32] Hugo Grotius, *The Rights of War and Peace*, ed. Richard Tuck (Indianapolis, IN), 1162.

[33] David Kennedy, 'Primitive legal scholarship', *Harvard International Law Journal* 27.1 (1986), 1–98, at 9.

[34] Emer de Vattel, *Les droit des gens* [*The Law of Nations*] (1758), ed. Béla Kapossy and Richard Whatmore (Indianapolis, 2008), V.70.

[35] *LN*, III-I-4 and I-II-19. For a comparison with Grotius, see Simone Zurbuchen, 'Vattel's *Law of Nations* and the principle of non-intervention', *Grotiana* 31.1 (2010), 69–84.

[36] Edward Keene, *Beyond International Anarchy: Grotius, Colonialism and Order in World Politics* (Cambridge, 2002).

[37] Stephen Krasner, 'The durability of organized hypocrisy', in Quentin Skinner and Hent Kalmo (eds.), *Sovereignty in Fragments: The Past, Present and Future of a Contested Concept* (Cambridge, 2010), 96–113, at 97.

At the heart of the long-standing debate on intervention lies the dualism between the inviolability of sovereignty, on the one hand, and its infringement on the other, that *The Law of Nations* helped formulate in the first place. The terms of such a dualism may not need to be seen so stark and oppositional as some have suggested but may, in fact, admit of a softer contrast. If state sovereignty is absolute and unconditional, then it can be overruled through absolute intervention ('hard' dualists), and alternatively, if we admit pre-existing asymmetries of sovereignty, then the very meaning of intervention admits degrees ('soft' dualists). Although the reception of Vattel's view of international intervention has varied widely, two distinct clusters of interpretations can be broadly identified. The first one champions him as a 'hard' interventionist, where a weakening of domestic sovereignty – through internal rebellion, insurrection, or civil war – demands outside intervention, whereas the second cluster towers him as a 'soft' interventionist, where weakened domestic sovereignty – through global structural political and economic inequalities – make intervention harder to justify. The difference between these two approaches also reflects two other distinctions: one consists in the high or low degree of external scrutinizing of sovereignty (what some have called the externalization of sovereignty)[38] and the other in the high or low level of exercising, what Vattel calls our 'offices of humanity between nations' (*LN*, II-I-1).

The legacy of Vattel, particularly in the period of decolonization since the mid-twentieth century, has tended to adopt the 'hard-dualism' interpretation of a sharp opposition: because states are viewed as perfectly equal in their attainment of sovereignty, any disturbance in such an equilibrium is seen as unstable for everyone else and demands restorative efforts. On this highly dualistic account, states are either 'failed,' if they fall short of any of the requirements for external sovereignty that would allow them to elevate their status to full equality, or 'successful,' if they fit perfectly into the established practice of full and equal sovereignty. International intervention here is limited to the basic Vattelian principle that 'every nation is obliged to perform the duty of self-preservation' and when it fails to do so, others have an imperfect duty to step in (*LN*, II-I-2). Vattel's endorsement of a muscular foreign policy that allows for more powerful states to interfere with states in need of political or economic assistance (particularly those emerging from an internal conflict such as a civil war), continues to exercise great influence on the global stage today. His standard reception in neoliberal thought calls for

[38] Stephane Beaulac, 'Emer de Vattel and the externalization of sovereignty', *Journal of the History of International Law* 5.2 (2003), 237–292.

interstate dynamics that perpetuate asymmetries of power and potentially exacerbate an already unequal global order.[39]

Seen as an apologist for international intervention and liberal paternalism, Vattel contributes to an approach in international affairs that privileges external interference for the sake of establishing domination and dependence of powerful states over politically and economically disadvantaged ones and fits comfortably into a discourse of intervention centered on the preservation of 'untrammeled sovereignty.'[40] His championing within a 'good governance' discourse that considers 'outlaw' states, which do not conform to established forms of economic practices (as set by international institutions like the World Bank and the IMF), has been used to advance the rhetoric of a 'right to globalization.'[41] The principle of state sovereignty, as promoted by Vattel's 'perfect equality of rights between independent nations,' has become the great equalizer across the globe in a post-1945 race to attain external recognition in a world of states (*LN*, II-1-3). For better or worse, Vattel has come to be used in wide-ranging discourses about the principle of sovereign equality and its violations in ways that he himself would have not anticipated.

But the line between full (*de jure*) and semi (*de facto*) equality can be rather fictional and drawn by the most powerful players precisely as a tool for creating inequity among states as a precondition for external interference. The rush to sovereign statehood, or 'contagion of sovereignty,' slow at first and limited to a few great powers in the early nineteenth century, accelerated dramatically to spread across the newly decolonized world of Africa and Asia in the second half of the twentieth century.[42] The quest for an equal standing in juridical statehood, propelled by the disintegration of former European empires, increasingly altered the sovereignty landscape: some of the requisite conditions for self-determination remained either unfulfilled or simply were interfered with by external agents (whether global financial institutions or powerful states) for the 'betterment' of newly emerging states. A state should 'give its aid when the occasion arises, and according to its ability,' and Vattel endorsed benign tutelage as one way of doing so, so that 'a learned nation, if applied to

39 Jennifer Pitts, 'Intervention and sovereign equality: Legacies of Vattel', in Stefano Recchia and Jennifer Welsh (eds.), *Just and Unjust Military Intervention: European Thinkers from Vitoria to Mill* (Cambridge, 2013), 132–153.

40 Andrew Hurrell, 'Vattel: Pluralism and its limits', in Ian Clarke and Iver B. Neumann (eds.), *Classical Theories of International Relations* (New York, 1996), 233–255.

41 Antony Anghie, *Imperialism, Sovereignty and the Making of International Law* (Cambridge, 2004), 245–272, at 270.

42 David Armitage, 'The contagion of sovereignty: Declarations of independence since 1776', *South African Historical Journal* 52 (2005), 1–18.

for masters and teachers in the sciences, by another nation desirious of shaking off its native barbarism, ought not to refuse such a request.' (*LN*, II-1-6). Intervention took a significantly less overt form and one which Vattel could have hardly predicted at the time of glaring imperial subjugation.

The decolonizing momentum of the latter twentieth century prioritized external recognition from outside over internal consolidation. Domestic sovereignty, consequently, may even be compromised at the expense of achieving an equal status in the international community. Increasingly, the question of whether a people has actually been consolidated internally has taken backstage, and the drive for sovereign equality, central to Vattel's thinking, propelled the act of external recognition to serve as a ticket of admission to the international community. 'Quasi-States' were duly engendered as sovereign alongside a world of 'States,' the venerable creation of the post-Westphalian order.[43] A differentiated mosaic of tiered sovereign states justified its existence by couching assertions of statehood in a universality of equal sovereign exercise as opposed to a sustained capacity for self-governance. Rather than recognize a pre-existing hierarchical structural inequality between the first and the third worlds, states have been granted juridical protection and an increased accommodation of highly diverse members. 'A dwarf is as much a man as a giant is,' Vattel famously claimed, and 'a small republic is no less a sovereign state than the most powerful kingdom' (*LN*, prelim. 75). Regarded as inseparable ever since Thomas Hobbes first formulated their union, state and sovereignty have come to be envisioned as distinct, especially since the beginning of the twentieth century.

The uncoupling of sovereignty from the state led to the rethinking of war in the international politics of the mid-twentieth century. The reception of Vattel, especially in the context of the jurisprudence of war, revolved around the question of the legal, rather than moral, status of interstate war.[44] The military defeat of the Nationalist Socialist regime in 1945 confronted thinkers with the question of how to judge the rise and fall of the Third Reich. This was not only a moral and historical but also a legal question that sought to place war in the broader context of international law after two world wars. For Carl Schmitt, who traced the rise and fall of the Eurocentric global order, these recent developments in the practice of international statehood would come to challenge the rigid division between the domestic and the foreign

[43] Robert Jackson, *Quasi-States: Sovereignty, International Relations and the Third World* (Cambridge, 1991).

[44] Lorenzo Cello, 'The legitimacy of international interventions in Vattel's The Law of Nations', *Global Intellectual History* 2 (2017), 1–19.

and to reject the moral status of warfare. In his defense of the European achievement to create the first truly global order of international law, Schmitt praises Vattel's 'marvelous product of human reason': in limiting war to conflicts among sovereign states, Vattel enabled 'the strongest possible rationalization and humanization of war.'[45] Unlike the religious wars and colonial wars of the past, the new type of wars was limited to states which recognized each other as 'lawful enemies.' By removing the principle of just war and defending regular war, as one scholar has noted, Vattel 'formalized the doctrine of war as a morally non-discriminatory conflict.'[46]

The moralizing of war, and the accompanying interventionism as total war in the name of righteousness, has now been contained, and, in the view of German political thinkers engaged in learning from the political legacy of the Enlightenment, it was Vattel who in effect helped civilize war by bracketing it to legal entities.[47] Contrary to previous interpretations of his views on intervention, such as those of Edmund Burke in the eighteenth century, who used Vattel to defend the Glorious Revolution of 1688 as a case of just war, the dominant reading in the twentieth century saw Vattel's critical role in excluding the natural law of morality from international law.[48] The problem of war and foundational violence was removed from questionable discourses of moral right or religious truth, and consequently any justification for intervention would be limited to the international legal sphere. The principle, derived from Vattel, that nobody has a moral right or finality on one's side produced the regulative effect of amoralizing conflict itself and constraining aggression. There can be no such conflict as just war.

In his seminal 1959 study, *Critique and Crisis*, Reinhart Koselleck (Schmitt's own student) relied on Vattel's exclusion of natural law from international politics in order to draw out a distinction between the 'necessary' and the 'voluntary' law of nations. The latter category, which affirmed the conditions that did not limit just war to one side only, was introduced in order to limit the force of the former, which, if maintained by states, would declare

45 Carl Schmitt, *Nomos of the Earth in the International Law of the Jus Publicum Europaeum*, translated by G. L. Ulmen (New York, 2003), 142, 151, respectively.

46 Ian Hunter, 'Vattel's Law of Nations: Diplomatic casuistry for the protestant nation,' *Grotiana* 31 (2010), 108–140, at 134. See also Chapter 7, by Pablo Kalmanovitz.

47 Pablo Kalmanovitz, 'Sovereignty, pluralism, and regular war: Wolff and Vattel's Enlightenment critique of just war', *Political Theory* 46.2 (2017), 1–21. See also Chapter 7, by Pablo Kalmanovitz.

48 On Burke's use of Vattel, see David Armitage, 'Edmund Burke and reason of state', *Journal of the History of Ideas* 61.4 (2000), 617–634.

justice on one side only and lead to endless conflict.[49] Koselleck's reception of Vattel led him to defend the rationalization of war by stripping it from any moral appeals and brought the practice of international law closer to Hobbes's account of it. In broadly following Schmitt's account of how Vattel prioritized political circumstances of moral laws, Koselleck similarly asserted that doing so opened up a political space free from moral judgments. At one point, however, he accused Vattel of 'breaching [his own] principle of non-intervention that was to guarantee the intra-state order.' If a state fails in its function to neutralize internal conflict, 'then it was permissible for other states to violate its sovereignty, if need be.'[50] For Koselleck, Vattel had ultimately violated his own claim to subordinating the moral to the political and compromised the rational basis for non-intervention.[51] In his critical study of just and unjust wars, Michael Walzer similarly concluded that we should read Vattel as the proponent, rather than the opponent of intervention for the sake of maintaining Europe's balance of power.[52] Late twentieth-century receptions of Vattel have generally come to accept his more ambiguous view that, in the end, intervention admits of a more nuanced spectrum, which potentially creates space for a more problematic justification, such as in cases of 'humanitarian' intervention.

CONCLUSION

The turn of the nineteenth century is widely seen in histories of international law as a watershed moment, when the naturalism of the eighteenth century paved the way for positivism in the nineteenth and twentieth centuries. Such a standard understanding of the period tends to see Vattel as central to these developments: his views on how states relate to one another incorporated the natural law discourse of his predecessors while also opened up practical possibilities for the enactment of express agreements and treaty making. This chapter reassesses such a narrative by tracing the question of the scope of the law of nations through the reception and use of Vattel, particularly in the international law literature. 'Vattel's natural law was not part of any substantive

49 Isaac Nakhimovsky, 'Carl Schmitt's Vattel and "The Law of Nations" between Enlightenment and revolution', *Grotiana* 31 (2010), 141–161.

50 Reinhart Koselleck, *Critic and Crisis: Enlightenment and the Pathogenesis of Modern Society* (Cambridge, MA, 1988), 46–47.

51 Ian Hunter has similarly observed that Vattel created a 'bi-level field of judgment': see Ian Hunter, 'Law, war, and casuistry in Vattel's *Jus Gentium*', *Parergon* 28.2 (2011), 87–104, at 93.

52 Michael Walzer, *Just and Unjust Wars: A Moral Argument with Historical Illustrations* [1977] (New York, 2006), 80–81.

tradition of war or peace, statehood, or the international order,' a recent account of his place in international legal history has argued. 'It was all of that at the same time, offering for later jurists an argumentative toolbox.'[53] The changing reception of Vattel's work from the first to the second half of the nineteenth century illustrates not only the increasing professionalization of international lawyers, but also his authoritative status in Europe's imperial expansion. The reception of Vattel throughout the nineteenth and twentieth centuries was wide, especially in the anglophone world, and his legacy in the formation of what has come to be known as international law is unparalleled.[54] His most enduring effect on colonial jurisprudence can be seen in judicial thought of the relations between European and non-European peoples. Vattel's use in modern international law has, similarly, drawn on the ambiguous status of the universality of the law of nations.

FURTHER READING

Beaulac, S., 'Emer de Vattel and the externalization of sovereignty,' *Journal of the History of International Law* 5 (2003), 237–292.

Brierly, J. L., The Law of Nations: An Introduction to the International Law of Peace (Oxford, 1963).

Hunter, I., 'Vattel's Law of Nations: Diplomatic casuistry for the protestant nation', *Grotiana* 31 (2010), 108–140.

Kalmanovitz, P., 'Sovereignty, pluralism, and regular war: Wolff and Vattel's Enlightenment critique of just war,' *Political Theory* 46.2 (2017), 1–21.

Koselleck, R., Critic and Crisis: Enlightenment and the Pathogenesis of Modern Society (Cambridge, MA, 1988).

Nakhimovsky, I., 'Carl Schmitt's Vattel and "The Law of Nations" between Enlightenment and revolution,' *Grotiana* 31 (2010), 141–161.

Schmitt, C., Nomos of the Earth in the International Law of the Jus Publicum Europaeum, translated by G. L. Ulmen (New York, 2003).

53 Martti Koskenniemi, 'What should international legal history become?', in Stefan Kadelbach, Thomas Kleinlein and David Roth-Isigkeit (eds.), *System, Order and International Law. The Early History of International Legal Thought from Machiavelli to Hegel* (Oxford, 2017), 387.

54 More than ten translations of his book in England in the first seven decades after original publication, and an additional eighteen in the United States until the 1870s.

15

Vattel's Reception in International Relations

RICHARD DEVETAK

It should not be hard to make a case for Emer de Vattel's significance to the study of international relations. His *Le Droit des Gens* [*Law of Nations*] (1758) was one of the most influential and popular treatises of international law and diplomacy published in the eighteenth century. It went through multiple editions and was translated into several languages. In addition to becoming something of a diplomat's 'bible' in the nineteenth century, it also had an impact on the thinking of political leaders such as the American founders.[1] One would think that this makes Vattel's writings on the law of nations consequential to a discipline dedicated to understanding international matters of state. But that has not been the case. International Relations (IR) has developed into a highly theoretical discipline in which the history of 'modern international thought' has generally been marginal.[2] To the extent it has featured, it has generally been used instrumentally and selectively. Vattel's name remains a rarity in the stories the discipline of IR tells about its subject and its intellectual development. The names of Machiavelli and Hobbes figure much more prominently, even though much less of their writing was directly concerned with relations between states. Accounting for Vattel's reception in the discipline of IR thus requires an understanding of the discipline's twentieth century development to understand why such a pivotal thinker in the development of international thought has been largely ignored.

1 For the reception and circulation of Vattel's *Law of Nations*, see E. Fiocchi Malaspina, L'Eterno Ritorno del *Droit des Gens* di Emer de Vattel (secc. XIII-XIX): L'impatto sulla Cultura Giuridica in Prospettiva Globale (Frankfurt am Main, 2017).

2 The phrase 'modern international thought' was originally used by M. Wight, *Systems of States*, ed. H. Bull (Leicester, 1977), 72. More recently it has been used by D. Armitage, *Foundations of Modern International Thought* (Cambridge, 2013).

INTERNATIONAL RELATIONS: AN UNRECEPTIVE DISCIPLINE?

Before examining Vattel's reception and influence in IR, a few words on the discipline's twentieth century origins and development and its changing intellectual trends and trajectory are necessary. Since the 1960s, IR has been decisively shaped by the dominance of American social science.[3] It was in this context that something of an Atlantic divide emerged, with the United States showing a stronger preference for the quest to make IR scientific than Britain, where more historical, institutional and interpretive approaches developed in the early twentieth century persisted.[4] It was in the context of this Atlantic divide that the so-called English School of international relations took shape, defending an approach that incorporates history, philosophy and law into a more interpretive theoretical perspective.[5] Though the English School was concerned with developing a theory of international society, it was committed to exploring the 'richness and complexity of modern international thought'.[6] Disciplinary developments in the United States, however, saw a steep decline in engagement with the history of political thought in IR. That shift is well illustrated by the career of one of the most esteemed and influential IR theorists, Kenneth Waltz. His early work engaged with the political thought of Augustine, Spinoza, Rousseau, Kant and others to elaborate rival intellectual approaches to understanding the causes of war.[7] Twenty years later, Waltz adopted a scientific conception of theory based on Lakatosian philosophy of science.[8] Engagement with the history of political thought did not disappear

3 S. Hoffmann, 'An American social science: International relations', *Daedalus* 106.3 (1977), 41–60.

4 For the contemporary defence of 'classical' approaches against 'scientism', see H. Bull, 'International theory: The case for a classical approach', *World Politics* 18.3 (1966), 361–377. On the *methodenstreit* and rise of theory in IR, see R. Devetak, *Critical International Theory: An Intellectual History* (Oxford, 2018), chapter 1. For more general disciplinary histories of IR, see B. Schmidt, 'On the history and historiography of international relations', in W. Carlsnaes, T. Risse and B. A. Simmons (eds), *Handbook of International Relations* (London, 2002); R. Vitalis, *White World Order, Black Power Politics: The Birth of American International Relations* (Ithaca, 2015).

5 The label 'English School' is something of a misnomer given that many of the associated scholars were not English. Hedley Bull and Coral Bell were Australian, Charles Manning was South African and R. J. Vincent was Welsh. For accounts of the English School see T. Dunne, *Inventing International Society: A History of the English School* (London, 1998); A. Linklater and H. Suganami, *The English School of International Relations: A Contemporary Reassessment* (Cambridge, 2006).

6 M. Wight, *Systems of States*, 72.

7 K. Waltz, *Man, the State and War: A Theoretical Analysis* (New York, 1959).

8 K. Waltz, *Theory of International Politics* (New York, 1979), ch. 1 on 'Laws and theories'. Waltz embraced a stance designed to combat the inductivism which, he argued, was incapable of

completely, but it was incidental to the development of law-based explanatory theory. Kuhn's lapidary comment about the development of science applies here: 'science destroys its past',[9] leaving no need for an account of past thinking as it is superseded by purportedly more advanced forms of theoretical knowledge.

The rise of scientific approaches did not prevent renewed engagement with the history of political thought and philosophy. Scholars such as R. B. J. Walker and Andrew Linklater embarked on an effort in the early 1980s to develop critical theories of IR by exploring the intellectual resources of early modern thinkers.[10] While sympathetic to the humanist style of 'traditional' IR theory, exponents of critical international theory were dissatisfied with the state-centric, 'high politics' focus of the discipline and sought to widen its ethical focus and diversify its intellectual resources so as to respond better to the crises and challenges of late modernity.[11]

By the 1990s, the social scientific approaches had evolved to incorporate social constructivism. While constructivist approaches have included a historical sociological dimension, the driving imperative remains a theoretical explanation. The point is to determine the social forces underpinning norms and ideas. As a result, norms and ideas are seen as little more than reflections of underlying social factors or are reified into abstractions that take on life independent of human individuals. But the growth in recent years of 'international intellectual history', to use David Armitage's term, has certainly created more receptive conditions in IR for contextual histories of international thought.[12]

determining 'which [empirical] materials to select and how to arrange them' to form hypotheses or laws (at p.5). Theory building required the theorist to obtain distance from sense experience in order to 'idealize', 'aggregate' and 'abstract'. See also I. Lakatos, *The Methodology of Scientific Research Programs: Philosophical Papers, Volume 1*, ed. J. Worrall and G. Currie (Cambridge, 1978).

9 T. Kuhn, 'Comment', *Comparative Studies in Society and History* 11.4 (1969), 403–412, at 407.

10 For classic statements, see R. B. J. Walker, *Political Theory and the Transformation of World Politics*, World Order Studies Program Occasional Paper No. 8 (Princeton, 1980); A. Linklater, *Men and Citizens in the Theory of International Relations* (London, 1982).

11 See Devetak, *Critical International Theory*.

12 Armitage, *Foundations*, 1. For accounts of contextual intellectual history in IR, see D. Bell, 'Writing the world: Disciplinary history and beyond', *International Affairs* 85.1 (2009), 3–22; L. Cello, 'Taking history seriously in IR: Towards a historicist approach', *Review of International Studies* 44.2 (2018), 236–251; R. Devetak, '"The battle is all there is": Philosophy and history in international relations', *International Relations* 31.3 (2017), 261–281; C. Vergerio, 'Context, reception, and the study of great thinkers in the study of international relations', *International Theory* 11.1 (2019), 110–137.

That said, the English School kept alive an interest in what Martin Wight called 'the intellectual history of the modern European states-system',[13] even if it did so with rather procrustean categories and without the finely tuned methods of contextual intellectual historians. As Hedley Bull remarked, whereas the scientific approach 'began by rejecting the literature of the past', Wight 'began with the resolve to rediscover, to assemble and to categorize' past thought.[14] He did so by delineating three traditions of international thought that he referred to as realism or Machiavellianism, revolutionism or Kantianism and rationalism or Grotianism.[15] The Grotian tradition represented a '*via media*' or '*juste milieu*' between the extremes of *Realpolitik* and revolutionary universalism, allowing for the existence of international society despite a condition of anarchy.[16] Together with Hugo Grotius, Vattel was seen as a progenitor of the theorising of international society's rules, norms and institutions.

The English School's approach to international society combined the humanist disciplines of history, philosophy and law in defence of what they called the 'classical approach'.[17] Though they did not incorporate into their approach the methods of contextual intellectual history we associate with the Cambridge School, they were in no doubt about the importance of intellectual history and relating 'theorists to the circumstances of their time'.[18]

The following section describes the intellectual context in which the English School developed its approach, focusing particularly on its reception of the 'Grotian tradition' of international law that emerged in the early twentieth century. This was not the only intellectual context for the formation of the English School, but it fed into the 'Grotian conception of international

[13] M. Wight, *Systems of States*, 38.

[14] H. Bull, 'Martin Wight and the theory of international relations: The second Martin Wight Memorial Lecture', *British Journal of International Studies* 2.2 (1976), 101–116.

[15] M. Wight, *International Theory: The Three Traditions*, ed. G. Wight and B. Porter (Leicester, 1991). Bull also invoked these three traditions of thought in H. Bull, *The Anarchical Society: A Study of Order in World Politics* (London, 1977), 24–27. For excellent treatments of Wight's oeuvre, see M. Chiaruzzi, *Politica di Potenza nell'età del Leviatano* (Bologna, 2008); and I. Hall, *The International Thought of Martin Wight* (London, 2006). On Wight and Bull's conception of international society in relation to a range of early modern thinkers, see U. Vollerthun, *The Idea of International Society: Erasmus, Vitoria, Gentili, Grotius*, ed. J. L. Richardson (Oxford, 2017).

[16] M. Wight, 'Western values in international relations', in H. Butterfield and M. Wight (eds.), *Diplomatic Investigations: Essays on the Theory of International Politics* (London, 1966), 91.

[17] Bull, 'International theory', 361. See also, M. Forsyth, 'The classical theory of international relations', *Political Studies* 26.3 (1978), 411–416.

[18] H. Bull, 'Natural law and international relations', *British Journal of International Studies* 5.2 (1979), 171–181, at 178.

society' that they saw as part of the intellectual history of the states-system and with which they held an affinity. It was largely through the English School's exploration of ideas informing the analyses and histories of the states-system that Vattel's reception in IR took place. While risking too close an association between Grotius and Vattel, the English School's main concern was to revive a mode of thinking identified with natural law and diplomacy as a *via media* between the poles of realism and idealism.

DEVELOPMENTS IN INTERNATIONAL LAW: THE 'GROTIAN TRADITION'

The English School's treatment of Vattel is framed by debates in early twentieth century international law, particularly by the construction of a Grotian tradition by Cornelis van Vollenhoven and Sir Hersch Lauterpacht. Hedley Bull is explicit in acknowledging the role played by Vollenhoven and Lauterpacht in promoting a Grotian conception of international law.[19] But their thinking was a continuation of earlier developments in international law going back to the mid-nineteenth century.

In the late nineteenth century, as Martti Koskenniemi has shown, international lawyers began to conceive their role as cultivating 'the legal conscience of the civilized world'. This liberal, cosmopolitan and progressive version of international law was at odds with the more conservative, statist and 'positivist' version that emerged in the late eighteenth century, partly in reaction to the French Revolution and Napoleonic Wars. Proponents of the progressive version of international law sought to break with the tradition of positive law associated with Georg Friedrich von Martens because it had failed to dialectically sublate the opposition between facts and norms into a higher legal consciousness.[20]

Across the Atlantic in the first decades of the twentieth century, a similar direction was underway with the influential James Brown Scott. He was instrumental in consolidating a similarly liberal, progressive and historically self-conscious form of international law inspired by the Spanish theologian

[19] H. Bull, 'The Grotian conception of international society', in Butterfield and Wight (eds), *Diplomatic Investigations*, 51–52. On the reception of Grotius in IR, see H. Bull, B. Kingsbury and A. Roberts (eds.), *Hugo Grotius and International Relations* (Oxford, 1990); R. Jeffery, *Hugo Grotius in International Thought* (London, 2006), chapter 4; and E. Keene, 'The reception of Hugo Grotius in international relations theory', *Grotiana* 20/21 (1999/2000), 135–158.

[20] I. Hunter, 'About the dialectical historiography of international law', *Global Intellectual History* 1.1 (2016), 1–32.

and jurist, Francisco de Vitoria, and grafting it onto Herbert Spencer's popular conception of evolutionary growth. Scott made the case for viewing Vitoria, as opposed to Grotius, as the 'founder of international law'. This made sense to Scott because he wanted to link the origins of international law to the 'discovery of America and the recognition of human rights'.[21] But the implications for how international law should be conceived were largely the same as for the Grotians. International law had to find inspiration in a founding thinker who extolled the spirit of a legal and moral conscience against war and unrestrained state sovereignty.

Central to this progressive conception of international law was the analogy between individuals and states. Consistent with metaphysical philosophies of natural law, Scott argued that individuals and states were subject to the same standard of morality. 'The state as a political corporation has no rights of its own. It is merely an agency of the citizens of the state for the execution of their will'.[22] Here Scott's thinking converged with Lauterpacht's argument for the 'essential identity of states and individuals'.[23] The rules governing states were essentially the same as those governing individuals. In this respect, their arguments rested on what Bull called the 'domestic analogy'; the transfer of assumptions about achieving order among individuals in domestic society to the experience of states at the international level.[24] This was a consequence of the claim that 'states *are composed of* individual human beings', not just that 'states *are like* individuals'.[25] The implication is that a single universal morality exists that applies to both individuals and states.

Writing in the aftermath of the Great War, Vollenhoven treated postwar efforts to regulate inter-state relations through law and multilateral institutions as evidence of international law's progressive evolution.[26] The history told in Vollenhoven's *Three Stages in the Evolution of the Law of Nations* grows out of the same dialectical philosophy of history that had become popular since

[21] P. Amorosa, *Rewriting the History of the Law of Nations: How James Brown Scott made Francisco de Vitoria the Founder of International Law* (Oxford, 2019), 8.

[22] J. B. Scott, 'A single standard of morality for the individual and the state', *Proceedings of the American Society of International Law at Its Annual Meeting* 26 (28–30 April 1932), 10–29, at 19.

[23] H. Lauterpacht, 'The Grotian tradition in international law', *British Yearbook of International Law* 23.1 (1946), 1–53, at 26–28.

[24] See H. Bull's original discussions of the 'domestic analogy' in 'Society and anarchy in international relations', in H. Butterfield and M. Wight (eds.), Diplomatic Investigations, 35; and *Anarchical Society*, 46, 49–51. For an extended treatment of the analogy, see H. Suganami, *The Domestic Analogy and World Order Proposals* (Cambridge, 1989).

[25] Lauterpacht, 'The Grotian tradition', 27 (emphasis in original).

[26] C. Vollenhoven, *The Three Stages in the Evolution of the Law of Nations* (Dordrecht, 1919); and C. Vollenhoven, 'Grotius and the study of law', *American Journal of International Law* 19.1 (1925), 1–11.

Hegel and that underpinned developments in late nineteenth-century international law.[27] It was a history in which the Grotian 'spirit' opposed and transcended the Vattelian and could finally be realised after the Great War through establishment of the League of Nations.

Vattel fell foul of Vollenhoven because he defended reason of state, allowing states the right to depart from the necessary law of nations to determine how to deal with a threat to its security.[28] Not unlike Kant, Vollenhoven saw Vattel as an apologist for war and the licentiousness behaviour of states.[29] His *Law of Nations* was, despite its ostensible purpose, counter-productive to international law because of its indecision and flexibility: 'The success of a mother who suffers herself to be bullied by her children; of a schoolmaster who abolishes home-tasks, tells stories and gives a holiday; of a cabinet minister who grants and puts down in the Estimates whatever the members of parliament come to ask of him'.[30]

Vollenhoven presented the evolution of international law as the gradual movement towards Grotius's conception of the law of nations. 'Grotius's spirit', says Vollenhoven, finally resurfaced in August 1914 in response to the onset of war.[31] Central to the Grotian conception of the law of nations was the criminalisation of war based on the just war doctrine of universal justice. Grotius's thought, says Vollenhoven, had become 'incarnate in millions of citizens, in spite of all diplomacy'.[32] Public opinion had now aligned with Grotius, and against Vattel, in denying states the unrestricted right to wage war.[33] In a later article, Vollenhoven observed that 'we have been learning to regard law as a thing of incessant historical development, perhaps of evolution'.[34] The 'hour of Grotius' had finally arrived.[35]

BEYOND THE GROTIAN TRADITION: VATTEL AND THE PLURALIST THEORY OF INTERNATIONAL RELATIONS

Bull's treatment of the 'Grotian tradition' juxtaposed two tendencies within international law: one, which he associated with Grotius and Vollenhoven, he

[27] I. Hunter, 'Dialectical historiography'.

[28] Vollenhoven, *Three Stages*, 31.

[29] I. Kant, 'Perpetual peace: A philosophical sketch', in H. Reiss (ed.), *Kant's Political Writings*, translated by H. B. Nisbet (Cambridge, 1970), 93–130, at 103.

[30] Vollenhoven, *Three Stages*, 33, quoted in Bull, 'Grotian conception', 69.

[31] Vollenhoven, *Three Stages*, 59.

[32] Ibid., 62.

[33] Ibid., 65.

[34] Vollenhoven, 'Grotius and the Study of Law', 6–7.

[35] Vollenhoven, *Three Stages*, 65–66.

called 'solidarism'; the other, which he associated with Vattel and Oppenheim, he called 'pluralism'. Grotians detected a growing consensus among states about the need to restrict the lawful grounds for war in the commitment of multilateral institutions to codify and enforce rules embodying the higher offices of humanity. Solidarists found evidence of the progressive growth in international conscience embodied in the League of Nations Covenant, the Kellogg–Briand Pact, the UN Charter and so on. Underpinning this approach was a conception of law's source in a single universal morality that subjects states to the same morality as applies to individuals and that refuses to regard the domestic and international as distinct spheres of political life. Bull attributed this, in Grotius at least, to 'a medieval residue'; describing him as a midwife standing 'at the birth of international society'.[36]

Pluralists, by contrast, are sceptical of solidarists' claims about the depth of legal and moral consensus among states. They do not deny the existence of international law but believe states 'are capable of agreeing only for certain minimum purposes'.[37] This perspective, 'which Vattel did a great deal to establish', offers:

> a conception of international society founded upon the observation of the actual area of agreement between states ... It seeks not to burden international law with a weight it cannot carry; and to have it leave room for the operation of those political forces, beyond the control of law, on which the existence of international society also depends.[38]

The pluralist conception of international society occupies an ambivalent position in relation to the Grotian tradition. To an extent it stands outside the Grotian tradition by embracing tenets usually associated with realism. On the other, it represents an extension and modification of the Grotian tradition in that it retains a conception of international society against Hobbesian anarchy and Kantian transcendence.[39] In particular, according to Bull, Vattel's pluralist conception of international society represents a tradition of thought that emerged in the eighteenth century in which discourses of natural law were conjoined with diplomacy and the balance of power.[40] Bull's argument that 'international society is unique' due to 'qualities that are

36 Bull, 'Grotian conception', 66.
37 Ibid., 52.
38 Ibid., 69 and 72.
39 Bull, 'Society and anarchy', 39.
40 Ibid., 39.

peculiar to the situation of sovereign states' owes a major debt to Vattel.[41] The law of nations, Vattel (*LN*, prelim. 3) averred, 'is the science which teaches the rights subsisting between nations or states, and the obligations correspondent to those rights'. While natural law theories had long been concerned with specifying rights and duties, it was Vattel (*LN*, prelim. 6) who conceived the law of nations to be a 'distinct science' (*une science particulière*) of relations between states, in other words of the states-system. The rules that applied to states in their interactions could not be straightforwardly deduced from the natural laws applying to individuals.

This was an important dimension of Vattel's thinking for the modern study of IR because it helped to legitimise it as a discipline with its own subject: the states-system or international society. IR could claim to be a field of enquiry separate and distinct from political theory given the latter's conventional focus on the state and society. The basic proposition on which the discipline's existence and identity has rested is that *international* politics are fundamentally different from *domestic* politics; that they have historically yielded different rules and institutions and allowed for different political practices and purposes. While the first Chair and Department of International Politics was established in 1919, doubts persisted into the second half of the century about whether IR constituted an independent discipline.[42] In an article originally published in 1960, Wight provocatively asked, 'why is there no international theory?'[43] Unlike political theory, which he defined as 'speculation about the state' from Plato onwards, international theory, defined as 'speculation about relations between states', lacked a single, substantial body of thought; it was scattered across the writings of classical international lawyers, irenists, Machiavellians, the memoirs of statesmen and the '*parerga*' of political philosophers and historians, Wight lamented. While 'many great minds' had been drawn, 'at the margin of their activities', to consider international relations, '[f]ew political thinkers have made it their business to study the states-system, the diplomatic community itself'.[44] The recovery of Vattel, therefore, as a thinker who made the states-system and its associated diplomatic practices central to his law of nations, might also be considered as part of the broader attempt to carve out a discrete subject matter for a discipline still anxious about its separation from political theory.

41 Ibid., 45. Bull developed this argument further in *Anarchical Society*, chapter 2.

42 M. Kaplan, 'Is international relations a discipline?', *Journal of Politics* 23.3 (1961), 462–476.

43 M. Wight, 'Why is there no international theory?', in Butterfield and Wight (eds.), *Diplomatic Investigations*, 37–54.

44 Ibid., 19–22.

It was in this context, during the 1960s and 1970s, that British IR scholars turned their attention to the history of what was beginning to be called 'international political theory' or what Wight called 'international theory'.[45] In the American discipline at this time a clear divide had emerged between the behaviouralists, who sought to introduce more rigorous scientific methods and techniques, and those like Hans J. Morgenthau, who continued to theorise with intellectual tools formed in humanist disciplines of law, history, philosophy and political theory.[46] On both sides of the Atlantic a common aim among 'traditionalists' was to develop modes of theorising specific to international relations and to build a canon of classic texts and thinkers. Despite training in jurisprudence and political philosophy, Morgenthau and other German émigrés paid surprisingly little attention to natural law theories. The British, on the other hand, were more willing to explore natural law theories as indispensable to an understanding of the historical shaping of international relations. Indeed, they saw Vattel's *Law of Nations* as embodying thought that was constitutive of the European international society as it emerged in the eighteenth and nineteenth centuries.[47] This led Bull to describe his own stance as 'part of the "empirical equivalent" of the natural-law theory'.[48]

In an edited collection that grew out of a London School of Economics study group, Peter Butler wrote the first, and still one of the few, essays focused exclusively on Vattel's significance for the study of international relations. His exposition began by noting Vattel's deviation from previous writers on the laws of nature and nations. They 'had failed to realise that natural law in its pure form . . . cannot be immediately applied to nations'.[49] It needed to be modified in a manner appropriate to its subject matter; in this case, according to Vattel (*LN*, prelim. 12), 'the great society established by nature between all nations'.[50]

45 See the subtitle of Donelan's *Reason of State* for 'international political theory', and Wight's 'Why is there no international theory?' for the latter term. Michael Donelan (ed.), *The Reason of States: A Study in International Political Theory* (London, 2016 (first published 1978)). For an early use of the expression 'international thought', see F. Melian Stawell, *The Growth of International Thought* (London, 1929).

46 For contemporary critiques of the abstract rationalism of the scientific outlook, see Bull, 'International theory'; and Hans J. Morgenthau, 'The intellectual and political functions of a theory of international relations', in Hans J. Morgenthau (ed.), *The Decline of Democratic Politics* (Chicago, 1962), 62–78.

47 Bull, *Anarchical Society*, 33–36.

48 Ibid., 6.

49 P. Butler, 'Legitimacy in a states-system: Vattel's Law of Nations', in M. Donelan (ed.), *The Reason of States* (London, 1978), 46.

50 Ibid., 46.

Key to understanding this modification, Butler stated, is Vattel's 'double law' (*LN*, preface 17), namely, his distinction between the voluntary and necessary laws of nations.[51] The *necessary* law of nations Vattel defined as absolutely binding on states 'in point of conscience' (*LN*, prelim. 7). It refers to the 'immutable' and 'indispensable' natural law that applies to both individuals and states (*LN*, prelim. 7–8). It embodies 'the eternal rules of justice' (*LN*, III-XII-188). This is the single universal law of nature that Grotian international lawyers invoked and which Vattel acknowledged derived from Grotius. But the centrepiece of Vattel's contribution, according to Butler, is his elaboration of the *voluntary* law of nations. As Andrew Hurrell remarked in another of the rare essays on Vattel's relevance to international relations, it is 'voluntary law that is central to the political existence of international society'.[52] It provides the basis on which that society exists.

States are not obliged to act in accordance with conscience when it comes to international relations because the actors and environment are so unique: states not only claim moral and legal equality, they also possess 'liberty and independence' in the 'natural society of nations' (*LN*, prelim. 15).[53] Indeed, as Vattel pithily stated, 'The law of nations is the law of sovereigns' (*LN*, preface 18); it is the law designed specifically for them, their ministers, diplomats and other 'conductors of states'. This changes natural law's application and the moral obligations it imposes on states as opposed to individuals. It introduced a kind of clutch mechanism that gave rulers and diplomats variable control over the degree to which the necessary laws of nature constrained or empowered statecraft.[54] In this regard, Vattel marks a clear break with the Grotian tradition's precept that states and individuals are subject to identical moral standards.

For Vattel, states in a state of nature could not be governed by the same natural laws that govern individuals. His argument on this point, as Hurrell reminds us, derives from Hobbes who argued that the state of nature was more dangerous to individuals than to states in the same condition.[55] Because states 'uphold . . . the industry of their subjects', said Hobbes, 'there does not follow from it, that misery, which accompanies the liberty of particular men'.[56] The

[51] Ibid., 46.

[52] A. Hurrell, 'Vattel: Pluralism and its limits', in I. Clarke and I. Neumann (eds.), *Classical Theories of International Relations* (London, 1996), 237.

[53] Butler, 'Legitimacy in a states-system', 52.

[54] See R. Devetak, 'Law of nations as reason of state: Diplomacy and the balance of power in Vattel's *Law of Nations*', *Parergon* 28.2 (2011), 105–128, at 106.

[55] Hurrell, 'Vattel', 235.

[56] T. Hobbes, *Leviathan*, ed. J. C. A. Gaskin (Oxford, 2008), 85.

international condition of anarchy is far more tolerable to states, which are 'less vulnerable to violent attack', than the original state of nature is to individual humans.[57] Though Hobbes recognised the law of nations '[c]oncerning the offices of one sovereign to another', he said little about the obligations that followed from it.[58]

Vattel's ambition to provide an account of international society and the obligations it comprises has made him attractive to scholars interested in the rules and norms governing international relations. As Butler explained, membership of international society creates imperfect obligations, because, unlike a domestic society, states recognise no superior authority.[59] While sovereign states in international relations have a *perfect* right to request other states to adhere to obligations issuing from the necessary law of nations, other states have only *imperfect* obligations under the voluntary law of nations (*LN*, prelim. 18). 'A nation has the right to ask for these kind offices [of humanity]', says Vattel (*LN*, II-1-8), 'but not to demand them'.

Vattel's insistence on dividing the law of nations into domestic and international rules, perfect and imperfect obligations, has drawn criticism from critical international theorists. In another rare IR analysis of Vattel, Andrew Linklater situated the Swiss thinker in a dialectical philosophy of history that investigates 'the bifurcated nature of modern moral and political experience' dividing ethical obligations between 'men and citizens'.[60] Distinguishing Vattel's thought, says Linklater, was 'his belief that the natural morality which survives the division of mankind into sovereign states will be enacted only at their discretion'.[61] States have only imperfect duties, allowing them to 'ignore international obligations at will, or violate the rights of others' whensoever they choose.[62] By permitting states to decide for themselves what is lawful and just, Vattel was '"subjectivising" … the natural law', allowing the particularism of state sovereignty to trump any residual universalism.[63] Linklater's argument here is that the introduction of an ethically subjective notion of obligation betrays natural law's single universal morality, yielding a 'voluntaristic international order' with minimal duties to humanity.

57 Bull, *Anarchical Society*, 49.
58 Hobbes, *Leviathan*, 235.
59 Butler, 'Legitimacy in a states-system', 53.
60 Linklater, *Men and Citizens*, 39.
61 Ibid., 84.
62 Ibid., 85.
63 Ibid., 87 and 92–93. For an argument that Vattel's conception of duties beyond borders is stronger than Linklater's reading suggests, see L. Glanville, 'Responsibility to perfect: Vattel's conception of duties beyond borders', *International Studies Quarterly* 61.2 (2017), 385–395.

ENQUIRIES INTO THE EMERGENCE OF SOVEREIGNTY AND THE MODERN STATES-SYSTEM

The increased engagement with political theory and the history of political thought led to enquiries into the origins and emergence of the modern states-system and its defining actor, the sovereign state. Again, it was the English School scholars, Wight and Bull, who pioneered examination of the modern states-system's emergence through intellectual developments, especially in the modern natural law tradition. Their focus was more on the way that thinkers saw, described and analysed things in their context.[64]

For example, Bull described the effort to understand European international change in the sixteenth and seventeenth centuries as a clash between 'thinkers like Machiavelli, Bacon and Hobbes [who] saw the emerging states as confronting one another in the social and moral vacuum left by the receding *respublica Christiana*', and those like the 'Papal and Imperialist writers [who] fought a rearguard action on behalf of the ideas of the universal authority of the Pope and Emperor'.[65] A third way of thinking, Bull pronounced, drew upon natural law theories to assert that the emergent states 'making themselves supreme over local rivals and independent of outside authorities were nevertheless bound by common interests and rules'.[66] It was not until the eighteenth and nineteenth centuries, Bull argued, that the modern states-system, or 'European international society' as he called it, emerged with greater clarity. Thinkers like Vattel provided 'a clear statement of the principle that international society is a society of states or nations'.[67] This established an intellectual architecture in which a range of political ideas, rules and institutions could be accommodated: the principle of national or popular sovereignty, positive international law, diplomacy, rules of coexistence and non-intervention, and acceptance of war as a *political* conflict.[68]

F. H. Hinsley provided a similar historical narrative, devoting a long chapter in his account of *Sovereignty* to 'the concept of sovereignty in the history of relations between states'.[69] This is a story of what Stephen Krasner would later

[64] As Donelan put it, the historical imperative was not the Rankean one of knowing history 'as it was really was', 'but history as it looks to the people concerned', 'the past as they see it'. M. Donelan, 'Introduction', in Donelan (ed.), *The Reason of States*, 11–24, at 12–13.
[65] Bull, *Anarchical Society*, 27–28.
[66] Ibid., 28.
[67] Ibid., 34.
[68] Ibid., 35–37.
[69] F. H. Hinsley, *Sovereignty*, 2nd ed. (London, 1986), chapter 5.

call 'Westphalian' or 'Vattelian sovereignty'.[70] IR conventionally distinguishes the meaning and function of sovereignty in its domestic and international contexts.[71] Domestically, 'internal sovereignty' refers to the notion that there is a single supreme authority that rules over a given territory and community. This is the notion that Hobbes's *Leviathan* elaborated to extinguish civil war and restore political order. Internationally, 'external sovereignty' refers not to supremacy but to the assertion of independence from outside authorities.[72] These two dimensions of sovereignty are considered complementary, 'the inward and outward expressions … of the same idea'.[73] By labelling the external expression of sovereignty 'Vattelian', Krasner is acknowledging, like other IR scholars, Vattel's importance to the intellectual consolidation of the modern states-system. According to Hinsley, Vattel offered a 'legal version of the new political understanding of Europe as an international system'.[74] It is important to note that the two sides of sovereignty only became 'complementary' when they were conjoined by thinkers such as Vattel. There is nothing natural about the complementarity, and the concept of 'internal sovereignty' long antedated the concept of 'external sovereignty', as Hinsley's account demonstrates.[75]

By the 1980s and 1990s, IR had witnessed the emergence of social constructivism when thinkers such as Nicholas Onuf, John Ruggie and Alexander Wendt, among others, challenged dominant positivist and realist approaches by theorising how intersubjective beliefs shape the social facts of international relations.[76] One of the chief concerns of social constructivism was to treat the modern states-system as a historically and socially contingent phenomenon. The task was to explore 'the origins of the present system of sovereign states and [ask] how it might change in the future'.[77] It is worth remembering that academics expended a lot of effort during the 1980s and 1990s grappling with globalisation and its implications for, among other

[70] S. D. Krasner, 'Abiding sovereignty', *International Political Science Review* 22.3 (2001), 229–251.

[71] See Bull, *Anarchical Society*, 8.

[72] Ibid., 8.

[73] Hinsley, *Sovereignty*, 158.

[74] Ibid., 194–195.

[75] A point also noted by H. Thompson, 'The case for external sovereignty', *European Journal of International Relations* 12.2 (2006), 251–274, at 253.

[76] N. Onuf, *World of our Making: Rules and Rule in Social Theory and International Relations* (Columbia, 1989); J. G. Ruggie, *Constructing the World Polity: Essays on International Institutionalization* (London, 1998); A. Wendt, *Social Theory of International Politics* (Cambridge, 1999).

[77] C. Reus-Smit, *The Moral Purpose of the State: Culture, Social Identity, and Institutional Rationality in International Relations* (Princeton, 1999), xi.

things, the system of sovereign states.[78] Understanding immanent trends and transformations inspired IR theorists to cast an eye back to the 'construction' of the modern states-system.

In an early example of social constructivist IR theory, Ruggie took Waltz to task for failing to account for the most fundamental 'contextual change in international politics in this millennium: the shift from the medieval to the modern international systems'.[79] Waltz failed, according to Ruggie, because his neorealist theory was unable to account for the international system's changing 'principles of separability'. By this he means '*the principles on the basis of which the constituent units are separated* from one another'.[80] The transition to the modern states-system was made possible, Ruggie argued, by modifications in the concept of sovereignty. These modifications were a solution to the 'legitimation crisis' brought on by the break-up of the medieval system.

The two thinkers who pioneered the solution, Ruggie claimed, were John Locke and Vattel, whose political thought 'came to be the most widely accepted legitimations for their respective realms, bourgeois society and the interstate system'.[81] In relation to domestic society, Locke legitimised a conception of property as the minimal basis on which society could exist. Analogously, Vattel asserted a minimal condition for international society based on sovereign states' natural liberty. Both Locke and Vattel 'developed an autonomous legitimation of the political order based simply on the minimalist social needs of its component parts'.[82] The 'modern system of rule', Ruggie contended, 'consists of the institutionalization of public authority within mutually exclusive jurisdictional domains'.[83] Ruggie offered a social constructivist version of Hinsley's historical argument about internal and external sovereignty forming a complementary pairing. The medieval system of overlapping and intersecting levels of power and authority was extinguished by a modern system predicated on the separation of sovereign jurisdictions by clearly marked boundaries; boundaries which now functioned to distinguish the inside of a sovereign state from the outside, thus institutionalising a generally recognised 'principle of separability' and legitimising the independence of states.

78 I. Clark, *Globalization and International Relations Theory* (Oxford, 1999).
79 J. G. Ruggie, 'Continuity and transformation in the world polity: Towards a neorealist synthesis', *World Politics* 35.2 (1983), 261–285, at 273.
80 Ibid., 274 (emphasis in original).
81 Ibid., 277.
82 Ibid., 278.
83 Ibid., 275.

In a later article, Ruggie argued that the 'central attribute of modernity in international politics has been a peculiar and historically unique configuration of territorial space'.[84] He argued that an IR theory must be able to account for change, including changes in the mode by which human groups are divided, as these create new constitutive units which act according to different political and strategic logics.[85] Ruggie's account of the transition to modernity used Locke and Vattel as little more than ciphers. The intellectual richness of both thinkers is irrelevant. His purpose, after all, was to make a theoretical point about conceptualising change rather than expounding the ideas fully and contextually. This is a common practice in a discipline that is heavily theory-driven. But for English School scholars such as Bull and Wight, theoretical analysis was not to be gained at the expense of historical veracity.

VATTEL AND THE SOCIETY OF STATES

A central concept in the study of international relations is the 'society of states'. The English School, in particular, has expounded the concept at length both in analytical and historical studies.[86] A society of states exists, according to Bull,

> when a group of states, conscious of certain common interests and common values, form a society in the sense that they conceive themselves to be bound by a common set of rules in their relations with one another, and share in the working of common institutions.[87]

By 'society of states' or 'international society', Bull means to refer to the same thing Wight refers to as the 'states-system' or 'system of states'.[88] This latter terminology originated in the seventeenth century with Pufendorf's discussions of the 'monstrous' Holy Roman Empire of Germany; it resembled, he

[84] J. G. Ruggie, 'Territoriality and beyond: Problematizing modernity in international relations', *International Organization* 47.1 (1993), 139–174, at 144.

[85] Ibid., 162–163.

[86] Bull's *Anarchical Society* is the classic analytical treatment of international society; M. Wight's *Systems of States* and H. Bull and A. Watson (eds.), *Expansion of International Society* (Oxford, 1984) are classic historical treatments. For a more recent study of international society, see T. Dunne and C. Reus-Smit (eds.), *The Globalization of International Society* (Oxford, 2017).

[87] Bull, *Anarchical Society*, 13.

[88] Bull, in *Anarchical Society*, 9–10 distinguished the *society* of states from a *system* of states (or international *system*) on the basis that systems exist 'when two or more states have sufficient contact between them … to cause them to behave … as parts of a whole' but lack the conscious recognition of common interests, values and institutions that characterise a society.

said, '*a System of* several *States*'.[89] Pufendorf's conceptual innovation was intended to describe the Holy Roman Empire, not 'international relations', but in the eighteenth and nineteenth centuries historians from the Scotsman William Robertson to the German Arnold Heeren would use the term to describe the international political order of Europe and later the world.[90] It is worth quoting at length Vattel's well-known description of the society of states, as it encapsulates the concept so well:

> Europe forms a political system, an integral body, closely connected by the relations and different interests of the nations inhabiting this part of the world. It is not, as formerly, a confused heap of detached pieces, each of which thought herself very little concerned in the fate of the others, and seldom regarded things which did not immediately concern her. The continual attention of sovereigns to every occurrence, the constant residence of ministers, and the perpetual negotiations, make of modern Europe a kind of republic, of which the members – each independent, but all linked together by the ties of common interest – unite for the maintenance of order and liberty. (*LN*, III-III-47)[91]

Bull and Wight's understanding of international society strongly resembles Vattel's description of the society of states, agreeing that it is sustained through recognition of common interests in preserving the system of independent states through diplomacy and the balance of power. What is surprising, however, is that neither Bull nor Wight draws upon Vattel directly. Instead,

89 See S. Pufendorf, *The Present State of Germany*, translated by E. Bohun, ed. M. J. Seidler (Indianapolis, 2007), 175. On Pufendorf's analysis of the German Empire and his analytical concept of state system, see P. Schröder, 'The constitution of the holy Roman Empire after 1648: Samuel Pufendorf's assessment in his Monzambano', *Historical Journal* 42.4 (1999), 961–983; P. Schröder, *Trust in Early Modern International Political Thought, 1598–1713* (Cambridge, 2017), 119–136; M. J. Seidler, '"Monstrous" Pufendorf: Sovereignty and system in the dissertations', in C. Cuttica and G. Burgess (eds.), *Monarchism and Absolutism in Early Modern Europe* (London, 2012), 159–175.

90 W. Robertson, *History of the Reign of Charles the Fifth, with an Account of the Emperor's Life after his Abdication by William H. Prescott* (London, 1869), 39–40; A. Heeren, *A Manual of the Political System of Europe and Its Colonies, from Its Formation at the Close of the Fifteenth Century, to Its Reestablishment upon the Fall of Napoleon*, translater unknown, 1834 translation (Freeport, 1971). On the emergence of the concept of states-system and its use in the historiography of international relations, see R. Devetak, 'Historiographical foundations of modern international thought: Histories of the European states-system from Florence to Göttingen', *History of European Ideas* 41.1 (2015), 62–77.

91 On Vattel's conception of the society of states, see S. Zurbuchen, 'Emer de Vattel on the society of nations and the political system of Europe', in S. Kadelbach, T. Kleinlein and David Roth-Isigkeit (eds.), *System, Order, and International Law: The Early History of International Legal Thought from Machiavelli to Hegel* (Oxford, 2017), 263–282.

they invoke Heeren's definition as 'the union of several contiguous states, resembling each other in their manners, religion, and degree of social improvement, and cemented together by a reciprocity of interests'.[92]

The English School's argument was that the distinctive institutions that comprise the society of states – Bull identifies them as the balance of power, international law, diplomacy, war and great power management – have contributed to order in relations among sovereign states.[93] Whilst international relations occur in a condition of 'formal anarchy', 'substantively, the interactions of states exhibit a degree of order' that would not be expected in a Hobbesian state of nature.[94] This was Bull's point of departure in his classic book, *The Anarchical Society*. There is a remarkable degree of international order, he argued, as most states, most of the time, are not fighting wars but respecting basic rules of co-existence as a *modus vivendi*.[95] Bull's explanation lies in his account of international society which is, to a considerable extent, Vattelian in inspiration and content.

Bull and Wight shared with Vattel two defining suppositions: first, that states share a common interest in maintaining order through international rules and institutions; and second, that these rules and institutions should not be conceived through a 'domestic analogy'. That is, states form a society that is disanalogous to domestic society; it is a society with its own rules and institutions. The rules of international society, says Bull, do not all have 'the status of law'.[96] Their fundamental purpose is to sustain order through 'rules of coexistence'. In Terry Nardin's words, the order international society maintains is procedural rather than substantive.[97] Europe, in other words, forms a pluralistic society whose members are independent states bound together by common rules and institutions, despite the diversity of religious and cultural beliefs, domestic political arrangements and material power.

One of the defining features of the society of states as understood by Vattel is that it is a bulwark against hegemony or universal empire. It has the effect of preventing any single state from being able to impose its will on all the rest. The mechanism most attuned to preventing hegemony and therefore critical

92 Heeren, quoted in Wight, *System of States*, 22; and Bull, *Anarchical Society*, 13.

93 For Bull's analysis of international society's five 'institutions', see *Anarchical Society*, chapters 5–9.

94 H. Suganami, 'The international society perspective on world politics reconsidered', *International Relations of the Asia-Pacific* 2.1 (2002), 1–28, at 4.

95 On Bull's treatment of international order, see R. J. Vincent, 'Hedley Bull and order in international politics', *Millennium* 17.2 (1988), 195–213.

96 Bull, *Anarchical Society*, xiii–xiv.

97 T. Nardin, *Law, Morality and the Relations of States* (Princeton, 1983).

to international society's preservation is the balance of power. In the words of the Treaty of Utrecht, it is the mechanism best suited 'to settle and establish the peace and tranquillity' of Europe.[98] Europe could overcome the sectarian anarchy of the sixteenth and seventeenth centuries without having to opt for universal empire. It could opt instead for a third choice: the equilibrium produced by the balance of power.[99] The balance of power, as an integral feature of the society of states, has two dimensions that have been identified by IR scholars: a negative, anti-hegemonial dimension and a positive, constructive dimension.

The negative dimension of the balance of power ensures that 'no potentate be able absolutely to predominate, and prescribe laws to others' (*LN*, III-III-47). This anti-hegemonial function frequently requires the use of force, as Vattel was well aware. He declared that states had a right, indeed a duty, to use force to resist the hegemonic ambitions of other states. He even extended that right to pre-emption, arguing 'that if that formidable potentate certainly entertain designs of oppression and conquest, ... other states have a right to anticipate him' (*LN*, III-III-49). Force, Vattel recognised, was integral to the balance of power and, by extension, to the maintenance of international society. After all, the purpose of the balancing mechanism was not to establish peace, but to prevent the European system of independent states collapsing under pressure of a 'universal monarchy'.[100]

The positive or 'associative' dimension, to use Richard Little's term, affirmed a Europe of free and equal states, in other words, the 'liberties of Europe'.[101] The society of states takes on the appearance then of what Adam

[98] 'Treaty of Peace and Friendship between Great Britain and Spain, signed at Utrecht, 13 July 1713', English translation, in C. Parry (ed.), *The Consolidated Treaty Series* (Dobbs Ferry, NY, 1969), 325–348, at 325.

[99] In one of his several essays on the topic Wight argued that the political alternatives to the balance of power were 'universal anarchy' or 'universal dominion'. M. Wight, 'The balance of power', in Butterfield and Wight (eds.), *Diplomatic Investigations*, 174–175. See also Bull, *Anarchical Society*, 101, who uses Vattel's definition of the balance of power to begin his discussion of the topic.

[100] On early modern European discourses of 'universal monarchy', balance of power and 'liberties of Europe', see R. Devetak, '"The fear of universal monarchy": Balance of power as an ordering practice of liberty', in T. Dunne, T. Flockhart and M. Koivisto (eds.), *Liberal World Orders* (Oxford, 2013), 121–137; P. Schröder, 'The concepts of universal monarchy and balance of power in the first half of the seventeenth century – A case study', in M. Koskenniemi, W. Rech and M. Fonseca (eds.), *International Law and Empire: Historical Explorations* (Oxford, 2017), 83–100.

[101] R. Little, 'Deconstructing the balance of power: Two traditions of thought', *Review of International Studies* 15.1 (1989), 87–100.

Watson called a 'continuous mobile equilibrium'.[102] The upshot, in Vattel's words, is that Europe can no longer be seen either as 'a confused heap of detached pieces' or as a universal empire. It is an order *sui generis* with its own principles of legitimacy, with common rules of conduct, and its own specific set of rights and duties, all of which are geared towards a common interest in co-existence. The extent to which Vattel conceives this common interest to apply beyond Europe remains a point of contention.[103]

VATTEL AND THE CONDUCT OF STATES

Vattel's treatment of the 'double law' holds important implications for the conduct of states. Key to his approach is the notion that states possess a moral personality (*LN*, prelim. 67, 83, 85).[104] The natural liberty and independence of states means that as moral persons they possess free and independent judgement; that is, they are at liberty to decide for themselves the circumstances under which they might offer assistance to another state, take up arms against them or withdraw from an agreement. For example, while it is an obligation under the necessary law of nations to observe treaties (*pacta sunt servanda*), it is no violation of the voluntary law of nations for a state to break a treaty if it judges the treaty to be 'pernicious' to its interests or risk its 'ruin' (*LN*, II-XII-160).[105]

On matters of defence and security, the same independence of judgement applies. On the one hand, a sovereign who wages an unjust war 'is chargeable with all the evils, all the horrors of war' (*LN*, III-XI-183–184). Judged from a purportedly universal moral standpoint of the necessary law of nations, war cannot be objectively just on both sides (*LN*, III-III-39). But on the other hand, in the 'state of nature' who is to determine which state has justice on their side? (*LN*, III-XII-188). By virtue of its natural liberty and independence, each state will determine the justice of its cause 'according to the dictates of her own conscience'. Given the non-existence of anything approximating Christian Wolff's *civitas maxima*, which is presided over by a rector, there is

[102] A. Watson, *The Evolution of International Society: A Comparative Historical Analysis* (London, 1992), 198.

[103] For rival perspectives on this contention, see I. Hunter, '"A *Jus gentium* for America": The rules of war and the rule of law in the revolutionary United States', *Journal of the History of International Law* 14.2 (2012), 173–206; and J. Pitts, *Boundaries of the International: Law and Empire* (Cambridge, MA, 2018), chapter 3.

[104] See B. Holland, 'The moral person of the state: Emer de Vattel and the foundations of international legal order', *History of European Ideas* 37.4 (2011), 438–445.

[105] See Butler, 'Legitimacy in a states-system', 49.

no place for a superior judge, no position above states from which the justice or morality of a particular war may be judged. Every state invariably claims justice on its side.

Consequently, under the voluntary law of nations, 'regular war', which is war declared between sovereign states, 'is to be accounted just on both sides' (*LN*, III-XII-190). This signified a departure from Grotius and the scholastic just war tradition, putting Vattel in closer proximity to Gentili.[106] For both Gentili and Vattel, each belligerent must be regarded as a 'just enemy' (*justus hostis*), with an equal right to wage war. The notion that war was a 'morally non-discriminatory conflict between equally "just enemies"' was intended to reduce the inhumanity of war.[107] 'There would be no stability in the affairs of mankind', Vattel (*LN*, III-XIII-196) observed, 'if we were allowed to draw a distinction between a just and an unjust war'. It would lead to endless quarrel, potentially making conflict 'more bloody, more calamitous in its effects, and also more difficult to terminate' (*LN*, III-XII-188).[108]

Tolerating what might be judged an unjust war according to the dictates of conscience is a practical necessity for states. This is Vattel's prudential accommodation to political realities in international relations; his recognition that international order could only be maintained 'if the conscience of a sovereign took its bearings not from moral law alone, but primarily from given political circumstances', as Reinhart Koselleck put it.[109] This line of argument has been rehearsed by critics of liberal instruments of world order. Danilo Zolo, for example, has argued that the war on terror and humanitarian intervention are symptomatic of the recriminalisation of war that followed upon the dismantling of *jus publicum Europaeum*.[110]

[106] I. Hunter, 'Law, war, and empire in early modern protestant *jus gentium*: The casuistries of Gentili and Vattel', in *Alberico Gentili: Giustizia, Guerra, Impero: Atti del Convegno XIV Giornata Gentiliana*, San Ginesio 24–25 settembre 2010 (San Ginesio, 2014), 151–168.

[107] P. Schröder, 'Carl Schmitt's appropriation of the early modern European tradition of political thought on the state and interstate relations', *History of Political Thought* 33.2 (2012), 348–371, at 366. See also I. Hunter, 'Vattel's Law of Nations: Diplomatic casuistry for the protestant nation', *Grotiana* 31 (2010), 108–140, at 134; S. Zurbuchen, 'Vattel's *Law of Nations* and just war theory', *History of European Ideas* 35.4 (2009), 408–417; and P. Kalmanovitz, 'Sovereignty, pluralism, and regular war: Wolff and Vattel's Enlightenment critique of just war', *Political Theory* 46.2 (2018), 218–241.

[108] See R. Koselleck, *Critique and Crisis: Enlightenment and the Pathogenesis of Modern Society* (Cambridge, 1988), 46; and A. Colombo, *La Guerra Ineguale: Pace e Violenza nel Tramonto della Società Internazionale* (Bologna, 2006).

[109] Koselleck, *Critique and crisis*, 45.

[110] D. Zolo, *Victors' Justice: From Nuremberg to Baghdad*, translated by W. Weir (London, 2009). Zolo draws heavily on C. Schmitt, *The Nomos of the Earth in the International Law of the Jus Publicum Europaeum*, translated by G. Ulmen (New York, 2004).

What appears like a tension or even contradiction in Vattel's thinking – noting that 'war cannot be just on both sides' (*LN*, III-III-39), yet concluding that regular wars are 'accounted just' on both sides (*LN*, III-III-195) – is actually a consequence of his casuistical thinking. As Ian Hunter has persuasively argued, Vattel's thinking exemplifies an 'art of diplomatic casuistry ... geared to the exigencies of diplomacy and statecraft'.[111] In Vattel's reconstruction of modern natural law, the necessary law of nations 'is continuously adjusted – moderated, modified, even suspended' to allow for the range of exceptions relating to the natural liberty of states under the voluntary law of nations.[112] In the most recent IR study of Vattel, Lorenzo Cello has explored the intellectual resources Vattel supplies, especially his diplomatic casuistry, to analyse the legitimacy of international intervention.[113] Against conventional attempts by IR theorists to understand intervention by invoking the principle of non-intervention as a logical extension of state sovereignty, Cello argues that Vattel's diplomatic casuistry, grounded in the ethical office of the statesperson, 'means thinking about the legitimacy of intervention in terms of the inevitable mediation of responsibilities within and between offices'.[114] The introduction of diplomatic casuistry into the discussion of Vattel enables IR scholars to move beyond the competing interpretations of him as a confused realist or idealist and recalls a mode of moral reasoning marginalised by the dominance of deontological and social scientific theories of IR.

CONCLUSION

Vattel's *Law of Nations* is arguably the first treatise in the natural law tradition principally concerned to address empirical problems of international relations with theoretical sophistication.[115] Yet international relations scholars have paid little attention to Vattel. This is partly explained by the dominance of the 'isms' – various forms of theorising that are insensitive to intellectual history or

[111] Hunter, 'Vattel's Law of Nations', 126.

[112] Ibid., 114–115. See also Hunter, 'Law, war, and empire'.

[113] L. Cello, 'The legitimacy of international interventions in Vattel's *The Law of Nations*', *Global Intellectual History* 2.2 (2017), 105–123.

[114] Cello, 'The legitimacy of international interventions', 117. See also R. J. Vincent's classic English School study of intervention. R. J. Vincent, *Nonintervention and International Order* (Princeton, 1974).

[115] Christian Wolff's *Law of Nations*, published in 1749, was similarly devoted to international relations but treated its subject in a much more abstract and empirically abstemious manner. C. Wolff, *The Law of Nations treated by the Scientific Method*, translated by J. H. Drake, ed. T. Ahnert (Indianapolis, 2017).

that issue from dialectical philosophies of history predicated on the unfolding of a single universal moral code.[116]

Better engagement with Vattel in IR was made possible by scholars interested in the intellectual history of the modern European states-system and its expansion. The main route was through the English School whose conception of international society was influenced by Vattel as much as Grotius. Scholars such as Wight and Bull engaged with theorists of natural law and the law of nations as part of their intellectual history of the modern states-system. Vattel provided the intellectual architecture to understand the development of rules and institutions specific to the society of states. His 'double law' was, in a way, a precursor to Bull's rejection of the 'domestic analogy'. The upshot was that the rules and institutions necessary for political life were different for the domestic and international realms. The law of nations that applied to international relations was proposed as a 'distinct science'. Consequently, the society of states could be understood to possess its own unique rules and institutions and its own form of political morality: a diplomatic casuistry grounded in the ethical office of the statesperson.

The growth of contextual forms of intellectual history has been crucial in developing a better appreciation of Vattel's writings in IR, and in opening the discipline to alternative modes of theorising. In a discipline that has become enamoured of various theoretical 'isms', Vattel's defence of casuistry, pluralism and the ethic of office represents an intolerable challenge to theories predicated on a single universal morality. But for those scholars and practitioners who remain sceptical of ethical universalism and theoretical abstraction in the study of international relations, Vattel's *Law of Nations* remains a crucial intellectual resource.

FURTHER READING

H. Bull, 'Society and anarchy in international relations', in H. Butterfield and M. Wight (eds.), *Diplomatic Investigations: Essays in the Theory of International Politics* (London, 1966), 55–70.

The Anarchical Society: A Study of Order in World Politics (London, 1977).

P. Butler, 'Legitimacy in a states-system: Vattel's *Law of Nations*', in M. Donelan (ed.), *The Reason of States* (London, 1978).

L. Cello, 'The legitimacy of international interventions in Vattel's The Law of Nations', *Global Intellectual History* 2.2 (2017), 105–123.

[116] See D. Lake, 'Why "isms" are evil: Theory, epistemology, and academic sects as impediments to understanding and progress', *International Studies Quarterly* 55.2 (2011), 465–480.

I. Hunter, 'Vattel's Law of Nations: Diplomatic casuistry for the protestant nation', *Grotiana* 31 (2010), 108–140.

A. Hurrell, 'Vattel: Pluralism and its limits', in I. Clarke and I. Neumann (eds.), *Classical Theories of International Relations* (London, 1996), 233–255.

A. Linklater, *Men and Citizens in the Theory of International Relations* (London, 1982).

A. Linklater and H. Suganami, *The English School of International Relations: A Contemporary Reassessment* (Cambridge, 2006).

C. Vollenhoven, *The Three Stages in the Evolution of the Law of Nations* (Dordrecht, 1919).

U. Vollerthun, *The Idea of International Society: Erasmus, Vitoria, Gentili, Grotius*, ed. J. L. Richardson (Oxford, 2017).

M. Wight, *Systems of States*, ed. H. Bull (Leicester, 1977).

International Theory: The Three Traditions, ed. G. Wight and B. Porter (Leicester, 1991).

Index

For EU product safety concerns, contact us at Calle de José Abascal, 56–1°,
28003 Madrid, Spain or eugpsr@cambridge.org.

www.ingramcontent.com/pod-product-compliance
Lightning Source LLC
LaVergne TN
LVHW011704200926
848484LV00004B/1069

* 9 7 8 1 1 0 8 4 8 9 4 4 7 *